A Handbook of
Criminal Law Terms

BRYAN A. GARNER
Editor

DAVID W. SCHULTZ
ELIZABETH C. POWELL
LANCE A. COOPER
Assistant Editors

WEST
GROUP

St. Paul, Minnesota
2000

PREFACE

If you've ever read a criminal-law treatise, you've probably felt a lump in your throat. The subject deals with base matters, and sometimes it can be frightening. Yet precisely because it deals with the darker side of life, it almost always maintains a high level of human interest.

In criminal law as in other legal subjects, clear thinking is crucial. And the first step toward clear thinking involves critical thought about how we use words and phrases. To avoid slipping into any number of fallacies, we need to know precisely what we're talking about. For that purpose, a good glossary can be indispensable.

This one pulls together the terminology from several related but distinct fields, such as substantive criminal law, criminal procedure, criminology, and penology. It is probably the most inclusive such glossary ever assembled.

One of the great challenges of this project was that, even though many terms are quite ancient, the legal vocabulary is constantly growing. The field known as *criminalistics* dates only from the mid-20th century, but many terms are even newer. There are police terms such as *preventive detention* and *protective sweep*. Judge-made law continues innovating phrases such as *independent-source rule* and *open-fields doctrine*. New categories such as *credit-card crime* and *cyberstalking* reflect technological and social changes. Meanwhile, legislation continues to be a source of new terms, such as *Brady Act* and *Megan's law*.

Whatever your needs — whether you're involved in a *Fatico hearing*, alleging a *Falconer error*, or challenging an *FCPV* — my colleagues and I hope this book will help you thread the maze of legal language.

For his painstaking review and expert comments on the manuscript, we wish to thank Professor Stephen A. Saltzburg of George Washington University Law School.

Finally, Karen Magnuson served as copy editor, as she has on several of my other book projects. Her work has been invaluable.

BRYAN A. GARNER

Dallas, Texas
January 2000

A Handbook
of Criminal
Law Terms

A

abandonment, *n*. See RENUNCIATION.

abduction (ab-**dək**-shən), *n*. **1.** The act of
leading someone away by force or fraudulent
persuasion. • Some jurisdictions have added
various elements to this basic definition, such
as that the abductor must have the intent to
marry or defile the person, that the abductee
must be a child, or that the abductor must
intend to subject the abductee to concubinage
or prostitution. **2.** *Archaic*. At common law,
the crime of taking away a female person
without her consent by use of persuasion,
fraud, or violence, for the purpose of marriage,
prostitution, or illicit sex.—**abduct,** *vb*.—**abductor,** *n*.—**abductee,** *n*. See KIDNAPPING.

aberrant behavior (a-**ber**-ənt). A single act
of unplanned or thoughtless criminal behavior.
• Many courts have held that aberrant behavior justifies a downward departure—that is, a
more lenient sentence—under the federal sentencing guidelines, based on a comment in the
introduction to the *Guidelines Manual* to the
effect that the guidelines do not deal with

single acts of aberrant behavior. *U.S. Sentencing Guidelines Manual*, ch. 1, pt. A, ¶ 4.

abet (ə-**bet**), *vb.* **1.** To aid, encourage, or assist (someone), esp. in the commission of a crime <abet a known felon>. **2.** To support (a crime) by active assistance <abet a burglary>.— **abetment,** *n.* See AID AND ABET. Cf. INCITE.

abettor. A person who aids, encourages, or assists in the commission of a crime.—Also spelled *abetter.* See *principal in the second degree* under PRINCIPAL.

abnormal law. The law as it applies to persons who are under legal disabilities such as infancy, alienage, insanity, criminality, and (formerly) coverture.

abortion, *n.* **1.** The spontaneous or artificially induced expulsion of an embryo or fetus. • In *Roe v. Wade*, the Supreme Court first recognized a woman's right to choose to end her pregnancy as a privacy right stemming from the Due Process Clause of the 14th Amendment. 410 U.S. 113, 93 S.Ct. 1409 (1973). **2.** *Archaic.* At common law, the misdemeanor of causing a miscarriage or premature delivery of a fetus by means of any instrument, medicine, drug, or other means. • Many American states made this a statutory felony until the *Roe v.*

2

Wade decision.—Also termed *procuring an abortion*.—**abort,** *vb.*—**abortionist,** *n.*

abscond (ab-**skond**), *vb.* **1.** To depart secretly or suddenly, esp. to avoid arrest or prosecution. **2.** To leave a place, usu. hurriedly, with another's money or property.—**abscondence** (ab-**skon**-dənts), *n.*

absolute contraband. See CONTRABAND.

absolute disparity. The difference between the percentage of a group in the general population and the percentage of that group in the pool of prospective jurors on a venire. ● For example, if African–Americans make up 12% of a county's population and 8% of the potential jurors on a venire, the absolute disparity of African–American veniremembers is 4%. The reason for calculating the disparity is to analyze a claim that the jury was not impartial because the venire from which it was chosen did not represent a fair cross-section of the jurisdiction's population. Some courts criticize the absolute-disparity analysis, favoring instead the comparative-disparity analysis, in the belief that the absolute-disparity analysis understates the deviation. See FAIR-CROSS-SECTION REQUIREMENT; DUREN TEST; STATISTICAL-DECISION THEORY. Cf. COMPARATIVE DISPARITY.

absolute pardon. See PARDON.

absolute presumption. See *conclusive presumption* under PRESUMPTION.

absolute privilege. See PRIVILEGE (1).

absolution (ab-sə-**loo**-shən). **1.** Release from a penalty; the act of absolving. **2.** An acquittal of a criminal charge.

abstract of conviction. A summary of the court's finding on an offense, esp. a moving violation.

abstract question. See HYPOTHETICAL QUESTION.

abuse (ə-**byoos**), *n*. **1.** A departure from legal or reasonable use; misuse. **2.** Physical or mental maltreatment.

abuse of the elderly. Physical or psychological abuse of an elderly person by a caretaker. ● Examples include deprivation of food or medication, beatings, oral assaults, and isolation.—Also termed *elder abuse*.

carnal abuse. See *sexual abuse*.

child abuse. The act or series of acts of physically or emotionally injuring a child. ● Child abuse may be intentional (as with sexual molestation) or negligent (as with some types of child neglect).—Also termed *cruelty to a child*; *cruelty to children.* See BATTERED-CHILD SYNDROME. Cf. CHILD NEGLECT.

elder abuse. See *abuse of the elderly.*

sexual abuse. 1. An illegal sex act, esp. one performed against a minor by an adult.— Also termed *carnal abuse.* **2.** See RAPE (2).

spousal abuse. Physical, sexual, or psychological abuse inflicted by one spouse on the other spouse. See BATTERED-WOMAN SYNDROME.

abuse (ə-**byooz**), *vb.* **1.** To depart from legal or reasonable use in dealing with (a person or thing); to misuse. **2.** To injure (a person) physically or mentally. **3.** To damage (a thing).

abuse excuse. The defense that a defendant is unable to tell right from wrong because of physical or mental abuse suffered as a child. ● Like the traditional excuse of insanity, the abuse excuse is asserted by a defendant in an effort to avoid all culpability for the crime charged.

abuse of the elderly. See ABUSE.

abuse-of-the-writ doctrine. The principle that a petition for a writ of habeas corpus may not raise claims that should have been, but were not, asserted in a previous petition. Cf. SUCCESSIVE-WRIT DOCTRINE.

abusive (ə-**byoo**-siv), *adj.* **1.** Characterized by wrongful or improper use <abusive trial tactics>. **2.** Of or relating to a person who treats another badly <abusive parent>.—**abusively,** *adv.*

accessorial (ak-sə-**sor**-ee-əl), *adj.* Of or relating to the accessory in a crime <accessorial guilt>.

accessory (ak-**ses**-ə-ree), *n.* A person who aids or contributes in the commission or concealment of a crime. ● An accessory is usu. liable only if the crime is a felony.—**accessory,** *adj.*—**accessoryship,** *n.* Cf. PRINCIPAL.

accessory after the fact. An accessory who knows that a crime has been committed and who helps the offender try to escape arrest or punishment. ● Most penal statutes establish the following four requirements: (1) someone else must have committed a felony, and it must have been completed before the accessory's act; (2) the accessory must not be guilty as a principal; (3) the accessory must personally help the principal try to avoid the consequences of the felony; and (4) the accessory's assistance must be rendered with guilty knowledge.—Sometimes shortened to *accessory after.*

accessory at the fact. See *principal in the second degree* under PRINCIPAL.

accessory before the fact. An accessory who assists or encourages another to commit a crime but who is not present when the offense is actually committed. • Most jurisdictions have abolished this category of accessory and instead treat such an offender as an accomplice.—Sometimes shortened to *accessory before*. See ACCOMPLICE.

access to counsel. See RIGHT TO COUNSEL.

accidental killing. Homicide resulting from a lawful act performed in a lawful manner under a reasonable belief that no harm could occur.—Also termed *death by misadventure*; *homicide by misadventure*; *killing by misadventure*; *homicide per infortunium*. See *justifiable homicide* under HOMICIDE. Cf. *involuntary manslaughter* under MANSLAUGHTER.

accomplice (ə-**kom**-plis). **1.** A person who is in any way involved with another in the commission of a crime, whether as a principal in the first or second degree or as an accessory. • Although the definition includes an accessory before the fact, not all authorities treat this term as including an accessory after the fact. **2.** A person who knowingly, voluntarily, and intentionally unites with the principal offender in committing a crime and thereby becomes punishable for it. See ACCESSORY. Cf. PRINCIPAL.

7

accomplice liability. See LIABILITY.

accomplice witness. See WITNESS.

accountant-client privilege. See PRIVILEGE (3).

accumulative sentences. See *consecutive sentences* under SENTENCE.

accusation, *n*. **1.** A formal charge of criminal wrongdoing. • The accusation is usu. presented to a court or magistrate having jurisdiction to inquire into the alleged crime. **2.** An informal statement that a person has engaged in an illegal or immoral act.

> ***malicious accusation.*** An accusation against another for an improper purpose and without probable cause. See MALICIOUS PROSECUTION.

accusatorial system. See ADVERSARY SYSTEM.

accusatory (ə-**kyoo**-zə-tor-ee), *adj*. Of, relating to, or constituting an accusation.

accusatory body. A body (such as a grand jury) that hears evidence and determines whether a person should be charged with a crime.

accusatory instrument. See CHARGING INSTRUMENT.

accusatory part. The section of an indictment in which the offense is named.

accusatory pleading. See PLEADING.

accusatory procedure. See ADVERSARY SYSTEM.

accusatory stage. The point in a criminal proceeding when the suspect's right to counsel attaches. • This occurs usu. after arrest and once interrogation begins. Cf. CRITICAL STAGE.

accuse, *vb.* To charge (a person) judicially or publicly with an offense; to make an accusation against <she accused him of the crime> <he was accused as an accomplice>.

accused, *n.* A person who has been blamed for wrongdoing; esp., a person who has been arrested and brought before a magistrate or who has been formally charged with a crime (as by indictment or information).

accuser. A person who accuses another of a crime.

accusing jury. See GRAND JURY.

acquaintance rape. See RAPE.

acquiescence (ak-wee-**es**-ənts). A person's tacit or passive acceptance; implied consent to an act.

acquisitive offense. See OFFENSE.

acquit, *vb*. To clear (a person) of a criminal charge.

acquittal, *n*. The legal certification, usu. by jury verdict, that an accused person is not guilty of the charged offense.

>**acquittal in fact.** An acquittal by a jury verdict of not guilty.

>**acquittal in law.** An acquittal by operation of law, as of someone who has been charged merely as an accessory after the principal has been acquitted.

>**implied acquittal.** An acquittal in which a jury convicts the defendant of a lesser-included offense without commenting on the greater offense. • Double jeopardy bars the retrial of a defendant who has received an implied acquittal.

acquitted, *adj*. Judicially discharged from an accusation; absolved.

act, *n*. **1.** Something done or performed, esp. voluntarily; a deed. **2.** The process of doing or performing; an occurrence that results from a person's will being exerted on the external world; ACTION (1).—Also termed *positive act*; *act of commission*.

action. 1. The process of doing something; conduct or behavior. **2.** A thing done; ACT (1). **3.** A civil or criminal judicial proceeding.

criminal action. An action instituted by the government to punish offenses against the public.

penal action. **1.** A criminal prosecution. **2.** A civil proceeding in which either the state or a common informer sues to recover a penalty from a defendant who has violated a statute. ● Although civil in nature, a penal action resembles a criminal proceeding because the result of a successful action is a monetary penalty intended, like a fine, to punish the defendant. See COMMON INFORMER.

active case. See CASE.

active concealment. See CONCEALMENT.

active euthanasia. See EUTHANASIA.

act of attainder. See BILL OF ATTAINDER.

act of commission. See ACT.

actual cause. See *but-for cause* under CAUSE (1).

actual escape. See ESCAPE (2).

actual-evidence test. See SAME-EVIDENCE TEST.

actual force. See FORCE.

actual innocence. See INNOCENCE.

actual malice. See MALICE.

actual physical control. Direct bodily power over something, esp. a vehicle. ● Many jurisdictions require a showing of "actual physical control" of a vehicle by a person charged with driving while intoxicated.

actus reus (**ak**-təs **ree**-əs *also* **ray**-əs). [Law Latin "guilty act"] The wrongful deed that comprises the physical components of a crime and that generally must be coupled with *mens rea* to establish criminal liability; a forbidden act <the *actus reus* for theft is the taking of or unlawful control over property without the owner's consent>.—Also termed *deed of crime*; *overt act*. Cf. MENS REA.

addict (**a**-dikt), *n.* A person who habitually uses a substance, esp. a narcotic drug.—**ad-**

dict (ə-**dikt**), *vb.*—**addictive,** *adj.*—**addiction,** *n.*

> ***drug addict.*** A person who is psychologically or physiologically dependent on a narcotic drug.

addictive drug. See DRUG.

additional grand jury. See *special grand jury* under GRAND JURY.

additional instruction. See JURY INSTRUCTION.

adequate cause. See *adequate provocation* under PROVOCATION.

adequate provocation. See PROVOCATION.

adjudication withheld. See *deferred judgment* under JUDGMENT.

adjudicative fact. See FACT.

adjudicative law. See CASELAW.

adjudicatory hearing. See HEARING.

administrative crime. See CRIME.

administrative search. See SEARCH.

administrative warrant. See WARRANT.

admissibility (ad-mis-ə-**bil**-ə-tee), *n.* The quality or state of being allowed to be entered into evidence in a hearing, trial, or other proceeding.

conditional admissibility. The evidentiary rule that when a piece of evidence is not itself admissible, but is admissible if certain other facts make it relevant, the evidence becomes admissible on condition that counsel later introduce the connecting facts. ● If counsel does not satisfy this condition, the opponent is entitled to have the conditionally admitted piece of evidence struck from the record, and to have the judge instruct the jury to disregard it.

curative admissibility. The rule that an inadmissible piece of evidence may be admitted if offered to cure or counteract the effect of some similar piece of the opponent's evidence that itself should not have been admitted.

limited admissibility. The principle that testimony or exhibits may be admitted into evidence for a restricted purpose. ● Common examples are admitting prior contradictory testimony to impeach a witness but not to establish the truth, and admitting evidence against one party but not another. The trial court must, upon request, instruct the jury

14

properly about the applicable limits when admitting the evidence. Fed. R. Evid. 105.

multiple admissibility. The evidentiary rule that, though a piece of evidence is inadmissible under one rule for the purpose given in offering it, it is nevertheless admissible if relevant and offered for some other purpose not forbidden by the rules of evidence.

admissible (ad-**mis**-ə-bəl), *adj.* Capable of being legally admitted; allowable; permissible <admissible evidence>.

admissible evidence. See EVIDENCE.

admission (ad-**mish**-ən), *n.* Any statement or assertion made by a party to a case and offered against that party; an acknowledgment that facts are true.—**admit,** *vb.* Cf. CONFESSION.

admission against interest. A person's statement acknowledging a fact that is harmful to the person's position as a litigant. ● An admission against interest must be made either by a litigant or by one in privity with or occupying the same legal position as the litigant; as an exception to the hearsay rule, it is admissible whether or not the person is available as a witness. A declaration against interest, by contrast, is made by a nonlitigant who is not in privity with a litigant; a declaration against interest is also admissible as an exception to the hearsay rule, but only when the declarant is unavailable as a witness. See *declaration against interest* under DECLARATION.

admission by employee or agent. An admission made by a party-opponent's agent during employment and concerning a matter either within the scope of the agency or authorized by the party-opponent.

admission by party-opponent. An opposing party's admission, which is not considered hearsay if it is offered against that party and is (1) the party's own statement, in either an individual or a representative capacity; (2) a statement of which the party has manifested an adoption or belief in its truth; (3) a statement by one authorized by the party to make such a statement; (4) a statement by the party's agent concerning a matter within the scope of the agency or employment and made during the existence of the relationship; or (5) a statement by a coconspirator of the party during the course of and in furtherance of the conspiracy. Fed. R. Evid. 801(d)(2).

admission by silence. The failure of a party to speak after an assertion of fact by another party that, if untrue, would naturally compel a person to deny the statement.

adoptive admission. An action by a party that indicates approval of a statement made by another, and thereby acceptance that the statement is true.

extrajudicial admission. An admission made outside court proceedings.

implied admission. An admission reasonably inferable from a party's action or statement, or a party's failure to act or speak.—Also termed *tacit admission.*

incidental admission. An admission made in some other connection or involved in the admission of some other fact.

incriminating admission. An admission of facts tending to establish guilt.

quasi-admission. An act or utterance, usu. extrajudicial, that creates an inconsistency with and discredits, to a greater or lesser degree, a present claim or other evidence of the person creating the inconsistency.

tacit admission. See *implied admission.*

admonition (ad-mə-**nish**-ən), *n.* A warning or cautionary statement, as by a judge to a lawyer or a jury <the judge's admonition that the jurors consider only the evidence before them>.—**admonish** (ad-**mon**-ish), *vb.*—**admonitory** (ad-**mon**-ə-tor-ee), *adj.*

adoptive admission. See ADMISSION.

adoptive-admissions rule. The principle that a statement offered against an accused is not inadmissible hearsay if the accused is aware of the statement and has, by words or conduct, indicated acceptance that the statement is true. See *adoptive admission* under ADMISSION.

adult (ə-**dəlt** *or* **ad**-əlt), *n.* A person who has attained the legal age of majority, generally 17 in criminal cases and 18 for other purposes.— Also termed *major*.—**adult** (ə-**dəlt**), *adj.*

adult correctional institution. See PRISON.

adulterator (ə-**dəl**-tə-ray-tər), *n.* A corrupter; a forger or counterfeiter.

adultery (ə-**dəl**-tə-ree), *n.* Voluntary sexual intercourse between a married person and someone other than that person's spouse. ● Adultery is variously defined and punished in some state statutes, but it is seldom prosecuted.—Formerly also termed *spouse-breach.*— **adulterous,** *adj.* Cf. FORNICATION; INFIDELITY.

  double adultery. Adultery by persons who are both married to other persons.

  incestuous adultery. Adultery by persons who are closely related.

18

open and notorious adultery. *Archaic.* Adultery in which the persons reside together publicly as if they were married, even though they are not, and about which the community is generally aware.

single adultery. Adultery in which only one of the persons is married.

adult offender. See OFFENDER.

adversary system. A procedural system, such as the Anglo–American legal system, in which contesting parties present a case before an independent decision-maker.—Also termed *adversary procedure*; (in criminal cases) *accusatorial system*; *accusatory procedure*. Cf. INQUISITORIAL SYSTEM.

adverse witness. See *hostile witness* under WITNESS.

advice of counsel. 1. The guidance given by lawyers to their clients. **2.** In a malicious-prosecution lawsuit, a defense requiring both a complete presentation of facts by the defendant to his or her attorney and honest compliance with the attorney's advice. **3.** A defense in which a party seeks to avoid liability by claiming that he or she acted reasonably and in good faith on the attorney's advice. ● Such a defense usu. requires waiver of the attorney-client privilege, and the attorney cannot have

19

knowingly participated in implementing an illegal plan.

advisory counsel. See *standby counsel* under COUNSEL.

advisory jury. See JURY.

advisory opinion. See OPINION.

advocate-witness rule. See LAWYER-WITNESS RULE.

affectively spontaneous crime. See CRIME.

affidavit (af-ə-**day**-vit). A voluntary declaration of facts written down and sworn to by the declarant before an officer authorized to administer oaths. ● A great deal of evidence is submitted by affidavit, esp. in pretrial matters. Cf. DECLARATION (2).

>   *poverty affidavit.* An affidavit made by an indigent person seeking public assistance, appointment of counsel, waiver of court fees, or other free public services. 28 USCA § 1915.—Also termed *pauper's affidavit*; *in forma pauperis affidavit*; *IFP affidavit*.

affirmation, *n.* A pledge equivalent to an oath but without reference to a supreme being or to "swearing." ● While an oath is "sworn to," an affirmation is merely "affirmed," but either type of pledge may subject the person making it to the penalties for perjury.—**affirm,** *vb.*—**affirmatory,** *adj.* Cf. OATH.

affirmative charge. See *affirmative instruction* under JURY INSTRUCTION.

affirmative converse instruction. See JURY INSTRUCTION.

affirmative defense. See DEFENSE.

affirmative instruction. See JURY INSTRUCTION.

affirmative misconduct. See MISCONDUCT.

affirmative pregnant. A positive statement that ambiguously implies a negative; a statement that does not explicitly deny a charge, but instead answers an unasked question and thereby implies culpability, as when a person says "I returned your car yesterday" to the charge "You stole my car!" Cf. NEGATIVE PREGNANT.

affirmative proof. See PROOF.

affirmative testimony. See TESTIMONY.

affray (ə-**fray**). The fighting, by mutual consent, of two or more persons in some public place, to the terror of onlookers. ● The fighting must be mutual. If one person unlawfully attacks another who resorts to self-defense, the first is guilty of assault and battery, but there is no affray.—Also termed *fray*. Cf. RIOT; *unlawful assembly* under ASSEMBLY; ROUT.

> **casual affray.** See CHANCE-MEDLEY.

> **mutual affray.** See MUTUAL COMBAT.

aftercare. See *juvenile parole* under PAROLE.

AG. *abbr*. ATTORNEY GENERAL.

against the peace and dignity of the state. A concluding phrase in an indictment, used to condemn the offending conduct generally (as opposed to the specific charge of wrongdoing contained in the body of the instrument). ● This phrase derives from the Law Latin *contra pacem domini regis* ("against the peace of the lord the king"), a charging phrase once used in indictments and in civil actions of trespass.

against the weight of the evidence. (Of a verdict or judgment) contrary to the credible evidence; not sufficiently supported by the evidence in the record. See WEIGHT OF THE EVIDENCE.

against the will. Contrary to a person's wishes. • Indictments use this phrase to indicate that the defendant's conduct was without the victim's consent.

agent. **1.** One who is authorized to act for or in place of another; a representative <a professional athlete's agent>. Cf. PRINCIPAL. **2.** Something that produces an effect <an intervening agent>. See CAUSE.

> ***government agent.*** **1.** A law-enforcement official, such as a police officer or an FBI agent. **2.** An informant, esp. an inmate, hired by law enforcement to obtain incriminating statements from another inmate. • An accused's Sixth Amendment right to counsel is triggered when the accused is questioned by a government agent.

> ***innocent agent.*** A person who lacks the mens rea for an offense but who is tricked or coerced by the principal into committing a crime. • The principal is legally accountable for the innocent agent's actions. See Model Penal Code § 2.06(2)(a).

> ***undercover agent.*** **1.** An agent who does not disclose his or her role as an agent. **2.** A police officer who gathers evidence of criminal activity without disclosing his or her identity to the suspect.

agent provocateur (**ay**-jənt prə-vok-ə-**tər** *or* **a**-zhaw*n* praw-vaw-kə-**tuur**), *n.* **1.** An undercover agent who instigates or participates in a crime, often by infiltrating a group involved in suspected illegal conduct, to expose and punish criminal activity. **2.** A person who entraps another, or entices another to break the law, and then informs against the other as a lawbreaker.

age of capacity. The age, usu. defined by statute as 18 years, at which a person is legally capable of agreeing to a contract, executing a will, maintaining a lawsuit, or the like.—Also termed *age of majority*; *legal age*; *lawful age*. See CAPACITY.

age of consent. The age, usu. defined by statute as 16 years, at which a person is legally capable of agreeing to marriage (without parental consent) or to sexual intercourse.

age of majority. 1. The age, usu. defined by statute as 18 years, at which a person attains full legal rights, esp. civil and political rights such as the right to vote.—Also termed *lawful age*. **2.** See AGE OF CAPACITY.

age of reason. The age at which a person becomes able to distinguish right from wrong and is thus legally capable of committing a crime. ● The age of reason varies from jurisdiction to jurisdiction, but 7 years is usu. the age below which a child is conclusively presumed not to have committed a crime, while 14 years is usu. the age below which a rebuttable presumption applies.

aggravated, *adj.* (Of a crime) made worse or more serious by circumstances such as violence, the presence of a deadly weapon, or the intent to commit another crime <aggravated robbery>. Cf. SIMPLE.

aggravated arson. See ARSON.

aggravated assault. See ASSAULT.

aggravated battery. See BATTERY.

aggravated harassment. See HARASSMENT.

aggravated kidnapping. See KIDNAPPING.

aggravated larceny. See LARCENY.

aggravated misdemeanor. See *serious misdemeanor* under MISDEMEANOR.

aggravated robbery. See ROBBERY.

aggravated sodomy. See SODOMY.

aggravating circumstance. See CIRCUM-
STANCE.

aggravating element. See *aggravating circumstance* under CIRCUMSTANCE.

aggravating factor. See *aggravating circumstance* under CIRCUMSTANCE.

aggravator. 1. One who commits a crime
with an aggravating circumstance. **2.** See *aggravating circumstance* under CIRCUMSTANCE.

aggregate sentence. See SENTENCE.

Aguilar–Spinelli **test** (ah-gee-**lahr** spi-**nel**-
ee *or* **ag**-wə-lahr). A standard for determining
whether hearsay (such as an informant's tip)
is sufficiently reliable to establish probable
cause for an arrest or search warrant. ● Under
this two-pronged test—which has been replaced by a broader, totality-of-the-circumstances approach—the reliability of both the
information and the informant must be assessed independently. *Aguilar v. Texas*, 378
U.S. 108, 84 S.Ct. 1509 (1964); *Spinelli v.
United States*, 393 U.S. 410, 89 S.Ct. 584
(1969). Cf. TOTALITY-OF-THE-CIRCUMSTANCES TEST.

aid and abet, *vb.* To assist or facilitate the
commission of a crime, or to promote its accomplishment. ● Aiding and abetting is a

crime in most jurisdictions.—Also termed *aid or abet*; *counsel and procure*.—**aider and abettor,** *n*.

aid and comfort. Help given by someone to a national enemy in such a way that the help amounts to treason.

aiding an escape. The crime of helping a prisoner escape custody.

aid or abet. See AID AND ABET.

aircraft piracy. See *air piracy* under PIRACY.

air piracy. See PIRACY.

alcoholometer. See BREATHALYZER.

Alford **plea.** A guilty plea that a defendant enters as part of a plea bargain, without actually admitting guilt. ● This plea is not considered compelled within the language of the Fifth Amendment if the plea represents a voluntary, knowing, and intelligent choice between the available options <the defendant—realizing the strength of the prosecution's evidence and not wanting to risk receiving the death penalty—entered into an *Alford* plea>. *North Carolina v. Alford*, 400 U.S. 25, 91 S.Ct. 160 (1970).

alias, *n.* An assumed or additional name that a person has used or is known by.—Also termed *assumed name*.

alias subpoena. See SUBPOENA.

alias summons. See SUMMONS.

alias writ. See WRIT.

alibi (al-ə-bɪ), *n.* [Latin "elsewhere"] **1.** A defense based on the physical impossibility of a defendant's guilt by placing the defendant in a location other than the scene of the crime at the relevant time. Fed. R. Crim. P. 12.1. **2.** The fact or state of having been elsewhere when an offense was committed.

alibi, *vb.* To offer or provide an alibi for <the conspirators alibied for each other>.

alibi witness. See WITNESS.

ALI test. See SUBSTANTIAL-CAPACITY TEST.

aliunde (ay-lee-yən-dee), *adj.* [Latin] From another source; from elsewhere <evidence aliunde>. See *extrinsic evidence* under EVIDENCE.

aliunde rule. The doctrine that a verdict may not be impeached by a juror's testimony unless a foundation for the testimony is first made by competent evidence from another source.

allegation, *n*. **1.** The act of declaring something to be true. **2.** Something declared or asserted as a matter of fact, esp. in a legal pleading; a party's formal statement of a factual matter as being true or provable, without its having yet been proved.—**allege,** *vb*.

   disjunctive allegation. A statement in a pleading or indictment that expresses something in the alternative, usu. with the conjunction "or" <a charge that the defendant murdered or caused to be murdered is a disjunctive allegation>.

   material allegation. In a pleading, an assertion that is essential to the charge or defense <a material allegation in a battery case is harmful or offensive contact with a person>.

   primary allegation. The principal charge made against an adversary in a legal proceeding.

alleged (ə-**lejd**), *adj*. **1.** Asserted to be true as described <alleged offenses>. **2.** Accused but not yet tried <alleged murderer>.

Allen **charge.** A supplemental jury instruction given by the court to encourage a deadlocked jury, after prolonged deliberations, to reach a verdict. *Allen v. United States*, 164 U.S. 492, 17 S.Ct. 154 (1896).—Also termed *dynamite charge*; *dynamite instruction*; *nitroglycerine charge*; *shotgun instruction*; *third-degree instruction*.

allied offense. See OFFENSE.

allocute (**al**-ə-kyoot), *vb*. To deliver an allocution in court.

allocution (al-ə-**kyoo**-shən), *n*. **1.** A trial judge's formal address to a convicted defendant, asking him or her to speak in mitigation of the sentence to be imposed. ● This address is required under Fed. R. Crim. P. 32(c)(3)(C). **2.** An unsworn statement from a convicted defendant to the sentencing judge or jury in which the defendant can ask for mercy, explain his or her conduct, apologize for the crime, or say anything else in an effort to lessen the impending sentence. ● This statement is not subject to cross-examination.

   victim allocution. A crime victim's address to the court before sentencing, usu. urging a harsher punishment.

allocutory (ə-**lok**-yə-tor-ee), *adj*. Of or relating to an allocution <allocutory pleas for mercy>.

altercation. A vehement dispute; a noisy argument.

alter-ego rule. The principle that one who defends another against attack stands in the position of that other person and can use only the amount of force that the other person could use under the circumstances.

alternative-means doctrine. The principle that when a crime may be committed in more than one way, the jury must be unanimous on the defendant's guilt but need not be unanimous on the possible different methods of committing the crime, as long as each possible method is supported by substantial evidence.

alternative sentence. See SENTENCE.

ambulatory automatism. See AUTOMATISM.

amendment of indictment. The alteration of the charging terms of an indictment, either literally or in effect, after the grand jury has made a decision on it. ● The indictment usu. cannot be amended at trial in a way that would prejudice the defendant by having a trial on matters that were not contained in the indictment. To do so would violate the defendant's Fifth Amendment right to indictment by grand jury.

American Law Institute test. See SUBSTAN-
TIAL-CAPACITY TEST.

amnesty, *n*. A pardon extended by the government to a group or class of persons, usu.
for a political offense; the act of a sovereign
power officially forgiving certain classes of persons who are subject to trial but have not yet
been convicted <the 1986 Immigration Reform
and Control Act provided amnesty for undocu-
mented aliens already present in the coun-
try>. ● Unlike an ordinary pardon, amnesty is
usu. addressed to crimes against state sovereignty—that is, to political offenses with respect to which forgiveness is deemed more
expedient for the public welfare than prosecution and punishment. Amnesty is usu. general,
addressed to classes or even communities.—
Also termed *general pardon*.—**amnesty,** *vb*.
See PARDON.

>   *express amnesty*. Amnesty granted in di-
>   rect terms.

>   *implied amnesty*. Amnesty indirectly re-
>   sulting from a peace treaty executed be-
>   tween contending parties.

amnesty clause. A clause, esp. one found in a
peace treaty, that wipes out past offenses such
as treason, sedition, rebellion, and even war
crimes. ● A sovereign may grant amnesty to all

guilty persons or only to certain categories of offenders.

Amnesty International. An international nongovernmental organization founded in the early 1960s to protect human rights throughout the world. ● Its mission is to "secure throughout the world the observance of the Universal Declaration of Human Rights." Amnesty Int'l Statute, art. 1.

***Anders* brief.** A brief filed by a court-appointed defense attorney who wants to withdraw from the case on appeal based on a belief that the appeal is frivolous. ● In an *Anders* brief, the attorney seeking to withdraw must identify anything in the record that might arguably support the appeal. The court then decides whether the appeal is frivolous and whether the attorney should be permitted to withdraw. *Anders v. California*, 386 U.S. 738, 87 S.Ct. 1396 (1967).—Also termed *no-merit brief*.

animus (**an**-ə-məs). [Latin] **1.** Ill will; animosity. **2.** Intention.

> ***animus felonicus*** (**an**-ə-məs fe-**loh**-ni-kəs). The intention to commit a felony.

> ***animus furandi*** (**an**-ə-məs fyuu-**ran**-dɪ). The intention to steal.—Also termed *furandi animus*.

animus injuriandi (**an**-ə-məs in-joor-ee-**an**-dɪ). The intention to injure, esp. to insult.

animus malus (**an**-ə-məs **mal**-əs). Evil intent.

animus nocendi (**an**-ə-məs noh-**sen**-dɪ). The intention to harm.

anomalous jurisdiction. See JURISDICTION.

anonymous, *adj.* Not named or identified <the police arrested the defendant after a tip from an anonymous informant>.—**anonymity** (an-ə-**nim**-ə-tee), *n.*

anthropometry (an-thrə-**pom**-ə-tree). A system of measuring the human body, esp. the size relationships among the different parts. ● Before the advent of fingerprinting, minute measurements of the human body—taken and compared to other persons' measurements— were used to identify criminals and deceased persons.—**anthropometric,** *adj.* Cf. BERTILLON SYSTEM.

anticipatory offense. See *inchoate offense* under OFFENSE.

anticipatory search warrant. See SEARCH WARRANT.

anti-john law. A criminal-law statute punishing prostitutes' customers.

antimarital-facts privilege. See *marital privilege* (2) under PRIVILEGE (3).

appeal, *n.* A proceeding undertaken to have a decision reconsidered by bringing it to a higher authority; esp., the submission of a lower court's or agency's decision to a higher court for review and possible reversal <the case is on appeal>. Cf. CERTIORARI.

　appeal by right. An appeal to a higher court from which permission need not be first obtained.—Also termed *appeal as of right*; *appeal of right*.

　appeal in forma pauperis (in **for**-mə **paw**-pər-is). An appeal by an indigent party, for whom court costs are waived. Fed. R. App. P. 24. See IN FORMA PAUPERIS.

　delayed appeal. An appeal that takes place after the time for appealing has expired, but only when the reviewing court has granted permission because of special circumstances.

　interlocutory appeal. An appeal that occurs before the trial court's final ruling on the entire case. ● Some interlocutory appeals involve legal points necessary to the determination of the case, while others involve collateral orders that are wholly separate from the merits of the action.

limited appeal. An appeal from only certain portions of a decision, usu. only the adverse or unfavorable portions.

appeal, *vb.* To seek review (from a lower court's decision) by a higher court <petitioner appeals the conviction>.—**appealability,** *n.*

appeal as of right. See *appeal by right* under APPEAL.

appeal by right. See APPEAL.

appealer. See APPELLANT.

appeal in forma pauperis. See APPEAL.

appeal of right. See *appeal by right* under APPEAL.

appearance, *n.* A coming into court as a party or interested person, or as a lawyer on behalf of a party or interested person.—**appear,** *vb.*

initial appearance. A criminal defendant's first appearance in court to hear the charges read, to be advised of his or her rights, and to have bail determined. • The initial appearance is usu. required by statute to occur without undue delay. In a misdemeanor case, the initial appearance may be combined with the arraignment. See AR-RAIGNMENT.

appearance bond. See *bail bond* under BOND.

appearance docket. See DOCKET (1).

appearance doctrine. In the law of self-defense, the rule that a defendant's use of force is justified if the defendant reasonably believed it to be justified.

appearance ticket. See CITATION.

appellant (ə-**pel**-ənt). A party who appeals a lower court's decision, usu. seeking reversal of that decision.—Formerly also termed *appealer*. Cf. APPELLEE.

appellate (ə-**pel**-it), *adj*. Of or relating to an appeal or appeals generally.

appellate jurisdiction. See JURISDICTION.

appellate record. See RECORD ON APPEAL.

appellate review. See REVIEW.

appellee (ap-ə-**lee**). A party against whom an appeal is taken and whose role is to respond to that appeal, usu. seeking affirmance of the lower court's decision. Cf. APPELLANT.

application for leave to appeal. A motion requesting an appellate court to hear a party's appeal from a judgment when the party has no appeal by right or when the party's time limit for an appeal by right has expired. • The reviewing court has discretion whether to grant or reject such a motion.

appreciation test. A test for the insanity defense requiring proof by clear and convincing evidence that at the time of the crime, the defendant suffered from a severe mental disease or defect preventing him or her from appreciating the wrongfulness of the conduct. • This test, along with the accompanying plea of *not guilty by reason of insanity*, was established by the Insanity Defense Reform Act of 1984. 18 USCA § 17.—Also termed *Insanity Defense Reform Act of 1984 test*. See INSANITY DEFENSE.

apprehension, *n.* **1.** Seizure in the name of the law; arrest <apprehension of a criminal>. **2.** Perception; comprehension <the tort of assault requires apprehension by the victim of imminent contact>. **3.** Fear; anxiety <the witness testified with some apprehension>.—**apprehend,** *vb.*

approver (ə-**proo**-vər), *n*. Formerly, one who offers proof; esp., a criminal who confesses and testifies against one or more accomplices.

argumentative instruction. See JURY IN-STRUCTION.

armed, *adj*. **1.** Equipped with a weapon <an armed robber>. **2.** Involving the use of a weapon <armed robbery>.

armed robbery. See ROBBERY.

arraignment, *n*. The initial step in a criminal prosecution whereby the defendant is brought before the court to hear the charges and to enter a plea.—**arraign,** *vb*. Cf. PRELIMINARY HEARING; *initial appearance* under APPEARANCE.

array, *n*. **1.** A panel of potential jurors; VENIRE (1) <the array of mostly wealthy professionals seemed to favor the corporate defendant>. **2.** The jurors actually impaneled <the array hearing the case consisted of seven women and five men>. **3.** A list or roster of impaneled jurors <the defendant obtained a copy of the array to help prepare for voir dire>. **4.** Order; arrangement <the array of jurors from oldest to youngest>. **5.** A militia <the array organized antigovernment rallies>. **6.** A series of statistics or a group of elements <a mathematical array>.

array, *vb.* **1.** To impanel a jury for trial. **2.** To call out the names of jurors, one by one, as they are impaneled.

arrest, *n.* **1.** A seizure or forcible restraint. **2.** The taking or keeping of a person in custody by legal authority, esp. in response to a criminal charge.—**arrest,** *vb.*

>   *arrest in quarters.* A nonjudicial punishment that can be given to officers and warrant officers only by a general, a flag officer in command, or an officer exercising general court-martial jurisdiction. See BREACH OF ARREST.

>   *citizen's arrest.* An arrest of a private person by another private person on grounds that (1) a public offense was committed in the arrester's presence, or (2) the arrester has reasonable cause to believe that the arrestee has committed a felony.

>   *false arrest.* An arrest made without proper legal authority. Cf. FALSE IMPRISONMENT.

>   *house arrest.* See HOUSE ARREST.

>   *lawful arrest.* The taking of a person into legal custody either under a valid warrant or on probable cause that the person has committed a crime.

malicious arrest. An arrest made without probable cause and for an improper purpose; esp., an abuse of process by which a person procures the arrest (and often the imprisonment) of another by means of judicial process, without any reasonable cause. • Malicious arrest can be grounds for an action for abuse of process, false imprisonment, or malicious prosecution.

parol arrest (pə-**rohl** *or* **par**-əl). An arrest ordered by a judge or magistrate from the bench, without written complaint, and executed immediately, such as an arrest of a person who breaches the peace in open court. See CONTEMPT.

pretextual arrest. An arrest of a person for a minor offense for the opportunity to investigate the person's involvement in a more serious offense for which there are no lawful grounds to make an arrest.—Also termed *pretext arrest.*

rearrest. A warrantless arrest of a person who has escaped from custody, violated parole or probation, or failed to appear in court as ordered.

subterfuge arrest. An arrest of a suspect for the stated purpose of obtaining evidence of one crime but with the underlying intent to search the suspect for evidence of a different crime.

warranted arrest. An arrest made under authority of a warrant.

warrantless arrest. An arrest, without a warrant, based on probable cause of a felony, or for a misdemeanor committed in a police officer's presence.—Also termed *arrest without a warrant*. See WARRANT.

arrestee. A person who has been taken into custody by legal authority; a person who has been arrested.

arrest in quarters. See ARREST.

arrest record. 1. A form completed by a police officer when a person is arrested. **2.** A cumulative list of the instances when a person has been arrested.—Also termed *police blotter*; *bench blotter*; *blotter*; *log*.

arrest warrant. See WARRANT.

arrest without a warrant. See *warrantless arrest* under ARREST.

arson, *n*. **1.** At common law, the malicious burning of someone else's dwelling house or outhouse that is either appurtenant to the dwelling house or within the curtilage. **2.** Under modern statutes, the intentional and wrongful burning of someone else's property (as to destroy a building) or one's own property (as to fraudulently collect insurance). See Model Penal Code § 220.1(1).—Also termed (in sense 2) *statutory arson*. Cf. HOUSEBURNING; CRIMINAL DAMAGE TO PROPERTY.

> **aggravated arson.** Arson accompanied by some aggravating factor, as when the offender foresees or anticipates that one or more persons will be in or near the property being burned.

arsonable, *adj.* (Of property) of such a nature as to give rise to a charge of arson if maliciously burned <only real property, and not personal property, is arsonable>.

arsonist. One who commits arson; INCENDIARY (1).

arsonous, *adj.* Of, relating to, or involving arson <an arsonous purpose>.

artifice (**ahr**-tə-fis). A clever plan or idea, esp. one intended to deceive.

artificial presumption. See *presumption of law* under PRESUMPTION.

asportation (as-pər-**tay**-shən), *n.* The act of carrying away or removing (property or a person). ● Asportation is a necessary element of larceny.—Also termed *carrying away.*—**asport,** *vb.*—**asportative,** *adj.* See LARCENY.

assailant. 1. One who physically attacks another; one who commits an assault. **2.** One who attacks another using nonphysical means; esp., one who attacks another's position or feelings, as by criticism, argument, or abusive language.

assassination, *n.* The act of deliberately killing someone, esp. a public figure, usu. for hire or for political reasons.—**assassinate,** *vb.*—**assassin,** *n.*

assault, *n.* **1.** The threat or use of force on another that causes that person to have a reasonable apprehension of imminent harmful or offensive contact; the act of putting another person in reasonable fear or apprehension of an immediate battery by means of an act amounting to an attempt or threat to commit a battery. **2.** An attempt to commit battery, requiring the specific intent to cause physical injury.—Also termed (in senses 1 and 2) *simple assault.* **3.** Loosely, a battery. **4.** Popularly, any attack.—**assault,** *vb.*—**assaultive,** *adj.* Cf. BATTERY.

aggravated assault. Criminal assault accompanied by circumstances that make it more severe, such as the intent to commit another crime or the intent to cause serious bodily injury, esp. by using a deadly weapon. See Model Penal Code § 211.1(2).

assault to rape. See *assault with intent to commit rape.*

assault with a deadly weapon. An aggravated assault in which the defendant, controlling a deadly weapon, threatens the victim with death or serious bodily injury.

assault with intent. Any of several assaults that are carried out with an additional criminal purpose in mind, such as assault with intent to murder, assault with intent to rob, assault with intent to rape, and assault with intent to inflict great bodily injury. • These are modern statutory inventions that are often found in state penal codes.

assault with intent to commit rape. An assault carried out with the additional criminal purpose of raping the victim.—Also termed *assault to rape.*

atrocious assault. An assault involving savage brutality.

attempted assault. An attempt to commit an assault; an attempted battery that has not progressed far enough to be an assault, as when a person intends to harm someone physically but is captured after trying to locate the intended victim in his or her place of employment. • Traditionally, most commentators held that an attempted assault could not exist because assault was in itself an attempt to commit a crime. Many modern authorities, however, assert that an attempted assault can occur, and that it should be punishable.—Also termed *attempt to assault*. See ATTEMPT TO ATTEMPT.

civil assault. An assault considered as a tort and not as a crime. • Although the same assaultive conduct can be both a tort and a crime, this term isolates the legal elements that give rise to civil liability.

conditional assault. An assault expressing a threat on condition, such as "your money or your life."

criminal assault. An assault considered as a crime and not as a tort. • This term isolates the legal elements that give rise to criminal liability even though the act might also have been tortious.

excusable assault. An assault committed by accident or while doing a lawful act by lawful means, with ordinary caution and without any unlawful intent.

felonious assault. An assault that is of sufficient severity to be classified and pun-

ished as a felony. See *aggravated assault*;
assault with a deadly weapon.

indecent assault. See *sexual assault* (2).

malicious assault with a deadly weapon. An aggravated assault in which the victim is threatened with death or serious bodily injury from the defendant's use of a deadly weapon. ● Malice is inferred from both the nature of the assault and the weapon used.

sexual assault. 1. Sexual intercourse with another person who does not consent. ● Several state statutes have abolished the crime of rape and replaced it with the offense of sexual assault. **2.** Offensive sexual contact with another person, exclusive of rape. ● The Model Penal Code lists eight circumstances under which sexual contact results in an assault, as when the offender knows that the victim is mentally incapable of appreciating the nature of the conduct, either because of a mental disease or defect or because the offender has drugged the victim to prevent resistance. Model Penal Code § 213.4.—Also termed (in sense 2) *indecent assault*. Cf. RAPE.

simple assault. 1. See ASSAULT (1). **2.** See ASSAULT (2).

assault and battery. Loosely, a criminal battery. See BATTERY.

assaultee. A person who is assaulted.

assaulter. A person who assaults another.

assault to rape. See *assault with intent to commit rape* under ASSAULT.

assault with a deadly weapon. See ASSAULT.

assault with intent. See ASSAULT.

assault with intent to commit rape. See ASSAULT.

assembly. A group of persons organized and united for some common purpose.

> *unlawful assembly.* A meeting of three or more persons who intend either to commit a violent crime or to carry out some act, lawful or unlawful, that will constitute a breach of the peace. Cf. RIOT.

assenting-silence doctrine. The principle that an accusation will be taken as true, despite silence by the accused, if the accusation was made under circumstances in which silence can be fairly said to be an agreement. ● This doctrine is usu. held to be invalid as a measure of a criminal defendant's guilt.

assertive conduct. See CONDUCT.

assertory oath (ə-sər-tə-ree). See OATH.

assignation house. See DISORDERLY HOUSE.

assigned counsel. See COUNSEL.

Assimilative Crimes Act. A federal statute providing that state law applies to a crime committed within a federal enclave in that state (such as a reservation or military installation) if the crime is not punishable under federal law. 18 USCA § 13. ● This statute uses local laws as gap-fillers for federal criminal law.

assistance of counsel. Representation by a lawyer, esp. in a criminal case. See RIGHT TO COUNSEL.

effective assistance of counsel. A conscientious, meaningful legal representation, whereby the defendant is advised of all rights and the lawyer performs all required tasks reasonably according to the prevailing professional standards in criminal cases. See Fed. R. Crim. P. 44; 18 USCA § 3006A.

ineffective assistance of counsel. A representation in which the defendant is deprived of a fair trial because the lawyer handles the case unreasonably usu. either by performing incompetently or by not devoting full effort to the defendant, esp. because of a conflict of interest. • In determining whether a criminal defendant received ineffective assistance of counsel, courts generally consider several factors including: (1) whether the lawyer had previously handled criminal cases; (2) whether strategic trial tactics were involved in the allegedly incompetent action; (3) to what extent the defendant was prejudiced as a result of the lawyer's alleged ineffectiveness; and (4) whether the ineffectiveness was due to matters beyond the lawyer's control.

assisted self-determination. See *assisted suicide* under SUICIDE.

assisted suicide. See SUICIDE.

associate judge. See JUDGE.

associate justice. See JUSTICE (2).

assumed name. See ALIAS.

asylum. 1. A sanctuary or shelter. **2.** Protection of usu. political refugees from arrest by a foreign jurisdiction; a nation or embassy that affords such protection.—Also termed *political asylum*. **3.** An institution for the protection and relief of the unfortunate, esp. the mentally ill.—Also termed (in sense 3) *insane asylum.*

at large. Free; unrestrained; not under control <the suspect is still at large>.

atrocious assault. See ASSAULT.

atrocious felony. See FELONY.

attainder (ə-**tayn**-dər), *n.* At common law, the act of extinguishing a person's civil rights when that person is sentenced to death or declared an outlaw for committing a felony or treason.—**attaint** (ə-**taynt**), *vb.* See BILL OF ATTAINDER.

attaint (ə-**taynt**), *adj.* Maligned or tarnished reputationally; under an attainder for crime.

attempt, *n.* An overt act that is done with the intent to commit a crime but that falls short of completing the crime. ● Attempt is an inchoate offense distinct from the attempted crime. Under the Model Penal Code, an attempt includes any act that is a substantial step toward commission of a crime, such as enticing, lying in wait for, or following the intended victim or unlawfully entering a building where a crime is expected to be committed. Model Penal Code § 5.01.—Also termed *criminal attempt*; *offer.* See DANGEROUS-PROXIMITY TEST; INDISPENSABLE-ELE-

MENT TEST; LAST-PROXIMATE-ACT TEST; PHYSICAL-PROXIMITY TEST; PROBABLE-DESISTANCE TEST; RES IPSA LOQUITUR TEST. Cf. CONSPIRACY; SOLICITATION (2).—**attempt,** *vb*.

attempted assault. See ASSAULT.

attempted suicide. See SUICIDE.

attempt to assault. See *attempted assault* under ASSAULT.

attempt to attempt. A first step made toward a criminal attempt of some sort, such as a failed effort to mail someone a note inciting that person to engage in criminal conduct. • As a general rule, courts do not recognize an attempt to commit a crime that is itself an attempt. But some jurisdictions recognize this offense, esp. when the attempted crime is defined to be an independent substantive crime. For example, some jurisdictions recognize an attempted assault if assault is defined as placing a person in apprehension of bodily injury (as opposed to being defined merely as an attempted battery). In this situation, courts have been willing to punish conduct that falls short of the attempted crime but constitutes more than mere preparation to commit it. See *attempted assault* under ASSAULT.

attendance officer. See TRUANCY OFFICER.

attendant, *adj.* Accompanying; resulting <attendant circumstances>.

attendant circumstance. See CIRCUMSTANCE.

attenuation doctrine (ə-ten-yə-**way**-shən). The rule providing that evidence obtained by illegal means may nonetheless be admissible if the connection between the evidence and the illegal means is sufficiently attenuated or remote. • This is an exception to the fruit-of-the-poisonous-tree doctrine. See FRUIT-OF-THE-POISONOUS-TREE DOCTRINE.

attesting witness. See WITNESS.

attorney. 1. Strictly, one who is designated to transact business for another; a legal agent.—Also termed *attorney-in-fact*; *private attorney*. **2.** A person who practices law; LAWYER.—Also termed (in sense 2) *attorney-at-law*; *public attorney*. Cf. COUNSEL.—Abbr. att'y. Pl. **attorneys.**

attorney-client privilege. See PRIVILEGE (3).

attorney general. The chief law officer of a state or of the United States, responsible for advising the government on legal matters and representing it in litigation.—Abbr. AG. Pl. **attorneys general.**

attorney-in-fact. See ATTORNEY (1).

attorney of record. The lawyer who appears for a party in a case and who is entitled to receive, on the party's behalf, all formal documents from the court and from other parties.—Also termed *counsel of record*.

attorney-witness rule. See LAWYER-WITNESS RULE.

aural acquisition. Under the Federal Wiretapping Act, hearing or tape-recording a communication, as opposed to tracing its origin or destination. 18 USCA § 2510(4).

authoritative precedent. See *binding precedent* under PRECEDENT.

automatism (aw-**tom**-ə-tiz-əm), *n.* **1.** Action or conduct occurring without will, purpose, or reasoned intention, such as sleepwalking; behavior carried out in a state of unconsciousness or mental dissociation without full awareness. • Automatism may be asserted as a defense to negate the requisite mental state of voluntariness for commission of a crime. **2.** The state of a person who, though capable of action, is not conscious of his or her actions.— **automaton,** *n.*

ambulatory automatism. Automatism that consists in irresponsible or purposeless wanderings.

automobile exception. An exception to the warrant requirement in Fourth Amendment search-and-seizure law, holding that the police may, without a warrant, thoroughly search a movable vehicle for which the individual has a lessened expectation of privacy (such as a car or boat) if probable cause exists. ● For purposes of this doctrine, exigent circumstances are presumed to exist. Once the right to conduct a warrantless search arises, the actual search may take place at a later time. *Carroll v. United States*, 267 U.S. 132, 45 S.Ct. 280 (1925); *California v. Acevedo*, 500 U.S. 565, 111 S.Ct. 1982 (1991). See *exigent circumstances* under CIRCUMSTANCE.

automobile homicide. See *vehicular homicide* under HOMICIDE.

autopsy (**aw**-top-see). **1.** An examination of a dead body to determine the cause of death, esp. in a criminal investigation.—Also termed *postmortem*; *necropsy*. **2.** The evidence of one's own senses.

autoptic evidence (aw-**top**-tik). See *demonstrative evidence* under EVIDENCE.

autoptic proference (proh-**fər**-ənts). The presentation of an item for inspection by the court. See *demonstrative evidence* under EVI-DENCE.

avowal (ə-**vow**-əl), *n*. See OFFER OF PROOF.

AWOL. *abbr*. Absent without leave; missing without notice or permission.

B

baby-snatching. See *child-kidnapping* under KIDNAPPING.

BAC. *abbr.* BLOOD ALCOHOL CONTENT.

bad character. A person's predilection toward evil. ● In limited circumstances, proof of bad character may be introduced into evidence to discredit a witness. Fed. R. Evid. 608, 609. See *character evidence* under EVIDENCE.

bad check. See CHECK.

bad-conduct discharge. See DISCHARGE.

badger game. A scheme to extort money or some other benefit by arranging to catch someone in a compromising position and then threatening to make that person's behavior public.

bad-man theory. The jurisprudential doctrine or belief that a bad person's view of the law represents the best test of what the law actually is because that person will carefully calculate precisely what the rules allow and operate up to the rules' limits. ● This theory was first espoused by Oliver Wendell Holmes in his essay *The Path of the Law*, 10 Harv. L. Rev. 457 (1897). In the essay, Holmes asserted that a society's legal system is defined by predicting how the law will affect a person, as opposed to considering the ethics or morals supposedly underlying the law. Under Holmes's theory, the prediction is best made by viewing the law as would a "bad man" who is unconcerned with morals. Such a person is not concerned with acting morally or in accord with a grand philosophical scheme. Rather, that person is concerned with whether and to what degree certain acts will incur punishment by the public force of the law.—Also termed *prediction theory*.

bad motive. See MOTIVE.

bagman. A person who collects and distributes illegally obtained money; esp., an intermediary who collects a bribe for a public official.

bail, *n.* **1.** A security such as cash or a bond; esp., security required by a court for the release of a prisoner who must appear at a future time <bail is set at $500>. Cf. RECOGNIZANCE.

   cash bail. A sum of money (rather than a surety bond) posted to secure a prisoner's release from jail.—Also termed *stationhouse bail.*

   civil bail. A bond or deposit of money given to secure the release of a person arrested for

failing to pay a court-ordered civil debt. ●
The bail is conditioned on the payment of
the debt.

excessive bail. Bail that is unreasonably
high considering both the offense with
which the accused is charged and the risk
that the accused will not appear for trial. ●
The Eighth Amendment prohibits excessive
bail.

2. Release of a prisoner on security for a
future appearance <the court refused bail for
the accused serial killer>. **3.** One or more
sureties for a criminal defendant <the attorney stood as bail for her client>. See BAILER.

bail, *vb.* **1.** To obtain the release of (oneself or
another) by providing security for future appearance <his parents bailed him out of jail>.
2. To release (a person) after receiving such
security <the court bailed the prisoner>.

bailable, *adj.* (Of an offense or person) eligible for bail.

bailable offense. See OFFENSE.

bailable process. See PROCESS.

bail bond. See BOND.

bail bondsman. See BAILER.

bail dock. A small compartment in a courtroom used to hold a criminal defendant during trial.—Often shortened to *dock*.

bail-enforcement agent. See BOUNTY HUNTER.

bailer. One who provides bail as a surety for a criminal defendant's release.—Also spelled *bailor*.—Also termed *bail bondsman*; *bailsman*.

bail-jumping, *n.* The criminal offense of defaulting on one's bail. See Model Penal Code § 242.8.—**bail-jumper,** *n.*—**jump bail,** *vb.* See JUMP BAIL.

bailor. See BAILER.

bail-point scale. A system for determining a criminal defendant's eligibility for bail, whereby the defendant either will be released on personal recognizance or will have a bail amount set according to the total number of points given, based on the defendant's background and behavior.

bail revocation. The court's cancellation of bail granted previously to a criminal defendant.

bailsman. See BAILER.

balance of sentence suspended. A sentencing disposition in which a criminal defendant is sentenced to jail but credited with the time already served before trial, resulting in a suspension of the remaining sentence and release of the defendant from custody. Cf. SENTENCED TO TIME SERVED.

ballistics. 1. The science of the motion of projectiles, such as bullets. **2.** The study of a weapon's firing characteristics, esp. as used in criminal cases to determine a gun's firing capacity and whether a particular gun fired a given bullet.

B & E. *abbr.* Breaking and entering. See BURGLARY (2).

bank fraud. See FRAUD.

bankruptcy crime. See *bankruptcy fraud* under FRAUD.

bankruptcy fraud. See FRAUD.

Bank Secrecy Act. A federal statute that requires banks and other financial institutions to maintain records of customers' transactions and to report certain domestic and foreign transactions. ● This act, passed by Congress in 1970, is designed to help the federal government in criminal, tax, and other regulatory investigations. 12 USCA § 1829b; 31 USCA § 5311.

barebones indictment. See INDICTMENT.

barratry (**bar**-ə-tree *or* **bair**-), *n.* Vexatious incitement to litigation, esp. by soliciting potential legal clients. • Barratry is a crime in most jurisdictions.

bathtub conspiracy. See *intra-enterprise conspiracy* under CONSPIRACY.

Batson **challenge.** See CHALLENGE (1).

battered-child syndrome. The medical and psychological condition of a child who has suffered continuing injuries that could not be accidental and are therefore presumed to have been inflicted by someone close to the child.

battered-woman syndrome. The medical and psychological condition of a woman who has suffered physical, sexual, or emotional abuse at the hands of a spouse or partner. • This syndrome is sometimes proposed as a defense to justify a woman's killing of a man.—Sometimes (more specifically) termed *battered-wife syndrome*; (more broadly) *battered-spouse syndrome*.

battery, *n.* The use of force against another, resulting in harmful or offensive contact. ● Battery is a misdemeanor under most modern statutes.—Also termed *criminal battery.*—**batter,** *vb.* Cf. ASSAULT.

   aggravated battery. A criminal battery accompanied by circumstances that make it more severe, such as the use of a deadly weapon or the fact that the battery resulted in serious bodily harm.

   sexual battery. The forced penetration of or contact with another's sexual organs or the sexual organs of the perpetrator. See RAPE.

   simple battery. A criminal battery not accompanied by aggravating circumstances and not resulting in serious bodily harm.

bawd. *Archaic.* A person, usu. a woman, who solicits customers for a prostitute; a madam. See DISORDERLY HOUSE (2). Cf. PIMP.

bawdy house. See DISORDERLY HOUSE.

BCD. See *bad-conduct discharge* under DISCHARGE.

BCD special court-martial. See COURT-MARTIAL.

beat, *n.* A law-enforcement officer's patrol territory.

bench blotter. See ARREST RECORD.

bench conference. See SIDEBAR CONFERENCE (1).

bench legislation. See JUDGE-MADE LAW (2).

bench parole. See *bench probation* under PROBATION.

bench probation. See PROBATION.

bench trial. See TRIAL.

bench warrant. See WARRANT.

Benthamism. See *hedonistic utilitarianism* under UTILITARIANISM.

Berry **rule.** The doctrine that a defendant seeking a new trial on grounds of newly discovered evidence must show that (1) the evidence is newly discovered and was unknown to the defendant at the time of trial; (2) the evidence is material rather than merely cumulative or impeaching; (3) the evidence will probably produce an acquittal; and (4) the failure to learn of the evidence was not due to the defendant's lack of diligence. *Berry v. State*, 10 Ga. 511 (1851).

bertillon system (bər-tə-lon *or* bair-tee-**yaw***n*). A system of anthropometry once used to identify criminals by measuring and describing them. • The bertillon system is named for Alphonse Bertillon, the French anthropologist who developed the technique early in the 20th century. Fingerprinting has largely replaced the bertillon system. Cf. ANTHROPOMETRY.

best evidence. See EVIDENCE.

best-evidence rule. The evidentiary rule providing that, to prove the contents of a writing (or a recording or photograph), a party must produce the original writing (or a mechanical, electronic, or other familiar duplicate, such as a photocopy) unless it is unavailable, in which case secondary evidence—the testimony of the drafter or a person who read the document— may be admitted. Fed. R. Evid. 1001–1004.— Also termed *documentary-originals rule*; *original-writing rule*; *original-document rule*.

bestiality (bes-chee-**al**-ə-tee). Sexual activity between a human and an animal. • Some authorities restrict the term to copulation between a human and an animal of the opposite sex. See SODOMY.

beyond a reasonable doubt. See REASONABLE DOUBT.

bias, *n.* Inclination; prejudice <the juror's bias prompted a challenge for cause>.—**bias,** *vb.*—**biased,** *adj.*

   judicial bias. Bias that a judge has toward one or more of the parties to a case over which the judge presides. ● Judicial bias is usu. insufficient to justify disqualifying a judge from presiding over a case. To justify disqualification or recusal, the judge's bias usu. must be personal or based on some extrajudicial reason.

bifurcated trial. See TRIAL.

bigamous (**big**-ə-məs), *adj.* **1.** (Of a person) guilty of bigamy. **2.** (Of a marriage) involving bigamy.

bigamy, *n.* The act of marrying one person while legally married to another. ● Bigamy is a criminal offense if it is committed knowingly. See Model Penal Code § 230.1(1).—**bigamist,** *n.* Cf. POLYGAMY.

billa vera (**bil**-ə **veer**-ə). See TRUE BILL.

bill of attainder. 1. *Archaic.* A special legislative act that imposes a death sentence on a person without a trial. **2.** A special legislative act prescribing punishment, without a trial, for a specific person or group. • Bills of attainder are prohibited by the U.S. Constitution (art. I, § 9, cl. 3; art. I, § 10, cl. 1).—Also termed *act of attainder*. See ATTAINDER; BILL OF PAINS AND PENALTIES.

bill of indictment. An instrument presented to a grand jury for the jury's determination whether sufficient evidence exists to formally charge the accused with a crime. See INDICTMENT; NO BILL; TRUE BILL.

bill of information. See INFORMATION.

bill of pains and penalties. A legislative act that, though similar to a bill of attainder, prescribes punishment less severe than capital punishment. • Bills of pains and penalties are included within the U.S. Constitution's ban of bills of attainder. U.S. Const. art I, § 9.

bill of particulars. A formal, detailed statement of the claims or charges brought by a prosecutor, usu. filed in response to the defendant's request for a more specific complaint.— Also termed *statement of particulars*. See MOTION FOR MORE DEFINITE STATEMENT.

bill of rights. 1. (*usu. cap.*) A section or addendum, usu. in a constitution, defining the situations in which a politically organized society will permit free, spontaneous, and individual activity, and guaranteeing that governmental powers will not be used in certain ways; esp., the first ten amendments to the U.S. Constitution. **2.** (*cap.*) One of the four great charters of English liberty (1 W. & M., 1689), embodying in statutory form all the principles of the other three charters, namely, Magna Carta, the Petition of Right (3 Car. I, 1628), and the Habeas Corpus Act (31 Car. 2, 1679).

binding authority. See *binding precedent* under PRECEDENT.

binding instruction. See *mandatory instruction* under JURY INSTRUCTION.

binding precedent. See PRECEDENT.

bind over, *vb.* **1.** To put (a person) under a bond or other legal obligation to do something, esp. to appear in court. **2.** To hold (a person) for trial; to turn (a defendant) over to a sheriff or warden for imprisonment pending further judicial action. • A court may bind over a defendant if it finds at a preliminary examination that enough evidence exists to require a trial on the charges made against the defendant.—**binding over,** *n.*—**bindover,** *adj*.

bindover hearing. See PRELIMINARY HEARING.

blackmail, *n.* A threatening demand made without justification; EXTORTION.—**blackmail,** *vb.* Cf. GRAYMAIL.

black maria. *Slang.* A locked van used by the police to transport prisoners to and from jail.

black market. An illegal market for goods that are controlled or prohibited by the government, such as the underground market for prescription drugs.

black-rage insanity defense. See INSANITY DEFENSE.

blanket search warrant. See SEARCH WARRANT.

blasphemy (**blas**-fə-mee), *n.* Irreverence toward God, religion, a religious icon, or something considered sacred. • Blasphemy was a crime at common law and remains so in some U.S. jurisdictions, but it is rarely if ever enforced because of its questionable constitutionality under the First Amendment.—**blaspheme** (blas-**feem** *or* **blas**-feem), *vb.*—**blasphemous** (**blas**-fə-məs), *adj.*—**blasphemer,** (**blas**-fee-mər), *n.*

blind plea. See PLEA.

***Blockburger* test.** See SAME-EVIDENCE TEST.

blockbusting. The act or practice, usu. by a real-estate broker, of persuading one or more property owners to sell their property quickly, and often at a loss, to avoid an imminent influx of minority groups. • Blockbusting is illegal in many states.

blood alcohol content. The concentration of alcohol in one's bloodstream, expressed as a percentage. • Blood alcohol content is used to determine whether a person is legally intoxicated, esp. under a driving-while-intoxicated law. In many states, a blood alcohol content of .08% is enough to charge a person with an offense.—Abbr. BAC.—Also termed *blood alcohol count, blood alcohol concentration.* See DRIVING UNDER THE INFLUENCE; DRIVING WHILE IN-TOXICATED.

blood feud. A state of hostility between families in which one family seeks to avenge the killing of one of its members by killing a member of the other family. See VENDETTA.

blood money. A reward given for the apprehension of a person charged with a crime, esp. capital murder.

blotter. See ARREST RECORD.

blue-ribbon jury. See JURY.

board of pardons. A state agency, of which the governor is usu. a member, authorized to pardon persons convicted of crimes.

board of parole. See PAROLE BOARD.

board of review. In some cities, a board that reviews allegations of police misconduct.

bodily harm. See HARM.

bodily injury. See INJURY.

body execution. See EXECUTION; CAPIAS.

bogus check. See *bad check* under CHECK.

bond, *n*. **1.** An obligation; a promise. **2.** A written promise to pay money or do some act if certain circumstances occur or a certain time elapses.

  bail bond. A bond given to a court by a criminal defendant's surety to guarantee that the defendant will duly appear in court in the future and, if the defendant is jailed, to obtain the defendant's release from confinement. ● The effect of the release on bail bond is to transfer custody of the defendant from the officers of the law to the custody of the surety on the bail bond, whose undertaking is to redeliver the defendant to legal

71

custody at the time and place appointed in the bond.—Also termed *appearance bond*; *recognizance*. See BAIL.

interim bond. **1.** A bond set by a police officer when a person is arrested for a minor offense, such as a misdemeanor, without a warrant. • Although the bond allows the arrestee to be released, it requires that the person be available for arraignment. **2.** A bond set by a judge or magistrate and attached to a misdemeanor warrant.

peace bond. A bond required by a court from a person who has breached or threatened to breach the peace. See BREACH OF THE PEACE.

ten-percent bond. A bail bond in the amount of 10% of the bond otherwise required for a defendant's release. • This type of bond usu. allows a defendant to arrange a bond without the services of a bondsman or other surety.

unsecured bail bond. A bond that holds a defendant liable for a breach of the bond's conditions (such as failure to appear in court), but that is not secured by a deposit of or lien on property. See RECOGNIZANCE.

bondsman. One who guarantees a bond; a surety.

boodle. *Slang*. Money paid as a bribe, usu. to a public official.

book, *vb*. To record the name of (a person arrested) in a sequential list of police arrests, with details of the person's identity (usu. including a photograph and a fingerprint), particulars about the alleged offense, and the name of the arresting officer <the defendant was booked immediately after arrest>.— **booking,** *n*.

boot camp. See *shock incarceration* under IN-CARCERATION.

bootleg, *vb*. To manufacture, reproduce, or distribute (something) illegally or without authorization <he was bootlegging copyrighted videotapes>.

bootlegger, *n*. A person who manufactures, transports, or sells something illegally, esp. alcoholic beverages. See MOONSHINE.

border search. See SEARCH.

bounced check. See *bad check* under CHECK.

bounty hunter. A person who for a fee pursues someone charged with, or suspected of committing, a crime; esp., a person hired by a bail-bond company to find and arrest a criminal defendant who has breached the bond agreement by failing to appear in court as ordered.—Also termed *bail-enforcement agent*.

Brady Act. A federal law establishing a national system for quickly checking the background of a prospective handgun purchaser. • The formal name of the law is the Brady Handgun Violence Prevention Act. The U.S. Supreme Court held unconstitutional the law's interim provision, which required chief state law-enforcement officers (usu. sheriffs) to conduct background checks until the national system was in place. The act is named for James Brady, a campaigner for gun-control laws who, as a member of President Ronald Reagan's staff, was wounded by gunfire during an attempted presidential assassination in 1981. 18 USCA §§ 921–930.

Brady **material.** Information or evidence that is favorable to a criminal defendant's case and that the prosecution has a duty to disclose. • The prosecution's withholding of such information violates the defendant's due-process rights. *Brady v. Maryland*, 373 U.S. 83, 83 S.Ct. 1194 (1963). Cf. JENCKS MATERIAL.

brain death. See DEATH.

breach of arrest. A military offense committed by an officer who, being under arrest in quarters, leaves those quarters without a superior officer's authorization. See *arrest in quarters* under ARREST.

breach of peace. See BREACH OF THE PEACE.

breach of prison. See PRISON BREACH.

breach of the peace. The criminal offense of creating a public disturbance or engaging in disorderly conduct, particularly by making an unnecessary or distracting noise.—Also termed *breach of peace*; *disturbing the peace*; *disturbance of the peace*; *public disturbance*. See *disorderly conduct* under CONDUCT.

break. *vb.* **1.** To violate or disobey (a law) <to break the law>. **2.** To escape from (a place of confinement) without permission <break out of prison>. **3.** To open (a door, gate, etc.) and step through illegally <he broke the close>.

breaking, *n.* In the law of burglary, the act of entering a building without permission.

breaking a case. 1. The voicing by one appellate judge to another judge on the same panel of a tentative view on how a case should be decided. ● These informal expressions assist the judges in ascertaining how close they are to agreement. **2.** The solving of a case by the police.

breaking and entering. See BURGLARY (2).

breaking bulk, *n*. Larceny by a bailee, esp. a carrier, who opens containers, removes items from them, and converts the items to personal use.—Also termed *breaking bale.*—**break bulk,** *vb*.

Breathalyzer. A device used to measure the blood alcohol content of a person's breath, esp. when the police suspect that the person was driving while intoxicated. • Breathalyzer test results are admissible as evidence if the test was properly administered.—Also termed *alcoholometer*; *drunkometer*; *intoxilyzer*; *intoximeter.*—**breathalyze,** *vb*. See BLOOD ALCOHOL CONTENT.

bribe, *n*. A price, reward, gift, or favor bestowed or promised with a view to pervert the judgment of or influence the action of a person in a position of trust.

bribee. One who receives a bribe.—Also termed *bribe-taker*.

bribe-giver. See BRIBER.

briber. One who offers a bribe.—Also termed *bribe-giver*.

bribery, *n*. The corrupt payment, receipt, or solicitation of a private favor for official action. • Bribery is a felony in most jurisdictions. See Model Penal Code § 240.1.—**bribe,** *vb*. Cf. KICKBACK.

> ***commercial bribery.*** **1.** The knowing solicitation or acceptance of a benefit in exchange for violating an oath of fidelity, such as that owed by an employee, partner, trustee, or attorney. Model Penal Code § 224.8(1). **2.** A supposedly disinterested appraiser's acceptance of a benefit that influences the appraisal of goods or services. Model Penal Code § 224.8(2). **3.** Corrupt dealing with the agents or employees of prospective buyers to secure an advantage over business competitors.

bribe-taker. See BRIBEE.

bring to book. To arrest and try (an offender) <the fugitives were brought to book and convicted>.

broadside objection. See *general objection* under OBJECTION.

***Bruton* rule (broot**-ən). The principle that when a codefendant's confession contains references to a second codefendant, and the confessor refuses to testify, the use of that confession in a joint trial violates the second codefendant's Sixth Amendment right to confront witnesses. • This violation is known as a *Bruton error. Bruton v. United States*, 391 U.S. 123, 88 S.Ct. 1620 (1968).

buggery, *n*. Sodomy or bestiality.—**bugger,** *vb*.—**bugger,** *n*. See SODOMY.

bugging, *n*. A form of electronic surveillance by which conversations may be electronically intercepted, overheard, and recorded, usu. covertly; eavesdropping by electronic means. See WIRETAPPING.

bullpen. *Slang*. **1.** An area in a prison where inmates are kept in close confinement. **2.** A detention cell where prisoners are held until they are brought into court.

burden of going forward with evidence. See BURDEN OF PRODUCTION.

burden of persuasion. A party's duty to convince the fact-finder to view the facts in a way that favors that party. • In criminal cases the prosecution's burden is "beyond a reasonable doubt," while in civil cases, the plaintiff's burden is usu. "by a preponderance of the evidence."—Also termed *persuasion burden*; *risk of nonpersuasion*; *risk of jury doubt*.—Also loosely termed *burden of proof*.

burden of production. A party's duty to introduce enough evidence on an issue to have the issue decided by the fact-finder, rather than decided against the party in a peremptory ruling such as a directed verdict.—Also termed *burden of going forward with evidence*; *burden of producing evidence*; *production burden*; *degree of proof.*

burden of proof. 1. A party's duty to prove a disputed assertion or charge. ● The burden of proof includes both the *burden of persuasion* and the *burden of production.*—Also termed *onus probandi.* **2.** Loosely, BURDEN OF PERSUASION.

Bureau of Prisons. A federal agency that oversees all federal penal and correctional facilities, assists states and local governments in improving their correctional facilities, and provides notice of prisoner releases. 18 USCA §§ 4041 et seq. ● The Bureau of Prisons falls within the purview of the U.S. Attorney General. See NATIONAL INSTITUTE OF CORRECTIONS.

burglar, *n.* One who commits burglary.

burglarious (bər-**glair**-ee-əs), *adj.* Of or relating to burglary <burglarious intent>.—**burglariously,** *adv.*

79

burglarize, *vb.* To commit a burglary <the defendant burglarized three houses>.—Also termed (esp. in BrE) *burgle*.

burglary, *n.* **1.** The common-law offense of breaking and entering another's dwelling at night with the intent to commit a felony. **2.** The modern statutory offense of breaking and entering any building—not just a dwelling, and not only at night—with the intent to commit a felony. ● Some statutes make petit larceny an alternative to a felony for purposes of proving burglarious intent.—Also termed (in sense 2) *breaking and entering* (B & E); *statutory burglary.* Cf. ROBBERY.

burglary tool. (*often pl.*) An implement designed to assist a person in committing a burglary. ● In many jurisdictions, it is illegal to possess such a tool if the possessor intends to commit a burglary.

burgle. See BURGLARIZE.

bursting-bubble theory. The principle that a presumption disappears once the presumed facts have been contradicted by credible evidence.

but-for cause. See CAUSE (1).

but-for test. The doctrine that causation exists only when the result would not have occurred without the party's conduct.—Also termed *had-not test*. See *but-for cause* under CAUSE (1).

but so insane as not to be responsible. See GUILTY BUT MENTALLY ILL.

bylaw. See ORDINANCE.

bystander. One who is present when an event takes place, but who does not become directly involved in it.

C

cahoots (kə-**hoots**). *Slang*. Partnership, esp. in an illegal act; collusion <the lawyer was in cahoots with her client>.

***Calandra* rule** (kə-**lan**-drə). The doctrine that a grand-jury witness may be compelled to answer questions about certain items, even though the items were obtained by the police illegally. *United States v. Calandra*, 414 U.S. 338, 94 S.Ct. 613 (1974).

capacitate (kə-**pas**-ə-tayt), *vb*. To qualify; to make legally competent.—**capacitation** (kə-pas-ə-**tay**-shən), *n*.

capacity. The mental ability to understand the nature and effect of one's acts <his acute pain reduced his capacity to understand the hospital's admission form>.—Also termed *mental capacity*. See COMPETENCY.

   criminal capacity. The mental ability that a person must possess to be held accountable for a crime; the ability to understand right from wrong. See INSANITY; INFANCY.

   diminished capacity. An impaired mental condition—short of insanity—that is caused by intoxication, trauma, or disease and that prevents the person from having the mental state necessary to be held responsible for a crime. ● In some jurisdictions, a defendant's diminished capacity can be used to determine the degree of the offense or the severity of the punishment.—Also termed *diminished responsibility*; *partial responsibility*; *partial insanity*. Cf. INSANITY.

capacity defense. See DEFENSE.

capias (**kay**-pee-əs *or* **kap**-ee-əs). [Latin "that you take"] Any of various types of writs that require an officer to take a named defendant into custody.—Also termed *writ of capias*; *body execution*.

capital, *adj.* Punishable by execution; involving the death penalty <a capital offense>.

capital crime. See *capital offense* under OF- FENSE.

capital offense. See OFFENSE.

capital punishment. See DEATH PENALTY.

career criminal. See RECIDIVIST.

career offender. See OFFENDER.

carjacking. The forcible theft of a vehicle from a motorist.

carnal abuse. See *sexual abuse* under ABUSE.

carnal knowledge. *Archaic*. Sexual intercourse, esp. with an underage female.—Sometimes shortened to *knowledge*.

carrying away. See ASPORTATION.

case. 1. A proceeding, action, suit, or controversy at law or in equity <the parties settled the case>.

active case. A case that is still pending.

case at bar. A case under the immediate consideration of the court.—Also termed *case at bench*; *instant case*; *present case*.

case of first impression. A case that presents the court with issues of law that have not previously been decided in that jurisdiction.

inactive case. A pending case that is not proceeding toward resolution. ● This may occur for several reasons, such as nonservice, want of prosecution, or (in a criminal case) the defendant's having absconded.

instant case. See *case at bar*.

present case. See *case at bar*.

2. A criminal investigation <the Manson case>. **3.** An individual suspect or convict in relation to any aspect of the criminal-justice system <the probation officer said he considers Mr. Jones a difficult case>. **4.** An argument <the debater made a compelling case for gun control>. **5.** An instance, occurrence, or situation <a case of mistaken identity> <a terminal case of cancer>.

case-in-chief. 1. The evidence presented at trial by the party with the burden of proof. **2.** The part of a trial in which a party presents evidence to support its claim or defense. Cf. REBUTTAL.

caselaw. The collection of reported cases that form the body of law within a given jurisdiction.—Also written *case law*; *case-law*.—Also termed *decisional law*; *adjudicative law*; *jurisprudence*; *organic law*.

case of first impression. See CASE.

cash bail. See BAIL.

castle doctrine. An exception to the retreat rule allowing the use of deadly force by a person who is protecting his or her home and its inhabitants from attack, esp. from a trespasser who intends to commit a felony or inflict serious bodily harm.—Also termed *dwelling defense*; *defense of habitation*. See RE-TREAT RULE.

casual affray. See CHANCE-MEDLEY.

categorical question. See QUESTION (1).

causal (**kaw**-zəl), *adj.* **1.** Of, relating to, or involving causation <a causal link exists between the defendant's action and the victim's injury>. **2.** Arising from a cause <a causal symptom>. Cf. CAUSATIVE.

causal challenge. See *challenge for cause* under CHALLENGE (2).

causality (kaw-**zal**-ə-tee). The principle of causal relationship; the relation between cause and effect <the foreseeability test is one of duty and of causality>.—Also termed *causation*.

causation (kaw-**zay**-shən). **1.** The causing or producing of an effect. **2.** See CAUSALITY.

causative (**kaw**-zə-tiv), *adj.* **1.** Effective as a cause or producing a result <causative factor of the accident>. **2.** Expressive of causation <the causative relationship between drinking and assault>. Cf. CAUSAL.

cause, *n.* **1.** Something that produces an effect or result <the cause of the accident>.

> *but-for cause.* The cause without which the event could not have occurred.—Also termed *actual cause*; *cause in fact*; *factual cause*.

> *concurrent cause.* **1.** One of two or more causes that simultaneously create a condition that no single cause could have brought about. **2.** One of two or more causes that simultaneously create a condition that any one cause could have created alone.

> *contributing cause.* A factor that—though not the primary cause—plays a part in producing a result.

> *direct and proximate cause.* See *proximate cause*.

> *direct cause.* See *proximate cause*.

> *effective cause.* See *immediate cause*.

> *efficient cause.* See *proximate cause*.

> *factual cause.* See *but-for cause*.

> *immediate cause.* The last event in a chain of events, though not necessarily the proximate cause of what follows.—Also termed *effective cause*.

intervening cause. An event that comes between the initial event in a sequence and the end result, thereby altering the natural course of events that might have connected a wrongful act to an injury. ● If the intervening cause is strong enough to relieve the wrongdoer of any liability, it becomes a *superseding cause.* A *dependent intervening cause* is one that is not an act and is never a superseding cause. An *independent intervening cause* is one that operates on a condition produced by an antecedent cause but in no way resulted from that cause.—Also termed *intervening act; intervening force; supervening cause.* See *superseding cause.*

jural cause. See *proximate cause.*

legal cause. See *proximate cause.*

primary cause. See *proximate cause.*

procuring cause. See *proximate cause.*

producing cause. See *proximate cause.*

proximate cause. **1.** A cause that is legally sufficient to result in liability. **2.** A cause that directly produces an event and without which the event would not have occurred.—Also termed *direct cause; direct and proximate cause; efficient cause; legal cause; procuring cause; producing cause; primary cause; jural cause.*

remote cause. A cause that does not necessarily or immediately produce an event or injury.

sole cause. The only cause that, from a legal viewpoint, produces an event or injury. • If it comes between a defendant's action and the event or injury at issue, it is treated as a *superseding cause*.

superseding cause. An intervening act that the law considers sufficient to override the cause for which the original wrongdoer was responsible, thereby exonerating that wrongdoer from culpability.—Also termed *sole cause*. Cf. *intervening cause*.

supervening cause. See *intervening cause*.

2. A ground for legal action <the prosecutor does not have cause to file charges>.

probable cause. See PROBABLE CAUSE.

3. A lawsuit; a case <the court has 50 causes on the motion docket>.

cause, *vb.* To bring about or effect <dry conditions caused the fire>.

cause-and-prejudice rule. The doctrine that a prisoner attacking a conviction or sentence (as by a petition for writ of habeas corpus) on the basis of a constitutional challenge that was not presented to the trial court must show good cause for failing to make the challenge at trial, and must show that the trial court's error actually prejudiced the prisoner. ● The cause that will excuse the defendant's procedural lapse must ordinarily be some objective factor that made presentation of the defense impractical at trial, such as the reasonable unavailability of the legal or factual basis of the defense at trial, or wrongful governmental interference. The defendant must then show that some actual prejudice, such as a constitutionally invalid sentence, resulted from the trial court's error. The cause-and-prejudice rule creates a higher burden than the defendant would face in a direct appeal because it is intended to provide protection from fundamental miscarriages of justice rather than from minor trial-court errors. But in death-penalty cases in which the defendant proves actual innocence, the court may grant relief even when the standards of the cause-and-prejudice rule have not been met. See *actual innocence* under INNOCENCE.

cause célèbre (**kawz** sə-**leb** *or* **kawz** say-**leb**-rə). [French "celebrated case"] A trial or decision in which the subject matter or the characters are unusual or sensational <the O.J. Simpson trial was a cause célèbre in the 1990s>.

cause in fact. See *but-for cause* under CAUSE (1).

cause list. See DOCKET (2).

cautionary instruction. See JURY INSTRUCTION.

cease-and-desist order. A court's or agency's order prohibiting a person from continuing a particular course of conduct. See INJUNCTION; RESTRAINING ORDER.

cert. *abbr.* CERTIORARI.

certification, *n.* A procedure by which a federal appellate court asks the U.S. Supreme Court or the highest state court to review a question of law arising in a case pending before the appellate court and on which it needs guidance. ● Certification is commonly used with state courts, but the U.S. Supreme Court has steadily restricted the number of cases it reviews by certification. See 15 USCA § 1254(2). Cf. CERTIORARI.

certification hearing. See *transfer hearing* under HEARING.

certified juvenile. See JUVENILE.

certified question. A point of law on which a federal appellate court seeks guidance from either the U.S. Supreme Court or the highest state court by the procedure of certification.

certiorari (sər-shee-ə-**rair**-ı *or* **rair**-ee *or* **rah**-ree). [Law Latin "to be more fully informed"] An extraordinary writ issued by an appellate court, at its discretion, directing a lower court to deliver the record in the case for review. • The U.S. Supreme Court uses certiorari to review most of the cases that it decides to hear.—Abbr. cert.—Also termed *writ of certiorari.*

certworthy, *adj. Slang.* (Of a case or issue) deserving of review by writ of certiorari.—**certworthiness,** *n.*

chain conspiracy. See CONSPIRACY.

chain gang. A group of prisoners chained together to prevent their escape while working outside a prison.

chain of custody. The movement and location of real evidence from the time it is obtained to the time it is presented in court.

chain-referral scheme. See PYRAMID SCHEME.

challenge, *n.* **1.** An act or instance of formally questioning the legality or legal qualifications of a person, action, or thing <a challenge to the opposing party's expert witness>.

Batson challenge. A defendant's objection to peremptory challenges of jurors whereby the defendant raises an inference that the prosecution used peremptory challenges to exclude potential jurors on the basis of race. *Batson v. Kentucky*, 476 U.S. 79, 106 S.Ct. 1712 (1986).

2. A party's request that a judge disqualify a potential juror or an entire jury panel <the prosecutor used his last challenge to disqualify a priest>.—Also termed *jury challenge.*

causal challenge. See *challenge for cause.*

challenge for cause. A party's challenge supported by a specified reason, such as bias or prejudice, that would disqualify that potential juror.—Also termed *causal challenge*; *general challenge*; *challenge to the poll.*

challenge propter affectum (**prop**-tər ə-**fek**-təm). A challenge because some circumstance, such as kinship with a party, renders the potential juror incompetent to serve in the particular case.

challenge propter defectum (**prop**-tər də-**fek**-təm). A challenge based on a claim that the juror is incompetent to serve on any jury for reasons such as alienage, infancy, or nonresidency.

challenge propter delictum (**prop**-tər də-**lik**-təm). A challenge based on a claim that the potential juror has lost citizenship rights, as by being convicted of an infamous crime. See CIVIL DEATH (1).

challenge to the array. A legal challenge to the manner in which the entire jury panel was selected, usu. for a failure to follow prescribed procedures designed to produce impartial juries. • Such a challenge is either a principal challenge (if some defect renders the jury prima facie incompetent, as where the officer selecting veniremembers is related to the prosecutor or defendant) or a challenge for favor (as where the defect does not amount to grounds for a principal challenge, but there is a probability of partiality).— Also termed *challenge to the jury array*.

challenge to the poll. See *challenge for cause*.

general challenge. See *challenge for cause*.

peremptory challenge. One of a party's limited number of challenges that need not be supported by any reason, although a party may not use such a challenge in a way that discriminates against a protected minority.—Often shortened to *peremptory*.— Also termed *peremptory strike*. See STRIKE (1).

3. An objection to a member of the court serving in a court-martial case. • A military judge can be challenged only for cause.

challenge, *vb*. **1.** To dispute or call into question <the columnist challenged the wisdom of the court's ruling>. **2.** To formally object to the legality or legal qualifications of <the defendant challenged the person's eligibility for jury duty>.

challenge for cause. See CHALLENGE (2).

challenge to the array. See CHALLENGE (2).

challenge to the poll. See *challenge for cause* under CHALLENGE (2).

chamber, *n*. A room or compartment; specif. (usu. pl.), the private office of a judge <a hearing in chambers>.

chance-medley. [fr. Anglo–Norman *chance medlee* "chance scuffle"] A spontaneous fight during which one participant kills another participant in self-defense.—Also termed *chaud-medley*; *casual affray*. Cf. MEDLEY.

chance verdict. See VERDICT.

change of venue. 1. The transfer of a case from one locale to another. **2.** The transfer of a case begun in one court to another court in the same district, usu. because of questions of fairness.—Also termed *transfer of venue*. See VENUE.

character evidence. See EVIDENCE.

character witness. See WITNESS.

charge, *n*. **1.** A formal accusation of a crime as a preliminary step to prosecution <a murder charge>.—Also termed *criminal charge*. **2.** See JURY CHARGE <review the charge for appealable error>.

charge, *vb*. **1.** To accuse (a person) of criminal conduct <the police charged him with murder>. **2.** To instruct a jury on matters of law <the judge charged the jury on self-defense>.—Also termed *instruct*.

chargeable, *adj*. (Of an act) capable or liable of being charged as a criminal offense <taking that money for personal use would be chargeable>.

charge and specification. A written description of an alleged offense.

charge bargain. See PLEA BARGAIN.

chargee (chahr-**jee**). One charged with a crime.

charge sheet. 1. A police record showing the names of each person brought into custody, the nature of the accusations, and the identity of the accusers. **2.** In military law, a four-part charging instrument containing (1) information about the accused and the witnesses, (2) the charges and specifications, (3) the preferring of charges and their referral to a summary, special, or general court-martial for trial, and (4) for a summary court-martial, the trial record.

charging grand jury. See GRAND JURY.

charging instrument. A formal document—usu. either an indictment or an information—that sets forth an accusation of a crime.—Also termed *accusatory instrument*.

chaud-medley. See CHANCE-MEDLEY.

cheating. The fraudulent obtaining of another's property by means of a false symbol or token, or by other illegal practices.—Also termed *cheating at common law*; *common-law cheat*; *cheat*. See FRAUD.

　　cheating by false pretenses. The act of purposely obtaining both the possession and ownership of money, goods, wares, or merchandise by means of misrepresentations, with the intent to defraud. See FALSE PRETENSES. Cf. *larceny by trick* under LARCENY.

check, *n.* A draft signed by the maker or drawer, drawn on a bank, payable on demand, and unlimited in negotiability.

> ***bad check.*** A check that is not honored because the account either contains insufficient funds or does not exist.—Also termed *hot check*; *worthless check*; *rubber check*; *bounced check*; *bogus check*.

> ***raised check.*** A check whose face amount has been increased, usu. without the knowledge of the issuer.

check, *vb.* **1.** To control or restrain <handcuffs checked the defendant's movement>. **2.** To verify or audit <an accountant checked the invoices>. **3.** To investigate <the police checked up on the suspect>.

check-kiting. The illegal practice of writing a check against a bank account with insufficient funds to cover the check, in the hope that the funds from a previously deposited check will reach the account before the bank debits the amount of the outstanding check.—Also termed *kiting*; *check-flashing*.

checkpoint search. See SEARCH.

chief judge. See JUDGE.

chief justice. See JUSTICE (2).

child. **1.** At common law, a person who has not reached the age of 14, though the age now varies from jurisdiction to jurisdiction. **2.** A boy or girl; a young person. **3.** A son or daughter. **4.** A baby or fetus. See JUVENILE; MINOR.

delinquent child. A legal infant who has either violated criminal laws or engaged in disobedient or indecent conduct, and is in need of treatment, rehabilitation, or supervision. See JUVENILE DELINQUENT.

disobedient child. See *incorrigible child.*

incorrigible child. A child who refuses to obey his or her parents or guardians or has been adjudicated delinquent under laws governing unruly children.—Also termed *disobedient child.*

neglected child. **1.** A child whose parents or legal custodians are unfit to care for him or her for reasons of cruelty, immorality, or incapacity. **2.** A child whose parents or legal custodians refuse to provide the necessary care and medical services for the child.

child abuse. See ABUSE.

child destruction. See FETICIDE.

child endangerment. The putting of a child in a place or position that exposes him or her to danger to life or health.—Also termed *endangering the welfare of a child.*

child-kidnapping. See KIDNAPPING.

child molestation. See MOLESTATION.

child neglect. The failure of a person responsible for a minor to care for the minor's emotional or physical needs. Cf. *child abuse* under ABUSE.

child pornography. See PORNOGRAPHY.

children's court. See JUVENILE COURT.

child-sexual-abuse-accommodation syndrome. The medical and psychological condition of a child who has suffered repeated instances of sexual abuse, usu. from a relative or family friend.—Also termed *child-sexual-abuse syndrome.*

child-slaying. See INFANTICIDE.

child-stealing. See *child-kidnapping* under KIDNAPPING.

child support. A parent's legal obligation to contribute to the economic maintenance and education of a child. ● The obligation is enforceable both civilly and criminally.

***Chimel* search.** See *protective search* under SEARCH.

choate (**koh**-it), *adj*. **1.** Complete in and of itself. **2.** Having ripened or become perfected.—**choateness,** *n*. Cf. INCHOATE.

choice of evils. See NECESSITY (1).

choice-of-evils defense. See *lesser-evils defense* under DEFENSE.

chop-shop, *n*. A garage where stolen automobiles are dismantled so that their parts can be sold separately.

CID. *abbr*. CIVIL INVESTIGATIVE DEMAND.

circle conspiracy. See *wheel conspiracy* under CONSPIRACY.

circuit, *n*. **1.** A judicial division in which hearings occur at several locations, as a result of which judges often travel to different courthouses. **2.** A judicial division of the United States—that is, one of the 13 circuits where the U.S. courts of appeals sit.

circuit judge. See JUDGE.

circuit justice. See JUSTICE (2).

circumstance, *n.* (*often pl.*) An accompanying or accessory fact, event, or condition, such as a piece of evidence that indicates the probability of an event.—**circumstantial,** *adj.*

> ***aggravating circumstance.*** **1.** A fact or situation that increases the degree of liability or culpability for a criminal act. **2.** A fact or situation that relates to a criminal offense or defendant and that is considered by the court in imposing punishment (esp. a death sentence). • Aggravating circumstances in death-penalty cases are usu. prescribed by statute. For a list of aggravating circumstances in a capital-murder case, see Model Penal Code § 210.6(3).—Also termed *aggravating element*; *aggravating factor*; *aggravator*. Cf. *mitigating circumstance*.

> ***attendant circumstance.*** A fact that is situationally relevant to a particular event or occurrence. • A fact-finder often reviews the attendant circumstances of a crime to learn, for example, the perpetrator's motive or intent.

> ***exigent circumstances.*** A situation in which a police officer must take immediate action to effectively make an arrest, search,

or seizure for which probable cause exists, and thus may do so without first obtaining a warrant. • Exigent circumstances may exist if (1) a person's life or safety is threatened, (2) a suspect's escape is imminent, or (3) evidence is about to be removed or destroyed.—Also termed *emergency circumstances*; *special circumstances*.

extenuating circumstance. See *mitigating circumstance.*

extraordinary circumstances. A highly unusual set of facts that are not commonly associated with a particular thing or event.

incriminating circumstance. A fact or situation showing either that a crime was committed or that a particular person committed it.

mitigating circumstance. **1.** A fact or situation that does not justify or excuse a wrongful act or offense but that reduces the degree of culpability and thus may reduce the punishment. **2.** A fact or situation that does not bear on the question of a defendant's guilt but that is considered by the court in imposing punishment and esp. in lessening the severity of a sentence. For a list of mitigating circumstances in a capital-murder case, see Model Penal Code

§ 210.6(4).—Also termed *extenuating circumstance*. Cf. *aggravating circumstance*.

circumstantial evidence. See EVIDENCE.

citation, *n.* **1.** A court-issued writ that commands a person to appear at a certain time and place to do something demanded in the writ, or to show cause for not doing so. **2.** A police-issued order to appear before a judge on a given date to defend against a stated charge, such as a traffic violation.—Also termed *appearance ticket*.

cite, *vb.* To summon before a court of law <the witness was cited for contempt>.

citizen-informant. A witness who, without expecting payment and with the public good in mind, comes forward and volunteers information to the police or other authorities.

citizen's arrest. See ARREST.

city judge. See *municipal judge* under JUDGE.

civil assault. See ASSAULT.

civil bail. See BAIL.

civil commitment. See COMMITMENT.

civil commotion. A public uprising by a large number of people who, acting together, cause harm to people or property. • A civil commotion usu. involves many more people than a riot. Cf. RIOT.

civil conspiracy. See CONSPIRACY.

civil death. 1. *Archaic.* At common law, the loss of rights—such as the rights to vote, make contracts, inherit, and sue—by a person who has been outlawed or convicted of a serious crime, or who is considered to have left the temporal world for the spiritual by entering a monastery. **2.** In some states, the loss of rights—such as the rights to vote and hold public office—by a person serving a life sentence. Cf. *civil disability* under DISABILITY.— Also termed *legal death*.

civil disability. See DISABILITY.

civil disorder. A public disturbance involving three or more people who commit violent acts that cause immediate danger or injury to people or property. See RIOT.

civil forfeiture. See FORFEITURE.

civil infraction. See INFRACTION.

civil injury. See INJURY.

civil investigative demand. 1. A request for information served by the U.S. Attorney General on any person who may have documents or information relevant to a civil antitrust investigation or to an investigation authorized by section 3 of the Antitrust Enforcement Assistance Act (15 USCA § 6202). ● A civil investigative demand can be issued before a civil or criminal action is begun, and can be served on anyone—not just potential defendants—thought to possess information pertinent to the investigation. If the Attorney General begins a civil or criminal action, this demand may not be served on persons within the scope of the proceeding. **2.** A similar request for information served by a different governmental entity, esp. a state attorney general.—Abbr. CID.

civilization. The transformation of a criminal matter to a civil one by law or judgment. Cf. CRIMINALIZATION.

civil law. 1. (*usu. cap.*) One of the two prominent legal systems in the Western World, originally administered in the Roman Empire and still influential in continental Europe, Latin America, Scotland, and Louisiana, among other parts of the world. Cf. COMMON LAW (2). **2.** The body of law imposed by the state, as opposed to moral law. **3.** The law of civil or private rights, as opposed to criminal law or administrative law.

C.J. *abbr.* **1.** See *chief justice* under JUSTICE (2). **2.** See *chief judge* under JUDGE. **3.** See *circuit judge* under JUDGE.

claim of appeal. See NOTICE OF APPEAL.

clandestine (klan-**des**-tin), *adj.* Secret or concealed, esp. for illegal or unauthorized purposes.

clean-slate rule. The doctrine that the double-jeopardy prohibition does not apply to the retrial of a defendant who appealed and obtained a reversal of an earlier conviction.

clear, *vb.* To acquit or exonerate <she was cleared of all wrongdoing>.

clear and convincing evidence. See EVIDENCE.

clear and convincing proof. See *clear and convincing evidence* under EVIDENCE.

clear-and-present-danger test. The doctrine allowing the government to restrict the First Amendment freedoms of speech and press if necessary to prevent immediate and severe danger to interests that the government may lawfully protect. • This test was formulated by Justice Oliver Wendell Holmes in *Schenck v. United States*, 249 U.S. 47, 39 S.Ct. 247 (1919).

clear error. See ERROR.

clear-view doctrine. See PLAIN-VIEW DOCTRINE.

clemency (**klem**-ən-see), *n.* Mercy or leniency; esp., the power of the President or a governor to pardon a criminal or commute a criminal sentence.—Also termed *executive clemency.*—**clement** (**klem**-ənt), *adj.* See PARDON; COMMUTATION.

clergyman-penitent privilege. See *priest-penitent privilege* under PRIVILEGE (3).

clerical error. See ERROR.

clerical misprision. See MISPRISION.

client's privilege. See *attorney-client privilege* under PRIVILEGE (3).

close-jail execution. See EXECUTION.

closing argument. In a trial, a lawyer's final statement to the judge or jury before deliberation begins, in which the lawyer requests the judge or jury to consider the evidence and to

apply the law in his or her client's favor. •
Generally, the judge afterwards instructs the
jury on the law that governs the case.—Also
termed *closing statement*; *final argument*; *jury
summation*; *summing up*; *summation*.

coconspirator. A person who engages in a
criminal conspiracy with another; a fellow conspirator. See CONSPIRATOR.

> **unindicted coconspirator.** See *unindicted
> conspirator* under CONSPIRATOR.

coconspirator's exception. An exception to
the hearsay rule whereby one conspirator's
acts and statements, if made during and in
furtherance of the conspiracy, are admissible
against a defendant even if the statements are
made in the defendant's absence.—Also
termed *coconspirator exception*; *coconspirator's
rule*. See HEARSAY.

codefendant. One of two or more defendants
charged with the same offense.—Also termed
joint defendant.

Code of Military Justice. The collection of
substantive and procedural rules governing
the discipline of members of the armed forces.
10 USCA §§ 801 et seq.—Also termed *Uniform
Code of Military Justice* (UCMJ).

coerce (koh-ərs), *vb*. To compel by force or threat <coerce a confession>.

coerced confession. See CONFESSION.

coercion (koh-ər-shən), *n*. **1.** Compulsion by physical force or threat of physical force. • An act such as signing a will is not legally valid if done under coercion.

> *criminal coercion*. Coercion intended to restrict another's freedom of action by: (1) threatening to commit a criminal act against that person; (2) threatening to accuse that person of having committed a criminal act; (3) threatening to expose a secret that either would subject the victim to hatred, contempt, or ridicule or would impair the victim's credit or goodwill, or (4) taking or withholding official action or causing an official to take or withhold action. Model Penal Code § 212.5.

2. Conduct that constitutes the improper use of economic power to compel another to submit to the wishes of one who wields it.—Also termed *economic coercion*. **3.** Formerly, a husband's actual or supposed control or influence over his wife's actions. • Under the common-law doctrine of coercion, a wife who committed a crime in her husband's presence was presumed to have been coerced by him and thus

110

had a complete defense. Courts have abolished this doctrine.—**coercive,** *adj.*—**coercer,** *n.*

cognate offense. See OFFENSE.

cognitive test. A test of the defendant's ability to know certain things, specifically the nature of his or her conduct and whether the conduct was right or wrong. ● This test is used in assessing whether a defendant may rely on an insanity defense.

cohabitation (koh-hab-ə-**tay**-shən), *n.* The fact or state of living together, esp. as partners in life, usu. with the suggestion of sexual relations.—**cohabit** (koh-**hab**-it), *vb.*—**cohabitative** (koh-**hab**-ə-tay-tiv), *adj.*—**cohabitant** (koh-**hab**-ə-tənt), *n.*

> *illicit cohabitation.* At common law, the act of a man and a woman openly living together without being married to each other.—Also termed *lewd and lascivious cohabitation.*

> *notorious cohabitation.* The act of a man and a woman openly living together under circumstances that make the arrangement illegal under statutes that are now rarely enforced.

coindictee. One of two or more persons who have been jointly indicted. Cf. *joint indictment* under INDICTMENT.

cold blood. A killer's state of mind when committing a willful and premeditated homicide <a shooting in cold blood>. See COOL BLOOD. Cf. HEAT OF PASSION.

collateral attack. An attack on a final judgment entered in a different proceeding. • A petition for a writ of habeas corpus is one type of collateral attack.—Also termed *indirect attack*. Cf. DIRECT ATTACK.

collateral consequence. A penalty for committing a crime, in addition to the penalties included in the criminal sentence. • An example is the loss of a professional license.

collateral defense. See DEFENSE.

collateral fact. See FACT.

collateral matter. Any matter on which evidence could not have been introduced for a relevant purpose. • If a witness has erred in testifying about a detail that is collateral to the relevant facts, then another party cannot call witnesses to contradict that point—cross-examination alone must suffice.

collateral proceeding. See PROCEEDING.

collective punishment. A penalty inflicted on a group of persons without regard to individual responsibility for the conduct giving rise to the penalty. • Collective punishment was outlawed in 1949 by the Geneva Convention.

colloquy (**kol**-ə-kwee). Any formal discussion, such as an oral exchange between a judge, the prosecutor, the defense counsel, and a criminal defendant in which the judge ascertains the defendant's understanding of the proceedings and of the defendant's rights.

collusion (kə-**loo**-zhən), *n.* An agreement to defraud another or to do or obtain something forbidden by law.

comment on the evidence. A statement made to the jury by the judge or by counsel on the probative value of certain evidence. • Lawyers typically make such comments in closing argument, and judges may make such comments in federal court. But most state-court judges are not permitted to do so when examining a witness, instructing the jury, and the like (in which case the comment is sometimes termed an *impermissible comment on the evidence*).

commercial bribery. See BRIBERY.

commercial crime. See CRIME.

commercialized obscenity. See OBSCENITY.

commission, *n.* **1.** A warrant or authority, from the government or a court, that empowers the person named to execute official acts. **2.** The act of doing or perpetrating (as a crime) <the perpetrator fled to Mexico after commission of the assault>.

commissioner. See MAGISTRATE.

commit, *vb.* **1.** To perpetrate (a crime). **2.** To send (a person) to prison or to a mental health facility, esp. by court order.

commitment, *n.* **1.** The act of confining a person in a prison, mental hospital, or other institution <commitment of the felon to prison>. **2.** The order directing an officer to take a person to a penal or mental institution <the judge signed the commitment after ruling that it was in the best interest of the troubled teen>.

   civil commitment. A commitment of a person who is ill, incompetent, drug-addicted, or the like, as contrasted with a criminal sentence.

   diagnostic commitment. Presentencing confinement of an individual, usu. to determine the individual's competency to stand trial or to determine the appropriate sentence to be rendered.

discretionary commitment. A commitment that a judge may or may not grant, depending on whether the government has proved—usu. by clear and convincing evidence—that the commitment is necessary for the well-being of the defendant or society (as when the defendant is insane and dangerous). ● Most states allow discretionary commitment.

mandatory commitment. An automatically required commitment for a defendant found not guilty by reason of insanity. ● This type of commitment is required under federal law, but in only a minority of states.

new court commitment. The confinement in prison of a person who is being admitted on a new conviction—that is, someone who is not being returned to prison for a parole violation.

commitment document. An order remanding a defendant to prison in order to carry out a judgment and sentence.

commitment warrant. See *warrant of commitment* under WARRANT.

committing magistrate. See MAGISTRATE.

common and notorious thief. See *common thief* under THIEF.

common assault. 1. See ASSAULT (2). **2.** See ASSAULT (2).

common-authority rule. The principle that a person may consent to a police officer's search of another person's property if both persons use, control, or have access to the property. ● Under this rule, the consenting person must have been legally able to permit the search in his or her own right, and the defendant must have assumed the risk that a fellow occupant might permit a search. See THIRD-PARTY CONSENT.

common design. 1. The intention by two or more people to join in committing an unlawful act. **2.** An intention to commit more than one crime.—Also termed *common scheme*; *common plan*.

common enterprise. See JOINT ENTERPRISE.

common informer. A person who sues to recover a penalty in a penal action. ● In some jurisdictions, such an action may be instituted either by the attorney general on behalf of the state or by a common informer. See INFORMER; *penal action* under ACTION.

common-interest doctrine. See *joint-defense privilege* under PRIVILEGE (3).

common jury. See *petit jury* under JURY.

common law, *n.* **1.** The body of law derived from judicial decisions, rather than from statutes or constitutions; CASELAW <federal common law>. Cf. STATUTORY LAW. **2.** The body of law based on the English legal system, as distinct from a civil-law system <all states except Louisiana have the common law as their legal system>. Cf. CIVIL LAW (1). **3.** General law common to the country as a whole, as opposed to special law that has only local application <the issue is whether the common law trumps our jurisdiction's local rules>. **4.** The body of law deriving from law courts as opposed to those sitting in equity <a defense founded in common law>. **5.** The body of law to which no constitution or statute applies <the common law used by lawyers to settle disputes>.

common-law cheat. See CHEATING.

common-law contempt. See *criminal contempt* under CONTEMPT.

common-law crime. See CRIME.

common-law extortion. See EXTORTION (1).

common plan. See COMMON DESIGN.

common scheme. See COMMON DESIGN.

common thief. See THIEF.

commonwealth attorney. A prosecutor in some jurisdictions, such as Virginia.

communication. **1.** The expression or exchange of information by speech, writing, or gestures. **2.** The information so expressed or exchanged.

> *confidential communication.* A communication made within a certain protected relationship—such as husband-wife, attorney-client, or priest-penitent—and legally protected from forced disclosure.

> *privileged communication.* A communication that is protected by law from forced disclosure. See PRIVILEGE (3).

communicative evidence. See *testimonial evidence* under EVIDENCE.

community control. A criminal sentence consisting in intensive and strict supervision of an offender in the community, as by restricting the offender's movements, conducting electronic surveillance, and severely sanctioning the offender for violations of any of the sentence terms.

community correctional center. See JAIL.

community policing. A law-enforcement technique in which police officers are assigned to a particular neighborhood or area to develop relationships with the residents for the purpose of enhancing the chances of detecting and thwarting criminal activity.

commutation (kom-yə-**tay**-shən), *n.* The executive's substitution in a particular case of a less severe punishment for a more severe one that has already been judicially imposed on the defendant. Cf. PARDON; REPRIEVE.

comparative criminology. See CRIMINOLOGY.

comparative disparity. The percentage of underrepresentation of a particular group among potential jurors on a venire, in comparison with the group's percentage of the general population. ● Comparative disparity is calculated by subtracting a group's percentage of representation on the venire from the group's percentage of the population—that is, calculating the group's absolute-disparity representation—then dividing that percentage by the group's percentage-representation in the population, and multiplying the result by 100. For example, if African-Americans make up 12% of a county's population, and 8% of the potential jurors on the venire, the absolute disparity of

African-Americans is 4%. And the comparative disparity is 33%, because 4 divided by 12 is .33, or 33%. Many courts criticize the comparative-disparity analysis, and favor an absolute-disparity analysis, because the comparative-disparity analysis is said to exaggerate the deviation. The reason for calculating the disparity is to analyze a claim that the jury was not impartial because it was not selected from a pool of jurors that fairly represented the makeup of the jurisdiction. See DUREN TEST; FAIR-CROSS-SECTION REQUIREMENT; STATISTICAL-DECISION THEORY. Cf. ABSOLUTE DISPARITY.

compel, *vb.* **1.** To cause or bring about by force or overwhelming pressure <a lawyer cannot be compelled to testify about a privileged communication>. **2.** (Of a legislative mandate or judicial precedent) to convince (a court) that there is only one possible resolution of a legal dispute <the wording of the statute compels us to affirm>.

compellable, *adj.* Capable of or subject to being compelled, esp. to testify <an accused person's spouse is not a compellable witness for the prosecution>.

compelling-state-interest test. A method for determining the constitutional validity of a law, whereby the government's interest in the law is balanced against the individual's constitutional right to be free of the law, and only if the government's interest is strong enough will the law be upheld. ● The compelling-state-interest test is used most commonly in equal-protection analysis when the disputed law requires strict scrutiny. See STRICT SCRUTINY.

competence, *n.* **1.** A basic or minimal ability to do something; qualification, esp. to testify <competence of a witness>. **2.** The capacity of an official body to do something <the court's competence to enter a valid judgment>. **3.** Authenticity <the documents were supported by a business-records affidavit, leaving their competence as evidence beyond doubt>.— **competent,** *adj.* Cf. COMPETENCY.

competency, *n.* **1.** The mental ability to understand problems and make decisions. **2.** A criminal defendant's ability to stand trial, measured by the capacity to understand the proceedings, to consult meaningfully with counsel, and to assist in the defense.—Also termed *competency to stand trial.*—**competent,** *adj.* Cf. COMPETENCE.

competency hearing. See PATE HEARING.

competency proceeding. See PROCEEDING.

competency to stand trial. See COMPETENCY.

competent evidence. See EVIDENCE.

competent witness. See WITNESS.

complainantless crime. See *victimless crime* under CRIME.

complaint. A formal charge accusing a person of an offense. Cf. INDICTMENT; INFORMATION.

   preliminary complaint. A complaint issued by a court to obtain jurisdiction over a criminal suspect for a hearing on probable cause or on whether to bind the suspect over for trial.

complicated larceny. See *mixed larceny* under LARCENY.

complicity (kəm-**plis**-ə-tee), *n.* Association or participation in a criminal act; the act or state of being an accomplice. • Under the Model Penal Code, a person can be an accomplice as a result of either that person's own conduct or the conduct of another (such as an innocent agent) for which that person is legally accountable. Model Penal Code § 2.06.—**complicitous** (kəm-**plis**-ə-təs), *adj.* See ACCOMPLICE; *innocent agent* under AGENT.

compos mentis (**kom**-pəs **men**-tis), *adj.* [Latin "master of one's mind"] Of sound mind;

having use and control over one's own mental faculties. Cf. NON COMPOS MENTIS.

compound (kom- *or* kəm-**pownd**), *vb.* **1.** To agree for consideration not to prosecute (a crime). ● Compounding a felony in this way is itself a felony. **2.** Loosely, to aggravate; to make (a crime, etc.) more serious by further bad conduct.

compounder (kom- *or* kəm-**pown**-dər). One who knows of a crime by another and agrees, for a promised or received reward, not to prosecute.

compounding a crime. The offense of either agreeing not to prosecute a crime that one knows has been committed or agreeing to hamper the prosecution.

compound larceny. See *mixed larceny* under LARCENY.

comprint (**kom**-print). A surreptitious and illegal printing of another bookseller's copy of a work. See *criminal infringement* under IN-FRINGEMENT.

compromise verdict. See VERDICT.

compulsion, *n.* **1.** The act of compelling; the state of being compelled. **2.** An uncontrollable inclination to do something. **3.** Objective necessity; duress.—**compel,** *vb.*

compulsory process. See PROCESS.

computer crime. See CRIME.

con. *abbr.* **1.** Confidence <con game>. **2.** Convict <ex-con>.

con. See CONFIDENCE GAME.

concealed weapon. See WEAPON.

concealment, *n.* **1.** The act of refraining from disclosure; esp., an act by which one prevents or hinders the discovery of something. **2.** The act of removing from sight or notice; hiding.

> *active concealment.* The concealment by words or acts of something that one has a duty to reveal.

> *fraudulent concealment.* The affirmative suppression or hiding, with the intent to deceive or defraud, of a material fact or circumstance that one is legally (or, sometimes, morally) bound to reveal.

> *passive concealment.* The act of maintaining silence when one has a duty to speak.

concert-of-action rule. See WHARTON'S RULE.

conclusion, *n.* **1.** The final part of a speech or writing (such as a jury argument or a pleading). **2.** A judgment arrived at by reasoning; an inferential statement. **3.** See OPINION (2). **4.** The closing, settling, or final arranging (as of a treaty or contract). **5.** *Archaic.* An act by which one estops oneself from doing anything inconsistent with it.

conclusive evidence. See EVIDENCE.

conclusive presumption. See PRESUMPTION.

conclusive proof. See *conclusive evidence* (1) under EVIDENCE.

concomitant evidence. See EVIDENCE.

concurrent cause. See CAUSE (1).

concurrent-sentence doctrine. The principle that an appellate court affirming a conviction and sentence need not hear a challenge to a conviction on another count if the conviction on the other count carries a sentence that is equal to or less than the affirmed conviction.

concurrent sentences. See SENTENCE.

concurrent writ. See WRIT.

condemn, *vb.* To judicially pronounce some-one guilty.

condemnation (kon-dem-**nay**-shən), *n.* The act of judicially pronouncing someone guilty; conviction.

conditional admissibility. See ADMISSIBILITY.

conditional assault. See ASSAULT.

conditional contraband. See CONTRABAND.

conditional pardon. See PARDON.

conditional presumption. See *rebuttable presumption* under PRESUMPTION.

conditional privilege. See *qualified privilege* under PRIVILEGE (1).

conditional proof. See PROOF.

conditional purpose. A possible defense against a crime if the conditions make commit-ting the crime impossible (e.g., "I will steal the money if it's there," and the money is not there).

conditional release. See RELEASE.

conditional sentence. See SENTENCE.

condonation (kon-də-**nay**-shən), *n.* A victim's act of consenting to or excusing a crime after the crime has been committed. • Condonation is not usu. a valid criminal defense.

conduct, *n.* Personal behavior, whether by action or inaction; the manner in which a person behaves.—**conduct,** *vb.*

> *assertive conduct.* Nonverbal behavior that is intended to be a statement, such as pointing one's finger to identify a suspect in a police lineup. • Assertive conduct is a statement under the hearsay rule, and thus it is not admissible unless a hearsay exception applies. Fed. R. Evid. 801(a)(2).—Also termed *implied assertion.*

> *contumacious conduct* (kon-t[y]oo-**may**-shəs). A willful disobedience of a court order. See CONTUMACY.

> *disorderly conduct.* Behavior that tends to disturb the public peace, offend public morals, or undermine public safety. See BREACH OF THE PEACE.

> *disruptive conduct.* Disorderly conduct in the context of a governmental proceeding. See CONTEMPT.

> *nonassertive conduct.* Nonverbal behavior that is not intended to be a statement, such as fainting while being questioned as a sus-

pect by a police officer. ● Nonassertive conduct is not a statement under the hearsay rule, and thus it is admissible. Fed. R. Evid. 801.

outrageous conduct. Conduct so extreme that it exceeds all reasonable bounds of human decency.

confess, *vb.* To admit (an allegation) as true; to make a confession.—**confessor,** *n.*

confession, *n.* A criminal suspect's acknowledgment of guilt, usu. in writing and often including details about the crime. Cf. ADMISSION; STATEMENT.

coerced confession. A confession that is obtained by threats or force.

direct confession. A confession in which an accused person acknowledges having committed the crime.

extrajudicial confession. A confession made out of court, and not as a part of a judicial examination or investigation. ● An extrajudicial confession must be corroborated by some other proof of the corpus delicti, or else it is insufficient to warrant a conviction. Cf. *judicial confession.*

implied confession. A confession in which the person does not plead guilty but invokes the mercy of the court and asks for a light sentence.

indirect confession. A confession that is inferred from the defendant's conduct.

interlocking confessions. Confessions by two or more suspects whose statements are substantially the same and consistent concerning the elements of the crime. ● Such confessions are admissible in a joint trial.

involuntary confession. A confession induced by the police or other law-enforcement authorities who make promises to, coerce, or deceive the suspect.

judicial confession. A plea of guilty or some other direct manifestation of guilt in court or in a judicial proceeding. Cf. *extrajudicial confession*.

naked confession. A confession unsupported by any evidence that a crime has been committed, and therefore usu. highly suspect.

oral confession. A confession that is not made in writing. ● Oral confessions are admissible, though as a practical matter police interrogators prefer to take written or recorded confessions since juries typically view these as being more reliable.

plenary   confession   (**plee**-nə-ree   *or*
plen-ə-). A complete confession; one that is
believed to be conclusive against the person
who made it.

threshold confession. A spontaneous confession made promptly after arrest and
without interrogation by the police. ● The
issue whether the defendant's statement is
a threshold confession usu. arises when the
defendant challenges the admissibility of the
confession on grounds that he or she suffered an impermissibly long delay before being brought before a magistrate. Courts
generally admit this type of confession into
evidence if the confession was given before
the delay occurred.

confidence game. A means of obtaining
money or property whereby a person intentionally misrepresents facts to gain the victim's trust so that the victim will transfer
money or property to the person.—Often
shortened to *con game*; *con.*

confidential communication. See COMMUNI-
CATION.

confidential source. A person who provides
information to a law-enforcement agency or to
a journalist on the express or implied guarantee of anonymity. ● Confidentiality is protected
both under the Federal Freedom of Informa-

tion Act (for disclosures to law enforcement) and under the First Amendment (for disclosures to journalists).

confinee. A person held in confinement.

confinement, *n.* The act of imprisoning or restraining someone; the state of being imprisoned or restrained <solitary confinement>.— **confine,** vb.

confiscable (kən-**fis**-kə-bəl *or* **kon**-fə-skə-bəl), *adj.* (Of property) liable to confiscation; subject to forfeiture <confiscable contraband>.

confiscate (**kon**-fə-skayt), *vb.* **1.** To appropriate (property) as forfeited to the government. **2.** To seize (property) by authority of law.

conflicting evidence. See EVIDENCE.

conflicting presumption. See PRESUMPTION.

conflict of interest. **1.** A real or seeming incompatibility between one's private interests and one's public or fiduciary duties. **2.** A real or seeming incompatibility between the interests of two of a lawyer's clients, such that the lawyer is disqualified from representing both clients if the dual representation adversely affects either client or if the clients do not consent.

Confrontation Clause. The Sixth Amendment provision guaranteeing a criminal defendant's right to directly confront an accusing witness and to cross-examine that witness.

con game. See CONFIDENCE GAME.

congressional immunity. See IMMUNITY (1).

conjoint robbery. See ROBBERY.

connivance (kə-**nı**-vənts), *n.* The ignoring of a wrongdoer's illegal conduct; esp., a secret or indirect condonation of another's unlawful act.

connive (kə-**nıv**), *vb.* **1.** To knowingly overlook another's wrongdoing. **2.** Loosely, to conspire.

conscience. 1. The moral sense of right or wrong; esp., a moral sense applied to one's own judgment and actions. **2.** In law, the moral rule that requires justice and honest dealings between people.

consecutive sentences. See SENTENCE.

consensual (kən-**sen**-shoo-əl), *adj.* Having, expressing, or occurring with full consent <consensual relations>.

132

consensual crime. See *victimless crime* under CRIME.

consent, *n.* Agreement, approval, or permission as to some act or purpose, esp. given voluntarily by a competent person. ● Consent may be a defense to a crime if the victim has the capacity to consent and if the consent negates an element of the crime or thwarts the harm that the law seeks to prevent. See Model Penal Code § 2.11.—**consent,** *vb.*

consent search. See SEARCH.

consequential contempt. See CONTEMPT.

conservator of the peace. See PEACE OFFICER.

consolidated sentence. See *general sentence* under SENTENCE.

consonant statement. See STATEMENT.

conspiracy, *n.* An agreement by two or more persons to commit an unlawful act; a combination for an unlawful purpose. ● Conspiracy is a separate offense from the crime that is the object of the conspiracy. A conspiracy ends when the unlawful act has been committed or (in some states) when the agreement has been abandoned. See Model Penal Code § 5.03(7).—

Also termed *criminal conspiracy*.—**conspiratorial,** *adj.* Cf. ATTEMPT; SOLICITATION (2).

bathtub conspiracy. See *intra-enterprise conspiracy*.

chain conspiracy. A single conspiracy in which each person is responsible for a distinct act within the overall plan, such as an agreement to produce, import, and distribute narcotics in which each person performs only one function. ● All participants are interested in the overall scheme and liable for all other participants' acts in furtherance of that scheme.

circle conspiracy. See *wheel conspiracy*.

civil conspiracy. An agreement between two or more persons to commit an unlawful act that causes damage to a person or property.

conspiracy in restraint of trade. See RESTRAINT OF TRADE.

hub-and-spoke conspiracy. See *wheel conspiracy*.

intracorporate conspiracy. A conspiracy existing between a corporation and its own officers, agents, or employees. ● To be prosecutable under federal law, the conspiracy must involve at least two persons (i.e., not just the corporation and one person). 18 USCA § 371.

intra-enterprise conspiracy. A conspiracy existing between two subsidiaries, divisions, or other parts of the same firm.—Also termed *bathtub conspiracy.*

seditious conspiracy. A criminal conspiracy to forcibly (1) overthrow or destroy the U.S. government, (2) oppose its authority, (3) prevent the execution of its laws, or (4) seize or possess its property. 18 USCA § 2384.

wheel conspiracy. A conspiracy in which a single member or group (the "hub") separately agrees with two or more other members or groups (the "spokes"). ● The person or group at the hub is the only part liable for all the conspiracies.—Also termed *circle conspiracy; hub-and-spoke conspiracy.*

conspirator, *n.* A person who takes part in a conspiracy.

unindicted conspirator. A person who has been identified by law enforcement as a member of a conspiracy, but who has not been named in the fellow conspirator's indictment. ● Prosecutors typically name someone an unindicted conspirator because any statement that the unindicted conspirator has made in the course and furtherance of the conspiracy is admissible against the indicted defendants.—Also termed *unindicted coconspirator*.

conspire, *vb.* To engage in conspiracy; to join in a conspiracy.

constable (**kon**-stə-bəl), *n.* **1.** A peace officer responsible for minor judicial duties, such as serving writs and warrants, but with less authority and smaller jurisdiction than a sheriff. **2.** In the United Kingdom, a police officer; also, the title of a police officer.—**constabulary** (kən-**stab**-yə-ler-ee), *adj.*—**constabulary** (body or force), *n.*

constituent element. An essential component of a crime.

constitutional law. 1. The body of law deriving from the U.S. Constitution and dealing primarily with governmental powers, civil rights, and civil liberties. **2.** The body of legal rules that determine the constitution of a state or country with a flexible constitution. Cf. STATUTORY LAW; COMMON LAW.

constructive breaking into a house. A breaking made out by construction of law, as when a burglar gains entry by threat or fraud.

constructive contempt. See *indirect contempt* under CONTEMPT.

constructive conversion. See CONVERSION.

constructive custody. See CUSTODY.

constructive escape. See ESCAPE (2).

constructive force. See FORCE.

constructive intent. See INTENT.

constructive larceny. See LARCENY.

constructive malice. See *implied malice* under MALICE.

constructive murder. See *felony murder* under MURDER.

constructive search. See SEARCH.

constructive taking. See TAKING.

contemner. A person who is guilty of contempt before an instrumentality of government, such as a court or legislature.—Also spelled *contemnor*.

contemporary community standard. The gauge by which a fact-finder decides whether material is obscene, judging by its patent offensiveness and its pruriency in the locale at a given time. See OBSCENITY.

137

contempt. Conduct that defies the authority or dignity of a court or legislature. ● Because such conduct interferes with the administration of justice, it is punishable, usu. by fine or imprisonment.—Also termed *contempt of court*. See CONTUMACY.

> *consequential contempt.* **1.** Contempt that, although not amounting to gross insolence or direct opposition, tends to create a universal disregard of the power and authority of courts and judges. **2.** See *indirect contempt*.

> *constructive contempt.* See *indirect contempt*.

> *criminal contempt.* An act that obstructs justice or attacks the integrity of the court. ● A criminal-contempt proceeding is punitive in nature.—Also termed *common-law contempt*.

> *direct contempt.* A contempt (such as an assault of a testifying witness) committed in the immediate vicinity of a court; esp., a contempt committed in a judge's presence. ● A direct contempt is usu. immediately punishable when the transgression occurs.

> *indirect contempt.* Contempt that is committed outside of court, as when a party disobeys a court order. ● Indirect contempt is punishable only after proper notice to the

contemner and a hearing.—Also termed *constructive contempt*; *consequential contempt*.

contempt proceeding. See PROCEEDING.

continuing jurisdiction. See JURISDICTION.

continuing objection. See OBJECTION.

continuing offense. See OFFENSE.

continuous crime. See CRIME.

contraband (**kon**-trə-band), *n*. **1.** Illegal or prohibited trade; smuggling. **2.** Goods that are unlawful to import, export, or possess.—**contraband,** *adj*.

absolute contraband. Goods used primarily for war, such as arms and ammunition, as well as clothing and equipment of a military character.

conditional contraband. Goods susceptible of being used for warlike and peaceful purposes, such as coal and food.

contraband per se. Property whose possession is unlawful regardless of how it is used.

derivative contraband. Property whose possession becomes unlawful when it is used in committing an illegal act.

139

contributing cause. See CAUSE (1).

contributing to the delinquency of a minor. The offense of an adult's engaging in conduct involving a minor—or in the presence of a minor—likely to result in delinquent conduct. • Examples include encouraging a minor to shoplift, to lie under oath, or to commit vandalism.—Also termed *contributing to delinquency*. See JUVENILE DELINQUENCY. Cf. IMPAIRING THE MORALS OF A MINOR; CORRUPTION OF A MINOR.

control. See ACTUAL PHYSICAL CONTROL.

controlled substance. Any type of drug whose possession and use is regulated by law, including a narcotic, a stimulant, or a hallucinogen. See DRUG.

controlled-substance act. A federal or state statute that is designed to control the distribution, classification, sale, and use of certain drugs. • Most states have enacted these laws, which are usu. modeled on the Uniform Controlled Substances Act.

control test. See IRRESISTIBLE-IMPULSE TEST.

control theory. The theory that people will engage in criminal behavior unless certain personally held social controls (such as a strong investment in conventional, legitimate activities or a belief that criminal behavior is morally wrong) are in place to prevent them from doing so. Cf. ROUTINE-ACTIVITIES THEORY; RATIONAL-CHOICE THEORY; STRAIN THEORY.

control-your-kid law. See PARENTAL-RESPONSIBILITY STATUTE.

contumacious conduct. See CONDUCT.

contumacy (**kon**-t[y]uu-mə-see), *n*. Contempt of court; the refusal of a person to follow a court's order or direction.—**contumacious,** *adj*. See CONTEMPT.

conversion, *n*. The wrongful possession or disposition of another's property as if it were one's own; an act or series of acts of willful interference, without lawful justification, with an item of property in a manner inconsistent with another's right, whereby that other person is deprived of the use and possession of the property.—**convert,** *vb*.

constructive conversion. Conversion consisting of an action that in law amounts to the appropriation of property. • Constructive conversion could be, for example, an appropriation that was initially lawful.

conversion by detention. Conversion by detaining property in a way that is adverse to the owner or other lawful possessor. •

141

The mere possession of property without title is not conversion. The defendant must have shown an intention to keep it in defiance of the owner or lawful possessor.

conversion by estoppel. A judicial determination that a conversion has taken place—though in truth one has not—because a defendant is estopped from offering a defense. • This occurs, for example, under the traditional rule that a bailee is estopped from denying the bailor's title even if the bailor has no title to the chattel.

conversion by taking. Conversion by taking property out of the possession of another with the intention of exercising a permanent or temporary dominion over it, despite the owner's entitlement to use it at all times.

conversion by wrongful delivery. Conversion by depriving an owner of goods by delivering them to someone else so as to change the possession.

conversion by wrongful destruction. Conversion by willfully consuming or otherwise destroying a chattel belonging to another person.

conversion by wrongful disposition. Conversion by depriving an owner of goods by giving some other person a lawful title to them.

direct conversion. The act of appropriating the property of another to one's own benefit, or to the benefit of another. • A direct conversion is per se unlawful, and the traditional requirements of demand and refusal of the property do not apply.

fraudulent conversion. Conversion that is committed by the use of fraud, either in obtaining the property or in withholding it.

involuntary conversion. The loss or destruction of property through theft, casualty, or condemnation.

convict (**kon**-vikt), *n.* A person who has been found guilty of a crime and is serving a sentence of confinement for that crime; a prison inmate.

convict (kən-**vikt**), *vb.* To find (a person) guilty of a criminal offense upon a criminal trial, a plea of guilty, or a plea of nolo contendere (no contest).

conviction (kən-**vik**-shən), *n.* **1.** The act or process of judicially finding someone guilty of a crime; the state of having been proved guilty. **2.** The judgment (as by a jury verdict) that a person is guilty of a crime.

summary conviction. A conviction of a person for a violation or minor misdemeanor as the result of a trial before a magistrate sitting without a jury.

conviction rate. Within a given area or for a given time, the number of convictions (including plea bargains) as a percentage of the total number of prosecutions undertaken.

cool blood. In the law of homicide, a condition in which the defendant's emotions are not in such an excited state that they interfere with his or her faculties and reason.—Also termed *cool state of blood*. See COLD BLOOD. Cf. HEAT OF PASSION.

cooling time. Time to recover cool blood after great excitement, stress, or provocation, so that one is considered able to contemplate, comprehend, and act with reference to the consequences that are likely to follow. See COOL BLOOD.

cool state of blood. See COOL BLOOD.

cop a plea, *vb. Slang.* (Of a criminal defendant) to plead guilty to a lesser charge as a means to avoid standing trial for a more serious offense. See PLEA BARGAIN.

coprincipal. One of two or more participants in a criminal offense who either perpetrate the crime or aid a person who does so.

coroner (**kor-** *or* **kahr-**ə-nər). A public official whose duty is to investigate the causes and circumstances of any death that occurs suddenly, suspiciously, or violently. See MEDICAL EXAMINER.

coroner's inquest. See INQUEST (1).

coroner's jury. See JURY.

corporal oath. See OATH.

corporal punishment. See PUNISHMENT.

corporate crime. See CRIME.

corpus delicti (**kor-**pəs də-**lik-**tɪ *or* -tee). [Latin "body of the crime"] **1.** The fact of a transgression; ACTUS REUS. **2.** Loosely, the material substance on which a crime has been committed; the physical evidence of a crime, such as the corpse of a murdered person.

corpus delicti **rule.** The doctrine that prohibits a prosecutor from proving the corpus delicti based solely on a defendant's extrajudicial statements. ● The prosecution must establish the *corpus delicti* with corroborating evidence to secure a conviction.

correction, *n.* (*usu. pl.*) The punishment and treatment of a criminal offender through a program of imprisonment, parole, and probation <Department of Corrections>.—**correct,** *vb.*—**correctional,** *adj.*

correction, house of. See HOUSE OF CORRECTION.

correctional institution. See PRISON.

correctional system. A network of governmental agencies that administer a jurisdiction's prisons and parole system.

corroborate (kə-**rob**-ə-rayt), *vb.* To strengthen or confirm; to make more certain <the witness corroborated the defendant's testimony>.

corroborating evidence. See EVIDENCE.

corroborating witness. See WITNESS.

corroboration (kə-rob-ə-**ray**-shən), *n.* Confirmation or support by additional evidence or authority <corroboration of the witness's testimony>.—**corroborate,** *vb.*—**corroborative** (kə-**rob**-ə-rə-tiv), *adj.*—**corroborator** (kə-**rob**-ə-ray-tər), *n.*

corroborative evidence. See *corroborating evidence* under EVIDENCE.

corrupt, *adj.* Having an unlawful or depraved motive; esp., influenced by bribery.

corrupt, *vb.* To change (a person's morals or principles) from good to bad.

corruption. Depravity, perversion, or taint; an impairment of integrity, virtue, or moral principle; esp., the impairment of a public official's duties by bribery.

corruption in office. See *official misconduct* under MISCONDUCT.

corruption of a minor. The crime of engaging in sexual activity with a minor; specif., the offense of having sexual intercourse or engaging in sexual activity with a person who is not the actor's spouse and who (1) is under the legal age of consent, the actor being considerably older than the victim (usu. four or more years), or (2) is less than 21 years old (or other age established by the particular jurisdiction), the actor being the person's guardian or otherwise responsible for the victim's welfare. Model Penal Code § 213.3. ● In some jurisdictions, the definition has been broadened to include aiding or encouraging a minor to commit a criminal offense. Cf. IMPAIRING THE MORALS OF A MINOR.

corruptly, *adv.* In a corrupt or depraved manner; by means of corruption or bribery. • As used in criminal-law statutes, *corruptly* usu. indicates a wrongful desire for pecuniary gain or other advantage.

corrupt-motive doctrine. The rule that conspiracy is punishable only if the agreement was entered into with an evil purpose, not merely with an intent to do the illegal act. • This doctrine—which originated in *People v. Powell*, 63 N.Y. 88 (1875)—has been rejected by the Model Penal Code.—Also termed *Powell doctrine*.

counsel, *n.* **1.** Advice or assistance <the lawyer's counsel was to petition immediately for a writ of habeas corpus>. **2.** One or more lawyers who represent a client <the client acted on advice of counsel>.—In the singular, also termed *counselor*. Cf. ATTORNEY; LAWYER.

advisory counsel. See *standby counsel.*

assigned counsel. An attorney appointed by the court to represent a person, usu. an indigent person.—Also termed *court-appointed attorney.*

counsel of record. See ATTORNEY OF RECORD.

independent counsel. An attorney hired to provide an unbiased opinion about a case or

148

to conduct an impartial investigation; esp., an attorney appointed by a governmental branch or agency to investigate alleged misconduct within that branch or agency. See *special prosecutor* under PROSECUTOR. Cf. *special counsel*.

special counsel. An attorney employed by the state or political subdivision to assist in a particular case when the public interest so requires.—Also termed *special attorney*. Cf. *independent counsel*.

standby counsel. An attorney who is appointed to represent a pro se criminal defendant if the defendant's self-representation ends. • The standby counsel may also provide some advice and guidance to the defendant during the self-representation.—Also termed *advisory counsel*.

counsel, assistance of. See ASSISTANCE OF COUNSEL.

counsel, right to. See RIGHT TO COUNSEL.

counsel and procure. See AID AND ABET.

counsel of record. See ATTORNEY OF RECORD.

count, *n.* The part of an indictment charging the suspect with a distinct offense.

multiple counts. Several separate charged offenses contained in a single indictment.

separate count. One of two or more criminal charges contained in one indictment, each charge constituting a separate indictment for which the accused may be tried.

Counterfeit Access Device and Computer Fraud and Abuse Act of 1984. A federal statute that criminalizes various computer-related activities such as accessing without permission a computer system belonging to a bank or the federal government, or using that access to improperly obtain anything of value. 18 USCA § 1030.

counterfeiter. A person who makes an unauthorized imitation of something (esp. a document, currency, or another's signature) with the intent to deceive or defraud.

counterfeiting, *n.* The unlawful forgery, copying, or imitation of an item, esp. money or a negotiable instrument (such as a security or promissory note) or other officially issued item of value (such as a postage stamp), or the unauthorized possession of such an item, with the intent to deceive or defraud by claiming or passing the item as genuine. See 18 USCA §§ 470 et seq.—**counterfeit,** *vb.*—**counterfeit,** *n.*—**counterfeit,** *adj.*

counterpart writ. See WRIT.

county agent. See JUVENILE OFFICER.

county attorney. An attorney who represents a county in civil matters and, in some
jurisdictions, who prosecutes criminal offenders.

county judge. See JUDGE.

court, *n.* **1.** A governmental body consisting of
one or more judges who sit to adjudicate disputes and administer justice <a question of
law for the court to decide>. **2.** The judge or
judges who sit on such a governmental body
<the court asked the parties to approach the
bench>. **3.** A legislative assembly <in Massa-
chusetts, the General Court is the legisla-
ture>. **4.** The locale for a legal proceeding <an
out-of-court statement>. **5.** The building
where the judge or judges convene to adjudicate disputes and administer justice <the lawyers agreed to meet at the court at 8:00
a.m.>.—Also termed (in sense 5) *courthouse.*

court-appointed attorney. See *assigned
counsel* under COUNSEL.

court calendar. See DOCKET (2).

court for the trial of impeachments. A tribunal empowered to try a government officer or other person brought before it by the process of impeachment. • The U.S. Senate and the British House of Lords have this authority, as do the upper houses of most state legislatures.—Also termed *impeachment court*; *court of impeachment*.

courthouse. See COURT (5).

court-martial, *n.* An ad hoc military court convened under military authority to try someone accused of violating the Code of Military Justice, particularly a member of the armed forces. Pl. **courts-martial.—court-martial,** *vb.*

    BCD special court-martial. A special court-martial in which a possible punishment is a bad-conduct discharge (a "BCD").

    general court-martial. A proceeding that is presided over by a military judge, and no fewer than five members (who serve as jurors), and that has jurisdiction over all the members of the armed forces. • It is the highest military trial court.

    special court-martial. A proceeding that is presided over by a military judge and no fewer than three members (who serve as jurors) to hear noncapital offenses and prescribe a sanction of hard labor, dismissal, or extended confinement (up to six months). • It is the intermediate level of courts-martial.

summary court-martial. A proceeding presided over by a single commissioned officer who is jurisdictionally limited in what sanctions can be imposed. • It is the lowest level of courts-martial.

court-martial order. A written order containing the result of a court-martial trial.

Court of Criminal Appeals. 1. For each armed service, an intermediate appellate court that reviews court-martial decisions. • The court was established by the Military Justice Act of 1968. 10 USCA §§ 859–876.—Formerly termed *Court of Military Review* (abbr. CMR). **2.** In some jurisdictions, such as Texas and Oklahoma, the highest appellate court that hears criminal cases.

court officer. See OFFICER OF THE COURT.

court of impeachment. See COURT FOR THE TRIAL OF IMPEACHMENTS.

Court of Military Review. See COURT OF CRIMINAL APPEALS (1).

court order. See ORDER (2).

court probation. See *bench probation* under PROBATION.

creative sentence. See *alternative sentence* under SENTENCE.

credible evidence. See EVIDENCE.

credible witness. See WITNESS.

credit-card crime. The offense of using a credit card to purchase something with knowledge that (1) the card is stolen or forged, (2) the card has been revoked or canceled, or (3) the card's use is unauthorized. Model Penal Code § 224.6.—Also termed *credit-card fraud*.

CRF. *abbr.* CRIMINAL-REFERRAL FORM.

crime. A social harm that the law makes punishable; the breach of a legal duty treated as the subject-matter of a criminal proceeding.—Also termed *criminal wrong*. See OFFENSE.

administrative crime. An offense consisting of a violation of an administrative rule or regulation that carries with it a criminal sanction.

affectively spontaneous crime. A criminal act that occurs suddenly and without premeditation in response to an unforeseen stimulus. • For example, a husband who discovers his wife in bed with another man and shoots him could be said to have committed an affectively spontaneous crime.

capital crime. See *capital offense* under OF-FENSE.

commercial crime. A crime that affects commerce; esp., a crime directed toward the property or revenues of a commercial establishment. • Examples include robbery of a business, embezzlement, counterfeiting, forgery, prostitution, illegal gambling, and extortion. See 26 CFR § 403.38.

common-law crime. A crime that is punishable under the common law, rather than by force of statute. Cf. *statutory crime.*

complainantless crime. See *victimless crime.*

computer crime. A crime requiring knowledge of computer technology, such as sabotaging or stealing computer data or using a computer to commit some other crime.

consensual crime. See *victimless crime.*

continuous crime. **1.** A crime that continues after an initial illegal act has been consummated; a crime that involves ongoing elements. • An example is illegal U.S. drug importation. The criminal act is completed not when the drugs enter the country, but when the drugs reach their final destination. **2.** A crime (such as driving a stolen vehicle) that continues over an extended period. Cf. *instantaneous crime*.

corporate crime. A crime committed either by a corporate body or by its representatives acting on its behalf. ● Examples include price-fixing and consumer fraud.—Also termed *organizational crime*. Cf. *occupational crime*.

credit-card crime. See CREDIT-CARD CRIME.

crime against the environment. See ENVIRONMENTAL CRIME.

crime malum in se. See MALUM IN SE.

crime malum prohibitum. See MALUM PROHIBITUM.

crime of omission. An offense that carries as its material component the failure to act.

crime of passion. A crime committed in the heat of an emotionally charged moment, with no opportunity to reflect on what is happening. See HEAT OF PASSION.

crime of violence. See *violent crime*.

crime without victims. See *victimless crime.*

economic crime. A nonphysical crime committed to obtain a financial gain or a professional advantage.

environmental crime. See ENVIRONMENTAL CRIME.

expressive crime. A crime committed for the sake of the crime itself, esp. out of frustration, rage, or other emotion rather than for financial gain. Cf. *instrumental crime.*

federal crime. See FEDERAL CRIME.

general-intent crime. A crime that involves performing a particular act only, rather than performing a further act or seeking a further result.

hate crime. A crime motivated by the victim's race, color, ethnicity, religion, or national origin. • Certain groups have lobbied to expand the definition by statute to include a crime motivated by the victim's disability, gender, or sexual orientation. Cf. *hate speech* under SPEECH.

high crime. A crime that is offensive to public morality, though not necessarily a felony. • Under the U.S. Constitution, a government officer's commission of a "high crime" is, along with treason and bribery, grounds for removal from office. U.S. Const. art. II, § 4. See IMPEACHABLE OFFENSE.

inchoate crime. See *inchoate offense* under OFFENSE.

index crime. See *index offense* under OFFENSE.

infamous crime (**in**-fə-məs). **1.** At common law, a crime for which part of the punishment was infamy, so that one who committed it would be declared ineligible to serve on a jury, hold public office, or testify. • Examples are perjury, treason, and fraud. **2.** A crime punishable by imprisonment in a penitentiary. • The Fifth Amendment requires a grand-jury indictment for the prosecution of infamous (or capital) crimes, which include all federal felony offenses. See *indictable offense* under OFFENSE. Cf. *noninfamous crime.*

instantaneous crime. A crime that is fully completed by a single act, as arson or murder, rather than a series of acts. • The statute of limitations for an instantaneous crime begins to run with its completion. Cf. *continuous crime.*

instrumental crime. A crime committed to further another end or result; esp., a crime committed to obtain money to purchase a good or service. Cf. *expressive crime.*

international crime. See INTERNATIONAL CRIME.

major crime. See FELONY.

noninfamous crime. A crime that does not qualify as an infamous crime. Cf. *infamous crime.*

occupational crime. A crime that a person commits for personal gain while on the job. Cf. *corporate crime.*

organizational crime. See *corporate crime.*

organized crime. See ORGANIZED CRIME.

personal-condition crime. See *status crime.*

personal crime. A crime (such as rape, robbery, or pickpocketing) that is committed against an individual's person.

political crime. See POLITICAL OFFENSE.

predatory crime. A crime that involves preying upon and victimizing individuals. • Examples include robbery, rape, and carjacking.

preliminary crime. See *inchoate offense* under OFFENSE.

quasi-crime. **1.** An offense not subject to criminal prosecution (such as contempt or violation of a municipal ordinance) but for which penalties or forfeitures can be imposed. • The term includes offenses that give rise to *qui tam* actions and forfeitures for the violation of a public duty. **2.** An offense for which someone other than the actual perpetrator is held liable, the perpetrator being presumed to act on the command of the responsible party.

serious crime. See *serious offense* under OFFENSE.

signature crime. A distinctive crime so similar in pattern, scheme, or modus operandi to previous crimes that it identifies a particular defendant as the perpetrator.

status crime. A crime of which a person is guilty by being in a certain condition or of a specific character, such as vagrancy.—Also termed *status offense*; *personal-condition crime.*

statutory crime. A crime punishable by statute. Cf. *common-law crime.*

street crime. Crime generally directed against a person in public, such as mugging, theft, or robbery.—Also termed *visible crime*.

strict-liability crime. A crime that does not require a *mens rea* element, such as speeding or attempting to carry a weapon aboard an aircraft.

substantive crime. See *substantive offense* under OFFENSE.

vice crime. A crime of immoral conduct, such as gambling or prostitution.

victimless crime. A crime that is considered to have no direct victim, usu. because only consenting adults are involved. • Examples are possession of illicit drugs and deviant sexual intercourse between consenting adults.—Also termed *consensual crime*; *crime without victims*; *complainantless crime*.

violent crime. A crime that has as an element the use, attempted use, threatened use, or substantial risk of use of physical force against the person or property of another. 18 USCA § 16.—Also termed *crime of violence*.

visible crime. See *street crime*.

war crime. See WAR CRIME.

white-collar crime. See WHITE-COLLAR CRIME.

crime against humanity. In international law, a brutal crime that is not an isolated incident but that involves large and systematic actions, often cloaked with official authority, and that shocks the conscience of humankind. • Among the specific crimes that fall within this category are mass murder, extermination, enslavement, deportation, and other inhumane acts perpetrated against a population, whether in wartime or not.

crime against international law. See CRIME AGAINST THE LAW OF NATIONS.

crime against peace. An international crime in which the offenders plan, prepare, initiate, or wage a war of aggression or a war in violation of international peace treaties, agreements, or assurances.

crime against the environment. See ENVIRONMENTAL CRIME.

crime against the law of nations. 1. A crime punishable under internationally prescribed criminal law or defined by an international convention and required to be made punishable under the criminal law of the member states. **2.** A crime, such as piracy or a war crime, punishable under international criminal law. **3.** A crime punishable under international law; an act that is internationally agreed to be

162

of a criminal nature, such as genocide, piracy, or engaging in the slave trade.—Also termed *crime against international law*.

crime against the person. See CRIMES AGAINST PERSONS.

crime-fraud exception. The doctrine that neither the attorney-client privilege nor the attorney-work-product privilege protects attorney-client communications that are in furtherance of a current or planned crime or fraud. *Clark v. United States*, 289 U.S. 1, 53 S.Ct. 465 (1933); *In re Grand Jury Subpoena Duces Tecum*, 731 F.2d 1032 (2d Cir. 1984).

crime malum in se. See MALUM IN SE.

crime malum prohibitum. See MALUM PROHIBITUM.

crimen (**krı**-mən), *n*. [Latin] **1.** An accusation or charge of a crime. **2.** A crime. Pl. *crimina* (**krim**-ə-nə).

   crimen falsi (**krı**-mən **fal**-sı *or* **fawl**-sı). [Latin "the crime of falsifying"] **1.** A crime in the nature of perjury. **2.** Any other offense that involves some element of dishonesty or false statement. See Fed. R. Evid. 609(a)(2).

crimen furti (**krī**-mən **fər**-tī). [Latin "the crime of stealing"] See THEFT.

crimen incendii (**krī**-mən in-**sen**-dee-ī). [Latin "the crime of burning"] See ARSON.

crimen raptus (**krī**-mən **rap**-təs). [Latin "the crime of rape"] See RAPE.

crimen roberiae (**krī**-mən rə-**beer**-ee-ee). [Latin "the crime of robbery"] See ROBBERY.

crime of omission. See CRIME.

crime of passion. See CRIME.

crime of violence. See *violent crime* under CRIME.

crimes against persons. A category of criminal offenses in which the perpetrator uses or threatens to use force. • Examples include murder, rape, aggravated assault, and robbery.—Also termed *crimes against the person.* Cf. *offense against the person* under OFFENSE.

crimes against property. A category of criminal offenses in which the perpetrator seeks to derive an unlawful benefit from—or do damage to—another's property without the use or threat of force. • Examples include burglary, theft, and arson (even though arson may result in injury or death).—Also termed *property crimes*. Cf. *offense against property* under OFFENSE.

crime score. A number assigned from an established scale, indicating the relative seriousness of an offense based on the nature of the injury or the extent of property damage. • Prosecutors use crime scores and defendant scores to promote uniform treatment of similar cases and to alert them to which cases need extensive pretrial preparation. Cf. DEFENDANT SCORE.

crime statistics. Figures compiled by a governmental agency to show the incidence of various types of crime within a defined geographic area during a specified time.

crime without victims. See *victimless crime* under CRIME.

criminal, *adj.* **1.** Having the character of a crime; in the nature of a crime <criminal mischief>. **2.** Connected with the administration of penal justice <the criminal courts>.

criminal, *n.* **1.** One who has committed a criminal offense. **2.** One who has been convicted of a crime.

   dangerous criminal. A criminal who has either committed a violent crime or used force in trying to escape from custody.

episodic criminal. **1.** A person who commits crimes sporadically. **2.** A person who commits crimes only during periods of intense stress, as in the heat of passion.

habitual criminal. See RECIDIVIST.

state criminal. **1.** A person who has committed a crime against the state (such as treason); a political criminal. **2.** A person who has committed a crime under state law.

criminal action. See ACTION.

criminal anarchy. The doctrine that advocates the violent overthrow of government. ● To promote this doctrine is a criminal offense. 18 USCA § 2385.

criminal anthropology. See CRIMINOLOGY.

criminal assault. See ASSAULT.

criminal attempt. See ATTEMPT.

criminal bankruptcy. See *bankruptcy fraud* under FRAUD.

criminal battery. See BATTERY.

criminal behavior. Conduct that causes social harm and is defined and punished by law.

criminal capacity. See CAPACITY.

criminal charge. See CHARGE (1).

criminal code. See PENAL CODE.

criminal coercion. See COERCION.

criminal conspiracy. See CONSPIRACY.

criminal contempt. See CONTEMPT.

criminal damage to property. 1. Injury, destruction, or substantial impairment to the use of property (other than by fire or explosion) without the consent of a person having an interest in the property. **2.** Injury, destruction, or substantial impairment to the use of property (other than by fire or explosion) with the intent to injure or defraud an insurer or lienholder. Cf. ARSON.

criminal defendant. One who is accused in a criminal proceeding.

criminal desertion. See DESERTION.

criminal forfeiture. See FORFEITURE.

criminal fraud. See FRAUD.

criminal homicide. See HOMICIDE.

criminal infringement. See INFRINGEMENT.

criminal instrument. 1. Something made or adapted for criminal use. Model Penal Code § 5.06(1)(a). **2.** Something commonly used for criminal purposes and possessed under circumstances showing an unlawful purpose. Model Penal Code § 5.06(1)(b).—Also termed *instrument of crime*.

criminal-instrumentality rule. The principle that when a criminal act is committed, that act—rather than the victim's negligence that made the crime possible—will be considered to be the crime's proximate cause.

criminal intent. See INTENT.

criminalism. 1. A pathological tendency toward criminality. **2.** *Archaic.* The branch of psychiatry dealing with habitual criminals.

criminalist (**krim**-ə-nəl-ist). **1.** A person who practices criminalistics as a profession. **2.** *Archaic.* One versed in criminal law. **3.** *Archaic.* A psychiatrist who treats criminals. **4.** *Archaic.* A habitual criminal.

criminalistics (krim-ə-nə-**lis**-tiks), *n.* The science of crime detection, usu. involving the subjection of physical evidence to laboratory analysis, including ballistic testing, blood-fluid and tissue analysis, and other tests that are helpful in determining what happened. Cf. CRIMINOLOGY.

criminality (krim-ə-**nal**-ə-tee). **1.** The state or quality of being criminal. **2.** An act or practice that constitutes a crime.

criminalization (**krim**-ə-nəl-ə-**zay**-shən), *n.* **1.** The act or an instance of making a previously lawful act criminal, usu. by passing a statute. Cf. DECRIMINALIZATION; CIVILIZATION. **2.** The process by which a person develops into a criminal.

criminalize (**krim**-ə-nəl-ɪz), *vb.* To make illegal; to outlaw.

criminal jurisdiction. See JURISDICTION.

criminal justice. 1. The methods by which a society deals with those who are accused of having committed crimes. See LAW ENFORCEMENT (1). **2.** The field of study pursued by those seeking to enter law enforcement as a profession. • Many colleges offer degrees in criminal justice, typically after two to four years of study.—Also termed (in sense 2) *police science*; *law enforcement*.

criminal-justice system. The collective institutions through which an accused offender passes until the accusations have been disposed of or the assessed punishment concluded. ● The system typically has three components: law enforcement (police, sheriffs, marshals), the judicial process (judges, prosecutors, defense lawyers), and corrections (prison officials, probation officers, and parole officers).—Also termed *law-enforcement system*.

criminal law. The body of law defining offenses against the community at large, regulating how suspects are investigated, charged, and tried, and establishing punishments for convicted offenders.—Also termed *penal law*.

criminal lawyer. See LAWYER.

criminal libel. See LIBEL.

criminally negligent homicide. See *negligent homicide* under HOMICIDE.

criminal mischief. See MALICIOUS MISCHIEF.

criminal negligence. See NEGLIGENCE.

criminal nonsupport. See NONSUPPORT.

criminal policy. The branch of criminal science concerned with limiting harmful conduct in society. ● It draws on information provided by criminology, and its subjects for investigation are (1) the appropriate measures of social organization for preventing harmful activities, and (2) the treatment to be accorded to those who have caused harm, whether the offenders are to be given warnings, supervised probation, medical treatment, or more serious deprivations of life or liberty, such as imprisonment or capital punishment.

criminal possession. See POSSESSION.

criminal procedure. The rules governing the mechanisms under which crimes are investigated, prosecuted, adjudicated, and punished. • It includes the protection of accused persons' constitutional rights.

criminal proceeding. See PROCEEDING.

criminal process. See PROCESS.

criminal prosecution. See PROSECUTION.

criminal protector. An accessory after the fact to a felony; one who aids or harbors a wrongdoer after the commission of a crime.

criminal-referral form. A form once required (from 1988 to 1996) for reporting every instance when a bank employee or affiliate committed or aided in committing a crime

171

such as credit-card fraud, employee theft, or check-kiting. ● This form, like the suspicious-transaction report, has since been superseded by the suspicious-activity report.—Abbr. CRF. See SUSPICIOUS-ACTIVITY REPORT.

criminal registration. See REGISTRATION.

criminal responsibility. See RESPONSIBILITY.

criminal sanction. See SANCTION.

criminal science. The study of crime with a view to discovering the causes of criminality, devising the most effective methods of reducing crime, and perfecting the means for dealing with those who have committed crimes. ● The three main branches of criminal science are criminology, criminal policy, and criminal law.

criminal sexual conduct in the first degree. See FIRST-DEGREE SEXUAL CONDUCT.

criminal solicitation. See SOLICITATION (2).

criminal statute. See STATUTE.

criminal syndicalism. See SYNDICALISM.

criminal trespass. See TRESPASS.

172

criminal wrong. See CRIME.

criminate, *vb*. See INCRIMINATE.

crimination (krim-ə-**nay**-shən), *n*. **1.** See IN-CRIMINATION. **2.** An accusation or strong censure.

criminative (**krim**-ə-nay-tiv), *adj*. Of, relating to, or involving incrimination or accusation. Cf. INFIRMATIVE.

criminogenic, *adj*. Tending to cause crime or criminality.—**criminogenesis,** *n*.

criminology, *n*. The study of crime and criminal punishment as social phenomena; the study of the causes of crime, comprising (1) criminal biology, which examines causes that may be found in the mental and physical constitution of an offender (such as hereditary tendencies and physical defects), and (2) criminal sociology, which deals with inquiries into the effects of environment as a cause of criminality.—Also termed *criminal anthropology*.—**criminological,** *adj*.—**criminologist,** *n*. Cf. CRIMINALISTICS; PENOLOGY.

  comparative criminology. The scholarly study of the similarities and differences between the criminal-justice systems of different nations.

environmental criminology. The scholarly study of areas where crime occurs and of why offenders are active in those areas.— Also termed *geography of crime*; *ecology of crime*.

critical evidence. See EVIDENCE.

critical stage. A point in a criminal prosecution when the accused's rights or defenses might be affected by the absence of legal representation. • Under the Sixth Amendment, a critical stage triggers the accused's right to appointed counsel. Examples of critical stages include preliminary hearings, jury selection, and (of course) trial. Cf. ACCUSATORY STAGE.

cross-error. See ERROR.

cross-examination, *n.* The questioning of a witness at a trial or hearing by the party opposed to the party who called the witness to testify. • The purpose of cross-examination is to discredit a witness before the fact-finder in any of several ways, as by bringing out contradictions and improbabilities in earlier testimony, by suggesting doubts to the witness, and by trapping the witness into admissions that weaken the testimony. The cross-examiner is typically allowed to ask leading questions but is traditionally limited to matters covered on direct examination and to credibility issues.—

Also termed *cross-interrogation*.—**cross-ex-amine,** *vb*. Cf. DIRECT EXAMINATION; RECROSS-EX-AMINATION.

cross-question. See QUESTION (1).

cruel and unusual punishment. See PUNISH-MENT.

cruelty. The intentional and malicious inflic-tion of mental or physical suffering on a living creature, esp. a human; abusive treatment; outrage.

cruelty to a child. See *child abuse* under ABUSE.

cruelty to animals. A malicious or criminally negligent act that causes an animal to suffer pain or death.

cruelty to children. See *child abuse* under ABUSE.

culpability (kəl-pə-**bil**-ə-tee), *n*. Blameworthi-ness; the quality of being culpable. • Except in cases of absolute liability, criminal culpability requires a showing that the person acted pur-posely, knowingly, recklessly, or negligently with respect to each material element of the offense. See Model Penal Code § 2.02.

culpable (kəl-pə-bəl), *adj.* Guilty; blamewor-thy.

culpable intoxication. See *voluntary intoxication* under INTOXICATION.

culpable negligence. See *criminal negligence* under NEGLIGENCE.

culprit. 1. A person accused or charged with the commission of a crime. **2.** A person who is guilty of a crime. • *Culprit* may be a running together of *cul*, shortened from the Latin *culpabilis* ("guilty"), and *prit*, from Old French *prest* ("ready"), two words formerly used to orally plead at the outset of a criminal case.

cumulative evidence. See EVIDENCE.

cumulative offense. See OFFENSE.

cumulative punishment. See PUNISHMENT.

cumulative sentences. See *consecutive sentences* under SENTENCE.

cumulative testimony. See TESTIMONY.

curative admissibility. See ADMISSIBILITY.

curative instruction. See JURY INSTRUCTION.

curfew (**kər**-fyoo). A regulation that forbids people (or certain classes of them) from being outdoors between certain hours.

curtilage (**kər**-tə-lij). The land or yard adjoining a house, usu. within an enclosure. ● Under the Fourth Amendment, the curtilage is an area usu. protected from warrantless searches. See OPEN-FIELDS DOCTRINE. Cf. MESSUAGE.

custodial interrogation. See INTERROGATION.

custody, *n*. **1.** The care and control of a thing or person for inspection, preservation, or security.

　　constructive custody. Custody of a person (such as a parolee or probationer) whose freedom is controlled by legal authority but who is not under direct physical control.

　　penal custody. Custody intended to punish a criminal offender.

　　physical custody. Custody of a person (such as an arrestee) whose freedom is directly controlled and limited.

　　preventive custody. Custody intended to prevent further dangerous or criminal behavior.

　　protective custody. The government's confinement of a person for that person's own security or well-being, such as a witness whose safety is in jeopardy or an incompetent person who may harm others.

2. The detention of a person by virtue of lawful process or authority.—Also termed *legal custody*.—**custodial,** *adj*.

cyberstalking. The act of threatening, harassing, or annoying someone through multiple e-mail messages, as through the Internet, esp. with the intent of placing the recipient in fear that an illegal act or an injury will be inflicted on the recipient or a member of the recipient's family or household.

cybertheft. The act of using an online computer service, such as one on the Internet, to steal someone else's property or to interfere with someone else's use and enjoyment of property. ● Examples of cybertheft are hacking into a bank's computer records to wrongfully credit one account and debit another, and interfering with a copyright by wrongfully sending protected material over the Internet.

D

D. *abbr.* **1.** DISTRICT. **2.** DEFENDANT. **3.** DIGEST.

D.A. *abbr.* DISTRICT ATTORNEY.

dactylography (dak-tə-**log**-rə-fee), *n.* The scientific study of fingerprints as a method of identification.—**dactylographic** (dak-til-ə-**graf**-ik), *adj.*

dangerous, *adj.* **1.** (Of a condition, situation, etc.) perilous; hazardous; unsafe <a dangerous intersection>. **2.** (Of a person, an object, etc.) likely to cause serious bodily harm <a dangerous weapon> <a dangerous criminal>.

dangerous criminal. See CRIMINAL.

dangerous drug. See DRUG.

dangerous instrumentality. An instrument, substance, or condition so inherently dangerous that it may cause serious bodily injury or death without human use or interference. Cf. *deadly weapon* under WEAPON.

dangerous-propensity test. See DANGEROUS-TENDENCY TEST.

dangerous-proximity test. A common-law test for the crime of attempt, focusing on whether the defendant is dangerously close to

179

completing the offense. ● Factors include the gravity of the potential crime, the apprehension of the victim, and the uncertainty of the crime's occurrence. See ATTEMPT.

dangerous-tendency test. A propensity of a person or animal to inflict injury. ● The test is often used in dog-bite cases to determine whether an owner will be held liable for injuries caused by the owner's animal.—Also termed *dangerous-propensity test*.

dangerous weapon. See WEAPON.

***Darden* hearing.** An ex parte proceeding to determine whether disclosure of an informer's identity is pertinent to establishing probable cause when there is otherwise insufficient evidence to establish probable cause apart from the arresting officer's testimony about an informer's communications. ● The defense attorney may be excluded from the hearing but can usu. submit questions to be used by the judge in the examination. *People v. Darden*, 313 N.E.2d 49 (N.Y. 1974).

date rape. See RAPE.

***Daubert* hearing** (**daw**-bərt *or* doh-**ber**). A hearing conducted by federal district courts, usu. before trial, to determine whether proposed expert testimony meets the federal requirements for relevance and reliability, as clarified by the Supreme Court in *Daubert v. Merrell Dow Pharms., Inc.*, 509 U.S. 579, 113 S.Ct. 2786 (1993).

***Daubert* test.** A method that federal district courts use to determine whether expert testimony is admissible under Federal Rule of Evidence 702, which generally requires that expert testimony consist of scientific, technical, or other specialized knowledge that will assist the fact-finder in understanding the evidence or determining a fact in issue. • In its role as "gatekeeper" of the evidence, the trial court must decide whether the proposed expert testimony meets the requirements of relevance and reliability. The court applies the test outside the jury's presence, usu. during a pretrial *Daubert* hearing. At the hearing, the proponent must show that the expert's underlying reasoning or methodology, and its application to the facts, are scientifically valid. In ruling on admissibility, the court considers a flexible list of factors, including (1) whether the theory can be or has been tested, (2) whether the theory has been subjected to peer review or publication, (3) the theory's known or potential rate of error and whether there are standards that control its operation, and (4) the degree to which the relevant scientific community has accepted the theory. *Daubert v. Merrell Dow Pharms., Inc.*, 509 U.S. 579, 113 S.Ct.

2786 (1993). The Supreme Court has held that
similar scrutiny must be applied to nonscien-
tific expert testimony. *Kumho Tire Co. v. Car-
michael*, 119 S.Ct. 1167 (1999). Variations of
the *Daubert* test are applied in the trial courts
of most states.

day fine. See FINE.

D.C. *abbr*. DISTRICT COURT.

deadlocked jury. See *hung jury* under JURY.

deadly force. See FORCE.

deadly weapon. See WEAPON.

deadly weapon per se. See WEAPON.

dead time. See TIME.

death. The ending of life; the cessation of all
vital functions and signs.—Also termed *decease*; *demise*.

> ***brain death.*** The bodily condition of show-
> ing no response to external stimuli, no spon-
> taneous movements, no breathing, no reflex-
> es, and a flat reading (usu. for a full day) on
> a machine that measures the brain's electri-
> cal activity.—Also termed *legal death*.

> ***civil death.*** See CIVIL DEATH.

legal death. **1.** See *brain death*. **2.** See CIVIL DEATH.

natural death. **1.** Bodily death, as opposed to civil death. **2.** Death from causes other than accident or violence; death from natural causes. Cf. *violent death*.

violent death. Death accelerated by human intervention and resulting from a sharp blow, explosion, gunfire, or the like. Cf. *natural death*.

deathbed declaration. See *dying declaration* under DECLARATION.

death by misadventure. See ACCIDENTAL KILLING.

death case. A criminal case in which the death penalty may be or has been imposed.

death certificate. An official document issued by a public registry verifying that a person has died, with information such as the date and time of death, the cause of death, and the signature of the attending or examining physician.

death penalty. A sentence imposing death as punishment for a serious crime.—Also termed *capital punishment*.

death-qualified jury. See JURY.

death row. The area of a prison where those who have been sentenced to death are confined.

death sentence. See SENTENCE.

deathsman. An executioner; a hangman.

death trap. 1. A structure or situation involving an imminent risk of death. **2.** A situation that, although seemingly safe, is actually quite dangerous.

death warrant. See WARRANT.

decarceration. The release of a prisoner; the removal of a prisoner from confinement. Cf. INCARCERATION.

decease, *n*. See DEATH.

decease, *vb*. To die; to depart from life.

deceptive advertising. See FALSE ADVERTISING.

decisional law. See CASELAW.

declaration, *n*. **1.** An unsworn statement made by someone having knowledge of facts relating to an event in dispute.

declaration against interest. A statement by a person who is not a party to a case and is not available to testify at trial, discussing a matter that is within the declarant's personal knowledge and is adverse to the declarant's interest. • Such a statement is admissible into evidence as an exception to the hearsay rule. Fed. R. Evid. 804(b)(3). See *admission against interest* under ADMISSION.

declaration of pain. A person's exclamation of present pain, which operates as an exception to the hearsay rule. Fed. R. Evid. 803(3).

declaration of state of mind. A person's state-of-mind statement that operates as an exception to the hearsay rule. Fed. R. Evid. 803(3).

dying declaration. A statement by a person who believes that death is imminent, relating to the cause or circumstances of the person's death. • The statement is admissible in evidence as an exception to the hearsay rule.—Also termed *deathbed declaration*.

self-serving declaration. An out-of-court statement made to benefit one's own interest.

2. A formal, written statement—resembling an affidavit but not notarized or sworn to—that attests, under penalty of perjury, to facts known by the declarant. • Such a declaration, if properly prepared, is admissible in federal court with the same effect as an affidavit. 28 USCA § 1746.—Also termed *declaration under penalty of perjury*; *unsworn declaration under penalty of perjury*. Cf. AFFIDAVIT.

declaratory precedent. See PRECEDENT.

decriminalization, *n.* The legislative act or process of legalizing an illegal act <many doctors seek the decriminalization of euthanasia>.—**decriminalize,** *vb.* Cf. CRIMINALIZATION (1).

deed of crime. See ACTUS REUS.

deface (di-**fays**), *vb.* To mar or injure (a building, monument, or other structure).—**defacement,** *n.*

defalcation (dee-fal-**kay**-shən), *n.* See EMBEZZLEMENT.—**defalcate** (di-**fal**-kayt *or* dee-), *vb.*—**defalcator,** *n.*

defamation, *n.* **1.** The act of harming the reputation of another by making a false statement to a third person. • If the alleged defamation involves a matter of public concern, the plaintiff is constitutionally required to prove both the statement's falsity and the defendant's fault. **2.** A false written or oral statement that damages another's reputation.—**defame,** *vb.* See LIBEL; SLANDER.

defamatory libel. See LIBEL.

defective verdict. See VERDICT.

defend, *vb.* **1.** To deny, contest, or oppose (an allegation or claim) <the suspect vigorously defended against the charge>. **2.** To represent (someone) as an attorney <the accused retained a well-known lawyer to defend him>.

defendant (di-**fen**-dənt). A person accused in a criminal proceeding or sued in a civil proceeding.—Abbr. D.

defendant score. A number taken from an established scale, indicating the relative seriousness of the defendant's criminal history. Cf. CRIME SCORE.

defendant's gain. The amount of money or the value of property that a criminal defendant has obtained by committing a crime. • Some states, such as New York, consider the defendant's gain when assessing a criminal fine or ordering restitution.

defense (di-**fen**[t]s). **1.** A defendant's stated reason why the prosecutor has no valid case; esp., a defendant's answer, denial, or plea

187

<her defense was that she was 25 miles from the building at the time of the robbery>. **2.** A defendant's method and strategy in opposing the prosecution; a doctrine giving rise to such a method or strategy <the lawyer advised her client to adopt a passive defense and to avoid taking the witness stand>. **3.** One or more defendants in a trial <the defense rests>. **4.** Measures taken by an individual to protect against an attack. See SELF-DEFENSE.

affirmative defense. A defendant's assertion raising new facts and arguments that, if true, will defeat the prosecution's claim, even if all allegations in the complaint are true. • Examples of affirmative defenses include insanity and self-defense.

capacity defense. A defense based on the defendant's inability to be held accountable for an illegal act.

choice-of-evils defense. See *lesser-evils defense*.

collateral defense (kə-**lat**-ə-rəl). A defense of justification or excuse not involving a rebuttal of the allegation and therefore collateral to the elements that the prosecutor must prove. See EXCUSE (2); JUSTIFICATION (2).

defense of habitation. The defense that conduct constituting a criminal offense is justified if an aggressor unjustifiably threatens the defendant's abode or premises and the defendant engages in conduct that is (1) harmful to the aggressor, (2) sufficient to protect that place of abode or premises, and (3) reasonable in relation to the harm threatened.—Also termed *defense of premises*. See CASTLE DOCTRINE.

derivative defense. A defense that rebuts the criminal elements that a prosecutor must establish to justify the submission of a criminal case to a jury.

dwelling defense. See CASTLE DOCTRINE.

frivolous defense. A defense that has no basis in fact or law.

general-justification defense. See *lesser-evils defense*.

imperfect defense. A defense that fails to meet all legal requirements and usu. results only in a reduction in grade or sentence rather than an acquittal, as when a defendant is charged with manslaughter rather than murder because the defendant, while defending another, used unreasonable force to repel the attack. See *imperfect self-defense* under SELF-DEFENSE. Cf. *perfect defense*.

inconsistent defense. A defense so contrary to another defense that the acceptance of one requires abandonment of the other. ●

A person accused of murder, for example, cannot claim both self-defense and the alibi of having been in a different city when the murder took place.

insanity defense. See INSANITY DEFENSE.

justification defense. See JUSTIFICATION DEFENSE.

legal defense. A complete and adequate defense in a court of law.

lesser-evils defense. The defense that, while the defendant may have caused the harm or evil that would ordinarily constitute a criminal offense, in the present case the defendant has not caused a net harm or evil because of justifying circumstances and therefore should be exculpated.—Also termed *choice-of-evils defense*; *necessity*; *general-justification defense*.

meritorious defense (mer-ə-**tor**-ee-əs). **1.** A defense that addresses the substance or essentials of a case rather than dilatory or technical objections. **2.** A defense that appears likely to succeed or has already succeeded.

perfect defense. A defense that meets all legal requirements and results in the defendant's acquittal. See *perfect self-defense* under SELF-DEFENSE. Cf. *imperfect defense*.

sham defense. A fictitious, untrue defense, made in bad faith.

true defense. A defense admitting that a defendant committed the charged offense, but seeking to avoid punishment based on a legal excuse (such as insanity) or justification (such as self-defense).

defense attorney. A lawyer who represents a defendant in a civil or criminal case.—Also termed *defense counsel*; *defense lawyer*.

defense of habitation. See DEFENSE.

defense of others. A justification defense available if one harms or threatens another when defending a third person. See JUSTIFICATION (2).

defense of premises. See *defense of habitation* under DEFENSE.

defense of property. A justification defense available if one harms or threatens another when defending one's property. See JUSTIFICATION (2).

defense of self. See SELF-DEFENSE.

deferment, *n.* **1.** The act of delaying; postponement <deferment of a judicial decision>. **2.** A delay in serving confinement that results from a court-martial until the sentence has been approved and its execution has been ordered. • The convening authority may grant a deferment.—**defer,** *vb.*

deferred adjudication. See *deferred judgment* under JUDGMENT.

deferred-adjudication probation. See *deferred judgment* under JUDGMENT.

deferred judgment. See JUDGMENT.

deferred prosecution. See *deferred judgment* under JUDGMENT.

deferred sentence. See SENTENCE.

definite sentence. See *determinate sentence* under SENTENCE.

definitive sentence. See *determinate sentence* under SENTENCE.

degree of crime. 1. A division or classification of a single crime into several grades of guilt, according to the circumstances surrounding the crime's commission, such as aggravating factors present or the type of injury suffered. **2.** A division of crimes generally, such as felonies or misdemeanors.

degree of proof. See BURDEN OF PRODUCTION.

delayed appeal. See APPEAL.

delayed sentence. See SENTENCE.

deliberate (di-**lib**-[ə]-rit), *adj*. **1.** Intentional; premeditated; fully considered. **2.** Unimpulsive; slow in deciding.

deliberate elicitation. The purposeful yet covert drawing forth of an incriminating response (usu. not during a formal interrogation) from a suspect whose Sixth Amendment right to counsel has attached but who has not waived that right. • Deliberate elicitation may occur, for example, when a police officer engages an arrested suspect in conversation on the way to the police station. Deliberate elicitation violates the Sixth Amendment. *Massiah v. United States*, 377 U.S. 201, 84 S.Ct. 1199 (1964). See MASSIAH RULE.

deliberate-indifference instruction. See JEWELL INSTRUCTION.

deliberative-process privilege. See PRIVILEGE (1).

delinquency, *n*. A failure or omission; a violation of a law or duty. See JUVENILE DELINQUENCY.

delinquent, *adj*. (Of a person) guilty of serious antisocial or criminal conduct.

delinquent, *n*. A person guilty of serious antisocial or criminal conduct. See JUVENILE DELINQUENT.

delinquent child. See CHILD.

delinquent minor. See JUVENILE DELINQUENT.

demand for document inspection. See REQUEST FOR PRODUCTION.

demeanor evidence. See EVIDENCE.

demented, *adj*. Not of sound mind; insane.

demise. See DEATH.

demonstrative evidence. See EVIDENCE.

denounce, *vb*. **1.** To condemn openly, esp. publicly. **2.** To declare (an act or thing) to be a crime and prescribe a punishment for it. **3.** To accuse or inform against.

Department of Justice. The federal executive division that is responsible for federal law enforcement and related programs and services. ● The U.S. Attorney General heads this department, which has separate divisions for prosecuting cases under federal antitrust laws, tax laws, environmental laws, and criminal laws. The department also has a civil division that represents the U.S. government in cases involving tort claims and commercial litigation.—Abbr. DOJ.

departure, *n.* A deviation or divergence from a standard rule, regulation, measurement, or course of conduct <an impermissible departure from sentencing guidelines>.

downward departure. In the federal sentencing guidelines, a court's imposition of a sentence more lenient than the standard guidelines propose, as when the court concludes that a criminal's history is less serious than it appears.

forbidden departure. An impermissible deviation from the federal sentencing guidelines based on race, sex, national origin, creed, religion, or socioeconomic status.

lateral departure. In the federal sentencing guidelines, a sentence allowing a defendant to avoid incarceration through community or home confinement.—Also termed *lateral sentencing*.

upward departure. In the federal sentencing guidelines, a court's imposition of a sentence harsher than the standard guidelines propose, as when the court concludes that a criminal's history did not take into account additional offenses committed while the prisoner was out on bail.

depeculation (dee-pek-yə-**lay**-shən). Formerly, an embezzlement from the public treasury. Cf. PECULATION.

deposition (dep-ə-**zish**-ən). **1.** A witness's out-of-court testimony that is reduced to writing (usu. by a court reporter) for later use in court or for discovery purposes. **2.** The session at which such testimony is recorded.

> *deposition de bene esse* (dee **bee**-nee **es**-ee *also* day **ben**-ay **es**-ay). A deposition taken from a witness who will likely be unable to attend a scheduled trial or hearing. ● If the witness is not available to attend trial, the testimony is read at trial as if the witness were present in court. See *testimony de bene esse* under TESTIMONY.

depraved, *adj*. **1.** (Of a person) corrupt; perverted. **2.** (Of a crime) heinous; morally horrendous.

depraved-heart murder. See MURDER.

deputy, *n*. A person appointed or delegated to act as a substitute for another, esp. for an official.—**deputize, depute,** *vb*.

***general deputy.* 1.** A deputy appointed to act in another officer's place and execute all ordinary functions of the office. **2.** See *deputy sheriff* under SHERIFF.

special deputy. A deputy specially appointed to serve a particular purpose, such as keeping the peace during a riot.

deputy sheriff. See SHERIFF.

derivative contraband. See CONTRABAND.

derivative defense. See DEFENSE.

derivative entrapment. See ENTRAPMENT.

derivative evidence. See EVIDENCE.

desecrate, *vb.* To divest (a thing) of its sacred character; to defile or profane (a sacred thing).

desertion, *n.* The willful and unjustified abandonment of a person's duties or obligations, esp. to military service or to a spouse or family.—**desert,** *vb.*

criminal desertion. One spouse's willful failure without just cause to provide for the care, protection, or support of the other spouse who is in ill health or needy circumstances.

deserts. See JUST DESERTS.

design, *n.* **1.** A plan or scheme. **2.** Purpose or intention combined with a plan.

> **formed design.** The deliberate and fixed intention to kill, though not necessarily a particular person. See PREMEDITATION.

designedly, *adv.* Willfully; intentionally.

designer drug. See DRUG.

despoil (di-**spoil**), *vb.* To deprive (a person) of possessions illegally by violence or by clandestine means; to rob.—**despoliation** (di-spoh-lee-**ay**-shən), **despoilment,** *n.*

detainer. **1.** The confinement of a person in custody. **2.** A writ authorizing a prison official to continue holding a prisoner in custody.

detection. The act of discovering or revealing something that was hidden, esp. to solve a crime.

detention, *n.* The act or fact of holding a person in custody; confinement or compulsory delay.—**detain,** *vb.*

> **investigative detention.** The holding of a suspect without formal arrest during the investigation of the suspect's participation

198

in a crime. • Detention of this kind is constitutional only if probable cause exists.

pretrial detention. The holding of a defendant before trial on criminal charges either because the established bail could not be posted or because release was denied.—Also termed *temporary detention*.

preventive detention. Confinement imposed usu. on a criminal defendant who has threatened to escape, poses a risk of harm, or has otherwise violated the law while awaiting trial, or on a mentally ill person who may cause harm.

detention hearing. See HEARING.

detention in a reformatory. A juvenile offender's sentence of being sent to a reformatory school for some period.

determinate sentence. See SENTENCE.

deterrence, *n.* The act or process of discouraging certain behavior, particularly by fear; esp., as a goal of criminal law, the prevention of criminal behavior by fear of punishment.— **deter,** *vb.*—**deterrent,** *adj.* Cf. REHABILITATION (1); RETRIBUTION (1).

general deterrence. A goal of criminal law generally, or of a specific conviction and sentence, to discourage people from committing crimes.

special deterrence. A goal of a specific conviction and sentence to dissuade the offender from committing crimes in the future.

deterrent, *n.* Something that impedes; something that prevents <a deterrent to crime>.

deterrent punishment. See PUNISHMENT.

diagnostic commitment. See COMMITMENT.

digest, *n.* An index of legal propositions showing which cases support each proposition; a collection of summaries of reported cases, arranged by subject and subdivided by jurisdiction and court. ● The chief purpose of a digest is to make the contents of reports available and to separate, from the great mass of caselaw, those cases bearing on some specific point. The American Digest System covers the decisions of all American courts of last resort, state and federal, from 1658 to present.— Abbr. D; Dig.

diminished capacity. See CAPACITY.

diminished responsibility. See *diminished capacity* under CAPACITY.

diplomatic immunity. See IMMUNITY (1).

direct and proximate cause. See *proximate cause* under CAUSE (1).

direct attack. An attack on a judgment made in the same proceeding as the one in which the judgment was entered. ● Examples of direct attacks are appeals and motions for new trial. Cf. COLLATERAL ATTACK.

direct cause. See *proximate cause* under CAUSE (1).

direct confession. See CONFESSION.

direct contempt. See CONTEMPT.

direct conversion. See CONVERSION.

directed verdict. See VERDICT.

direct evidence. See EVIDENCE.

direct examination. The first questioning of a witness in a trial or other proceeding, conducted by the party who called the witness to testify.—Often shortened to *direct*.—Also termed *examination-in-chief*. Cf. CROSS-EXAMINATION; REDIRECT EXAMINATION.

direct injury. See INJURY.

direct question. See QUESTION (1).

disability. Incapacity in the eyes of the law
<most of a minor's disabilities are removed
when he or she turns 18>.—Also termed *incapacity*.

> *civil disability.* The condition of a person
> who has had a legal right or privilege re-
> voked as a result of a criminal conviction, as
> when a person's driver's license is revoked
> after a DWI conviction. Cf. CIVIL DEATH (2).

discharge (**dis**-chahrj), *n.* **1.** The dismissal of
a case. **2.** The canceling or vacating of a court
order. **3.** The release of a prisoner from confinement. **4.** The relieving of a witness, juror,
or jury from further responsibilities in a case.
5. The dismissal of a member of the armed
services from military service <the sergeant
was honorably discharged>.—**discharge** (dis-
chahrj), *vb.*

> *bad-conduct discharge.* A punitive dis-
> charge that a court-martial can give a mem-
> ber of the military, usu. as punishment for
> repeated minor offenses.—Abbr. BCD.

> *dishonorable discharge.* The most severe
> punitive discharge that a court-martial can
> give to a member of the military. ● A dishon-
> orable discharge may result from conviction
> for an offense recognized in civilian law as a

felony or of a military offense requiring severe punishment. Only a general court-martial can give a dishonorable discharge.

discipline, *n*. **1.** Punishment intended to correct or instruct; esp., a sanction or penalty
imposed after an official finding of misconduct.
2. Control gained by enforcing compliance or
order.—**discipline,** *vb*.—**disciplinary,** *adj*.

discovery, *n*. **1.** Compulsory disclosure, at a
party's request, of information that relates to
the litigation. • The primary discovery devices
are interrogatories, depositions, requests for
admissions, and requests for production. Although discovery typically comes from parties,
courts also allow limited discovery from non-
parties. **2.** The facts or documents disclosed
<the new associate spent all her time review-
ing discovery>.—**discover,** *vb*.—**discover-
able,** *adj*.

> *pretrial discovery*. Discovery conducted
> before trial to reveal facts and develop evi-
> dence. • Modern procedural rules have
> broadened the scope of pretrial discovery to
> prevent the parties from surprising each
> other with evidence at trial.

discretion (di-**skresh**-ən). **1.** A public official's power or right to act in certain circumstances according to personal judgment and
conscience.—Also termed *discretionary power*.

judicial discretion. The exercise of judgment by a judge or court based on what is fair under the circumstances and guided by the rules and principles of law; a court's power to act or not act when a litigant is not entitled to demand the act as a matter of right.—Also termed *legal discretion*.

prosecutorial discretion. A prosecutor's power to choose from the options available in a criminal case, such as filing charges, prosecuting, plea-bargaining, and recommending a sentence to the court.

2. The capacity to distinguish between right and wrong, sufficient to make a person responsible for his or her own actions.

discretionary commitment. See COMMITMENT.

discretionary power. See DISCRETION.

discretionary review. See REVIEW.

dishonorable discharge. See DISCHARGE.

disincarcerate, *vb.* To release (a person) from jail; to set free.

disinterested witness. See WITNESS.

disjunctive allegation. See ALLEGATION.

dismissal, *n.* Termination of an action or claim without further hearing, esp. before the trial of the issues involved.

disobedient child. See *incorrigible child* under CHILD.

disorderly conduct. See CONDUCT.

disorderly house. 1. A dwelling where people carry on activities that are a nuisance to the neighborhood. **2.** A dwelling where people conduct criminal or immoral activities. ● Examples are brothels and drug houses.—Also termed *bawdy house*; *house of prostitution*; *house of ill fame*; *lewd house*; *assignation house*.

disorderly person. 1. A person guilty of disorderly conduct. See *disorderly conduct* under CONDUCT. **2.** A person who breaches the peace, order, decency, or safety of the public, as defined by statute.

disposition hearing. See HEARING.

disposition without a trial. The final determination of a criminal case without a trial on the merits, as when a defendant pleads guilty or admits sufficient facts to support a guilty finding without a trial.

dispositive fact. See FACT.

disputable presumption. See *rebuttable presumption* under PRESUMPTION.

disqualification, *n*. **1.** Something that makes one ineligible; esp., a bias or conflict of interest that prevents a judge or juror from impartially hearing a case, or that prevents a lawyer from representing a party.

> *vicarious disqualification.* Disqualification of all the lawyers in a firm or in an office because one of the lawyers is ethically disqualified from representing the client at issue.—Also termed *imputed disqualification*.

2. The act of making ineligible; the fact or condition of being ineligible.—**disqualify,** *vb*. Cf. RECUSAL.

disruptive conduct. See CONDUCT.

dissent. See *dissenting opinion* under OPINION.

dissenting opinion. See OPINION.

district. 1. A territorial area into which a country, state, county, municipality, or other political subdivision is divided for judicial, political, electoral, or administrative purposes. **2.** A territorial area in which similar local businesses or entities are concentrated, such as a theater district or an arts district.—Abbr. D.

district attorney. A public official appointed or elected to represent the state in criminal cases in a particular judicial district; PROSECUTOR (1).—Abbr. D.A.—Also termed *public prosecutor*; *state's attorney*; *prosecuting attorney*. Cf. UNITED STATES ATTORNEY.

district court. A trial court having general jurisdiction within its judicial district.—Abbr. D.C.

district-court magistrate. See MAGISTRATE.

district judge. See JUDGE.

disturbance of the peace. See BREACH OF THE PEACE.

disturbing the peace. See BREACH OF THE PEACE.

diversion program. A program that refers certain criminal defendants before trial to community programs on job training, education, and the like, which if successfully completed may lead to the dismissal of the charges.—Also termed *pretrial diversion*; *pretrial intervention*. Cf. *deferred judgment* under JUDGMENT.

207

divertee. A defendant who participates in a diversion program. See DIVERSION PROGRAM.

divestiture (di-**ves**-tə-chər *or* dī-), *n.* **1.** The loss or surrender of an asset or interest. **2.** A court order to a party to dispose of assets or property.

divisible offense. See OFFENSE.

D.J. See *district judge* under JUDGE.

DNA identification. A method of comparing a person's deoxyribonucleic acid (DNA)—a patterned chemical structure of genetic information—with the DNA in a biological specimen (such as blood, tissue, or hair) to determine whether the person is the source of the specimen.—Also termed *DNA fingerprinting*; *genetic fingerprinting*. Cf. HLA TEST.

dock. See BAIL DOCK.

docket, *n.* **1.** A formal record in which a judge or court clerk briefly notes all the proceedings and filings in a court case <review the docket to determine the filing date>.—Also termed *judicial record*.

  appearance docket. A list of the parties and lawyers participating in an action, together with a brief abstract of the successive steps in the action.

judgment docket. A book that a court clerk keeps for the entry or recordation of judgments, giving official notice of existing judgment liens to interested parties.—Also termed *judgment book*; *judgment file*; *judgment record*.

2. A schedule of pending cases <the case is third on Monday's trial docket>.—Also termed *court calendar*; *cause list*; *trial calendar*.

preferred docket. A list of cases set for trial, arranged in order of priority. ● Criminal cases are, for example, generally given precedence over civil cases on the preferred docket because of the constitutional right to a speedy trial.

3. See DOCKET CALL.

docket call. A court session in which attorneys (and sometimes parties) appear in court to report the status of their cases.—Often shortened to *docket*.

doctor-patient privilege. See PRIVILEGE (3).

doctrine of precedent. 1. The rule that precedents not only have persuasive authority, but must be followed when similar circumstances

arise. ● This rule developed in the 19th century and prevails today. See STARE DECISIS. **2.** A
rule that precedents are reported, may be cited, and will probably be followed by courts. ●
This is the rule that prevailed in England until
the 19th century.

doctrine of specialty. The principle, included as a provision in most extradition treaties,
under which a person who is extradited to a
country to stand trial for certain criminal offenses may be tried only for those offenses and
not for any other pre-extradition offenses.—
Also termed *specialty doctrine*. See EXTRADITION.

documentary evidence. See EVIDENCE.

documentary-originals rule. See BEST-EVI-
DENCE RULE.

DOJ. *abbr.* DEPARTMENT OF JUSTICE.

domestic authority. A defense allowing a
person responsible for another (such as a parent responsible for a child) to use nondeadly
force when reasonably necessary to protect the
person being cared for.

domestic dispute. A disturbance, usu. at a
residence and usu. within a family, involving
violence and often resulting in a call to a law-
enforcement agency.—Also termed *domestic*

disturbance; *family disturbance*. See *domestic violence* under VIOLENCE.

domestic violence. See VIOLENCE.

dope. 1. A thick liquid used esp. for medicinal purposes. **2.** *Slang.* A drug, esp. a narcotic.

dossier (**dos**-ee-ay), *n*. [French] A file or brief; a bundle of papers pertaining to a particular matter, such as a criminal case.

double adultery. See ADULTERY.

double forgery. See FORGERY.

double hearsay. See HEARSAY.

double jeopardy. The fact of being prosecuted twice for substantially the same offense. ● Double jeopardy is prohibited by the Fifth Amendment. Cf. FORMER JEOPARDY.

Double Jeopardy Clause. The Fifth Amendment provision stating, "nor shall any person be subject for the same offence to be twice put in jeopardy of life or limb." ● The amendment was ratified in 1791.

doubt, reasonable. See REASONABLE DOUBT.

downward departure. See DEPARTURE.

driving under the influence. The offense of operating a motor vehicle in a physically or mentally impaired condition, esp. after consuming alcohol or drugs. • Generally, this is a lesser offense than driving while intoxicated. But in a few jurisdictions the two are synonymous.—Abbr. DUI.—Also termed *driving while ability-impaired* (DWAI); *driving under the influence of liquor* (DUIL); *operating under the influence* (OUI); *operating while intoxicated* (OWI); *operating a motor vehicle while intoxicated* (OMVI); *operating a motor vehicle under the influence* (OMVUI). Cf. DRIVING WHILE INTOXICATED.

driving while ability-impaired. See DRIVING UNDER THE INFLUENCE.

driving while intoxicated. The offense of operating a motor vehicle in a physically or mentally impaired condition after consuming enough alcohol to raise one's blood alcohol content above the statutory limit ((.08%) in many states), or after consuming drugs. • Penalties vary widely; for example, the maximum penalty in Missouri and Louisiana is a $500 fine and six months in jail, while the penalties in New York range from $500 to $5,000 in fines and up to four years in jail.—Abbr. DWI. Cf. DRIVING UNDER THE INFLUENCE.

dropsy testimony. See TESTIMONY.

drug, *n*. **1.** A substance intended for use in the diagnosis, cure, treatment, or prevention of disease. **2.** A natural or synthetic substance that alters one's perception or consciousness.—**drug,** *vb*. See CONTROLLED SUBSTANCE.

   addictive drug. A drug (such as heroin or nicotine) that, usu. after repeated consumption, causes physical dependence and results in well-defined physiological symptoms upon withdrawal.

   dangerous drug. A drug that has potential for abuse or injury, usu. requiring a label warning that it cannot be dispensed without a prescription.

   designer drug. A chemical substance that is created to duplicate the pharmacological effects of controlled substances, often by using the same chemicals contained in controlled substances, but manipulating their formulas.

drug abuse. The detrimental state produced by the repeated consumption of a narcotic or other potentially dangerous drug, other than as prescribed by a doctor to treat an illness or other medical condition.

drug addict. See ADDICT.

drug dependence. Psychological or physiological need for a drug.

drug-free zone. An area in which the possession or distribution of a controlled substance results in an increased penalty. • Drug-free zones are often established around public schools.

druggist. A person who mixes, compounds, dispenses, or otherwise deals in drugs and medicines, usu. either as a proprietor of a drugstore or as a pharmacist.

drug kingpin. An organizer, leader, manager, financier, or supervisor of a drug conspiracy; a person with great authority in running an illegal drug operation.

drug paraphernalia. Anything used, intended for use, or designed for use with a controlled substance. • Possession of drug paraphernalia is a crime.

drunk, *adj.* Intoxicated; (of a person) under the influence of intoxicating liquor to such a degree that the normal capacity for rational thought and conduct is impaired.

drunkard. A person who is habitually or often intoxicated.

drunkenness. 1. A state of intoxication; inebriation; the condition resulting from a person's ingestion of excessive amounts of intoxicating liquors sufficient to affect the person's normal capacity for rational thought and conduct. **2.** A habitual state of intoxication.

> *excessive drunkenness.* A state of drunkenness in which a person is so far deprived of reason and understanding that he or she is incapable of understanding the character and consequences of an act.

drunkometer (drəng-**kom**-ə-tər). See BREATH-ALYZER.

dual-criminality principle. The rule prohibiting the international extradition of a fugitive unless the offense involves conduct that is criminal in both countries.

dual-prosecution rule. The principle that the federal government and a state government may both prosecute a defendant for the same offense because both governments are separate and distinct entities. See DUAL-SOVEREIGNTY DOCTRINE.

dual-sovereignty doctrine. The rule that the federal government and a state government may both prosecute someone for a crime, without violating the constitutional protection against double jeopardy, if the person's act violated both jurisdictions' laws. See DUAL-PROSECUTION RULE.

due course of law. See DUE PROCESS.

duel, *n.* A single combat; specif., a prear-ranged combat with deadly weapons fought between two or more persons under prescribed rules, usu. in the presence of at least two witnesses, to resolve a previous quarrel or avenge a deed. ● In England and the United States, death resulting from a duel is treated as murder, and seconds may be liable as acces-sories.—Also termed *single combat.* Cf. MUTUAL COMBAT.

dueling, *n.* The common-law offense of fight-ing at an appointed time and place after an earlier disagreement. ● If one of the partici-pants is killed, the other is guilty of murder, and all who are present, abetting the crime, are guilty as principals in the second degree.

due process. The conduct of legal proceedings according to established rules and principles for the protection and enforcement of private rights, including notice and the right to a fair hearing before a tribunal with the power to decide the case.—Also termed *due process of law; due course of law.*

Due Process Clause. The constitutional pro-vision that prohibits the government from un-fairly or arbitrarily depriving a person of life, liberty, or property. ● There are two Due Process Clauses in the U.S. Constitution, one in the 5th Amendment applying to the federal government, and one in the 14th Amendment applying to the states (although the 5th Amendment's Due Process Clause also applies to the states under the incorporation doctrine).

due-process rights. The rights (as to life, liberty, and property) so fundamentally important as to require compliance with due-process standards of fairness and justice.

DUI. *abbr.* DRIVING UNDER THE INFLUENCE.

DUIL. *abbr.* Driving under the influence of liquor. See DRIVING UNDER THE INFLUENCE.

***Dunaway* hearing.** A hearing to determine whether evidence has been seized from an accused in violation of his or her Fourth Amendment rights, as by a search conducted without probable cause. *Dunaway v. New York*, 442 U.S. 200 (1979). See FOURTH AMENDMENT.

duplicitous (d[y]oo-**plis**-i-təs), *adj.* **1.** (Of a person) deceitful; double-dealing. **2.** (Of a pleading, esp. an indictment) alleging two or more matters in one plea; characterized by double pleading.

duplicitous indictment. See INDICTMENT.

duplicity (d[y]oo-**plis**-i-tee), *n.* **1.** Deceitfulness; double-dealing. **2.** The charging of the same offense in more than one count of an indictment. **3.** The charging of two distinct offenses in the same count of an indictment.

Duren **test.** A test to determine whether a jury's composition violates the fair-cross-section requirement and a criminal defendant's Sixth Amendment right to an impartial jury. • Under the test, a constitutional violation occurs if (1) in the venire from which the jury was selected, a distinctive group is not fairly and reasonably represented in relation to the group's population in the community, (2) the underrepresentation is the result of a systematic exclusion of the group from the jury-selection process, and (3) the government cannot reasonably justify the discrepancy. *Duren v. Missouri*, 439 U.S. 357, 99 S.Ct. 664 (1979). See FAIR-CROSS-SECTION REQUIREMENT; STATISTICAL-DECISION THEORY; ABSOLUTE DISPARITY; COMPARATIVE DISPARITY.

duress (d[y]uu-**res**). **1.** Strictly, the physical confinement of a person. **2.** Broadly, the threat of confinement or detention, or other threat of harm, used to compel a person to do something against his or her will or judgment. **3.** The use or threatened use of unlawful force—usu. that a reasonable person cannot resist—to compel someone to commit an unlawful act. •

Duress is a recognized criminal defense. See Model Penal Code § 2.09. See COERCION; EXTORTION.

> ***duress of circumstances.*** See NECESSITY (1).

> ***duress of the person.*** Compulsion of a person by imprisonment, by threat, or by a show of force that cannot be resisted.

> ***duress per minas*** (pər **mɪ**-nəs). [Law Latin] Duress by threat of loss of life, loss of limb, mayhem, or other harm to a person.

***Durham* rule.** A test for the insanity defense, holding that a defendant is not criminally responsible for an act that was the product of a mental disease or defect (*Durham v. United States*, 214 F.2d 862 (D.C. Cir. 1954)). ● Formerly used in New Hampshire and the District of Columbia, the *Durham* rule has been criticized as being too broad and is no longer accepted in any American jurisdiction.—Also termed *product test*. See INSANITY DEFENSE.

duty judge. See JUDGE.

DWAI. *abbr*. Driving while ability-impaired. See DRIVING UNDER THE INFLUENCE.

dwelling defense. See CASTLE DOCTRINE.

dwelling-house. 1. The house or other structure in which a person lives; a residence or abode. **2.** A building, a part of a building, a tent, a mobile home, or another enclosed space that is used or intended for use as a human habitation. ● The term has referred to connected buildings in the same curtilage but now typically includes only the structures connected either directly with the house or by an enclosed passageway.—Often shortened to *dwelling.*—Also termed (archaically) *mansion house.*

DWI. *abbr.* DRIVING WHILE INTOXICATED.

Dyer Act. A federal law, originally enacted in 1919, making it unlawful either (1) to transport a stolen motor vehicle across state lines, knowing it to be stolen, or (2) to receive, conceal, or sell such a vehicle, knowing it to be stolen. 18 USCA §§ 2311–2313.—Also termed *National Motor Vehicle Theft Act.*

dying declaration. See DECLARATION.

dynamite charge. See ALLEN CHARGE.

dynamite instruction. See ALLEN CHARGE.

E

earned time. See TIME.

earwitness. A witness who testifies about something that he or she heard but did not see. Cf. EYEWITNESS.

eavesdropping. The act of secretly listening to the private conversation of others without their consent. Cf. BUGGING; WIRETAPPING.

ecology of crime. See *environmental criminology* under CRIMINOLOGY.

economic coercion. See COERCION (2).

economic crime. See CRIME.

editorial privilege. See *journalist's privilege* (2) under PRIVILEGE (3).

effective assistance of counsel. See ASSISTANCE OF COUNSEL.

effective cause. See *immediate cause* under CAUSE (1).

efficient cause. See *proximate cause* under CAUSE (1).

effraction (ə-**frak**-shən). A breach made by the use of force.

effractor (ə-**frak**-tər). One who breaks through; a burglar.

Eighth Amendment. The constitutional amendment, ratified as part of the Bill of Rights in 1791, prohibiting excessive bail, excessive fines, and cruel and unusual punishment.

elder abuse. See *abuse of the elderly* under ABUSE.

electric chair. A chair that is wired so that electrodes can be fastened to a condemned person's head and one leg and a lethal charge passed through the body for the purpose of carrying out a death penalty. ● The electric chair was first used in 1890.

elemental fact. See *ultimate fact* under FACT.

elements of crime. The constituent parts of a crime—usu. consisting of the actus reus, mens rea, and causation—that the prosecution must prove to sustain a conviction. ● The term is more broadly defined by the Model Penal Code in § 1.13(9) to refer to each component of the actus reus, causation, the mens rea, any grading factors, and the negative of any defense.

emancipated minor. See MINOR.

emancipation. 1. The act by which one who was under another's power and control is freed. **2.** A surrender and renunciation of the correlative rights and duties concerning the care, custody, and earnings of a child; the act by which a parent (historically a father) frees a child and gives the child the right to his or her own earnings.—**emancipate,** *vb.*

embezzlement, *n.* The fraudulent taking of personal property with which one has been entrusted, esp. as a fiduciary. • The criminal intent for embezzlement—unlike larceny and false pretenses—arises after taking possession (not before or during the taking).—Also termed *defalcation*; *peculation*.—**embezzle,** *vb.* See LARCENY; FALSE PRETENSES.

embracer (im-**brays**-ər). The bribe-giver in the offense of embracery.—Also spelled *embraceor*.

embracery (im-**brays**-ə-ree), *n.* The attempt to corrupt or instruct a jury to reach a particular conclusion by means other than presenting evidence or argument in court, as by bribing or threatening jurors; a corrupt or wrongful attempt to influence a juror's vote on a verdict.—Also termed *jury-tampering*; *laboring a jury*.—Also spelled *imbracery*. Cf. JURY-FIXING; JURY-PACKING.

emergency circumstances. See *exigent circumstances* under CIRCUMSTANCE.

emergency doctrine. The principle that a police officer may conduct a search without a warrant if the officer has probable cause and reasonably believes that immediate action is needed to protect life or property.—Also termed *emergency exception*. See *exigent circumstances* under CIRCUMSTANCE.

emergency exception. See EMERGENCY DOCTRINE.

emergency search. See SEARCH.

emotional insanity. See INSANITY.

empty-chair defense. A trial tactic in a multi-party case whereby one defendant attempts to put all the fault on a defendant who plea-bargained before trial or on a person who was not charged.

encourage, *vb.* To instigate; to incite to action; to embolden; to help. See AID AND ABET.

endangering the welfare of a child. See CHILD ENDANGERMENT.

endless-chain scheme. See PYRAMID SCHEME.

enhanced, *adj*. Made greater; increased <because of his recidivism, Monte was subject to an enhanced sentence after his latest conviction>.

enterprise, *n*. Under federal anti-racketeering law, an individual, partnership, corporation, association, union, other legal entity, or group of individuals associated in fact, although not a legal entity. ● The enterprise must be ongoing and must exist as an entity separate from the allegedly illegal activity that it engages in. 18 USCA § 1961(4). See RACKETEER INFLUENCED AND CORRUPT ORGANIZATIONS ACT.

enterprise liability. See LIABILITY.

entice, *vb*. To lure or induce; esp., to wrongfully solicit (a person) to do something.

enticement, *n*. The act or an instance of wrongfully soliciting or luring a person to do something.

  enticement of a child. The act or offense of inviting, persuading, or attempting to persuade a child to enter a vehicle, building, room, or secluded place with the intent of committing an unlawful sexual act against the child.

entrapment, *n*. **1.** A law-enforcement officer's or government agent's inducement of a person

ENTRAPMENT

to commit a crime, by means of fraud or undue persuasion, in an attempt to later bring a criminal prosecution against that person. **2.** The affirmative defense of having been so induced. ● To establish entrapment (in most states), the defendant must show that he or she would not have committed the crime but for the fraud or undue persuasion.—**entrap,** *vb.*

> *derivative entrapment.* Entrapment in which the government uses a private person, acting either as an agent of the government or as an unwitting participant, to induce the subject of the entrapment to commit a crime.

> *sentencing entrapment.* Entrapment of a defendant who is predisposed to commit a lesser offense but who is unlawfully induced to commit a more serious offense that carries a more severe sentence.—Also termed *sentence-factor manipulation.*

entry, *n.* The act, right, or privilege of entering real property <they were given entry into the stadium>.

> *lawful entry.* **1.** The entry onto real property by a person not in possession, under a claim or color of right, and without force or fraud. **2.** The entry of premises under a search warrant. See SEARCH WARRANT.

unlawful entry. **1.** The crime of entering another's property, by fraud or other illegal means, without the owner's consent. **2.** An alien's crossing of a border into a country without proper documents.

environmental crime. A statutory offense involving harm to the environment, such as a violation of the criminal provisions in the Clean Air Act Amendments of 1970, the Federal Water Pollution Control Act of 1972 (commonly called the Clean Water Act), or the Endangered Species Act of 1973. ● Although the most significant environmental-crime statutes were passed in the 1970s, they date back to the late 19th century, with statutes such as the Pure Food and Drug Act of 1896 and the assorted statutes that ultimately became the Rivers and Harbors Act of 1899.—Also termed *crime against the environment.*

environmental criminology. See CRIMINOLO-GY.

episodic criminal. See CRIMINAL.

equal-access rule. The doctrine that contraband found on a defendant's premises will not support a conviction if other persons have the same access to the premises as the defendant. ● To invoke this defense successfully, the defendant must show that other persons did in fact have equal access to the premises; speculative evidence that trespassers might have come onto the premises will not bar a conviction.

equivocality test (i-kwiv-ə-**kal**-ə-tee). See RES IPSA LOQUITUR TEST.

erasure of record. See EXPUNGEMENT OF RECORD.

error, *n.* **1.** A mistake of law or of fact in a court's judgment, opinion, or order.

clear error. A trial judge's decision or action that appears to a reviewing court to have been unquestionably erroneous. • Even though a clear error occurred, it may not warrant reversal.

clerical error. An error resulting from a minor mistake or inadvertence, esp. in writing or copying something on the record, and not from judicial reasoning or determination. • Among the boundless examples of clerical errors are omitting an appendix from a document; typing an incorrect number; mistranscribing a word; and failing to log a call. A court can correct a clerical error at any time, even after judgment has been entered.—Also termed *scrivener's error.*

cross-error. An error brought by the party responding to a writ of error.

error apparent of record. See *plain error*.

fatal error. See *reversible error*.

fundamental error. See *plain error*.

harmful error. See *reversible error*.

harmless error. An error that does not affect a party's substantive rights or the case's outcome. ● A harmless error is not grounds for reversal.—Also termed *technical error*.

invited error. An error that a party cannot complain of on appeal because the party, through conduct, encouraged or prompted the trial court to make the erroneous ruling.

manifest constitutional error. An error by the trial court that has an identifiably negative impact on the trial to such a degree that the constitutional rights of a party are compromised. ● A manifest constitutional error can be reviewed by a court of appeals even if the appellant did not object at trial.

manifest error. An error that is plain and indisputable, and that amounts to a complete disregard of the controlling law or the credible evidence in the record.

plain error. An error that is so obvious and prejudicial that an appellate court should address it despite the parties' failure to raise a proper objection. ● A plain error is often said to be so obvious and substantial that failure to correct it would infringe a party's due-process rights and damage the integrity of the judicial process.—Also termed *fundamental error*; *error apparent of record.*

reversible error. An error that affects a party's substantive rights or the case's outcome, and thus is grounds for reversal if the party properly objected.—Also termed *harmful error*; *prejudicial error*; *fatal error.*

scrivener's error. See *clerical error.*

technical error. See *harmless error.*

2. An appeal <a proceeding in error>.

escape, *n.* **1.** The act or an instance of breaking free from confinement, restraint, or an obligation. **2.** An unlawful departure from legal custody without the use of force.—Also termed *actual escape.* Cf. PRISON BREACH.

constructive escape. A prisoner's obtaining more liberty than the law allows, while not fully regaining freedom.

3. At common law, a criminal offense committed by a peace officer who allows a prisoner to depart unlawfully from legal custody.—Also termed *voluntary escape.*—**escape,** *vb.*

negligent escape. A prisoner's departure from legal custody as a result of an officer's negligence.

escapee. A prisoner or other inmate who has escaped from lawful custody.

escape warrant. See WARRANT.

Escobedo **rule** (es-kə-**bee**-doh). The principle that a statement by an unindicted, targeted suspect in police custody is inadmissible at trial unless the police warn the suspect of the right to remain silent and provide an opportunity for the suspect to consult with retained or appointed counsel. • This rule was a precursor to the *Miranda* rule. *Escobedo v. Illinois*, 378 U.S. 478, 84 S.Ct. 1758 (1964). See MIRANDA RULE.

espionage (**es**-pee-ə-nahzh). The practice of using spies to collect information about what another government or company is doing or plans to do.

industrial espionage. One company's spying on another to steal the other company's trade secrets or other proprietary information.

231

Espionage Act. A federal law that criminal-izes and punishes espionage, spying, and relat-ed crimes. 18 USCA §§ 793 et seq.

euthanasia (yoo-thə-**nay**-zhə), *n.* The act or practice of killing or bringing about the death of a person who suffers from an incurable disease or condition, esp. a painful one, for reasons of mercy. ● Euthanasia is sometimes regarded by the law as second-degree murder, manslaughter, or criminally negligent homi-cide.—Also termed *mercy killing.*—**euthana-sic** (yoo-thə-**nay**-zik), *adj.* Cf. *assisted suicide* under SUICIDE.

> ***active euthanasia.*** Euthanasia performed by a facilitator (usu. a physician) who not only provides the means of death but also carries out the final death-causing act.

> ***involuntary euthanasia.*** Euthanasia of a competent, nonconsenting person.

> ***nonvoluntary euthanasia.*** Euthanasia of an incompetent, and therefore nonconsent-ing, person.

> ***passive euthanasia.*** The act of allowing a terminally ill person to die by either with-holding or withdrawing life-sustaining sup-port such as a respirator or feeding tube.

voluntary euthanasia. Euthanasia performed with the terminally ill person's consent.

euthanize (**yoo**-thə-nɪz), *vb.* To put to death by euthanasia. • This term is used chiefly in reference to animals.—Also termed *euthanatize*.

evidence, *n.* **1.** Something (including testimony, documents, and tangible objects) that tends to prove or disprove the existence of an alleged fact <the bloody glove is the key piece of evidence for the prosecution>. **2.** See *fact in evidence* under FACT. **3.** The collective mass of things, esp. testimony and exhibits, presented before a tribunal in a given dispute <the evidence will show that the defendant breached the contract>. **4.** The body of law regulating the burden of proof, admissibility, relevance, and the weight and sufficiency of what should be admitted into the record of a legal proceeding <under the rules of evidence, the witness's statement is inadmissible hearsay that is not subject to any exception>.—**evidence,** *vb.*

admissible evidence. Evidence that is relevant and is of such a character (e.g., not unfairly prejudicial or based on hearsay) that the court should receive it.—Also termed *competent evidence*; *proper evidence*.

autoptic evidence. See *demonstrative evidence*.

best evidence. Evidence of the highest quality available, as measured by the nature of the case rather than the thing being offered as evidence. ● The term is usu. applied to writings and recordings.—Also termed *primary evidence*; *original evidence*. See BEST-EVIDENCE RULE. Cf. *secondary evidence*.

character evidence. Evidence regarding someone's personality traits; evidence of a person's moral standing in a community, based on reputation or opinion. Fed. R. Evid. 404, 405, 608.

circumstantial evidence. **1.** Evidence based on inference and not on personal knowledge or observation.—Also termed *indirect evidence*; *oblique evidence*. Cf. *direct evidence* (1). **2.** All evidence that is not given by testimony.

clear and convincing evidence. Evidence indicating that the thing to be proved is highly probable or reasonably certain. ● This is a greater burden than preponderance of the evidence, the standard applied in most civil trials, but less than evidence beyond a reasonable doubt, the norm for criminal trials.—Also termed *clear and convincing proof*.

communicative evidence. See *testimonial evidence.*

competent evidence. **1.** See *admissible evidence.* **2.** See *relevant evidence.*

conclusive evidence. **1.** Evidence so strong as to overbear any other evidence to the contrary.—Also termed *conclusive proof.* **2.** Evidence that, though not irrebuttable, so preponderates as to oblige a fact-finder to come to a certain conclusion.

concomitant evidence. Evidence that, at the time of the act, the alleged doer of the act was present and actually did it.

conflicting evidence. Irreconcilable evidence that comes from different sources.

corroborating evidence. Evidence that differs from but strengthens or confirms other evidence (esp. that which needs support).—Also termed *corroborative evidence.* Cf. *cumulative evidence.*

credible evidence. Evidence that is worthy of belief; trustworthy evidence.

critical evidence. Evidence strong enough that its presence could tilt a juror's mind. ● Under the Due Process Clause, an indigent criminal defendant is usu. entitled to an expert opinion of the merits of critical evidence.

cumulative evidence. Additional evidence of the same character as existing evidence and that supports a fact established by the existing evidence (esp. that which does not need further support). Cf. *corroborating evidence.*

demeanor evidence. The behavior of a witness on the witness stand, to be considered by the fact-finder on the issue of credibility.

demonstrative evidence (di-**mon**-strə-tiv). Physical evidence that one can see and inspect (such as a model or photograph) and that, while of probative value and usu. offered to clarify testimony, does not play a direct part in the incident in question.—Also termed *illustrative evidence; real evidence; tangible evidence; autoptic evidence.* See *nonverbal testimony* under TESTIMONY. Cf. *testimonial evidence.*

derivative evidence. Evidence that is discovered as a result of illegally obtained evidence and is therefore inadmissible because of the primary taint. See EXCLUSIONARY RULE; FRUIT-OF-THE-POISONOUS-TREE DOCTRINE.

direct evidence. **1.** Evidence that is based on personal knowledge or observation and that, if true, proves a fact without inference or presumption.—Also termed *positive evidence*. Cf. *circumstantial evidence* (1); *negative evidence*. **2.** See *original evidence* (1).

documentary evidence. Evidence supplied by a writing or other document, which must be authenticated before the evidence is admissible.

evidence-in-chief. Evidence used by a party in making its case-in-chief.

exclusive evidence. The only facts that have any probative force at all on a particular matter in issue.

exculpatory evidence (ik-**skəl**-pə-tor-ee). Evidence tending to establish a criminal defendant's innocence. ● The prosecution has a duty to disclose exculpatory evidence in its possession or control when the evidence may be material to the outcome of the case. See BRADY MATERIAL.

expert evidence. Evidence about a scientific, technical, or professional issue given by a person qualified to testify because of familiarity with the subject or special training in the field.—Also termed *expert testimony*. Fed. R. Evid. 702–705. See DAUBERT TEST.

extrajudicial evidence. Evidence that does not come directly under judicial cognizance but nevertheless constitutes an intermediate link between judicial evidence and the fact requiring proof. ● It includes all facts that are known to the tribunal only by way of inference from some form of judicial evidence.

extrinsic evidence. Evidence that is not legitimately before the court. Cf. *intrinsic evidence*.

fabricated evidence. False or deceitful evidence that is unlawfully created, usu. after the relevant event, in an attempt to avoid liability or conviction.—Also termed *fabricated fact*.

false evidence. See *false testimony* under TESTIMONY.

forensic evidence. Evidence used in court; esp., evidence arrived at by scientific means, such as ballistic or medical evidence.

foundational evidence. Evidence that determines the admissibility of other evidence.

habit evidence. Evidence of one's regular response to a repeated specific situation. Fed. R. Evid. 406.

hearsay evidence. See HEARSAY.

illegally obtained evidence. Evidence obtained by violating a statute or a person's constitutional right, esp. the Fourth Amendment guarantee against unreasonable searches, the Fifth Amendment right to remain silent, or the Sixth Amendment right to counsel.

illustrative evidence. See *demonstrative evidence.*

immaterial evidence. **1.** Evidence lacking in probative value. **2.** Evidence offered to prove a matter that is not in issue.

impeachment evidence. Evidence used to undermine a witness's credibility. Fed. R. Evid. 607–610.

incompetent evidence. Evidence that is for any reason inadmissible.

incriminating evidence. Evidence tending to establish guilt or from which a fact-trier can infer guilt.

inculpatory evidence (in-**kəl**-pə-tor-ee). Evidence showing or tending to show one's involvement in a crime.

indirect evidence. See *circumstantial evidence* (1).

indispensable evidence. Evidence without which a particular fact cannot be proved.

insufficient evidence. Evidence that is inadequate to prove something, so that no presumption—even a conditional one—is raised.

intrinsic evidence. **1.** Evidence brought out by the examination of the witness testifying. **2.** Evidence existing within a writing. Cf. *extrinsic evidence.*

judicial evidence. Evidence produced in court, consisting of all facts brought to the attention of or admitted into evidence before the tribunal.

legal evidence. All admissible evidence, both oral and documentary, of such a character that it reasonably and substantially proves the point rather than merely raising suspicion or conjecture.

material evidence. Evidence having some logical connection with the consequential facts or the issues. Cf. *relevant evidence.*

mathematical evidence. Loosely, evidence that establishes its conclusions with absolute certainty.

mediate evidence. See *secondary evidence.*

medical evidence. Evidence furnished by a doctor, nurse, or other qualified medical person testifying in a professional capacity as an expert, or by a standard treatise on medicine or surgery.

moral evidence. Loosely, evidence that depends on a belief, rather than complete and absolute proof. • Generally, moral evidence is testimonial.

multiple evidence. Evidence with probative value on more than one issue but usu. admitted into evidence for one specific purpose.

negative evidence. Evidence suggesting that an alleged fact does not exist, such as a witness's testifying that he or she did not see an event occur. • Negative evidence is generally regarded to be weaker than positive evidence, because a positive assertion that a witness saw an event is a stronger statement than an assertion that a witness did not see it. But a negative assertion will sometimes be considered positive evidence, depending on the witness's opportunity to see the event. For instance, testimony that the witness watched the entire game and saw no riot in the stands is stronger than testimony stating only that the witness did not see a riot.—Also termed *negative testimony*. Cf. *direct evidence* (1).

newly discovered evidence. Evidence existing at the time of a motion or trial but then unknown to a party, who, upon later discovering it, may assert it as grounds for reconsideration or a new trial.

no evidence. See NO EVIDENCE.

oblique evidence. See *circumstantial evidence* (1).

opinion evidence. A witness's belief, thought, or inference about a disputed fact. Fed. R. Evid. 701–705. See OPINION; OPINION RULE.

original evidence. **1.** A witness's statement that he or she perceived a fact in issue by one of the five senses, or that the witness was in a particular physical or mental state.—Also termed *direct evidence.* Cf. HEARSAY. **2.** See *best evidence.*

parol evidence (pə-**rohl** *or* **par**-əl). **1.** Evidence given orally. **2.** See *extrinsic evidence* (1).

partial evidence. Evidence that establishes one of a series of facts.

personal evidence. See TESTIMONY.

positive evidence. See *direct evidence* (1).

preappointed evidence. Evidence prescribed in advance (as by statute) for the proof of certain facts.

preliminary evidence. Evidence that is necessary to begin a hearing or trial and that may be received conditionally in anticipation of other evidence linking it to issues in the case. Fed. R. Evid. 104.

presumptive evidence. **1.** Evidence deemed true and sufficient unless discredited by other evidence. **2.** *Archaic.* Circumstantial evidence as distinct from testimonial evidence.—Also termed *probable evidence.*

prima facie evidence (**prı**-mə **fay**-shə). Evidence that will establish a fact or sustain a judgment unless contradictory evidence is produced.

primary evidence. See *best evidence.*

privileged evidence. Evidence that is exempt from production to an opposing party (with certain, limited exceptions) because it is covered by one or more statutory and common-law protections, such as the attorney-client privilege. See *privileged communication* under COMMUNICATION.

probable evidence. See *presumptive evidence.*

probative evidence (**proh**-bə-tiv). Evidence that tends to prove or disprove a point in issue.

proffered evidence (**prof**-ərd). **1.** Evidence that is offered to the court to obtain a ruling on its admissibility. **2.** Evidence whose admissibility depends on the existence or non-existence of a preliminary fact.

proper evidence. See *admissible evidence.*

prospectant evidence (prə-**spek**-tənt). Evidence that, before someone does an act, suggests that the person might or might not do the act. • This evidence typically falls into any of five categories: (1) moral character or disposition, (2) physical and mental capacity, (3) habit or custom, (4) emotion or motive, and (5) plan, design, or intention.

real evidence. **1.** Physical evidence (such as a knife wound) that itself plays a direct part in the incident in question. **2.** See *demonstrative evidence.*

rebuttal evidence. Evidence offered to disprove or contradict the evidence presented by an opposing party.

relevant evidence. Evidence tending to prove or disprove a matter in issue. • Relevant evidence is both probative and material and is admissible unless excluded by a specific statute or rule. Fed. R. Evid. 401–403.—Also termed *competent evidence.* Cf. *material evidence.*

reputation evidence. Evidence of what one is thought by others to be. • Reputation evidence may be introduced as proof of character when character is in issue or is used circumstantially. Fed. R. Evid. 405(a).—Also termed *reputational evidence*.

retrospectant evidence (re-tra-**spek**-tənt). Evidence that, although it occurs after an act has been done, suggests that the alleged doer of the act actually did it <when goods have been stolen, and the thief is sought, a person's later possession of those goods amounts to retrospectant evidence that this person took them>.—Also termed *traces*.

satisfactory evidence. Evidence that is sufficient to satisfy an unprejudiced mind seeking the truth.—Also termed *sufficient evidence*; *satisfactory proof*.

scientific evidence. Testimony or opinion evidence that draws on technical or specialized knowledge and relies on scientific method for its evidentiary value. See DAUBERT TEST.

secondary evidence. Evidence that is inferior to the primary or best evidence and that becomes admissible when the primary or best evidence is lost or inaccessible. ● Examples include a copy of a lost instrument and testimony about its contents.—Also termed *mediate evidence*; *mediate testimony*; *substitutionary evidence*. Cf. *best evidence*.

secondhand evidence. See HEARSAY.

245

signature evidence. Highly distinctive evidence of a person's prior bad acts. ● While ordinarily inadmissible, signature evidence will be admitted if it shows, for example, that two crimes were committed through the same planning, design, scheme, or modus operandi, and in such a way that the prior act and the current act are uniquely identifiable as those of the defendant.

slight evidence. An inconsiderable or trifling quantity of evidence; esp., the small amount sufficient for a rational fact-finder to conclude that the state failed to disprove an affirmative defense beyond a reasonable doubt. See SLIGHT-EVIDENCE RULE.

state's evidence. Testimony provided by one criminal defendant—under a promise of immunity or reduced sentence—against another criminal defendant. See TURN STATE'S EVIDENCE.

substantial evidence. Evidence that a reasonable mind would accept as adequate to support a conclusion; evidence beyond a scintilla.

substantive evidence (**səb**-stən-tiv). Evidence offered to support a fact in issue, as opposed to impeachment or corroborating evidence.

substitutionary evidence. See *secondary evidence.*

sufficient evidence. See *satisfactory evidence.*

tainted evidence. Evidence that is inadmissible because it was directly or indirectly obtained by illegal means. See FRUIT-OF-THE-POISONOUS-TREE DOCTRINE.

tangible evidence. See *demonstrative evidence.*

testimonial evidence. A person's testimony offered to prove the truth of the matter asserted; esp., evidence elicited from a witness.—Also termed *communicative evidence.* Cf. *demonstrative evidence.*

traditionary evidence. Evidence derived from a deceased person's former statements or reputation. ● Traditionary evidence is admissible to prove ancestry, ancient boundaries, or similar facts, usu. when no living witnesses are available to testify.

unwritten evidence. Evidence given orally, in court or by deposition.

evidence-in-chief. See EVIDENCE.

evidential, *adj.* Of, relating to, relying on, or constituting evidence; EVIDENTIARY (1).

evidential fact. See *evidentiary fact* (2) under FACT.

evidentiary (ev-i-**den**-shə-ree), *adj.* **1.** Having the quality of evidence; constituting evidence; evidencing. **2.** Pertaining to the rules of evidence or the evidence in a particular case.

evidentiary fact. See FACT.

evidentiary hearing. See HEARING.

examination in chief. See DIRECT EXAMINATION.

examiner. See MEDICAL EXAMINER.

examining court. A lower court (usu. presided over by a magistrate) that determines probable cause and sets bail at a preliminary hearing in a criminal case. See PRELIMINARY HEARING.

examining trial. See PRELIMINARY HEARING.

excessive bail. See BAIL.

excessive drunkenness. See DRUNKENNESS.

excessive fine. See FINE.

excessive force. See FORCE.

248

excessive punishment. See PUNISHMENT.

excessive sentence. See SENTENCE.

excited utterance. A statement about a startling event made under the stress and excitement of the event. ● An excited utterance may be admissible as a hearsay exception. Fed. R. Evid. 803(2). Cf. PRESENT SENSE IMPRESSION.

exclusionary hearing. See HEARING.

exclusionary rule. 1. Any rule that excludes or suppresses evidence that does not satisfy a minimum standard of probative value <despite many exceptions, hearsay has long been inadmissible under an exclusionary rule>. **2.** A rule that excludes or suppresses evidence obtained in violation of an accused person's constitutional rights <in accordance with the exclusionary rule, the court did not admit the drugs into evidence because they had been obtained during a warrantless search of the defendant's home>. See FRUIT-OF-THE-POISONOUS-TREE DOCTRINE; GOOD-FAITH EXCEPTION.

exclusive evidence. See EVIDENCE.

exculpate (**ek**-skəl-payt *or* ek-**skəl**-payt), *vb*. To free from blame or accusation.—**exculpation** (ek-skəl-**pay**-shən), *n*.—**exculpatory** (ek-**skəl**-pə-tor-ee), *adj*. Cf. EXONERATE (1).

exculpatory evidence. See EVIDENCE.

exculpatory-no doctrine. The principle that a person cannot be charged with making a false statement for falsely denying guilt in response to an investigator's question. ● This doctrine is based on the Fifth Amendment right against self-incrimination.

excusable, *adj.* (Of an illegal act or omission) not punishable under the specific circumstances <excusable neglect>.

excusable assault. See ASSAULT.

excusable homicide. See HOMICIDE.

excuse (eks-**kyoos**), *n.* **1.** A reason that justifies an act or omission or that relieves a person of a duty. **2.** A defense that arises because the defendant is not blameworthy for having acted in a way that would otherwise be criminal. ● The following defenses are the traditional excuses: duress, entrapment, infancy, insanity, and involuntary intoxication.—Also termed *legal excuse.* Cf. JUSTIFICATION (2).—**excuse** (ek-**skyooz**), *vb.*—**excusatory** (ek-**skyooz**-ə-tor-ee), *adj.*

execute, *vb.* To put to death, esp. by legal sentence <Johnson was executed shortly after midnight>.

execution, *n.* **1.** The act of carrying out or putting into effect (as a court order) <execution of the court's decree>.

> ***body execution.*** A court order requiring an officer to take a named person into custody, usu. to bring the person before the court to pay a debt; CAPIAS.

> ***close-jail execution.*** A body execution stating that the person to be arrested should be confined in jail without the privilege of movement about the jail yard.

2. The carrying out of a death sentence <the Supreme Court stayed the execution>.—**execute,** *vb.*

executioner. A person who puts another person to death to carry out a death sentence; a person who carries out capital punishment on the state's behalf.

executive clemency. See CLEMENCY.

executive pardon. See PARDON.

executive privilege. See PRIVILEGE (3).

exemplar (eg-**zem**-plər *or* -plahr), *n.* **1.** An ideal or typical example; a standard specimen <handwriting exemplars>. **2.** Nontestimonial identification evidence, such as fingerprints, voiceprints, and DNA samples. See VOICE EX-EMPLAR.

exigency (**ek**-sə-jən-see), *n*. A state of urgency; a situation requiring immediate action.—**exigent,** *adj*.

exigent circumstances. See CIRCUMSTANCE.

exigent search. See SEARCH.

exonerate (eg-**zon**-ə-rayt), *vb*. To free from responsibility <exonerate from the payment of the fine>.—**exonerative** (eg-**zon**-ər-ay-tiv *or* -ə-tiv), *adj*. Cf. EXCULPATE.

ex parte hearing. See *ex parte proceeding* under PROCEEDING.

ex parte order. See ORDER.

ex parte proceeding. See PROCEEDING.

expectation of privacy. A belief in the existence of the right to be free of governmental intrusion in regard to a particular place or thing. ● To suppress a search on privacy grounds, a defendant must show the existence of the expectation and that the expectation was reasonable.

expert, *n.* A person who, through education or experience, has developed skill or knowledge in a particular subject, so that he or she may form an opinion that will assist the factfinder. Fed. R. Evid. 702.—**expertise** (ek-spər-**teez**), *n.* See DAUBERT TEST.

expert evidence. See EVIDENCE.

expert testimony. See *expert evidence* under EVIDENCE.

expert witness. See WITNESS.

express amnesty. See AMNESTY.

expressive crime. See CRIME.

express malice. See MALICE.

expungement of record. The removal of a conviction (esp. for a first offense) from a person's criminal record.—Also termed *expunction of record*; *erasure of record*.

extenuating circumstance. See *mitigating circumstance* under CIRCUMSTANCE.

extenuation (ek-sten-yoo-**ay**-shən), *n.* The act or fact of making the commission of a crime less severe.

extort, *vb.* **1.** To compel or coerce (a confession, etc.) by means that overcome one's power to resist. **2.** To gain by wrongful methods; to obtain in an unlawful manner; to exact wrongfully by threat or intimidation.—**extortive,** *adj.*

extortion, *n.* **1.** The offense committed by a public official who illegally obtains property under the color of office; esp., an official's collection of an unlawful fee.—Also termed *common-law extortion.* **2.** The act or practice of obtaining something or compelling some action by illegal means, as by force or coercion.—Also termed *statutory extortion.*—**extortionate,** *adj.*

extortionate credit transaction. See LOAN-SHARKING.

extradite (**ek**-strə-dıt), *vb.* **1.** To surrender or deliver (a fugitive) to another jurisdiction. **2.** To obtain the surrender of (a fugitive) from another jurisdiction.

extradition (ek-strə-**dish**-ən). The official surrender of an alleged criminal by one state or nation to another having jurisdiction over the crime charged; the return of a fugitive from justice, regardless of consent, by the authorities where the fugitive resides. Cf. RENDITION (2).

international extradition. Extradition in response to a demand made by the executive of one nation on the executive of another nation. • This procedure is regulated by treaties.

interstate extradition. Extradition in response to a demand made by the governor of one state on the governor of another state. • This procedure is provided for by the U.S. Constitution, by federal statute, and by state statutes.

Extradition Clause. The clause of the U.S. Constitution providing that any accused person who flees to another state must, on request of the executive authority of the state where the crime was committed, be returned to that state. U.S. Const. art. IV, § 2, cl. 2.

extradition treaty. A treaty governing the preconditions for, and exceptions to, the surrender of a fugitive from justice by the fugitive's country of residence to another country claiming criminal jurisdiction over the fugitive.

extradition warrant. See WARRANT.

extrajudicial admission. See ADMISSION.

extrajudicial confession. See CONFESSION.

extrajudicial evidence. See EVIDENCE.

extrajudicial oath. See OATH.

extraneous offense. See OFFENSE.

extraordinary circumstances. See CIRCUM-STANCE.

extraordinary grand jury. See *special grand jury* under GRAND JURY.

extraordinary writ. See WRIT.

extreme force. See *deadly force* under FORCE.

extrinsic evidence. See EVIDENCE.

eye for an eye. See LEX TALIONIS.

eyewitness. One who personally observes an event. Cf. EARWITNESS.

eyewitness identification. A naming or description by which one who has seen an event testifies from memory about the person or persons involved.

F

fabricate, *vb.* To invent, forge, or devise false-ly. ● To fabricate a story is to create a plausible version of events that is advantageous to the person relating those events. The term is softer than *lie.* See LIE.

fabricated evidence. See EVIDENCE.

fabricated fact. See *fabricated evidence* under EVIDENCE.

FAC. *abbr.* Failure to answer a (traffic) citation. ● In some jurisdictions, if someone fails to respond after receiving a ticket, the court notifies the relevant administrative agency, which records this information and suspends the defendant's driver's license until the FAC is vacated and any fines or fees are paid.

facially sufficient, *adj.* (Of a document) appearing valid on its face. ● A search-warrant affidavit's facial sufficiency will not protect it from attack if the affidavit is based on false testimony by the officer making the affidavit. See FRANKS HEARING.

facilitate, *vb.* To make the commission of a crime easier. ● Property (such as a vehicle or home) that facilitates the commission of certain offenses may be forfeited.—**facilitator,** *n.*

facilitation, *n.* The act or an instance of aiding or helping; esp., in criminal law, the act of making it easier for another person to commit a crime.

fact. 1. Something that actually exists; an aspect of reality <it is a fact that all people are mortal>. **2.** An actual or alleged event or circumstance, as distinguished from its legal effect, consequence, or interpretation <the jury made a finding of fact>. **3.** An evil deed; a crime <an accessory after the fact>.

adjudicative fact (ə-**joo**-di-kay-tiv *or* -kə-tiv). A controlling or operative fact, rather than a background fact; a fact that concerns the parties to a judicial or administrative proceeding and that helps the court or agency determine how the law applies to those parties. ● For example, adjudicative facts include those that the jury weighs.

collateral fact. A fact not directly connected to the issue in dispute, esp. because it involves a different transaction from the one at issue.

dispositive fact (dis-**poz**-ə-tiv). A fact that is decisive of a legal matter; evidence that definitively resolves a legal issue or controversy.

elemental fact. See *ultimate fact.*

evidentiary fact (ev-i-**den**-shə-ree). **1.** A fact that is necessary for or leads to the determination of an ultimate fact.—Also termed *predicate fact*. **2.** A fact that furnishes evidence of the existence of some other fact.—Also termed *evidential fact*. **3.** See *fact in evidence*.

fabricated fact. See *fabricated evidence* under EVIDENCE.

fact in evidence. A fact that a tribunal considers in reaching a conclusion; a fact that has been admitted into evidence in a trial or hearing.—Also written *fact-in-evidence*.—Also termed *evidentiary fact*. See EVIDENCE (2).

fact in issue. (*usu. pl.*) A fact to be determined by a fact-trier.—Also written *fact-in-issue*.—Also termed *principal fact*.

foundational fact. See *predicate fact*.

immaterial fact. A fact that is not essential to a matter in issue.

inferential fact. A fact established by conclusions drawn from other evidence rather than from direct testimony or evidence; a fact derived logically from other facts.

judicial fact. A fact that the court accepts as proved without hearing evidence.

jurisdictional fact. (*usu. pl.*) A fact that must exist for a court to properly exercise its jurisdiction over a case, party, or thing.

legal fact. A fact that triggers a particular legal consequence.

material fact. A fact that is significant or essential to the issue or matter at hand.

physical fact. A fact having a physical existence, such as a fingerprint left at a crime scene.

predicate fact (**pred**-ə-kit). A fact from which a presumption or inference arises.— Also termed *foundational fact*; *evidentiary fact*.

primary fact. A fact that can be established by direct testimony and from which inferences are made leading to ultimate facts. See *ultimate fact*.

principal fact. **1.** See *fact in issue*. **2.** See *ultimate fact*.

probative fact (**proh**-bə-tiv). A fact in evidence used to prove an ultimate fact, such as skid marks used to show speed as a predicate to a finding of negligence.

ultimate fact. A fact essential to the claim or the defense.—Also termed *elemental fact*; *principal fact*.

undisputed fact. An uncontested or admitted fact, esp. one that a court has not deemed necessary to include in a finding of fact.

fact-finder. One or more persons—such as jurors in a trial or administrative-law judges in a hearing—who hear testimony and review evidence to rule on a factual issue.—Also termed *finder of fact*; *fact-trier* or *trier of fact* (in a judicial proceeding); *fact-finding board* (for a group or committee). See FINDING OF FACT.

fact in evidence. See FACT.

fact in issue. See FACT.

fact question. See QUESTION OF FACT (3).

fact-trier. See FACT-FINDER.

factual cause. See *but-for cause* under CAUSE (1).

factual impossibility. See IMPOSSIBILITY.

factual presumption. See *presumption of fact* under PRESUMPTION.

failure of justice. See MISCARRIAGE OF JUSTICE.

failure-of-proof defense. The defense that a party's proof does not establish a fact essential to a claim or defense.

fair and impartial jury. See *impartial jury* under JURY.

fair and impartial trial. See FAIR TRIAL.

fair-cross-section requirement. The principle that a person's right to an impartial jury, guaranteed by the Sixth Amendment, includes a requirement that the pool of potential jurors fairly represent the composition of the jurisdiction's population. • The pool of potential jurors need not precisely match the composition of the jurisdiction. But the representation of each group must be fair—no group should be systematically excluded or underrepresented. A minimal disparity in a particular group's representation, such as an absolute disparity of 10%, will not ordinarily violate this principle unless some aggravating factor exists. See DUREN TEST; ABSOLUTE DISPARITY; COMPARATIVE DISPARITY; STATISTICAL-DECISION THEORY.

fair hearing. See HEARING.

fair notice. See FAIR WARNING.

fair trial. A trial by an impartial and disinterested tribunal in accordance with regular procedures; esp., a criminal trial in which the defendant's constitutional and legal rights are respected.—Also termed *fair and impartial trial*.

fair warning. The requirement that a criminal statute define an offense with enough precision so that a reasonable person can know what conduct is prohibited and so that a reasonably skilled lawyer can predict what conduct falls within the statute's scope.—Also termed *fair notice*.

faith and trust. See FLIM FLAM.

fake, *n.* Something that is not what it purports to be. See FORGERY (2); IMPOSTOR.

fake, *vb.* To make or construct falsely. See COUNTERFEIT.

Falconer **error.** A trial court's failure to instruct the jury that a guilty finding on a manslaughter charge requires acquittal on a murder charge. *Falconer v. Lane*, 905 F.2d 1129 (7th Cir. 1990).

false advertising, *n.* The tortious and sometimes criminal act of distributing an advertisement that is untrue, deceptive, or misleading.—Also termed *deceptive advertising*.

false arrest. See ARREST.

False Claims Act. A federal statute establishing civil and criminal penalties against persons who bill the government falsely, deliver less to the government than represented, or use a fake record to decrease an obligation to the government. 18 USCA §§ 286–287; 31 USCA §§ 3729–3733. • The Act may be enforced either by the attorney general or by a private person in a qui tam action.

false evidence. See *false testimony* under TESTIMONY.

false impersonation. See IMPERSONATION.

false imprisonment. A restraint of a person in a bounded area without justification or consent. • False imprisonment is a common-law misdemeanor and a tort. It applies to private as well as governmental detention. Cf. *false arrest* under ARREST.

false making. See FORGERY (1).

false oath. See PERJURY.

false personation. See *false impersonation* under IMPERSONATION.

false pretenses. The crime of knowingly obtaining title to another's personal property by misrepresenting a fact with the intent to defraud. ● Although unknown to English common law, false pretenses became a misdemeanor under a statute old enough to make it common law in the United States. Modern American statutes make it either a felony or a misdemeanor, depending on how valuable the property is.—Also termed *obtaining property by false pretenses*; *fraudulent pretenses*. Cf. *larceny by trick* under LARCENY; EMBEZZLEMENT.

false report. The criminal offense of informing law enforcement about a crime that did not occur.

false statement. See STATEMENT.

false swearing. See PERJURY.

false testimony. See TESTIMONY.

false verdict. See VERDICT.

falsify, *vb.* To make something false; to counterfeit or forge <the chiropractor falsified his records to help the defendant>. See COUNTERFEIT; FORGERY.

falsifying a record. The crime of making false entries or otherwise tampering with a

265

public record with the intent to deceive or injure, or to conceal wrongdoing. 18 USCA §§ 1506, 2071, 2073; Model Penal Code § 224.4.

family disturbance. See DOMESTIC DISPUTE.

fatal error. See *reversible error* under ERROR.

fatal variance. See VARIANCE.

Fatico **hearing** (**fat**-ə–koh). A sentencing hearing at which the prosecution and the defense may present evidence about what the defendant's sentence should be. *United States v. Fatico*, 603 F.2d 1053 (2d Cir. 1979).

faux **money.** Counterfeit money. See COUNTERFEITING.

FBI. *abbr*. FEDERAL BUREAU OF INVESTIGATION.

FCJ. *abbr*. A failure to comply with a judgment imposed for a traffic violation. • The defendant's driver's license is suspended until the FCJ is remedied and the fines and fees are paid.

FCPV. *abbr*. A failure to comply with parking-violation tickets. • If a person has a certain number of unpaid parking tickets (often six)

within a jurisdiction, the person will be barred
from obtaining or renewing a driver's license.

Federal Bureau of Investigation. A division of the U.S. Department of Justice charged
with investigating all violations of federal laws
except those specifically assigned to another
federal agency.—Abbr. FBI.

federal crime. A criminal offense under a
federal statute. • Most federal crimes are codified in Title 18 of the U.S. Code.

federal jurisdiction. See JURISDICTION.

Federal Kidnapping Act. A federal law punishing kidnapping for ransom or reward when
the victim is transported interstate or internationally. • The law presumes that a victim has
been transported in violation of the law if the
victim is not released within 24 hours. 18
USCA § 1201.—Also termed *Lindbergh Act*.

federal magistrate. See UNITED STATES MAGISTRATE JUDGE.

federal question. A legal issue involving the
interpretation and application of the U.S. Constitution, an act of Congress, or a treaty. •
Jurisdiction over federal questions rests with
the federal courts. 28 USCA § 1331.

federal-question jurisdiction. See JURISDIC-TION.

Federal Rules of Criminal Procedure. The rules governing criminal proceedings in the U.S. district courts.—Abbr. Fed. R. Crim. P.

Federal Rules of Evidence. The rules governing the admissibility of evidence at trials in federal courts.—Abbr. Fed. R. Evid.; FRE.

Fed. R. Crim. P. *abbr*. FEDERAL RULES OF CRIMINAL PROCEDURE.

Fed. R. Evid. *abbr*. FEDERAL RULES OF EVIDENCE.

feigned accomplice. See INFORMANT.

fellow-officer rule. The principle that an investigative stop or an arrest is valid if the law-enforcement officer lacks personal knowledge to establish reasonable suspicion or probable cause but acts on the knowledge of another officer and the collective knowledge of the law-enforcement office.—Also termed *Whiteley rule*.

felon, *n*. A person who has been convicted of a felony.

felonious (fə-**loh**-nee-əs), *adj*. **1.** Of, relating to, or involving a felony. **2.** Constituting or having the character of a felony. **3.** Proceeding from an evil heart or purpose; malicious; villainous. **4.** Wrongful; (of an act) done without excuse or color of right.

felonious assault. See ASSAULT.

felonious homicide. See HOMICIDE.

felonious intent. See *criminal intent* under INTENT.

felonious restraint. 1. The offense of knowingly and unlawfully restraining a person under circumstances that expose the person to serious bodily harm. Model Penal Code § 212.2(a). **2.** The offense of holding a person in involuntary servitude. Model Penal Code § 212.2(b).

felony, *n.* A serious crime usu. punishable by imprisonment for more than one year or by death. ● Examples include murder, rape, arson, and burglary. At common law, a felony was an offense for which conviction involved the forfeiture of the defendant's lands or goods, or both, to the Crown. Treason was traditionally included in the term *felony.*—Also termed *major crime*; *serious crime*. Cf. MISDE-MEANOR.

atrocious felony. A serious, usu. cruel felony involving personal violence. ● This term is now used less frequently than the specific type of crime alleged (e.g., first-degree murder or aggravated sexual assault).

serious felony. A major felony, such as burglary of a residence or an assault that causes great bodily injury. ● In many jurisdictions, a defendant's prior serious-felony convictions can be used to enhance another criminal charge.

violent felony. See *violent offense* under OFFENSE.

felony de se. See SUICIDE.

felony murder. See MURDER.

felony-murder rule. The doctrine holding that any death resulting from the commission or attempted commission of a felony is murder. ● Most states restrict this rule to inherently dangerous felonies such as rape, arson, robbery, and burglary. Cf. MISDEMEANOR-MANSLAUGHTER RULE.

femicide (**fem**-ə-sɪd). **1.** The killing of a woman. **2.** One who kills a woman.

fence, *n.* **1.** A person who receives stolen goods. **2.** A place where stolen goods are sold. See RECEIVING STOLEN PROPERTY.

fence, *vb.* To sell stolen property to a fence.

feticide (**fee**-tə-sɪd). The act or an instance of killing a fetus, usu. by assaulting and battering the mother; an intentionally induced miscarriage.—Also termed *child destruction*. Cf. INFANTICIDE (1).

field sobriety test. See SOBRIETY TEST.

field stop. See STOP AND FRISK.

Fifth Amendment. The constitutional amendment, ratified with the Bill of Rights in 1791, providing that a person cannot be (1) required to answer for a capital or otherwise infamous offense unless a grand jury issues an indictment or presentment, (2) subjected to double jeopardy, (3) compelled to engage in self-incrimination on a criminal matter, (4) deprived of life, liberty, or property without due process of law, and (5) deprived of private property for public use without just compensation.

Fifth Amendment, pleading the. See PLEADING THE FIFTH.

final argument. See CLOSING ARGUMENT.

final order. See ORDER.

finder of fact. See FACT-FINDER.

fine, *n.* A pecuniary criminal punishment or civil penalty payable to the public treasury.— **fine,** *vb.*

>   *day fine.* A fine payable over time, usu. as a percentage of the defendant's earnings on a weekly or monthly basis.

>   *excessive fine.* A fine that is unreasonably high and disproportionate to the offense committed. • The Eighth Amendment proscribes excessive fines. An example of an excessive fine is a civil forfeiture in which the property was not an instrumentality of the crime and the worth of the property was not proportional to the owner's culpability.

finger, *vb. Slang.* To identify (a person) as a perpetrator, usu. of a crime <in his grand-jury testimony, Vinson fingered Bauer as the gunman>.

fingerprint, *n.* **1.** The distinctive pattern of lines on a human fingertip <no two fingerprints are identical>. **2.** The impression of a fingertip made on any surface <the detective found several fingerprints on the knife>. **3.** An ink impression of the pattern of lines on a fingertip, usu. taken during the booking procedure after an arrest <after Dick had his fingerprints taken, he was put in the drunk

tank>.—Also termed *print*; *thumbprint*.—**fin-gerprint,** *vb.*—**fingerprinting,** *n.* Cf. DNA IDENTIFICATION.

firearm. A weapon that expels a projectile (such as a bullet or pellets) by the combustion of gunpowder or other explosive.

firebug. See INCENDIARY (1).

firing squad. 1. A group of persons assembled to carry out a capital-punishment sentence by shooting the prisoner with high-powered rifles at the same time from a short distance. **2.** A military detachment that fires a salute, usu. at the burial of the person honored.

first-degree murder. See MURDER.

first-degree principal. See *principal in the first degree* under PRINCIPAL.

first-degree sexual conduct. Sexual battery that involves an aggravating factor, as when the perpetrator commits an offense against a minor or when the perpetrator commits an offense in the course of committing another crime, such as a burglary.—Also termed *criminal sexual conduct in the first degree*.

first offender. See OFFENDER.

fitness hearing. See *transfer hearing* under
HEARING.

fix, *n.* A dose of an illegal drug <the defendant testified that he robbed the store because
he needed to buy a fix>.

fix bail, *vb.* To set the amount and terms of
bail <after hearing the officer's testimony, the
judge fixed bail for the defendant at
$100,000>. See BAIL.

fixed sentence. See SENTENCE.

fixing a jury. See JURY-FIXING.

flat sentence. See *determinate sentence* under
SENTENCE.

flat time. See TIME.

flee from justice. See FLIGHT.

flight. The act or an instance of fleeing, esp.
to evade arrest or prosecution <the judge denied bail because the defendant is a flight
risk>.—Also termed *flight from prosecution*;
flee from justice.

flight from prosecution. See FLIGHT.

flim flam. A scheme by which another is tricked for money; CONFIDENCE GAME.—Also termed *faith and trust*.

flip, *vb. Slang.* To turn state's evidence. See TURN STATE'S EVIDENCE.

forbidden departure. See DEPARTURE.

force, *n.* Power, violence, or pressure directed against a person or thing.

> *actual force.* Force consisting in a physical act, esp. a violent act directed against a robbery victim.—Also termed *physical force*.

> *constructive force.* Threats and intimidation to gain control or prevent resistance; esp., threatening words or gestures directed against a robbery victim.

> *deadly force.* Violent action known to create a substantial risk of causing death or serious bodily harm. ● A person may use deadly force in self-defense only if retaliating against another's deadly force.—Also termed *extreme force*. Cf. *nondeadly force*.

> *excessive force.* Unreasonable or unnecessary force under the circumstances.

> *extreme force.* See *deadly force*.

> *legal force.* See *reasonable force*.

***nondeadly force.* 1.** Force that is neither intended nor likely to cause death or serious bodily harm; force intended to cause only minor bodily harm. **2.** A threat of deadly force, such as displaying a knife.—Also termed *moderate force.* Cf. *deadly force.*

physical force. See *actual force.*

reasonable force. Force that is not excessive and that is appropriate for protecting oneself or one's property. ● The use of reasonable force will not render a person criminally or tortiously liable.—Also termed *legal force.*

unlawful force. Force that is directed against a person without that person's consent, and that is an offense or actionable tort. Model Penal Code § 3.11.

force, *vb.* To compel by physical means or by legal requirement <Barnes used a gun to force Jillian to use her ATM card>.

forcible detainer. 1. The wrongful retention of possession of property by one originally in lawful possession, often with threats or actual use of violence. **2.** See FORCIBLE ENTRY AND DETAINER.

forcible entry. At common law, the act or an instance of violently and unlawfully taking possession of lands and tenements against the will of those entitled to possession.

forcible entry and detainer. 1. The act of violently taking and keeping possession of lands and tenements without legal authority. **2.** A quick and simple legal proceeding for regaining possession of real property from someone who has wrongfully taken, or refused to surrender, possession.—Also termed *forcible detainer*.

foreman. See *presiding juror* under JUROR.

forensic evidence. See EVIDENCE.

forensic medicine. The branch of medicine that establishes or interprets evidence using scientific or technical facts, such as ballistics.—Also termed *medical jurisprudence*.

forensic pathology. The specific branch of medicine that establishes or interprets evidence dealing with diseases and disorders of the body, esp. those that cause death.

forensics (fə-**ren**-siks *also* -ziks). The branch of law enforcement dealing with legal evidence relating to firearms and ballistics.

foreperson. See *presiding juror* under JUROR.

forfeiture (**for**-fi-chər), *n.* **1.** The loss of a right, a privilege, or property because of a crime, breach of obligation, or neglect of duty. ● Title is simultaneously transferred to another, such as the government, a corporation, or a private person. **2.** Something (esp. money or property) lost or confiscated by this process; a penalty.—**forfeit,** *vb.*—**forfeitable,** *adj.*

> *civil forfeiture.* An in rem proceeding brought by the government against property that either facilitated a crime or was acquired as a result of criminal activity.

> *criminal forfeiture.* A governmental proceeding brought against a person as punishment for the person's criminal behavior.

forgery, *n.* **1.** The act of fraudulently making a false document or altering a real one to be used as if genuine <the contract was void because of the seller's forgery>.—Also termed *false making.* ● Though forgery was a misdemeanor at common law, modern statutes typically make it a felony. **2.** A false or altered document made to look genuine by someone with the intent to deceive <he was not the true property owner because the deed of trust was a forgery>.—Also termed *fake.* **3.** Under the Model Penal Code, the act of fraudulently altering, authenticating, issuing, or transferring a writing without appropriate authorization. ● Under the explicit terms of the Code, *writing* can include items such as coins and credit cards. Model Penal Code § 224.1(1).— **forge,** *vb.*—**forger,** *n.*

double forgery. A draft having a forged payor signature and a forged indorsement.

formed design. See DESIGN.

former jeopardy. The fact of having previously been prosecuted for the same offense. • A defendant enters a plea of former jeopardy to inform the court that he or she should not be prosecuted again. Cf. DOUBLE JEOPARDY.

former punishment. In military law, the rule that nonjudicial punishment for a minor offense may bar trial by court-martial for the same offense.

formula instruction. See JURY INSTRUCTION.

fornication, *n.* Voluntary sexual intercourse between two unmarried persons. • Fornication is a crime in some states, such as Virginia.— **fornicate,** *vb.* Cf. ADULTERY.

forswearing. See PERJURY.

foundational evidence. See EVIDENCE.

foundational fact. See *predicate fact* under FACT.

Fourth Amendment. The constitutional amendment, ratified with the Bill of Rights in 1791, prohibiting unreasonable searches and seizures and the issuance of warrants without probable cause. See PROBABLE CAUSE.

frame, *vb.* To incriminate (an innocent person) with false evidence, esp. fabricated.— **framable, frameable,** *adj.*

frame-up, *n.* A plot to make an innocent person appear guilty.

***Franks* hearing.** A hearing to determine whether a police officer's affidavit used to obtain a search warrant that yields incriminating evidence was based on false statements by the police officer. *Franks v. Delaware*, 438 U.S. 154, 98 S.Ct. 2674 (1978).

fratricide (**fra**-trə-sɪd *or* **fray**-). **1.** One who has killed one's brother or sister. **2.** The killing of one's brother or sister.

fraud, *n.* **1.** A knowing misrepresentation of the truth or concealment of a material fact to induce another to act to his or her detriment. ● Fraud is usu. a tort, but in some cases (esp. when the conduct is willful) it may be a crime. **2.** A misrepresentation made recklessly without belief in its truth to induce another person to act.

bank fraud. The criminal offense of knowingly executing, or attempting to execute, a scheme or artifice to defraud a financial institution, or to obtain property owned by or under the control of a financial institution, by means of false or fraudulent pretenses, representations, or promises. 18 USCA § 1344.

bankruptcy fraud. A fraudulent act connected to a bankruptcy case; esp., any of several prescribed acts performed knowingly and fraudulently in a bankruptcy case, such as concealing assets or destroying, withholding, or falsifying documents in an effort to defeat bankruptcy-code provisions. See 18 USCA § 152.—Also termed *criminal bankruptcy*; *bankruptcy crime*.

criminal fraud. Fraud that has been made illegal by statute and that subjects the offender to criminal penalties such as fines and imprisonment. • An example is the willful evasion of taxes accomplished by filing a fraudulent tax return. Cf. *larceny by trick* under LARCENY.

fraud on the court. In a judicial proceeding, a lawyer's or party's misconduct so serious that it undermines or is intended to undermine the integrity of the proceeding. • Examples are bribery of a juror and introduction of fabricated evidence.

fraud on the market. **1.** Fraud occurring when an issuer of securities gives out misinformation that affects the market price of stock, the result being that people who buy or sell are effectively misled even though they did not rely on the statement itself or anything derived from it other than the market price. **2.** The securities-law claim based on such fraud.

insurance fraud. Fraud committed against an insurer, as when an insured lies on a policy application or fabricates a claim.

intrinsic fraud. Deception that pertains to an issue involved in an original action. • Examples include the use of fabricated evidence, a false return of service, perjured testimony, and false receipts or other commercial documents.

mail fraud. An act of fraud using the U.S. Postal Service, as in making false representations through the mail to obtain an economic advantage. 18 USCA §§ 1341–1347.

wire fraud. An act of fraud using electronic communications, as by making false representations on the telephone to obtain money. • The federal Wire Fraud Act provides that any artifice to defraud by means of wire or other electronic communications (such as radio or television) in foreign or interstate commerce is a crime. 18 USCA § 1343.

fraudulent concealment. See CONCEALMENT.

fraudulent conversion. See CONVERSION.

fraudulent pretenses. See FALSE PRETENSES.

fray. See AFFRAY.

FRE. *abbr.* FEDERAL RULES OF EVIDENCE.

fresh complaint. A reasonably prompt lodging of a grievance; esp., a victim's prompt report of a sexual assault to someone trustworthy.

fresh-complaint rule. The theory that the credibility of a sexual-assault victim is bolstered if the victim reports the assault soon after it occurs. ● Most courts no longer recognize this theory.

fresh pursuit. 1. The right of a police officer to make a warrantless search of a fleeing suspect or to cross jurisdictional lines to arrest a fleeing suspect. **2.** The right of a person to use reasonable force to retake property that has just been taken.—Also termed *hot pursuit.*

friendly fire. Military or police gunfire that injures one's own side.

frisk, *n.* A pat-down search to discover a concealed weapon.—Also termed *pat-down*. See STOP AND FRISK. Cf. SEARCH.

frivolous defense. See DEFENSE.

front, *n.* A person or group that serves to conceal the true identity or activity of the person or group in control <the political party was a front for the terrorist group>.

fruit. Something (such as evidence) obtained during an activity or operation <the fruit of the officer's search>.

fruit-of-the-poisonous-tree doctrine. The rule that evidence derived from an illegal search, arrest, or interrogation is inadmissible because the evidence (the "fruit") was tainted by the illegality (the "poisonous tree"). ● Under this doctrine, for example, a murder weapon is inadmissible if the map showing its location and used to find it was seized during an illegal search.—Also termed *fruits doctrine*. See EXCLUSIONARY RULE; ATTENUATION DOCTRINE; INDEPENDENT-SOURCE RULE; INEVITABLE-DISCOVERY RULE.

fruits of a crime. The proceeds acquired through criminal acts.

Frye **test.** The defunct federal common-law rule of evidence on the admissibility of scientific evidence. • It required that the tests or procedures must have gained general acceptance in their particular field. In *Daubert v. Merrell Dow Pharms., Inc.*, 509 U.S. 579, 113 S.Ct. 2786 (1993), the Supreme Court held that scientific evidence must meet the requirements of the Federal Rules of Evidence, not the *Frye* test, to be admissible. *Frye v. United States*, 293 F. 1013 (D.C. Cir. 1923). See DAU-BERT TEST.

FST. See *field sobriety test* under SOBRIETY TEST.

fugitive. 1. A person who flees or escapes; a refugee. **2.** A criminal suspect or a witness in a criminal case who flees, evades, or escapes arrest, prosecution, imprisonment, service of process, or the giving of testimony, esp. by fleeing the jurisdiction or by hiding. See 18 USCA § 1073.—Also termed (in sense 2) *fugitive from justice*.

fugitive-disentitlement doctrine. An equitable rule that allows a trial or appellate court to limit a fugitive's access to civil and criminal courts in the United States.

fugitive-dismissal rule. The principle that an appellate court may dismiss a criminal defendant's appeal if the defendant is a fugitive.

Fugitive Felon Act. A federal statute that makes it a felony to flee across state lines to avoid state-felony prosecution or confinement, or to avoid giving testimony in a state-felony case. 18 USCA § 1073.

fugitive from justice. See FUGITIVE (2).

fugitive warrant. See WARRANT.

fugue (fyoog). An abnormal state of consciousness in which one appears to function normally but on recovery has no memory of what one did while in that condition.

full age. The age of legal majority; legal age.

full pardon. See *absolute pardon* under PARDON.

fundamental error. See *plain error* under ERROR.

fundamental-fairness doctrine. The rule that applies the principles of due process to a judicial proceeding. • The term is commonly considered synonymous with *due process*.

fundamental interest. See FUNDAMENTAL RIGHT.

fundamental-miscarriage-of-justice exception. The doctrine allowing a federal court in a habeas corpus proceeding to address a claim of constitutional error that, although ordinarily unreviewable, is subject to review because of a state-court procedural default that rendered the proceedings basically unfair. • For the exception to apply, among other things, the petitioner must show by a preponderance of the evidence that constitutional error resulted in the conviction of one who is probably innocent. If the defaulted claim applies only to sentencing, the exception permits review of the claim if the petitioner shows by clear and convincing evidence that, but for the constitutional error, no reasonable judge or jury would have found the petitioner legally eligible for the sentence received.

fundamental right. 1. A right derived from natural or fundamental law. **2.** A significant component of liberty, encroachments of which are rigorously tested by courts to ascertain the soundness of purported governmental justifications. • A fundamental right triggers strict scrutiny to determine whether the law violates the Due Process Clause or the Equal Protection Clause of the 14th Amendment. As enunciated by the Supreme Court, fundamental rights include voting, interstate travel, and various aspects of privacy (such as marriage and contraception rights).—Also termed *fundamental interest*. See STRICT SCRUTINY. Cf. SUSPECT CLASSIFICATION.

furandi animus (fyuu-**ran**-dɪ an-ə-məs). See *animus furandi* under ANIMUS.

furlough (**fər**-loh). A brief release from prison. See *study release* under RELEASE.

further instruction. See *additional instruction* under JURY INSTRUCTION.

G

gag order. **1.** A judge's order directing parties, attorneys, witnesses, or journalists to refrain from publicly discussing the facts of a case. • When directed to the press, such an order is generally unconstitutional under the First Amendment. **2.** A judge's order that an unruly defendant be bound and gagged during trial to prevent further interruptions.

gallows. A wooden frame consisting of two upright posts and a crossbeam, from which condemned criminals are hanged by a rope.

gambling device. Anything, such as cards, dice, or an electronic or mechanical contrivance, that allows a person to play a game of chance in which money may be won or lost. • Gambling devices are regulated by law, and the use or possession of a gambling device can be illegal.—Also termed *gaming device*.

gambling place. Any location where gambling occurs. 18 USCA § 1081.—Also termed *gaming house*; *gaming room*.

gambling verdict. See *chance verdict* under VERDICT.

game law. A federal or state law that regulates the hunting of game, esp. one that forbids the capturing or killing of specified game either entirely or seasonally, describes the means for killing or capturing game in season, or restricts the number and type of game animals that may be killed or captured in season. 16 USCA §§ 661–667; 18 USCA §§ 41–47.

gaming device. See GAMBLING DEVICE.

gaming house. See GAMBLING PLACE.

gaming room. See GAMBLING PLACE.

gang. A group of persons who go about together or act in concert, esp. for antisocial or criminal purposes. • Many gangs (esp. those made up of adolescents) have common identifying signs and symbols, such as hand signals and distinctive colors.—Also termed *street gang*.

Ganser's syndrome (**gahn**-zər *or* **gan**-sər). An abnormality characterized by the giving of irrelevant and nonsensical answers to questions. • Prisoners have been known to feign this syndrome in an attempt to obtain leniency.

gaoler. See JAILER.

gaol liberties. See JAIL LIBERTIES.

Garcia **hearing** (gahr-**see**-ə). A hearing held to ensure that a defendant who is one of two or more defendants represented by the same attorney understands (1) the risk of a conflict of interest inherent in this type of representation, and (2) that he or she is entitled to the services of an attorney who does not represent anyone else in the defendant's case. *United States v. Garcia*, 517 F.2d 272 (5th Cir. 1975).

Garrity **statement** (**gar**-ə-tee). A public employee's oral or written report (as of an incident) obtained under a threat of termination of employment. • A public employee usu. makes a *Garrity* statement in the course of an internal investigation (as by a police department). Because a *Garrity* statement is coerced, the statement and any evidence obtained as a result of it cannot be used in a later criminal prosecution against the public employee. The statement and evidence may be used only to evaluate the employee's performance. *Garrity v. New Jersey*, 385 U.S. 493, 87 S.Ct. 616 (1967).

gas chamber. A small, sealed room in which capital punishments are carried out by strapping the prisoner into a chair and releasing poisonous fumes.

GBMI. *abbr*. GUILTY BUT MENTALLY ILL.

general challenge. See *challenge for cause* under CHALLENGE (2).

general court-martial. See COURT-MARTIAL.

general criminal intent. See *general intent* under INTENT.

general deputy. See DEPUTY.

general deterrence. See DETERRENCE.

general intent. See INTENT.

general-intent crime. See CRIME.

general jail delivery. See JAIL DELIVERY.

general jurisdiction. See JURISDICTION.

general-justification defense. See *lesser-evils defense* under DEFENSE.

general legislation. See LEGISLATION.

general malice. See MALICE.

general mens rea. See *general intent* under INTENT.

general objection. See OBJECTION.

general pardon. See AMNESTY.

general plea in bar. See PLEA IN BAR.

general sentence. See SENTENCE.

general verdict. See VERDICT.

general verdict with interrogatories. See VERDICT.

general warrant. See WARRANT.

genetic fingerprinting. See DNA IDENTIFICATION.

Geneva Convention (jə-**nee**-və). An international agreement establishing the proper treatment of prisoners of war and of persons injured or killed in battle. • Drafted in 1864, the Convention has since been adopted in revised form by most nations.

genocide (**jen**-ə-sɪd). The systematic destruction of a substantial part of a national, ethnic, racial, or religious group, usu. with the intention of destroying the entire group. • Under the terms of the Geneva Convention of 1948, genocide is a crime (whether committed during war or peace) subject to prosecution either in the nation where it was committed or by an international tribunal having jurisdiction elsewhere.

geography of crime. See *environmental criminology* under CRIMINOLOGY.

give bail, *vb*. To post security for one's appearance in court <the court ordered the accused to give bail in the amount of $10,000>.—Also termed *post bail*.

GMI. *abbr*. GUILTY BUT MENTALLY ILL.

going witness. See WITNESS.

good behavior. Orderly conduct, which in the context of penal law allows a prisoner to reduce the time spent in prison. Cf. *good time* under TIME.

good-faith exception. An exception to the exclusionary rule whereby evidence obtained under a warrant later found to be invalid (esp. because it is not supported by probable cause) is nonetheless admissible if the police reasonably relied on the notion that the warrant was valid. ● The good-faith exception was adopted by the Supreme Court in *United States v. Leon*, 468 U.S. 897, 104 S.Ct. 3405 (1984).

good time. See TIME.

government. The prosecutors in a given criminal case <the government has objected to the introduction of that evidence>.

government agent. See AGENT.

grade, *n.* An incremental step in the scale of punishments for offenses, based on a particular offense's seriousness <several grades of murder>.

graded offense. See OFFENSE.

grading. The fixing of a criminal offense at a level of seriousness, such as first degree, second degree, or third degree (in reference to a felony), or Class A, Class B, or Class C (in reference to a misdemeanor). See DEGREE OF CRIME.

graft, *n.* **1.** The act of taking advantage of a position of trust to gain money or property dishonestly; esp., a public official's fraudulent acquisition of public funds. **2.** Money or property gained illegally or unfairly.

grand, *adj.* Of or relating to a crime involving the theft of money or property valued more than a statutorily established amount, and therefore considered more serious than those involving a lesser amount <grand theft>. See *grand larceny* under LARCENY. Cf. PETTY.

295

grand inquest. See INQUEST.

grand juror. See JUROR.

grand jury. A body of (often 23) people who are chosen to sit permanently for at least a month—and sometimes a year—and who, in ex parte proceedings, decide whether to issue indictments. • If the grand jury decides that evidence is strong enough to hold a suspect for trial, it returns a bill of indictment (a *true bill*) charging the suspect with a specific crime.— Also termed *accusing jury*; *presenting jury*; *jury of indictment*; *charging grand jury*. Cf. *petit jury* under JURY.

> **investigative grand jury.** A grand jury whose primary function is to examine possible crimes and develop evidence not currently available to the prosecution.—Also termed *investigatory grand jury*.

> **runaway grand jury.** A grand jury that acts essentially in opposition to the prosecution, as by perversely failing to return an indictment that the prosecution has requested.

> **screening grand jury.** A grand jury whose primary function is to decide whether to issue an indictment.

special grand jury. A grand jury specially summoned, usu. when the regular grand jury either has already been discharged or has not been drawn; a grand jury with limited authority.—Also termed *additional grand jury*; *extraordinary grand jury*.

Grand Jury Clause. The clause of the Fifth Amendment to the U.S. Constitution requiring an indictment by a grand jury before a person can be tried for serious offenses.

grand-jury witness. See WITNESS.

grand larceny. See LARCENY.

graymail. A criminal defendant's threat to reveal classified information during the trial in the hope of forcing the government to drop the criminal charge. Cf. BLACKMAIL.

great bodily injury. See *serious bodily injury* under INJURY.

grievous bodily harm. See *serious bodily injury* under INJURY.

grift, *vb.* To obtain money illicitly by adroit use of a scam, confidence game, or other fraudulent means.—**grifter,** *n.*

gross misdemeanor. See MISDEMEANOR.

gross negligence. See NEGLIGENCE.

guardhouse lawyer. See JAILHOUSE LAWYER.

guardian, *n.* One who has the legal authority and duty to care for another's person or property, esp. because of the other's infancy, incapacity, or disability. • A guardian may be appointed either for all purposes or for specific purposes.

>   *guardian ad litem* (ad lı-təm). A guardian, usu. a lawyer, appointed by the court to appear in a case on behalf of an incompetent or minor party.—Also termed *special guardian.*

guilt, *n.* The fact or state of having committed a wrong, esp. a crime <the state's burden was to prove guilt beyond a reasonable doubt>. Cf. INNOCENCE.

guiltless, *adj.* **1.** Free from guilt; not having committed a wrong <guiltless of the crime>. **2.** Having the quality or appearance of innocence <even though she confessed, the defendant looked guiltless>.

guilt phase. The part of a criminal trial during which the fact-finder determines whether the defendant committed a crime. Cf. PENALTY PHASE.

guilty, *adj.* **1.** Having committed a crime; responsible for a crime <guilty of armed rob-

bery>. **2.** Responsible for a civil wrong, such as a tort or breach of contract <guilty of fraudulent misrepresentation>.—**guiltily,** *adv.*

guilty, *n.* **1.** A plea of a criminal defendant who does not contest the charges. **2.** A jury verdict convicting the defendant of the crime charged.

guilty but mentally ill. A form of verdict in a criminal case whereby the jury rejects the defendant's insanity defense but still recommends psychiatric treatment because the defendant is mentally ill.—Abbr. GBMI; GMI.— Also termed *guilty but insane*; *guilty of the act, but so insane as not to be responsible.* See IN-SANITY DEFENSE.

guilty mind. See MENS REA.

guilty plea. See PLEA.

guilty verdict. See VERDICT.

gun-control law. A statute or ordinance that regulates the sale, possession, or use of firearms. ● Gun-control laws vary widely among the states, and many cities have gun-control ordinances. Federal law prohibits the illegal sale, possession, and use of firearms. 18 USCA §§ 921–930. See BRADY ACT.

H

habeas corpus (**hay**-bee-əs **kor**-pəs). [Law Latin "that you have the body"] A writ employed to bring a person before a court, most frequently to ensure that the party's imprisonment or detention is not illegal (*habeas corpus ad subjiciendum*). ● In addition to being used to test the legality of an arrest or commitment, the writ may be used to obtain review of (1) the regularity of the extradition process, (2) the right to or amount of bail, or (3) the jurisdiction of a court that has imposed a criminal sentence.—Abbr. H.C.—Sometimes shortened to *habeas*.—Also termed *writ of habeas corpus*.

habit evidence. See EVIDENCE.

habitual criminal. See RECIDIVIST.

habitual offender. See RECIDIVIST.

had-not test. See BUT-FOR TEST.

Hague Convention on the Civil Aspects of International Child Abduction. An international convention (established in 1980) that seeks to counteract child-snatching by noncustodial parents. ● The Hague Convention is a private legal mechanism available to parents seeking the return of, or access to, their children. More than 46 countries are parties to the

Convention, including the United States, which became a signatory on July 1, 1988.

halfway house. A transitional housing facility designed to rehabilitate people who have recently left a prison or medical-care facility, or who otherwise need help in adjusting to a normal life.—Also termed *residential community treatment center*.

hang, *vb.* (Of a jury) to be unable to reach a verdict <the jury was hung after 12 hours of continuous deliberation>. See *hung jury* under JURY.

hanging, *n.* The act of carrying out an execution by suspending the person above the ground by a rope around the person's neck. • Death is caused by asphyxiation (by being hoisted from the ground) or by a sudden breaking of the cervical vertebrae (by being dropped from a height).

hanging judge. See JUDGE.

hangman. *Archaic.* An executioner, esp. one who executes condemned criminals by hanging.

harassment (hə-**ras**-mənt *or* **har**-əs-mənt). Words, conduct, or action (usu. repeated or persistent) that, being directed at a specific

301

person, annoys, alarms, or causes substantial
emotional distress in that person and serves
no legitimate purpose. ● Harassment is actionable in some circumstances, as when a creditor
uses threatening or abusive tactics to collect a
debt.—**harass** (hə-**ras** *or* **har**-əs), *vb.*

   aggravated harassment. Harassment accompanied by aggravating factors; esp.,
harassment conducted through the mails or
by telephone, harassment based on a person's race, color, religion, or national origin,
or harassment by one previously convicted
of harassment.

harboring, *n.* The act of affording lodging,
shelter, or refuge to a person, esp. a criminal
or illegal alien.

hard labor. Work imposed on prisoners as
additional punishment, usu. for misconduct
while in prison. ● Several states (such as Louisiana, Maine, and New Jersey) impose hard
labor as a sentence for a variety of crimes.
Hard labor is also imposed in military sentencing.

harm, *n.* Injury, loss, or detriment.

   bodily harm. Physical pain, illness, or impairment of the body.

grievous bodily harm. See *serious bodily injury* under INJURY.

physical harm. Any physical impairment of land, chattels, or the human body.

social harm. An adverse effect on any social interest that is protected by the criminal law.

harmful error. See *reversible error* under ERROR.

harmless error. See ERROR.

hate crime. See CRIME.

hazardous negligence. See *gross negligence* (2) under NEGLIGENCE.

head shop. A retail establishment that sells items intended for use with illegal drugs.

hearing. 1. A judicial session, usu. open to the public, held for the purpose of deciding issues of fact or of law, sometimes with witnesses testifying <the court held a hearing on the admissibility of DNA evidence in the murder case>. **2.** In legislative practice, any proceeding in which legislators or their designees receive testimony about legislation that might be enacted <the shooting victim spoke at the

Senate's hearing on gun control>. See PRELIMI-
NARY HEARING.

adjudicatory hearing (ə-**joo**-di-kə-tor-ee).
A hearing held by a juvenile court to determine whether a juvenile has engaged in delinquent conduct; a trial of a youth accused
of a delinquency. See JUVENILE DELINQUENCY.
Cf. *detention hearing* (2); *disposition hearing.*

Daubert hearing. See DAUBERT HEARING.

detention hearing. 1. A hearing to determine whether an accused should be released
pending trial. See *pretrial detention* under
DETENTION. **2.** A hearing held by a juvenile
court to determine whether a juvenile accused of delinquent conduct should be detained, continued in confinement, or released pending an adjudicatory hearing. Cf.
adjudicatory hearing; *disposition hearing.*

disposition hearing. A hearing held to determine the most appropriate form of custody or treatment for a juvenile who has been
found at an adjudicatory hearing to be a
juvenile delinquent or a status offender. Cf.
adjudicatory hearing; *detention hearing* (2).

evidentiary hearing. A hearing at which
evidence is presented, as opposed to a hearing at which only legal argument is presented.

exclusionary hearing. A pretrial hearing conducted to review and determine the admissibility of alleged illegally obtained evidence.

fair hearing. A judicial or administrative hearing conducted in accordance with due process.

Fatico hearing. See FATICO HEARING.

Franks hearing. See FRANKS HEARING.

Garcia hearing. See GARCIA HEARING.

Jackson–Denno hearing. See JACKSON–DEN-NO HEARING.

Mapp hearing. See MAPP HEARING.

omnibus hearing. A hearing designed to bring judicial oversight over criminal cases at an early stage to make certain that the cases are being handled expeditiously and properly. • At an omnibus hearing, the court is primarily interested in ensuring that discovery is being conducted properly, that any necessary evidentiary hearings have been scheduled, and that all issues ripe for decision have been decided.

preliminary hearing. See PRELIMINARY HEARING.

presentence hearing. See PRESENTENCE HEARING.

revocation hearing. A hearing held to determine whether a parolee should be returned to prison for violating the terms of parole.

sentencing hearing. See PRESENTENCE HEARING.

suppression hearing. A pretrial hearing in which a criminal defendant seeks to prevent the introduction of evidence alleged to have been seized illegally.

transfer hearing. A hearing held to determine whether a juvenile alleged to have committed a delinquent act should be tried as an adult or as a juvenile.—Also termed *certification hearing*; *waiver hearing*; *fitness hearing*.

unfair hearing. A hearing that is not conducted in accordance with due process, as when the defendant is denied the opportunity to prepare or consult with counsel.

Wade hearing. See WADE HEARING.

hearsay. 1. Traditionally, testimony that is given by a witness who relates not what he or she knows personally, but what others have said, and that is therefore dependent on the credibility of someone other than the witness. • Such testimony is generally inadmissible under the rules of evidence. **2.** In federal law, a statement (either a verbal assertion or nonverbal assertive conduct), other than one made by the declarant while testifying at the trial or hearing, offered in evidence to prove the truth of the matter asserted. Fed. R. Evid. 801(c).— Also termed *hearsay evidence*; *secondhand evidence*. Cf. *original evidence* under EVIDENCE.

> **double hearsay.** A hearsay statement that contains further hearsay statements within it, none of which is admissible unless exceptions to the rule against hearsay can be applied to each level <the double hearsay was the investigation's report stating that Amy admitted to running the red light>. Fed. R. Evid. 805.—Also termed *multiple hearsay*; *hearsay within hearsay*.

hearsay rule. The rule that no assertion offered as testimony can be received unless it is or has been open to test by cross-examination or an opportunity for cross-examination, except as provided otherwise by the rules of evidence, by court rules, or by statute. • The chief reasons for the rule are that out-of-court statements amounting to hearsay are not made under oath and are not subject to cross-examination. Fed. R. Evid. 802. Rule 803 provides 23 explicit exceptions to the hearsay rule, regardless of whether the out-of-court declarant is available to testify, and Rule 804 provides 5 more exceptions for situations in which the declarant is unavailable to testify.

hearsay within hearsay. See *double hearsay* under HEARSAY.

heartbalm statute. A state law that abolishes the rights of action for alienation of affections, breach of promise to marry, criminal conversation, and seduction of a person over the legal age of consent.

heat of passion. Rage, terror, or furious hatred suddenly aroused by some immediate provocation, usu. another person's words or actions. ● At common law, the heat of passion could serve as a mitigating circumstance that would reduce a murder charge to manslaughter.—Also termed *sudden heat of passion*; *sudden heat*; *sudden passion*; *hot blood*. Cf. COLD BLOOD; COOL BLOOD.

hedonistic utilitarianism. See UTILITARIANISM.

heedlessness, *n.* The quality of being thoughtless and inconsiderate; esp., conduct whereby the actor disregards the rights or safety of others. ● Heedlessness is often construed to involve the same degree of fault as recklessness.—**heedless,** *adj*. See RECKLESS-NESS.

heightened scrutiny. See INTERMEDIATE SCRUTINY.

heinous (**hay**-nəs), *adj*. (Of a crime or its perpetrator) shockingly atrocious or odious.—**heinousness,** *n*.

HGN test. *abbr*. HORIZONTAL-GAZE NYSTAGMUS TEST.

high crime. See CRIME.

high misdemeanor. See *serious misdemeanor* under MISDEMEANOR.

high treason. See TREASON.

highway robbery. See ROBBERY.

hijack, *vb*. **1.** To commandeer (a vehicle or airplane), esp. at gunpoint. **2.** To steal or rob from (a vehicle or airplane in transit).

hit-and-run statute. A law requiring a motorist involved in an accident to remain at the scene and to give certain information to the police and others involved.

Hobbs Act. A federal anti-racketeering act making it a crime to interfere with interstate commerce by extortion, robbery, or physical violence. 18 USCA § 1951. See RACKETEER INFLUENCED AND CORRUPT ORGANIZATIONS ACT.

holding, *n*. **1.** A court's determination of a matter of law pivotal to its decision; a principle drawn from such a decision. **2.** A ruling on evidence or other questions presented at trial.

holding cell. See JAIL.

holding charge. A criminal charge of some minor offense filed to keep the accused in custody while prosecutors take time to build a bigger case and prepare more serious charges.

hold order. A notation in a prisoner's file stating that another jurisdiction has charges pending against the prisoner and instructing prison officials to alert authorities in that other jurisdiction instead of releasing the prisoner.

holdup. See STICKUP.

homicide (**hom**-ə-sɪd), *n*. The killing of one person by another.—**homicidal,** *adj*.

   criminal homicide. **1.** Homicide prohibited and punishable by law, such as murder or manslaughter. **2.** The act of purposely, knowingly, recklessly, or negligently causing the death of another human being. Model Penal Code § 210.1.

criminally negligent homicide. See *negligent homicide.*

excusable homicide. **1.** Homicide resulting from a person's lawful act, committed without intention to harm another. **2.** See *justifiable homicide* (1).

felonious homicide. Homicide committed unlawfully, without legal justification or excuse. ● This is the category into which murder and manslaughter fall.

homicide by abuse. Homicide in which the perpetrator, under circumstances showing an extreme indifference to human life, causes the death of the perpetrator's dependent—usu. a child or mentally retarded person.

homicide by misadventure. See ACCIDENTAL KILLING.

homicide per infortunium (pər in-fort[y]oo-nee-əm). [Latin "homicide by misfortune"] The unintentional killing of another while engaged in a lawful act; ACCIDENTAL KILLING.

innocent homicide. Homicide that does not involve criminal guilt.

justifiable homicide. **1.** The killing of another in self-defense when faced with the danger of death or serious bodily injury.— Also termed *excusable homicide*. See SELF-DE-FENSE. **2.** A killing mandated or permitted by the law, such as execution for a capital crime or killing to prevent a crime or a criminal's escape.

negligent homicide. Homicide resulting from the careless performance of a legal or illegal act in which the danger of death is apparent; the killing of a human being by criminal negligence.—Also termed *criminally negligent homicide*. See *criminal negligence* under NEGLIGENCE.

reckless homicide. The unlawful killing of another person with conscious indifference toward that person's life. Cf. MANSLAUGHTER.

vehicular homicide. The killing of another person by one's unlawful or negligent operation of a motor vehicle.—Also termed *automobile homicide*.

willful homicide. The act of intentionally causing a person's death, with or without legal justification.

horizontal-gaze nystagmus test. A field-so-briety test for intoxication, in which the suspect is told to focus on an object (such as a pencil) and to track its movement, usu. from side to side, by moving only the eyes. ● Intoxication is indicated if the eyes jerk or twitch while tracking the object.—Abbr. HGN test.

hostage. 1. An innocent person held captive by another who threatens to kill or harm that person if one or more demands are not met. ● Hostage-taking is a federal crime. 18 USCA § 1203. Cf. KIDNAPPING. **2.** A person who is given into an enemy's possession, in time of war, with his or her freedom or life to stand as security for the performance of some agreement made to the enemy by the belligerent power giving the hostage.

hosticide (**hos**-tə-sɪd), *n.* **1.** A person who kills an enemy. **2.** The killing of an enemy.

hostile witness. See WITNESS.

hot blood. See HEAT OF PASSION.

hot check. See *bad check* under CHECK.

hot pursuit. 1. See FRESH PURSUIT. **2.** The legitimate chase of a foreign vessel on the high seas just after that vessel has violated the law of the pursuing country while within that country's jurisdiction.

house arrest. The confinement of a person who is accused or convicted of a crime to his or her home usu. by attaching an electronically monitored bracelet to the criminal offender. • Most house-arrest programs require the offender to work and permit leaving the home only for reasons such as work, medical needs, or community-service obligations.

housebreaking. The crime of breaking into a dwelling or other secured building, with the intent to commit a felony inside; BURGLARY. • *Burglary* is now used more than *housebreaking*. In England, for example, *housebreaking* was replaced in 1968 with statutory burglary, though the term is still used in Scots law.

houseburning. The common-law misdemeanor of intentionally burning one's own house that is within city limits or that is close enough to other houses that they might be in danger of catching fire (even though no actual damage to them may result). Cf. ARSON.

house of correction. 1. A reformatory. **2.** A place for the confinement of juvenile offenders or those who have committed crimes of lesser magnitude.—Also termed *house of refuge*.

house of detention. See JAIL.

house of ill fame. See DISORDERLY HOUSE.

house of prostitution. See DISORDERLY HOUSE.

house of refuge. See HOUSE OF CORRECTION.

hovering act. A statute applying to a coastal country's criminal jurisdiction over ships, and persons aboard those ships, when the ships are outside the country's territory.

hub-and-spoke conspiracy. See *wheel conspiracy* under CONSPIRACY.

hung jury. See JURY.

husband-wife privilege. See *marital privilege* under PRIVILEGE (3).

hush money. *Slang.* A bribe to suppress the dissemination of certain information; a payment to secure silence.

hypothetical-person defense. An entrapment defense in which the defendant asserts that an undercover law-enforcement officer (or person acting at the law-enforcement officer's direction) encouraged the defendant to engage in the criminal conduct either by making false representations designed to convince the defendant that the conduct was not prohibited, or by using persuasive methods that created a substantial risk that the charged offense would be committed by a person who was not otherwise inclined to commit it. • This defense has been adopted by a minority of states and by the Model Penal Code.—Also termed *objective method*. See Model Penal Code § 2.13. Cf. SHERMAN–SORRELLS DOCTRINE.

hypothetical question. A trial device that solicits an expert witness's opinion based on assumptions treated as facts established by evidence.—Also termed *abstract question*.

I

ICC. *abbr.* INTERNATIONAL CRIMINAL COURT.

identification parade. See LINEUP.

identify, *vb.* To prove the identity of (a person or thing) <the witness identified the weapon>.

identity. The authenticity of a person or thing.

IFP. *abbr.* IN FORMA PAUPERIS.

IFP affidavit. See *poverty affidavit* under AFFIDAVIT.

ignorantia juris non excusat (ig-nə-**ran**-shee-ə **joor**-is non ek-**skyoo**-sat *or* -zat). [Latin] Lack of knowledge about a legal requirement or prohibition is never an excuse to a criminal charge. ● In English, the idea is commonly rendered *ignorance of the law is no excuse.*—Often shortened to *ignorantia juris.*—Also termed *ignorantia juris neminem excusat* (ignorance of the law excuses no one); *ignorantia legis non excusat*; *ignorantia juris haud excusat.*

ignore, *vb.* **1.** To refuse to notice, recognize, or consider. **2.** (Of a grand jury) to reject (an indictment) as groundless; to no-bill (a charge).

illegal, *adj.* Forbidden by law; unlawful <illegal dumping> <an illegal drug>.

illegal entry. 1. The unlawful act of going into a building with the intent to commit a crime. ● In some jurisdictions, illegal entry is a lesser included offense of burglary. **2.** The unauthorized entrance of an alien into the United States by arriving at the wrong time or place, by evading inspection, or by fraud.

illegality. 1. An act that is not authorized by law. **2.** The state of not being legally authorized. **3.** The state or condition of being unlawful.

illegally obtained evidence. See EVIDENCE.

illegal per se. Unlawful in and of itself.

illegal search. See *unreasonable search* under SEARCH.

illicit (i[l]-**lis**-ət), *adj.* Illegal or improper <illicit relations>.

illicit cohabitation. See COHABITATION.

illustrative evidence. See *demonstrative evidence* under EVIDENCE.

imbracery. See EMBRACERY.

immaterial, *adj.* (Of evidence) tending to prove some fact that is not properly at issue; lacking any logical connection with the consequential facts. Cf. IRRELEVANT.

immaterial evidence. See EVIDENCE.

immaterial fact. See FACT.

immaterial variance. See VARIANCE.

immaturity. See MINORITY.

immediate cause. See CAUSE (1).

immediate control. 1. The area within an arrestee's reach. • A police officer may conduct a warrantless search of this area to ensure the officer's safety and to prevent the arrestee from destroying evidence. **2.** Vehicular control that is close enough to allow the driver to instantly govern the vehicle's movements.

immediate intent. See INTENT.

immediately-apparent requirement. The principle that a police officer must have probable cause to believe that an item is contraband before seizing it. • This plain-view exception to the warrant requirement was first announced in *Coolidge v. New Hampshire*, 403 U.S. 443, 91 S.Ct. 2022 (1971).

imminent danger. The danger resulting from an immediate threatened injury sufficient to cause a reasonable and prudent person to defend himself or herself.

imminently dangerous. (Of a person, behavior, or thing) reasonably certain to place life or limb in peril. • This term is relevant in several legal contexts. For example, if a mental condition renders a person imminently dangerous to self or others, he or she may be committed to a mental hospital. And the imminently dangerous behavior of pointing a gun at someone's head could subject the actor to criminal liability.

immunity. 1. Any exemption from a duty, liability, or service of process; esp., such an exemption granted to a public official.

　congressional immunity. Either of two special immunities given to members of Congress: (1) the exemption from arrest while attending a session of the body to which the member belongs, excluding an arrest for treason, breach of the peace, or a felony, or

(2) the exemption from arrest or questioning for any speech given or debate entered into during a legislative session. U.S. Const. art. I, § 6, cl. 1.

diplomatic immunity. The general exemption of diplomatic ministers from the operation of local law, the exception being that a minister who is plotting against the security of the host nation may be arrested and sent out of the country. • A minister's family shares in diplomatic immunity to a great, though ill-defined, degree.

2. Freedom from prosecution granted by the government in exchange for the person's testimony. • By granting immunity, the government can compel testimony—despite the Fifth Amendment right against self-incrimination—because that testimony can no longer incriminate the witness.

pocket immunity. Immunity that results from the prosecutor's decision not to prosecute, instead of from a formal grant of immunity.—Also termed *informal immunity.*

testimonial immunity. Immunity from the use of the compelled testimony against the witness. • Any information derived from that testimony, however, is generally admissible against the witness.

transactional immunity. Immunity from prosecution for any event or transaction described in the compelled testimony. ● This is the broadest form of immunity.

use immunity. Immunity from the use of the compelled testimony (or any information derived from that testimony) in a future prosecution against the witness. ● After granting use immunity, the government can still prosecute if it shows that its evidence comes from a legitimate independent source.—Also termed *use/derivative-use immunity.*

impairing the morals of a minor. The offense of an adult's engaging in sex-related acts, short of intercourse, with a minor. ● Examples of this conduct are fondling, taking obscene photographs, and showing pornographic materials. Cf. CONTRIBUTING TO THE DELINQUENCY OF A MINOR; CORRUPTION OF A MINOR.

impartial jury. See JURY.

impeach, *vb.* **1.** To charge with a crime or misconduct; esp., to formally charge (a public official) with a violation of the public trust <President Nixon resigned from office to avoid being impeached>. ● Impeaching a federal official, such as the President, the Vice President, or a judge, requires that a majority of the U.S. House of Representatives vote to return at least one article of impeachment to the U.S. Senate, itemizing the charges and explaining their factual grounds. Even if an official is impeached, removal from office does not occur unless two-thirds of the senators vote for conviction. **2.** To discredit the veracity of (a witness) <the lawyer hoped that her star witness wouldn't be impeached on cross-examination>. **3.** To challenge the accuracy or authenticity of (a document) <the handwriting expert impeached the holographic will>.

impeachable offense. An offense for which a public official may legally be impeached, during the first step in a two-step process that may, depending on the vote in the U.S. Senate, lead to the official's removal from office. • The U.S. Constitution states that "[t]he President, Vice President and all civil Officers of the United States, shall be removed from Office on Impeachment for, and Conviction of, Treason, Bribery, or other high Crimes and Misdemeanors." The meaning of this language was much debated during the impeachment and trial of President Bill Clinton, against whom two articles of impeachment were returned by the House of Representatives. The question arose what type of misdemeanor will suffice, and whether the *high* in *high crimes* modifies *misdemeanors* as well. No definitive answer resulted from the proceedings.

impeachment. 1. The act (by a legislature) of
calling for the removal from office of a public
official, accomplished by presenting a written
charge of the official's alleged misconduct;
esp., the initiation of a proceeding in the U.S.
House of Representatives against a federal official, such as the President or a judge. •
Congress's authority to remove a federal official stems from Article II, Section 4 of the
Constitution, which authorizes the removal of
an official for "Treason, Bribery, or other high
Crimes and Misdemeanors." The grounds
upon which an official can be removed do not,
however, have to be criminal in nature. They
usu. involve some type of abuse of power or
breach of the public trust. Articles of impeachment—which can be approved by a simple
majority in the House—serve as the charging
instrument for the later trial in the Senate. If
the President is impeached, the Chief Justice
of the Supreme Court presides over the Senate
trial. The defendant can be removed from office by a two-thirds majority of the senators
who are present. In the United Kingdom, impeachment is by the House of Commons and
trial by the House of Lords. But no case has
arisen there since 1801, and many British
scholars consider impeachment obsolete. **2.**
The act of discrediting a witness, as by catching the witness in a lie or by demonstrating
that the witness has been convicted of a crimi-

nal offense. **3.** The act of challenging the accuracy or authenticity of evidence.

impeachment court. See COURT FOR THE TRIALS OF IMPEACHMENT.

impeachment evidence. See EVIDENCE.

impeachment of verdict. A party's attack on a verdict, alleging impropriety by a member of the jury.

imperfect defense. See DEFENSE.

imperfect justification. See JUSTIFICATION.

imperfect self-defense. See SELF-DEFENSE.

impermissible comment on the evidence. See COMMENT ON THE EVIDENCE.

impersonation. The act of impersonating someone.—Also termed *personation*.

   false impersonation. The crime of falsely representing oneself as another person, usu. a law-enforcement officer, for the purpose of deceiving someone. See 18 USCA §§ 912–917.—Also termed *false personation*.

implicate, *vb.* **1.** To show (a person) to be involved in (a crime, misfeasance, etc.) <when he turned state's evidence, he implicated three

other suspects>. **2.** To be involved or affected <three judges were implicated in the bribery>.

implication. 1. The act of showing involvement in something, esp. a crime or misfeasance <the implication of the judges in the bribery scheme>. **2.** An inference drawn from something said or observed <the implication was that the scheme involved several persons>.

   necessary implication. An implication so strong in its probability that anything to the contrary would be unreasonable.

implied acquittal. See ACQUITTAL.

implied admission. See ADMISSION.

implied amnesty. See AMNESTY.

implied assertion. See *assertive conduct* under CONDUCT.

implied confession. See CONFESSION.

implied intent. See INTENT.

implied malice. See MALICE.

impossibility. 1. The fact or condition of not being able to occur, exist, or be done. **2.** A fact or circumstance that cannot occur, exist, or be done. **3.** A fact or circumstance preventing the commission of a crime.

>*factual impossibility.* Impossibility due to the fact that the illegal act cannot physically be accomplished, such as trying to pick an empty pocket. ● Factual impossibility is not a defense to the crime of attempt.—Also termed *physical impossibility*; *impossibility of fact*.

>*legal impossibility.* **1.** Impossibility due to the fact that what the defendant intended to do is not illegal even though the defendant might have believed that he or she was committing a crime. ● A legal impossibility might occur, for example, if a person goes hunting while erroneously believing that it is not hunting season. This type of legal impossibility is a defense to the crimes of attempt, conspiracy, and solicitation.—Also termed *impossibility of law*; *true legal impossibility*. **2.** Impossibility due to the fact that an element required for an attempt has not been satisfied. ● This type of legal impossibility might occur, for example, if a person fires an unloaded gun at another when the crime of attempt requires that the gun be loaded. This is a defense to the crime of attempt.

impostor (im-**pos**-tər). One who pretends to be someone else to deceive others, esp. to receive the benefits of a negotiable instrument.—Also spelled *imposter*.

impound, *vb.* **1.** To place (something, such as a car or other personal property) in the custody of the police or the court, often with the understanding that it will be returned intact at the end of the proceeding. **2.** To take and retain possession of (something, such as a forged document to be produced as evidence) in preparation for a criminal prosecution.

impoundment. The action of impounding; the state of being impounded.

imprison, *vb.* To confine (a person) in prison.

imprisonment, *n.* **1.** The act of confining a person, esp. in a prison <the imprisonment of Jackson was entirely justified>. **2.** The state of being confined; a period of confinement <Jackson's imprisonment lasted 14 years>. See FALSE IMPRISONMENT.

impulse, *n.* A sudden urge or inclination that prompts an unplanned action.

> ***uncontrollable impulse.*** An impulse that is so overwhelming that it cannot be resisted. ● In some jurisdictions, an uncontrollable impulse serves as a defense to criminal conduct committed while in the grip of the impulse. See IRRESISTIBLE-IMPULSE TEST.

impunity (im-**pyoo**-nə-tee). An exemption or protection from punishment <because she was a foreign diplomat, she was able to disregard the parking tickets with impunity>. See IMMUNITY.

imputation, *n*. The act or an instance of ascribing something, esp. fault or crime, to a person; an accusation or charge.

imputed disqualification. See *vicarious disqualification* under DISQUALIFICATION.

inactive case. See CASE.

inadmissible, *adj*. (Of evidence) excludable by some rule of evidence.

inadvertent discovery. A law-enforcement officer's unexpected finding of incriminating evidence in plain view. • Even though this type of evidence is obtained without a warrant, it can be used against the accused under the plain-view exception to the warrant requirement.

in articulo mortis (in ahr-**tik**-yə-loh **mor**-tis). [Law Latin] At the point of death. Cf. IN EXTREMIS.

in camera (in **kam**-ə-rə), *adv*. & *adj*. [Law Latin "in a chamber"] **1.** In the judge's private chambers. **2.** In the courtroom with all spectators excluded. **3.** (Of a judicial action) taken when court is not in session.—Also termed (in reference to the opinion of one judge) *in chambers*.

in camera proceeding. See PROCEEDING.

incapacitated person. A person who is impaired by an intoxicant, by mental illness or deficiency, or by physical illness or disability to the extent that personal decision-making is impossible.

incapacitation, *n*. **1.** The action of disabling or depriving of legal capacity. **2.** The state of being disabled or lacking legal capacity.—**incapacitate,** *vb*.

incapacity. 1. Lack of physical or mental capabilities. **2.** Lack of ability to have certain legal consequences attach to one's actions. • For example, a five-year-old has an incapacity to make a binding contract. **3.** See DISABILITY. Cf. INCOMPETENCY.

    testimonial incapacity. The lack of capacity to testify.

incarceration, *n*. The act or process of confining someone; IMPRISONMENT.—**incarcerate,** *vb*.—**incarcerator,** *n*. Cf. DECARCERATION.

shock incarceration. Incarceration in a military-type setting, usu. for three to six months, during which the offender is subjected to strict discipline, physical exercise, and hard labor. See 18 USCA § 4046. • After successfully completing the program, the offender is usu. placed on probation.—Also termed *boot camp.* Cf. *shock probation* under PROBATION.

incendiary (in-**sen**-dee-er-ee), *n.* **1.** One who deliberately and unlawfully sets fire to property.—Also termed *arsonist*; *firebug.* **2.** An instrument (such as a bomb) or chemical agent designed to start a fire.—**incendiary,** *adj.*

incest, *n.* Sexual relations between family members or close relatives, including children related by adoption. • Incest was not a crime under English common law but was punished as an ecclesiastical offense. Modern statutes make it a felony.—**incestuous,** *adj.*

incestuous adultery. See ADULTERY.

in chambers. See IN CAMERA.

inchoate (in-**koh**-it), *adj.* Partially completed or imperfectly formed; just begun.—**inchoateness,** *n.* Cf. CHOATE.

inchoate crime. See *inchoate offense* under OFFENSE.

inchoate offense. See OFFENSE.

incidental admission. See ADMISSION.

incite, *vb.* To provoke or stir up (someone to commit a criminal act, or the criminal act itself). Cf. ABET.

incitee. A person who has been incited, esp. to commit a crime.

inciteful, *adj.* Tending to incite <inciteful speech>.

incitement, *n.* **1.** The act or an instance of provoking, urging on, or stirring up. **2.** The act of persuading another person to commit a crime; SOLICITATION (2).—**inciteful,** *adj.*

inciter. A person who incites another to commit a crime; an aider or abettor.

included offense. See *lesser included offense* under OFFENSE.

inclusionary-approach rule. The principle that evidence of a prior crime, wrong, or act is admissible for any purpose other than to show a defendant's criminal propensity as long as it is relevant to some disputed issue and its probative value outweighs its prejudicial effect.

incommunicado (in-kə-myoo-ni-**kah**-doh), *adj.* [Spanish] **1.** Without any means of communication. **2.** (Of a prisoner) having the right to communicate only with a few designated people.

incommutable (in-kə-**myoot**-ə-bəl), *adj.* (Of an offense) not capable of being commuted. See COMMUTATION.

incompetency, *n.* Lack of legal ability in some respect, esp. to stand trial or to testify <once the defense lawyer established her client's incompetency, the client did not have to stand trial>.—Also termed *incompetence; mental incompetence.*—**incompetent,** *adj.* Cf. INCAPACITY.

incompetency hearing. See PATE HEARING.

incompetent, *adj.* **1.** (Of a witness) unqualified to testify. **2.** (Of evidence) inadmissible.

incompetent evidence. See EVIDENCE.

inconsistent defense. See DEFENSE.

inconsistent presumption. See *conflicting presumption* under PRESUMPTION.

incorrigibility (in-kor-ə-jə-**bil**-ə-tee *or* in-kahr-). Serious or persistent misbehavior by a child, making reformation by parental control impossible or unlikely. Cf. JUVENILE DELINQUENCY.

incorrigible (in-**kor**-ə-jə-bəl *or* in-**kahr**-), *adj*. Incapable of being reformed; delinquent.

incorrigible child. See CHILD.

incriminate (in-**krim**-ə-nayt), *vb*. **1.** To charge (someone) with a crime <the witness incriminated the murder suspect>. **2.** To identify (oneself or another) as being involved in the commission of a crime or other wrongdoing <the defendant incriminated an accomplice>.—Also termed *criminate*.—**incriminatory,** *adj*.

incriminating, *adj*. Demonstrating or indicating involvement in criminal activity <incriminating evidence>.

incriminating admission. See ADMISSION.

incriminating circumstance. See CIRCUMSTANCE.

incriminating evidence. See EVIDENCE.

incriminating statement. See STATEMENT.

incrimination. 1. The act of charging someone with a crime. **2.** The act of involving someone in a crime.—Also termed *crimination*. See SELF-INCRIMINATION.

inculpate (in-**kəl**-payt *or* **in**-kəl-payt), *vb.* **1.** To accuse. **2.** To implicate (oneself or another) in a crime or other wrongdoing; INCRIMINATE.— **inculpation,** *n.*—**inculpatory** (in-**kəl**-pə-toree), *adj.*

inculpatory evidence. See EVIDENCE.

indecency, *n.* The state or condition of being outrageously offensive, esp. in a vulgar or sexual way. • Unlike obscene material, indecent speech is protected under the First Amendment.—**indecent,** *adj.* Cf. OBSCENITY.

indecent advertising. *Archaic.* In some jurisdictions, the statutory offense of advertising the sale of abortifacients and (formerly) contraceptives.

indecent assault. See *sexual assault* (2) under ASSAULT.

indecent exhibition. The act of publicly displaying or offering for sale something (such as a photograph or book) that is outrageously offensive, esp. in a vulgar or sexual way.

indecent exposure. An offensive display of one's body in public, esp. of the genitals. Cf. LEWDNESS; OBSCENITY.

indecent liberties. Improper behavior toward a child, esp. of a sexual nature.

indefinite detainee. See NONREMOVABLE INMATE.

indefinite sentence. See *indeterminate sentence* under SENTENCE.

indefinite sentencing. See INDETERMINATE SENTENCING.

independent counsel. See COUNSEL.

independent-source rule. The rule providing—as an exception to the fruit-of-the-poisonous-tree doctrine—that evidence obtained by illegal means may nonetheless be admissible if that evidence is also obtained by legal means unrelated to the original illegal conduct. See FRUIT-OF-THE-POISONOUS-TREE DOCTRINE. Cf. INEVITABLE-DISCOVERY RULE.

indeterminate conditional release. A release from prison granted once the prisoner fulfills certain conditions. • The release can be revoked if the prisoner breaches other conditions.

indeterminate sentence. See SENTENCE.

indeterminate sentencing. The practice of not imposing a definite term of confinement, but instead prescribing a range for the minimum and maximum term, leaving the precise term to be fixed in some other way, usu. based on the prisoner's conduct and apparent rehabilitation while incarcerated.—Also termed *indefinite sentencing*. See *indeterminate sentence* under SENTENCE.

index crime. See *index offense* under OFFENSE.

index offense. See OFFENSE.

indict (in-**dɪt**), *vb.* To charge (a person) with a crime by formal legal process, esp. by grand-jury presentation.

indictable misdemeanor. See *serious misdemeanor* under MISDEMEANOR.

indictable offense. See OFFENSE.

indictee (in-dɪ-**tee**). A person who has been indicted; one officially charged with a crime.

indictment (in-**dɪt**-mənt), *n.* **1.** The formal written accusation of a crime, made by a grand jury and presented to a court for prosecution against the accused person. **2.** The act or process of preparing or bringing forward such a formal written accusation. Cf. INFORMATION; PRESENTMENT (2).

barebones indictment. An indictment that cites only the language of the statute allegedly violated; an indictment that does not provide a factual statement.

duplicitous indictment (d[y]oo-**plis**-ə-təs). **1.** An indictment containing two or more offenses in the same count. **2.** An indictment charging the same offense in more than one count.

joint indictment. An indictment that charges two or more people with an offense.

indictor (in-**dɪt**-ər *or* in-**dɪ**-tor). A person who causes another to be indicted.

indigency, *n.* The state or condition of a person who lacks the means of subsistence; extreme hardship or neediness; poverty. ● For purposes of the Sixth Amendment right to appointed counsel, *indigency* refers to a defendant's inability to afford an attorney.—Also termed *indigence*.—**indigent,** *adj.* & *n.*

indigent defendant. A person who is too poor to hire a lawyer and who, upon indictment, becomes eligible to receive aid from a court-appointed attorney and a waiver of court costs. See IN FORMA PAUPERIS.

indirect attack. See COLLATERAL ATTACK.

indirect confession. See CONFESSION.

indirect contempt. See CONTEMPT.

indirect evidence. See *circumstantial evidence* (1) under EVIDENCE.

indispensable-element test. A common-law test for the crime of attempt, based on whether the defendant acquires control over anything that is essential to the crime. ● Under this test, for example, a person commits a crime by buying the explosives with which to detonate a bomb. See ATTEMPT.

indispensable evidence. See EVIDENCE.

inducement, *n.* **1.** The act or process of enticing or persuading another person to take a certain course of action. **2.** An enticement or urging of another person to commit a crime. **3.** The preliminary statement in a pleading; esp., in a criminal indictment, a statement of preliminary facts necessary to show the criminal character of the alleged offense. Cf. INNUENDO (2).—**induce,** *vb.*

industrial espionage. See ESPIONAGE.

ineffective assistance of counsel. See ASSISTANCE OF COUNSEL.

inevitable-discovery rule. The rule providing—as an exception to the fruit-of-the-poisonous-tree doctrine—that evidence obtained by illegal means may nonetheless be admissible if the prosecution can show that the evidence would eventually have been legally obtained anyway. See FRUIT-OF-THE-POISONOUS-TREE DOCTRINE. Cf. INDEPENDENT-SOURCE RULE.

in extremis (in ek-**stree**-mis). [Latin "in extremity"] **1.** In extreme circumstances. **2.** Near the point of death; on one's deathbed. ● Unlike *in articulo mortis*, the phrase *in extremis* does not always mean at the point of death. Cf. *in articulo mortis*.

infamous (**in**-fə-məs), *adj*. **1.** (Of a person) having a bad reputation. **2.** (Of conduct) that is punishable by imprisonment.

infamous crime. See CRIME.

infamous punishment. See PUNISHMENT.

infamy (**in**-fə-mee), *n*. **1.** Disgraceful repute. **2.** The loss of reputation or position resulting from a person's being convicted of an infamous crime. See *infamous crime* under CRIME.

infancy. 1. See MINORITY. **2.** Early childhood.

> *natural infancy.* At common law, the period ending at age seven, during which a child was presumed to be without criminal capacity.

infant, *n*. **1.** A newborn baby. **2.** See MINOR.

infanticide (in-**fant**-ə-sɪd). **1.** The act of killing a newborn child, esp. by the parents or with their consent. ● In archaic usage, the word referred also to the killing of an unborn child.—Also termed *child-slaying*; *neonaticide*. Cf. FETICIDE. **2.** The practice of killing newborn children. **3.** One who kills a newborn child.

infect, *vb*. **1.** To contaminate <the virus infected the entire network>. **2.** To taint with crime <one part of the city has long been infected with illegal drug-dealing>. **3.** To make (a ship or cargo) liable in the seizure of contraband, which is only a part of its cargo <claiming that the single package of marijuana had infected the ship, the Coast Guard seized the entire vessel>.—**infection,** *n*.—**infectious,** *adj*.

inferential fact. See FACT.

341

infidelity. Unfaithfulness to an obligation; esp., marital unfaithfulness. Cf. ADULTERY.

infirmative, *adj. Rare.* (Of evidence) tending to weaken or invalidate a criminal accusation <an infirmative fact>. Cf. CRIMINATIVE.

infirmative hypothesis. An approach to a criminal case in which the defendant's innocence is assumed, and incriminating evidence is explained in a manner consistent with that assumption.

in flagrante delicto (in flə-**gran**-tee də-**lik**-toh). [Latin "while the crime is ablaze"] In the very act of committing a crime or other wrong; red-handed <the sheriff caught them *in flagrante delicto*>.

informal immunity. See *pocket immunity* under IMMUNITY (2).

informal proceeding. See PROCEEDING.

informant. One who informs against another; esp., one who confidentially supplies information to the police about a crime, sometimes in exchange for a reward or special treatment.— Also termed *informer; feigned accomplice.*

informant's privilege. See PRIVILEGE (3).

in forma pauperis (in **for**-mə **paw**-pə-ris). [Latin "in the manner of a pauper"] In the manner of an indigent who is permitted to disregard filing fees and court costs <when suing, a poor person is generally entitled to proceed *in forma pauperis*>.—Abbr. *i.f.p.*

in forma pauperis **affidavit.** See *poverty affidavit* under AFFIDAVIT.

information. A formal criminal charge made by a prosecutor without a grand-jury indictment. • The information is used to prosecute misdemeanors in most states, and about half the states allow its use in felony prosecutions as well.—Also termed *bill of information.* Cf. INDICTMENT.

informer. 1. See INFORMANT. **2.** A private citizen who brings a penal action to recover a penalty. • Under some statutes, a private citizen is required to sue the offender for a penalty before any criminal liability can attach.— Also termed *common informer.* See COMMON INFORMER.

informer's privilege. See *informant's privilege* under PRIVILEGE (3).

infraction, *n.* A violation, usu. of a rule or local ordinance andusu. not punishable by incarceration. **infract,** *vb.* See VIOLATION (1).

civil infraction. An act or omission that, though not a crime, is prohibited by law and is punishable. ● In some states, many traffic violations are classified as civil infractions.

infringement, *n.* An act that interferes with one of the exclusive rights of a patent, copyright, or trademark owner.—**infringe,** *vb.*

criminal infringement. The statutory criminal offense of either (1) willfully infringing a copyright to obtain a commercial advantage or financial gain (17 USCA § 506; 18 USCA § 2319), or (2) trafficking in goods or services that bear a counterfeit mark (18 USCA § 2320). ● Under the second category, the law imposes criminal penalties if the counterfeit mark is (1) identical with, or substantially indistinguishable from, a mark registered on the Principal Register of the U.S. Patent and Trademark Office, and (2) likely to confuse or deceive the public.

in invitum (in in-**vi**-təm). [Latin] Against an unwilling person <the nonparty appealed after being compelled to participate in the proceedings *in invitum*>.

initial appearance. See APPEARANCE.

initiation of charges. The first report to the proper military authority of an alleged commission of an offense by a person subject to

the Uniform Code of Military Justice. Cf. PRE-
FERRING OF CHARGES.

injunction (in-**jəngk**-shən), *n*. A court order
commanding or preventing an action. ● To get
an injunction, the complainant must show that
there is no plain, adequate, and complete remedy at law and that an irreparable injury will
result unless the relief is granted.—Also
termed *writ of injunction*.

injury, *n*. **1.** The violation of another's legal
right, for which the law provides a remedy; a
wrong or injustice. See WRONG. **2.** Harm or
damage.—**injure,** *vb*.—**injurious,** *adj*.

bodily injury. Physical damage to a person's body.—Also termed *physical injury*.
See *serious bodily injury*.

civil injury. Physical harm or property
damage caused by breach of a contract or by
a criminal offense redressable through a civil action.

direct injury. **1.** An injury resulting directly from violation of a legal right. **2.** An
injury resulting directly from a particular
cause, without any intervening causes.

malicious injury. **1.** An injury resulting
from a willful act committed with knowledge
that it is likely to injure another or with

reckless disregard of the consequences. **2.** See MALICIOUS MISCHIEF.

physical injury. See *bodily injury.*

serious bodily injury. Serious physical impairment of the human body; esp., bodily injury that creates a substantial risk of death or that causes serious, permanent disfigurement or protracted loss or impairment of the function of any body part or organ. Model Penal Code § 210.0(3). • Typically, the fact-finder must decide in any given case whether the injury meets this general standard.—Also termed *serious bodily harm*; *grievous bodily harm*; *great bodily injury.*

inmate. A person confined in a prison, hospital, or other institution.

innocence, *n.* The absence of guilt; esp., freedom from guilt for a particular offense. Cf. GUILT.

actual innocence. The absence of facts that are prerequisites for the sentence given to a defendant. • In death-penalty cases, actual innocence is an exception to the cause-and-prejudice rule, and can result in a successful challenge to the death sentence on the basis of a defense that was not presented to the trial court. The prisoner must show by clear and convincing evidence that, but for constitutional error in the trial court, no reasonable judge or juror would find the defendant eligible for the death penalty. See *Sawyer v. Whitley*, 505 U.S. 333, 112 S.Ct. 2514 (1992). Cf. CAUSE-AND-PREJUDICE RULE.

legal innocence. The absence of one or more procedural or legal bases to support the sentence given to a defendant. • In the context of a petition for writ of habeas corpus or other attack on the sentence, legal innocence is often contrasted with actual innocence. Actual innocence, which focuses on the facts underlying the sentence, can sometimes be used to obtain relief from the death penalty based on trial-court errors that were not objected to at trial, even if the petitioner cannot meet the elements of the cause-and-prejudice rule. But legal innocence, which focuses on the applicable law and procedure, is not as readily available. Inadvertence or a poor trial strategy resulting in the defendant's failure to assert an established legal principle will not ordinarily be sufficient to satisfy the cause-and-prejudice rule or to establish the right to an exception from that rule. See CAUSE-AND-PREJUDICE RULE.

innocent, *adj.* Free from guilt; free from legal fault. Cf. NOT GUILTY (2).

innocent agent. See AGENT.

innocent homicide. See HOMICIDE.

innuendo (in-yoo-**en**-doh). [Latin "by hinting"] **1.** An oblique remark or indirect suggestion, usu. of a derogatory nature. **2.** An explanatory word or passage inserted parenthetically into a legal document. • In criminal law, an innuendo takes the form of a statement in an indictment showing the application or meaning of matter previously expressed, the meaning of which would not otherwise be clear. Cf. INDUCEMENT (3).

in-presence rule. The principle that a police officer may make a warrantless arrest of a person who commits a misdemeanor offense not only in the officer's actual presence but also within the officer's immediate vicinity.

inquest. 1. An inquiry by a coroner or medical examiner, sometimes with the aid of a jury, into the manner of death of a person who has died under suspicious circumstances, or who has died in prison.—Also termed *coroner's inquest*; *inquisition after death*. **2.** An inquiry into a certain matter by a jury empaneled for that purpose. **3.** The finding of such a specially empaneled jury. Cf. INQUISITION.

grand inquest. An impeachment proceeding.

inquest jury. See JURY.

inquisition. 1. The record of the finding of the jury sworn by the coroner to inquire into a person's death. **2.** A judicial inquiry, esp. in a derogatory sense. **3.** A persistent, grueling examination conducted without regard for the examinee's dignity or civil rights. Cf. INQUEST.

inquisition after death. See INQUEST (1).

inquisitor. 1. An officer who examines and inquires, such as a coroner or sheriff. **2.** A person who inquires; esp., one who examines another in a harsh or hostile manner.

inquisitorial system. A system of proof-taking used in civil law, whereby the judge conducts the trial, determines what questions to ask, and defines the scope and the extent of the inquiry. • This system prevails in most of continental Europe, in Japan, and in Central and South America. Cf. ADVERSARY SYSTEM.

insane, *adj.* Mentally deranged; suffering from one or more delusions or false beliefs that (1) have no foundation in reason or reality, (2) are not credible to any reasonable person of sound mind, and (3) cannot be overcome in a sufferer's mind by any amount of evidence or argument. See INSANITY.

insane asylum. See ASYLUM (3).

insane delusion. An irrational, persistent belief in an imaginary state of facts that deprives a person of the capacity to undertake acts of legal consequence, such as making a will.

insanity, *n.* Any mental disorder severe enough that it prevents a person from having legal capacity and excuses the person from criminal or civil responsibility. ● Insanity is a legal, not a medical, standard.—Also termed *legal insanity*; *lunacy.* Cf. *diminished capacity* under CAPACITY; SANITY.

> **emotional insanity.** Insanity produced by a violent excitement of the emotions or passions, although reasoning faculties may remain unimpaired; a passion that for a period creates complete derangement of intellect. ● Emotional insanity is sometimes described as an irresistible impulse to do an act. See IRRESISTIBLE-IMPULSE TEST.

> **temporary insanity.** Insanity that exists only at the time of a criminal act.

insanity defense. An affirmative defense alleging that a mental disorder caused the accused to commit the crime. ● Unlike other defenses, a successful insanity defense results not in acquittal but instead in a special verdict ("not guilty by reason of insanity") that usu. leads to the defendant's commitment to a mental institution.—Also termed *insanity plea*. See MCNAGHTEN RULES; SUBSTANTIAL-CAPACITY TEST; IRRESISTIBLE-IMPULSE TEST; DURHAM RULE; APPRECIATION TEST.

> **black-rage insanity defense.** An insanity defense based on an African-American defendant's hatred of white people. • This defense was first used in the mid-1990s.

Insanity Defense Reform Act of 1984 test. See APPRECIATION TEST.

insanity plea. See INSANITY DEFENSE.

insider trading. The use of material, nonpublic information in trading the shares of a company by a corporate insider or other person who owes a fiduciary duty to the company. • This is the classic definition. The Supreme Court has also approved a broader definition, known as the "misappropriation theory": the deceitful acquisition and misuse of information that properly belongs to persons to whom one owes a duty. Thus, under the misappropriation theory, it is insider trading for a lawyer to trade in the stock of XYZ Corp. after learning that a client of the lawyer's firm is planning a takeover of XYZ. But under the classic definition, that is not insider trading because the lawyer owed no duty to XYZ itself.—Also termed *insider dealing*.

inspection search. See *administrative search* under SEARCH.

instantaneous crime. See CRIME.

instant case. See *case at bar* under CASE.

instruct, *vb*. See CHARGE (2).

instructed verdict. See *directed verdict* under VERDICT.

instruction. See JURY INSTRUCTION.

instrumental crime. See CRIME.

instrument of crime. See CRIMINAL INSTRUMENT.

insufficient evidence. See EVIDENCE.

insurance fraud. See FRAUD.

intake, *n*. **1.** The official screening of a juvenile charged with an offense to determine where to place the juvenile pending formal adjudication or informal disposition. **2.** The body of officers who conduct this screening.

intend, *vb.* **1.** To have in mind a fixed purpose to reach a desired objective; to have as one's purpose <Daniel intended to become a lawyer>. **2.** To contemplate that the usual consequences of one's act will probably or necessarily follow from the act, whether or not those consequences are desired for their own sake <although he activated the theater's fire alarm only on a dare, the jury found that Wilbur intended to cause a panic>.

intent. The state of mind accompanying an act, esp. a forbidden act. ● While motive is the inducement to do some act, intent is the mental resolution or determination to do it. When the intent to do an act that violates the law exists, motive becomes immaterial. Cf. MOTIVE; SCIENTER.

> *constructive intent.* A legal principle that actual intent will be presumed when an act leading to the result could have been reasonably expected to cause that result.

> *criminal intent.* **1.** See MENS REA. **2.** An intent to commit an actus reus without any justification, excuse, or other defense. **3.** See *specific intent.*—Also termed *felonious intent.*

> *felonious intent.* See *criminal intent.*

general intent. The state of mind required for the commission of certain common-law crimes not requiring a specific intent or not imposing strict liability. • General intent usu. takes the form of recklessness (involving actual awareness of a risk and the culpable taking of that risk) or negligence (involving blameworthy inadvertence).—Also termed *general criminal intent*; *general mens rea*.

immediate intent. The intent relating to a wrongful act; the part of the total intent coincident with the wrongful act itself.

implied intent. A person's state of mind that can be inferred from speech or conduct, or from language used in an instrument to which the person is a party.

intent to kill. An intent to cause the death of another; esp., a state of mind that, if found to exist during an assault, can serve as the basis for an aggravated-assault charge.

manifest intent. Intent that is apparent or obvious based on the available circumstantial evidence, even if direct evidence of intent is not available.

specific intent. The intent to accomplish the precise criminal act that one is later charged with. • At common law, the specific-intent crimes were robbery, assault, larceny, burglary, forgery, false pretenses, embezzlement, attempt, solicitation, and conspiracy.—Also termed *criminal intent*. See SPECIFIC-INTENT DEFENSE.

transferred intent. Intent that has been shifted from the originally intended wrongful act to the wrongful act actually committed. • For example, if a person intends to kill one person but kills another, the intent may be transferred to the actual act. See TRANSFERRED-INTENT DOCTRINE.

ulterior intent. The intent that passes beyond a wrongful act and relates to the objective for the sake of which the act is done; MOTIVE. • For example, a thief's immediate intent may be to steal another's money, but the ulterior intent may be to buy food with that money.

intentional, *adj.* Done with the aim of carrying out the act.

intentional manslaughter. See *voluntary manslaughter* under MANSLAUGHTER.

intentional wrong. See WRONG.

intent to kill. See INTENT.

intercept, *vb.* To covertly receive or listen to (a communication). ● The term usu. refers to covert reception by a law-enforcement agency. See WIRETAPPING.

interested witness. See WITNESS.

interim bond. See BOND.

interim order. See ORDER.

interlocking confessions. See CONFESSION.

interlocutory appeal. See APPEAL.

interlocutory decision. See *interlocutory order* under ORDER.

interlocutory order. See ORDER.

intermediate order. See *interlocutory order* under ORDER.

intermediate scrutiny. A constitutional standard lying between the extremes of rational-basis review and strict scrutiny. ● Under the standard, if a statute contains a quasi-suspect classification (such as gender or legitimacy), the classification must be substantially related to the achievement of an important governmental objective.—Also termed *middle-level* *scrutiny*; *mid-level scrutiny*; *heightened scrutiny*. Cf. STRICT SCRUTINY; RATIONAL-BASIS TEST.

intermittent sentence. See SENTENCE.

international crime. A crime against international law, occurring when three conditions are satisfied: (1) the criminal norm must derive either from a treaty concluded under international law or from customary international law, and must have direct binding force on individuals without intermediate provisions of municipal law, (2) the provision must be made for the prosecution of acts penalized by international law in accordance with the principle of universal jurisdiction, so that the international character of the crime might show in the mode of prosecution itself (e.g., before the International Criminal Court), and (3) a treaty establishing criminal liability for the act must bind the great majority of countries.

International Criminal Court. A court that was established by the U.N. Security Council to adjudicate international crimes such as terrorism. • The court was repeatedly proposed and discussed throughout the 20th century, but was established only in 1998. In the absence of any international criminal code, the court applies general principles of international criminal law.—Abbr. ICC.

International Criminal Police Organization. An international law-enforcement group founded in 1923 and headquartered in Lyons, France. ● The organization gathers and shares information on transnational criminals with more than 180 member nations.—Also termed *Interpol*.

international extradition. See EXTRADITION.

Interpol (**in**-tər-pohl). See INTERNATIONAL CRIMINAL POLICE ORGANIZATION.

interpreted testimony. See TESTIMONY.

interrogatee (in-ter-ə-gə-**tee**). A person who is interrogated.—Also termed *interrogee* (in-ter-ə-**gee**).

interrogation, *n.* The formal or systematic questioning of a person; esp., intensive questioning by the police, usu. of a person arrested for or suspected of committing a crime. ● The Supreme Court has held that, for purposes of the Fifth Amendment right against self-incrimination, interrogation includes not only express questioning but also words or actions that the police should know are reasonably likely to elicit an incriminating response. *Rhode Island v. Innis*, 446 U.S. 291, 100 S.Ct. 1082 (1980).—**interrogate,** *vb.*—**interrogative,** *adj.*

358

custodial interrogation. Intense police questioning of a detained person. • Miranda warnings must be given before a custodial interrogation.

investigatory interrogation. Routine, non-accusatory questioning by the police of a person who is not in custody.

noncustodial interrogation. Police questioning of a suspect who has not been detained and can leave at will. • Miranda warnings are usu. not given before a noncustodial interrogation.

interrogative question. In civil-law jurisdictions, a question asked of a witness to elicit inadmissible evidence relating to the crime at issue in the case.

interrogator (in-**ter**-ə-gay-tər). One who poses questions to another.

interrogee. See INTERROGATEE.

Interstate Agreement on Detainers Act. A law, originally enacted in 1956, in which the federal government, certain states, and the District of Columbia agree that a state may obtain custody of a prisoner for trial even though the prisoner is already incarcerated in another state. • Under the Act, if a prisoner makes a written request for disposition of the charges in the second state, the second state must try the prisoner within 180 days of the request. 18 USCA App. Articles I–IX. See UNIFORM MANDATORY DISPOSITION OF DETAINERS ACT.

interstate extradition. See EXTRADITION.

interstate rendition. See RENDITION.

intervening act. See *intervening cause* under CAUSE (1).

intervening cause. See CAUSE (1).

intervening force. See *intervening cause* under CAUSE (1).

intimidation, *n.* Unlawful coercion; extortion.—**intimidate,** *vb.*—**intimidatory,** *adj.*—**intimidator,** *n.*

intoxicant, *n.* A substance (esp. liquor) that deprives a person of the ordinary use of the senses or of reason.

intoxication, *n.* A diminished ability to act with full mental and physical capabilities because of alcohol or drug consumption; drunkenness. See Model Penal Code § 2.08.—**intoxicate,** *vb.*

culpable intoxication. See *voluntary intoxication.*

involuntary intoxication. The ingestion of alcohol or drugs against one's will or without one's knowledge. ● Involuntary intoxication is an affirmative defense to a criminal or negligence charge.

pathological intoxication. An extremely exaggerated response to an intoxicant. ● This may be treated as involuntary intoxication if it is unforeseeable.

public intoxication. The appearance of a person who is under the influence of drugs or alcohol in a place open to the general public. ● In most American jurisdictions, public intoxication is considered a misdemeanor, and in some states, alcoholism is a defense if the offender agrees to attend a treatment program.

self-induced intoxication. See *voluntary intoxication.*

voluntary intoxication. A willing ingestion of alcohol or drugs to the point of impairment done with the knowledge that one's physical and mental capabilities would be impaired. ● Voluntary intoxication is not a defense to a general-intent crime, but may be admitted to refute the existence of a particular state of mind for a specific-intent crime.—Also termed *culpable intoxication*; *self-induced intoxication*.

intoxilyzer (in-**tok**-si-lI-zər). See BREATHALYZER.

intoximeter (in-tok-**sim**-ə-tər). See BREATHALYZER.

intracorporate conspiracy. See CONSPIRACY.

intra-enterprise conspiracy. See CONSPIRACY.

intrinsic evidence. See EVIDENCE.

intrinsic fraud. See FRAUD.

inventory search. See SEARCH.

investigate, *vb.* **1.** To inquire into (a matter) systematically; to make (a suspect) the subject of a criminal inquiry <the police investigated the suspect's involvement in the murder>. **2.** To make an official inquiry <after the judge dismissed the case, the police refused to investigate further>.

investigating magistrate. See MAGISTRATE.

investigative detention. See DETENTION.

investigative grand jury. See GRAND JURY.

investigatory detention. See STOP AND FRISK.

investigatory grand jury. See *investigative grand jury* under GRAND JURY.

investigatory interrogation. See INTERROGATION.

investigatory stop. See STOP AND FRISK.

invited error. See ERROR.

involuntary, *adj.* Not resulting from a free and unrestrained choice; not subject to control by the will.—**involuntariness,** *n.*

involuntary confession. See CONFESSION.

involuntary conversion. See CONVERSION.

involuntary euthanasia. See EUTHANASIA.

involuntary intoxication. See INTOXICATION.

involuntary manslaughter. See MANSLAUGHTER.

involuntary servitude. See SERVITUDE.

irrebuttable presumption. See *conclusive presumption* under PRESUMPTION.

irrelevant (i-**rel**-ə-vənt), *adj.* (Of evidence) having no probative value; not tending to prove or disprove a matter in issue.—**irrelevance,** *n.* Cf. IMMATERIAL.

irresistible-impulse test. A test for insanity, holding that a person is not criminally responsible for an act if mental disease prevented that person from controlling potentially criminal conduct. • The few jurisdictions that have adopted this test have combined it with the *McNaghten* rules.—Also termed *control test*; *volitional test.* See INSANITY DEFENSE; MCNAGHTEN RULES.

J

J. *abbr.* **1.** JUDGE. **2.** JUSTICE (2). **3.** JUDGMENT.

***Jackson–Denno* hearing.** A court proceeding held outside the jury's presence, to determine whether the defendant's confession was voluntary and therefore admissible as evidence. *Jackson v. Denno*, 378 U.S. 368, 84 S.Ct. 1774 (1964).—Also termed *Jackson v. Denno hearing*.

***Jackson* standard.** The principle that the standard of review on appeal—when a criminal defendant claims that there is insufficient evidence to support the conviction—is to determine whether, after considering the evidence in the light most favorable to the prosecution, any rational trier of fact could have found the essential elements of the crime beyond a reasonable doubt. *Jackson v. Virginia*, 443 U.S. 307, 99 S.Ct. 2781 (1979).

***Jackson v. Denno* hearing.** See JACKSON–DENNO HEARING.

jail, *n.* A place where persons awaiting trial or those convicted of misdemeanors are confined.—Also spelled (esp. in BrE) *gaol.*—Also termed *holding cell*; *lockup*; *jailhouse*; *house of detention*; *community correctional center.*—**jail,** *vb.* Cf. PRISON.

jail credit. Time spent by a criminal defendant in confinement awaiting trial. ● This time is usu. deducted from the defendant's final sentence (if convicted).

jail delivery. 1. An escape by several prisoners from a jail. **2.** *Archaic.* A clearing procedure by which all prisoners at a given jail are tried for the offenses that they are accused of having committed. **3.** *Archaic.* The commission issued to judges of assize, directing them to clear a jail by trying—and either acquitting or condemning—all the inmates. **4.** *Archaic.* The court charged with the trial of all ordinary criminal cases.

> ***general jail delivery.*** Collectively, acquittals in high numbers as a result of either lax or reckless administration of the law or defects in the law.

jailer. A keeper, guard, or warden of a prison or jail.—Also spelled (esp. in BrE) *gaoler*.

jailhouse. See JAIL.

jailhouse lawyer. A prison inmate who seeks release through legal procedures or who gives legal advice to other inmates.—Also termed *guardhouse lawyer*.

jail liberties. Bounds within which a jail or prison lies and throughout which certain prisoners are allowed to move freely, usu. after giving bond for the liberties. • The bounds are considered an extension of the prison walls. Historically, jail liberties were given in England to those imprisoned for debt. The prisoners were allowed to move freely within the city in which the prison was located.—Also spelled *gaol liberties*.—Also termed *jail limits*.

Jamaican switch. An illegal scheme whereby one conspirator convinces the victim of a need for help in handling a large sum of money, usu. by claiming to have found the money or by claiming to be an unsophisticated foreigner, and promises to share part of the money with the victim or asks the victim for help in finding a suitable charity to donate to, at which time the other conspirator appears and promises to assist if both the victim and first conspirator provide good-faith money, the intent being for the two conspirators to leave with all the money, including the victim's.

***James* hearing.** A court proceeding held to determine whether the out-of-court statements of a coconspirator should be admitted into evidence, by analyzing whether there was a conspiracy, whether the declarant and the defendant were part of the conspiracy, and whether the statement was made in furtherance of the conspiracy. *United States v. James,*

590 F.2d 575 (5th Cir. 1979); Fed. R. Evid. 801(d)(2)(E).

Jane Doe. A fictitious name for a female party to a legal proceeding, used because the party's true identity is unknown or because her real name is being withheld.—Also termed *Jane Roe*; *Mary Major*. Cf. JOHN DOE.

jaywalking, *n.* The act or instance of crossing a street without heeding traffic regulations, as by crossing between intersections or at a place other than a crosswalk.—**jaywalk,** *vb.*

Jedburgh justice (jed-bər-ə). See JUSTICE (1).

Jeddart justice (jed-ərt). See *Jedburgh justice* under JUSTICE (1).

Jedwood justice (jed-wəd). See *Jedburgh justice* under JUSTICE (1).

Jencks **material.** A prosecution witness's written or recorded pretrial statement that a criminal defendant, upon filing a motion after the witness has testified, is entitled to have in preparing to cross-examine the witness. • The defense may use a statement of this kind for impeachment purposes. *Jencks v. United States*, 353 U.S. 657, 77 S.Ct. 1007 (1957); Jencks Act, 18 USCA § 3500. Cf. BRADY MATERIAL.

jeopardy. The risk of conviction and punishment that a criminal defendant faces at trial. • Jeopardy attaches in a jury trial when the jury is empaneled, and in a bench trial when the first witness is sworn.—Also termed *legal jeopardy*. See DOUBLE JEOPARDY.

Jewell **instruction** (**joo**-wəl). A court's instruction to the jury that the defendant can be found to have the requisite criminal mental state despite being deliberately ignorant of some of the facts surrounding the crime. • If a defendant claims ignorance of some fact essential to the crime, such as not knowing that a particular bag contained drugs, but the surrounding circumstances would put a reasonable person on notice that there was a high probability of illegality, as when the defendant has taken the bag from a known drug-dealer and has noticed the smell of marijuana coming from the bag, then the court may instruct the jury that it is entitled to infer the defendant's guilty knowledge if the defendant deliberately avoided knowledge of the critical facts. *United States v. Jewell*, 532 F.2d 697 (9th Cir. 1976).—Also termed *deliberate-indifference instruction*.

JJ. *abbr*. **1.** Judges. **2.** Justices.

John Doe. A fictitious name used in a legal proceeding to designate a person whose identity is unknown, to protect a person's known identity, or to indicate that a true defendant does not exist. Cf. JANE DOE; RICHARD ROE.

John Doe summons. See SUMMONS.

John Doe warrant. See WARRANT.

joinder of offenses. The charging of an accused with two or more crimes as multiple counts in a single indictment or information. ● Unless later severed, joined offenses are tried together at a single trial. Fed. R. Crim. P. 8(a).

joint defendant. See CODEFENDANT.

joint-defense privilege. See PRIVILEGE (3).

joint enterprise. An undertaking by two or more persons who set out to commit an offense they have conspired to commit. —Also termed *common enterprise*. See CONSPIRACY.

joint indictment. See INDICTMENT.

joint offense. See OFFENSE.

joint trial. See TRIAL.

journalist's privilege. See PRIVILEGE (3).

joyriding, *n.* The illegal driving of someone else's automobile without permission, but with no intent to deprive the owner of it permanently. ● Under the Model Penal Code, the offender's reasonable belief that the owner would have consented is an affirmative defense. See Model Penal Code § 223.9.—Also termed *unauthorized use of a vehicle.*—**joyride,** *vb.*—**joyrider,** *n.*

J.P. *abbr.* JUSTICE OF THE PEACE.

J.P. court. See JUSTICE COURT.

judge, *n.* A public official appointed or elected to hear and decide legal matters in court.— Abbr. J. (and, in plural, JJ.).

associate judge. An appellate judge who is neither a chief judge nor a presiding judge.

chief judge. The judge who presides over the sessions and deliberations of a court, while also overseeing the administration of the court.—Abbr. C.J.

circuit judge. A judge who sits on a circuit court; esp., a federal judge who sits on a U.S. court of appeals.—Abbr. C.J.

city judge. See *municipal judge.*

county judge. A local judge having criminal or civil jurisdiction, or sometimes both, within a county.

district judge. A judge in a federal or state judicial district.—Abbr. D.J.

duty judge. A judge responsible for setting an arrestee's bail, usu. by telephone or videoconference.

hanging judge. A judge who is harsh with defendants, esp. those accused of capital crimes, and sometimes corruptly so.

judge pro tempore. See *visiting judge.*

lay judge. A judge who is not a lawyer.

municipal judge. A local judge having criminal or civil jurisdiction, or sometimes both, within a city.—Also termed *city judge.*

presiding judge. **1.** A judge in charge of a particular court or judicial district; esp., the senior active judge on a three-member panel that hears and decides cases. **2.** A chief judge.—Abbr. P.J.—Also termed *president judge.*

senior judge. **1.** The judge who has served for the longest time on a given court. **2.** A federal or state judge who qualifies for senior status and chooses this status over retirement.

special judge. A judge appointed or selected to sit—usu. in a specific case—in the absence or disqualification of the regular judge or otherwise as provided by statute.

temporary judge. See *visiting judge.*

trial judge. The judge before whom a case is tried. • This term is used most commonly on appeal from the judge's rulings.

visiting judge. A judge appointed by the presiding judge of an administrative region to sit temporarily on a given court, usu. in the regular judge's absence.—Also termed *temporary judge*; *judge pro tempore.*

judge-made law. 1. The law established by judicial precedent rather than by statute. See COMMON LAW. **2.** The law that results when judges construe statutes contrary to legislative intent.—Also termed (in sense 2) *judicial legislation*; *bench legislation.*

judgement. See JUDGMENT.

judge *pro tempore* (proh **tem**-pə-ree). See *visiting judge* under JUDGE.

judge trial. See *bench trial* under TRIAL.

judgment. A court's final determination of the rights and obligations of the parties in a case. • The term *judgment* includes a decree and any order from which an appeal lies.—

JUDGMENT

Abbr. J.—Also spelled (esp. in BrE) *judgement*. Cf. RULING; OPINION.

deferred judgment. A judgment placing a convicted defendant on probation, the successful completion of which will prevent entry of the underlying judgment of conviction. • This type of probation is common with minor traffic offenses.—Also termed *deferred adjudication*; *deferred-adjudication probation*; *deferred prosecution*; *probation before judgment*; *probation without judgment*; *pretrial intervention*; *adjudication withheld*.

judgment of acquittal. A judgment, rendered on the defendant's motion or court's own motion, that acquits the defendant of the offense charged when the evidence is insufficient. See *directed verdict* under VERDICT.

judgment of blood. See *death sentence* under SENTENCE.

judgment of conviction. The written record of a criminal judgment, consisting of the plea, the verdict or findings, the adjudication, and the sentence. Fed. R. Crim. P. 32(d)(1).

judgment of dismissal. A final determination of a case without a trial on its merits.

judgment book. See *judgment docket* under DOCKET (1).

judgment docket. See DOCKET (1).

judgment file. See *judgment docket* under DOCKET (1).

judgment of acquittal. See JUDGMENT.

judgment of blood. See *death sentence* under SENTENCE.

judgment of conviction. See JUDGMENT.

judgment of dismissal. See JUDGMENT.

judgment record. See *judgment docket* under DOCKET (1).

judicature. See JUDICIARY (3).

judicial bias. See BIAS.

judicial confession. See CONFESSION.

judicial discretion. See DISCRETION.

judicial evidence. See EVIDENCE.

judicial fact. See FACT.

judicial jurisdiction. See JURISDICTION.

judicial legislation. See LEGISLATION.

judicial oath. See OATH.

judicial opinion. See OPINION.

judicial order. See ORDER (2).

judicial privilege. See PRIVILEGE (3).

judicial proceeding. See PROCEEDING.

judicial process. See PROCESS.

judicial question. A question that is proper for determination by the courts, as opposed to a moot question or one properly decided by the executive or legislative branch. Cf. POLITICAL QUESTION.

judicial record. See DOCKET (1).

judicial review. 1. A court's power to review the actions of other branches or levels of government; esp., the courts' power to invalidate legislative and executive actions as being unconstitutional. **2.** The constitutional doctrine providing for this power. **3.** A court's review of a lower court's or an administrative body's factual or legal findings.

judicial writ. See WRIT.

judiciary (joo-**dish**-ee-er-ee *or* joo-**dish**-ə-ree), *n.* **1.** The branch of government responsible for interpreting the laws and administering justice. **2.** A system of courts. **3.** A body of judges.—Also termed (in sense 3) *judicature.*—**judiciary,** *adj.*

jump bail, *vb.* (Of an accused) to fail to appear in court at the appointed time, even after posting a bail bond and promising to appear.—Also termed *skip bail*. See BAIL-JUMPING.

jural cause. See *proximate cause* under CAUSE (1).

jurisdiction, *n.* **1.** A government's general power to exercise authority over all persons and things within its territory <New Jersey's jurisdiction>. **2.** A court's power to decide a case or issue a decree <the constitutional grant of federal-question jurisdiction>. **3.** A geographic area within which political or judicial authority may be exercised <the accused fled to another jurisdiction>. **4.** A political or judicial subdivision within such an area <other jurisdictions have decided the issue differently>.—**jurisdictional,** *adj.* Cf. VENUE.

   anomalous jurisdiction. **1.** Jurisdiction that is not granted to a court by statute, but that is inherent in the court's authority to govern lawyers and other officers of the court, such as the power to issue a preindictment order suppressing illegally seized property. **2.** An appellate court's provisional jurisdiction to review the denial of a motion to intervene in a case, so that if the court finds that the denial was correct, then its jurisdiction disappears—and it must dismiss the appeal for want of jurisdiction—because an order denying a motion to intervene is not a final, appealable order.

appellate jurisdiction. The power of a court to review and revise a lower court's decision. • For example, U.S. Const. art. III, § 2 vests appellate jurisdiction in the Supreme Court, while 28 USCA §§ 1291–1295 grant appellate jurisdiction to lower federal courts of appeals. Cf. *original jurisdiction.*

continuing jurisdiction. A court's power to retain jurisdiction over a matter after entering a judgment, allowing the court to modify its previous rulings or orders.

criminal jurisdiction. A court's power to hear criminal cases.

federal jurisdiction. **1.** The exercise of federal-court authority. **2.** The area of study dealing with the jurisdiction of federal courts.

federal-question jurisdiction. The exercise of federal-court power over claims arising under the U.S. Constitution, an act of Congress, or a treaty. 28 USCA § 1331.

general jurisdiction. A court's authority to hear a wide range of cases, civil or criminal, that arise within its geographic area.

judicial jurisdiction. The legal power and authority of a court to make a decision that binds the parties to any matter properly brought before it.

original jurisdiction. A court's power to hear and decide a matter before any other court can review the matter. Cf. *appellate jurisdiction.*

plenary jurisdiction (**plee**-nə-ree *or* **plen**-ə-ree). A court's full and absolute power over the subject matter and the parties in a case.

summary jurisdiction. **1.** A court's jurisdiction in a summary proceeding. **2.** The court's authority to issue a judgment or order (such as a finding of contempt) without the necessity of a trial or other process.

jurisdictional fact. See FACT.

jurisprudence. See CASELAW.

juror (**joor**-ər *also* **joor**-or). A person serving on a jury panel.

  grand juror. A person serving on a grand jury.

  petit juror (**pet**-ee). A trial juror, as opposed to a grand juror.

  presiding juror. The juror who chairs the jury during deliberations and speaks for the jury in court by announcing the verdict. • The presiding juror is usu. elected by the jury at the start of deliberations.—Also termed *foreman; foreperson.*

juror misconduct. See MISCONDUCT.

jury, *n.* A group of persons selected according to law and given the power to decide questions of fact and return a verdict in the case submitted to them.

  advisory jury. A jury empaneled to hear a case when the parties have no right to a jury trial. • The judge may accept or reject the advisory jury's verdict.

  blue-ribbon jury. A jury consisting of jurors who are the most highly educated on a given panel, sometimes used in a complex civil case (usu. by stipulation of the parties) and sometimes also for a grand jury (esp. those investigating governmental corruption). ● An even more elite group of jurors, involving specialists in a technical field, is called a *blue-blue-ribbon jury*.

common jury. See *petit jury*.

coroner's jury. A jury summoned by a coroner to investigate the cause of death.

deadlocked jury. See *hung jury*.

death-qualified jury. A jury that is fit to decide a case involving the death penalty because the jurors have no absolute ideological bias against capital punishment. Cf. *life-qualified jury*.

fair and impartial jury. See *impartial jury*.

grand jury. See GRAND JURY.

hung jury. A jury that cannot reach a verdict by the required voting margin.—Also termed *deadlocked jury*.

impartial jury. A jury that has no opinion about the case at the start of the trial and that bases its verdict on competent legal evidence.—Also termed *fair and impartial jury*.

inquest jury. A jury summoned from a particular district to appear before a sheriff, coroner, or other ministerial officer and in-

quire about the facts concerning a death.
See INQUEST.

jury of indictment. See GRAND JURY.

jury of the vicinage (**vis**-ə-nij). **1.** At common law, a jury from the county where the crime occurred. **2.** A jury from the county where the court is held. See VICINAGE.

life-qualified jury. In a case involving a capital crime, a jury selected from a venire from which the judge has excluded anyone unable or unwilling to consider a sentence of life imprisonment, instead of the death penalty, if the defendant is found guilty. Cf. *death-qualified jury.*

petit jury. (**pet**-ee). A jury (usu. consisting of 6 or 12 persons) summoned and empaneled in the trial of a specific case.—Also termed *petty jury; trial jury; common jury; traverse jury.* Cf. GRAND JURY.

presenting jury. See GRAND JURY.

special jury. A jury chosen from a panel that is drawn specifically for that case. ● Such a jury is usu. empaneled at a party's request in an unusually important or complicated case. See STRIKING A JURY.

struck jury. A jury selected by allowing the parties to alternate in striking from a list any person whom a given party does not wish to have on the jury, until the number is reduced to the appropriate number (traditionally 12).

traverse jury. See *petit jury.*

trial jury. See *petit jury.*

jury box. The enclosed part of a courtroom where the jury sits.—Also spelled *jury-box.*

jury challenge. See CHALLENGE (2).

jury charge. 1. See JURY INSTRUCTION. **2.** A set of jury instructions.—Often shortened to *charge.*

jury commissioner. An officer responsible for choosing the panels of potential jurors in a given county.

jury direction. See JURY INSTRUCTION.

jury duty. 1. The obligation to serve on a jury. **2.** Actual service on a jury.—Also termed *jury service.*

jury-fixing. The act or an instance of illegally procuring the cooperation of one or more jurors who actually influence the outcome of the trial.—Also termed *fixing a jury.* Cf. EMBRACERY; JURY-PACKING.

jury instruction. (*usu. pl.*) A direction or guideline that a judge gives a jury concerning the law of the case.—Often shortened to *instruction.*—Also termed *jury charge; charge; jury direction.*

> *additional instruction.* A jury charge, beyond the original instructions, that is usu. given in response to the jury's question about the evidence or some point of law.—Also termed *further instruction.*

> *affirmative converse instruction.* An instruction presenting a hypothetical that, if true, commands a verdict in favor of the defendant. • An affirmative converse instruction usu. begins with language such as "your verdict must be for the defendant if you believe...."

> *affirmative instruction.* An instruction that removes an issue from the jury's consideration, such as an instruction that whatever the evidence, the defendant cannot be convicted under the indictment count to which the charge is directed.—Also termed *affirmative charge.*

> *argumentative instruction.* An instruction that assumes facts not in evidence, that singles out or unduly emphasizes a particular issue, theory, or defense, or that otherwise invades the jury's province regarding

the weight, probative value, or sufficiency of the evidence.

binding instruction. See *mandatory instruction*.

cautionary instruction. **1.** A judge's instruction to the jurors to disregard certain evidence or consider it for specific purposes only. **2.** A judge's instruction for the jury not to be influenced by outside factors and not to talk to anyone about the case while the trial is in progress.

curative instruction. A judge's instruction that is intended to correct an erroneous instruction.

formula instruction. A jury charge intended to be the complete statement of the law on which the jury must base its verdict.

further instruction. See *additional instruction*.

Jewell instruction. See JEWELL INSTRUCTION.

mandatory instruction. An instruction requiring a jury to find for one party and against the other if the jury determines that, based on a preponderance of the evidence, a given set of facts exists.—Also termed *binding instruction*.

model jury instruction. A form jury charge usu. approved by a state bar association or similar group regarding matters arising in a typical case. • Courts usu. accept model jury instructions as authoritative.— Also termed *pattern jury instruction*; *pattern jury charge*; *model jury charge*.

ostrich instruction. An instruction stating that a defendant who deliberately avoided acquiring actual knowledge can be found to have acted knowingly.

pattern jury instruction. See *model jury instruction*.

peremptory instruction. A court's explicit direction that a jury must obey, such as an instruction to return a verdict for a particular party. See *directed verdict* under VERDICT.

special instruction. An instruction on some particular point or question involved in the case, usu. in response to counsel's request for such an instruction.

standard instruction. A jury instruction that has been regularly used in a given jurisdiction.

jury list. A list of persons who may be summoned to serve as jurors.

jury nullification. A jury's knowing and deliberate rejection of the evidence or refusal to apply the law either because the jury wants to send a message about some social issue that is larger than the case itself or because the result dictated by law is contrary to the jury's sense of justice, morality, or fairness.

jury of indictment. See GRAND JURY.

jury of the vicinage. See JURY.

jury-packing. The act or an instance of contriving to have a jury composed of persons who are predisposed toward one side or the other.—Also termed *packing a jury*. Cf. EMBRACERY; JURY-FIXING.

jury panel. See VENIRE (1).

jury pardon. A rule that permits a jury to convict a defendant of a lesser offense than the offense charged if sufficient evidence exists to convict the defendant of either offense.

jury pool. See VENIRE (1).

jury process. 1. The procedure by which jurors are summoned and their attendance is enforced. **2.** The papers served on or mailed to potential jurors to compel their attendance.

jury question. 1. An issue of fact that a jury decides. See QUESTION OF FACT. **2.** A special question that a court may ask a jury that will deliver a special verdict.

jury sequestration. See SEQUESTRATION.

jury service. See JURY DUTY.

jury summation. See CLOSING ARGUMENT.

jury-tampering. See EMBRACERY.

jury trial. See TRIAL.

jury wheel. A physical device or electronic system used for storing and randomly selecting names of potential jurors.

jus talionis. See LEX TALIONIS.

just deserts (di-**zərts**). What one really deserves; esp., the punishment that a person deserves for having committed a crime.—Also termed *deserts*.

justice. 1. The fair and proper administration of laws.

    Jedburgh justice (**jed**-bər-ə). A brand of justice involving punishment (esp. execution) first and trial afterwards. ● The term alludes to Jedburgh, a Scottish border town where in the 17th century raiders were said to have been hanged without the formality of a trial. Jedburgh justice differs from lynch law in that the former was administered by an established court (albeit after the fact).— Also termed *Jeddart justice*; *Jedwood justice*. Cf. LIDFORD LAW; LYNCH LAW.

2. A judge, esp. of an appellate court or a court of last resort.—Abbr. J. (and, in plural, JJ.).

associate justice. An appellate-court justice other than the chief justice.

chief justice. The presiding justice of an appellate court, usu. the highest appellate court in a jurisdiction and esp. the U.S. Supreme Court.—Abbr. C.J.

circuit justice. **1.** A justice who sits on a circuit court. **2.** A U.S. Supreme Court justice who has jurisdiction over one or more of the federal circuits, with power to issue injunctions, grant bail, or stay execution in those circuits.

justice court. A court, presided over by a justice of the peace, that has jurisdiction to hear minor criminal cases, matters involving small amounts of money, or certain specified claims (such as forcible-entry-and-detainer

389

suits).—Also termed *justice-of-the-peace court*;
J.P. court.

justice of the peace. A local judicial officer
having jurisdiction over minor criminal offenses and minor civil disputes, and authority
to perform routine civil functions (such as
administering oaths and performing marriage
ceremonies).—Abbr. J.P. Cf. MAGISTRATE.

justice-of-the-peace court. See JUSTICE
COURT.

justice's warrant. See *peace warrant* under
WARRANT.

justiciable (jə-**stish**-ee-ə-bəl *or* jəs-**tish**-ə-bəl),
adj. (Of a case or dispute) properly brought
before a court of justice; capable of being disposed of judicially <a justiciable controversy>.

justifiable homicide. See HOMICIDE.

justification, *n.* **1.** A lawful or sufficient reason for one's acts or omissions. **2.** A showing,
in court, of a sufficient reason why a defendant did what the prosecution charges the
defendant to answer for. ● Under the Model
Penal Code, the defendant must believe that
the action was necessary to avoid a harm or
evil and that the harm or evil to be avoided
was greater than the harm that would have

resulted if the crime had been committed. Model Penal Code § 3.02.—See *lesser-evils defense* under DEFENSE.—Also termed *justification defense; necessity defense.*—**justify,** *vb.*—**justificatory** (jəs-**ti**-fi-kə-tor-ee), *adj.*

> ***imperfect justification.*** A reason or cause that is insufficient to completely justify a defendant's behavior but that can be used to mitigate criminal punishment.

justification defense. A defense that arises when the defendant has acted in a way that the law does not seek to prevent. ● Traditionally, the following defenses were justifications: consent, self-defense, defense of others, defense of property, necessity (choice of evils), the use of force to make an arrest, and the use of force by public authority.—Sometimes shortened to *justification.* Cf. EXCUSE (2).

juvenile (**joo**-və-nəl *or* -nIl), *n.* A person who has not reached the age (usu. 18) at which one should be treated as an adult by the criminal-justice system; MINOR.—**juvenile,** *adj.*—**juvenility** (joo-və-**nil**-ə-tee), *n.*

> ***certified juvenile.*** A juvenile who has been certified to be tried as an adult.

juvenile court. A court having jurisdiction over cases involving children under a specified age, usu. 18.—Also termed *children's court.*

juvenile delinquency. Antisocial behavior by a minor; esp., behavior that would be criminally punishable if the actor were an adult, but instead is usu. punished by special laws pertaining only to minors. Cf. INCORRIGIBILITY.

juvenile delinquent. A minor guilty of criminal behavior, which is usu. punished by special laws not pertaining to adults.—Also termed *juvenile offender*; *youthful offender*; *delinquent minor*. See OFFENDER.

juvenile officer. A juvenile-court employee who works with the judge to direct and develop the court's child-welfare work.—Also termed *county agent*.

juvenile parole. See PAROLE.

juvenile petition. See PETITION.

K

kangaroo court. 1. A self-appointed tribunal or mock court in which the principles of law and justice are disregarded, perverted, or parodied. ● Kangaroo courts may be assembled by various groups, such as prisoners in a jail (to settle disputes between inmates) and players on a baseball team (to "punish" teammates who commit fielding errors). **2.** A court or tribunal characterized by unauthorized or irregular procedures, esp. so as to render a fair proceeding impossible. **3.** A sham legal proceeding.

***Ker–Frisbie* rule.** The principle that the government's power to try a criminal defendant is not impaired by the defendant's having been brought back illegally to the United States from a foreign country. *Ker v. Illinois*, 119 U.S. 436, 7 S.Ct. 225 (1886); *Frisbie v. Collins*, 342 U.S. 519, 72 S.Ct. 509 (1952).

key money. 1. Payment (as rent or security) required from a new tenant in exchange for a key to the leased property. **2.** Payment made (usu. secretly) by a prospective tenant to a landlord or current tenant to increase the chance of obtaining a lease in an area where there is a housing shortage. ● Key money in the first sense is a legal transaction; key money in the second sense is usu. an illegal bribe that violates housing laws.

kickback, *n.* A return of a portion of a monetary sum received, esp. as a result of coercion or a secret agreement <the contractor paid the city official a 5% kickback on the government contract>.—Also termed *payoff.* Cf. BRIBERY.

kidnap, *vb.* To seize and take away (a person) by force or fraud, often with a demand for ransom.

kidnapping. 1. At common law, the crime of forcibly abducting a person from his or her own country and sending the person to another. • This offense amounted to false imprisonment aggravated by moving the victim to another country. **2.** The crime of seizing and taking away a person by force or fraud.—Also termed *simple kidnapping*; (archaically) *man-stealing*.

　　aggravated kidnapping. Kidnapping accompanied by some aggravating factor (such as a demand for ransom or injury of the victim).

　　child-kidnapping. The kidnapping of a child, often without the element of force or fraud (as when someone walks off with another's baby stroller).—Also termed *child-stealing; baby-snatching*.

　　kidnapping for ransom. The offense of unlawfully seizing a person and then confining the person in a secret place while attempting to extort ransom. • This grave crime is sometimes made a capital offense. In addition to the abductor, a person who acts as a go-between to collect the ransom is generally considered guilty of the crime.

parental kidnapping. The kidnapping of a child by one parent in violation of the other parent's custody or visitation rights.

simple kidnapping. Kidnapping not accompanied by an aggravating factor.

killing by misadventure. See ACCIDENTAL KILLING.

kiting. See CHECK-KITING.

kleptomania (klep-tə-**may**-nee-ə), *n.* A compulsive urge to steal, esp. without economic motive.—**kleptomaniac,** *n.* & *adj.*

knock-and-announce rule. The requirement that the police knock at the door and announce their identity, authority, and purpose before entering a residence to execute an arrest or search warrant.—Also termed *knock-and-notice rule.*

knowing, *adj.* **1.** Having or showing awareness or understanding; well-informed <a

knowing waiver of the right to counsel>. **2.** Deliberate; conscious <a knowing attempt to commit fraud>.—**knowingly,** *adv.*

knowledge. 1. An awareness or understanding of a fact or circumstance. **2.** *Archaic.* See CARNAL KNOWLEDGE.

L

L. *abbr.* LAW (5).

la bomba (lə **bom**-bə). (*sometimes cap.*) An incendiary device consisting of a plastic bag filled with fuel and placed inside a paper bag stuffed with tissue and rigged with a fuse. • A person who uses such a device to start a fire violates the federal arson statute. 18 USCA § 844(j).

laboring a jury. See EMBRACERY.

Lacey Act. A federal law, originally enacted in 1900, that permits states to enforce their own game laws against animals imported from other states or countries. 16 USCA §§ 661 et seq. See GAME LAW.

***Lackey* claim.** A prisoner's assertion that incarceration on death row for a protracted period is cruel and unusual punishment. *Lackey v. Texas*, 514 U.S. 1045, 115 S.Ct. 1421 (1995) (denying cert.).

laesa majestas (**lee**-zə mə-**jes**-tas). See LESE MAJESTY.

landing law. A law prohibiting the possession or sale of fish or game that have been taken illegally.

lapping. An embezzlement technique by which an employee takes funds from one customer's accounts receivable and covers it by using a second customer's payment to pay the first account, then a third customer's payment to pay the second account, and so on.

larcenable (**lahr**-sə-nə-bəl), *adj*. Subject to larceny <because it cannot be carried away, real estate is not larcenable>.

larcenist. One who commits larceny. See LARCENY.

larcenous (**lahr**-sə-nəs), *adj*. **1.** Of, relating to, or characterized by larceny <a larcenous taking>. **2.** (Of a person) contemplating or tainted with larceny; thievish <a larcenous purpose>.

larcenous intent. A state of mind existing when a person (1) knowingly takes away the goods of another without any claim or pretense of a right to do so, and (2) intends to deprive the owner of them or to convert the goods to personal use. See LARCENY.

larceny (**lahr**-sə-nee), *n*. The unlawful taking and carrying away of someone else's personal property with the intent to deprive the possessor of it permanently. ● Common-law larceny has been broadened by some statutes to include embezzlement and false pretenses, all three of which are often subsumed under the statutory crime of "theft."

aggravated larceny. Larceny accompanied by some aggravating factor (as when the theft is from a person).

complicated larceny. See *mixed larceny.*

compound larceny. See *mixed larceny.*

constructive larceny. Larceny in which the perpetrator's felonious intent to appropriate the goods is construed from the defendant's conduct at the time of asportation, although a felonious intent was not present before that time.

grand larceny. Larceny of property worth more than a statutory cutoff amount, usu. $100. Cf. *petit larceny.*

larceny by bailee. Larceny committed by a bailee who converts the property to personal use or to the use of a third party.

larceny by extortion. See *theft by extortion* under THEFT.

larceny by trick. Larceny in which the taker misleads the rightful possessor, by misrepresentation of fact, into giving up possession of (but not title to) the goods.—Also termed *larceny by trick and deception; larce-*

ny by trick and device; *larceny by fraud and deception*. Cf. FALSE PRETENSES; *cheating by false pretenses* under CHEATING.

larceny from the person. Larceny in which the goods are taken directly from the person, but without violence or intimidation, the victim usu. being unaware of the taking. ● Pickpocketing is a typical example. This offense is similar to robbery except that violence or intimidation is not involved. Cf. ROBBERY.

larceny of property lost, mislaid, or delivered by mistake. See *theft of property lost, mislaid, or delivered by mistake* under THEFT.

mixed larceny. 1. Larceny accompanied by aggravation or violence to the person. Cf. *simple larceny*. **2.** Larceny involving a taking from a house.—Also termed *compound larceny*; *complicated larceny*.

petit larceny. Larceny of property worth less than an amount fixed by statute, usu. $100.—Also spelled *petty larceny*. Cf. *grand larceny*.

simple larceny. Larceny unaccompanied by aggravating factors; larceny of personal goods unattended by an act of violence. Cf. *mixed larceny* (1).

Larrison **rule** (**lar**-ə-sən). The doctrine that a defendant may be entitled to a new trial on the basis of newly discovered evidence of false testimony by a government witness if the jury might have reached a different conclusion without the evidence and it unfairly surprised the defendant at trial. *Larrison v. United States*, 24 F.2d 82 (7th Cir. 1928).

lascivious (lə-**siv**-ee-əs), *adj.* (Of conduct) tending to excite lust; lewd; indecent; obscene.

lascivious cohabitation. The offense committed by two persons not married to each other who live together as husband and wife and engage in sexual intercourse. • This offense, where it still exists, is seldom prosecuted.

last-link doctrine. The rule that an attorney need not divulge nonprivileged information if doing so would reveal information protected by the attorney-client privilege, particularly if the information would provide essential evidence to support indicting or convicting the client of a crime. • This doctrine is often relied on as an exception to the rule that a client's identity is not privileged. For example, if divulging the client's name would supply the last link of evidence to indict or convict the client of a crime, the name need not be disclosed.

last-proximate-act test. A common-law test for the crime of attempt, based on whether the defendant does the final act necessary to commit an offense (such as pulling the trigger of a gun, not merely aiming it). ● Most courts have rejected this test as being too lenient. See AT-TEMPT.

lateral departure. See DEPARTURE.

lateral sentencing. See *lateral departure* under DEPARTURE.

latrocination (la-trə-sə-**nay**-shən). [fr. Latin *latrocinium* "highway robbery"] *Archaic*. The act of robbing; a depredation; a theft.—Also termed *latrociny*. See LARCENY; THEFT.

laundering, *n*. The federal crime of transferring illegally obtained money through legitimate persons or accounts so that its original source cannot be traced. 18 USCA § 1956.—Also termed *money-laundering*.—**launder,** *vb*.

law. 1. The regime that orders human activities and relations through systematic application of the force of politically organized society, or through social pressure, backed by force, in such a society; the legal system <respect and obey the law>. **2.** The aggregate of legislation, judicial precedents, and accepted legal principles; the body of authoritative grounds of judicial and administrative action <the law of the land>. **3.** The set of rules or principles dealing with a specific area of a legal system <criminal law>. **4.** The judicial and administrative process; legal action and proceedings <when settlement negotiations failed, they submitted their dispute to the law>. **5.** A statute <Congress passed a law>.—Abbr. L. **6.** See COMMON LAW <law but not equity>. **7.** The legal profession <she spent her entire career in law>.

law enforcement. 1. The detection and punishment of violations of the law. ● This term is not limited to the enforcement of criminal laws. For example, the Freedom of Information Act contains an exemption from disclosure for information compiled for law-enforcement purposes and furnished in confidence. That exemption is valid for the enforcement of a variety of noncriminal laws (such as national-security laws) as well as criminal laws. See 5 USCA § 552(b)(7). **2.** See CRIMINAL JUSTICE (2). **3.** Police officers and other members of the executive branch of government charged with carrying out and enforcing the criminal law.

Law Enforcement Assistance Administration. A former federal agency (part of the Department of Justice) that was responsible for administering law-enforcement grants under the Omnibus Crime Control and Safe

Streets Act of 1968. ● It has been replaced by a variety of federal agencies, including the National Institute of Corrections and National Institute of Justice.—Abbr. LEAA.

Law Enforcement Information Network. A computerized communications system used in some states to document drivers' license records, automobile registrations, wanted persons' files, etc.—Abbr. LEIN.

law-enforcement officer. A person whose duty is to enforce the laws and preserve the peace. See PEACE OFFICER; SHERIFF.

law-enforcement system. See CRIMINAL-JUSTICE SYSTEM.

lawful, *adj.* Not contrary to law; permitted by law <the police officer conducted a lawful search of the premises>. See LEGAL.

lawful age. 1. See AGE OF CAPACITY. **2.** See AGE OF MAJORITY.

lawful arrest. See ARREST.

lawful authorities. Those persons (such as the police) with the right to exercise public power, to require obedience to their lawful commands, and to command or act in the public name.

lawful entry. See ENTRY.

lawful goods. Property that one may legally hold, sell, or export; property that is not contraband.

lawmaking. See LEGISLATION (1).

law of the case. 1. The doctrine holding that a decision rendered in a former appeal of a case is binding in a later appeal. **2.** An earlier decision giving rise to the application of this doctrine. Cf. LAW OF THE TRIAL; STARE DECISIS.

law of the circuit. 1. The law as announced and followed by a U.S. Circuit Court of Appeals. **2.** The rule that one panel of judges on a U.S. Circuit Court of Appeals should not overrule a decision of another panel of judges on the same court. **3.** The rule that an opinion of one U.S. Circuit Court of Appeals is not binding on another circuit but may be considered persuasive.

law of the trial. A legal theory or court ruling that is not objected to and is used or relied on in a trial <neither party objected to the court's jury instruction, so it became the law of the trial>. Cf. LAW OF THE CASE.

law question. See QUESTION OF LAW.

lawyer, *n.* One who is licensed to practice law.—**lawyerly, lawyerlike,** *adj.*—**lawyerdom,** *n.* Cf. ATTORNEY; COUNSEL.

criminal lawyer. A lawyer whose primary work is to represent criminal defendants. • This term is rarely if ever applied to prosecutors despite their integral involvement in the criminal-justice system.

jailhouse lawyer. See JAILHOUSE LAWYER.

lawyer-client privilege. See *attorney-client privilege* under PRIVILEGE (3).

lawyer-witness rule. The principle that an attorney who will likely be called as a fact witness at trial may not participate as an advocate in the case, unless the testimony will be about an uncontested matter or the amount of attorney's fees in the case, or if disqualifying the attorney would create a substantial hardship for the client. *Model Rules of Professional Conduct* Rule 3.7 (1987).—Also termed *advocate-witness rule*; *attorney-witness rule*.

lay judge. See JUDGE.

lay opinion testimony. See TESTIMONY.

lay witness. See WITNESS.

L-Claim proceeding. A hearing that is connected with a criminal proceeding brought under the Racketeer Influenced and Corrupt Organizations Act, and that is intended to ensure that property ordered to be forfeited belongs to the defendant. • A petition for an L-Claim proceeding is filed by someone other than the defendant who claims an interest in property that has been ordered to be forfeited. To succeed, an L-Claim petitioner must be able to show an interest in a specific asset that has been ordered forfeited. The proceeding's purpose is not to divide the defendant's estate among competing claimants, and general creditors of the defendant should not be allowed to maintain an L-Claim petition. The proceeding is referred to as an L-Claim proceeding because its legal basis is subsection *l* of RICO's penalty provision. 18 USCA § 1963(*l*)(2).

LEAA. *abbr.* LAW ENFORCEMENT ASSISTANCE ADMINISTRATION.

leading question. A question that suggests the answer to the person being interrogated; esp., a question that may be answered by a mere "yes" or "no." • Leading questions are generally allowed only in cross-examination.— Also termed *categorical question*; *suggestive question*; *suggestive interrogation*.

least-intrusive-means doctrine. A doctrine requiring the government to exhaust all other

investigatory means before seeking sensitive
testimony, as by compelling an attorney to
testify before a grand jury on matters that
may be protected by the attorney-client privilege.

legal, *adj.* **1.** Of or relating to law; falling
within the province of law <pro bono legal
services>. **2.** Established, required, or permitted by law; LAWFUL <it is legal to carry a
concealed handgun in some states>. **3.** Of or
relating to law as opposed to equity.

legal act. 1. Any act not condemned as illegal.
● For example, a surgeon's incision is a legal
act, while stabbing is an illegal one. **2.** An
action or undertaking that creates a legally
recognized obligation; an act that binds a person in some way.

legal-advice exception. 1. The rule that an
attorney may withhold as privileged the
client's identity and information regarding
fees, if there is a strong probability that disclosing the information would implicate the
client in the criminal activity for which the
attorney was consulted. **2.** An exemption contained in open-meetings legislation, permitting
a governmental body to meet in closed session
to consult with its attorney about certain matters.

legal age. See AGE OF CAPACITY.

legal aid. Free or inexpensive legal services provided to those who cannot afford to pay full price. • Legal aid is usu. administered locally by a specially established organization. See LEGAL SERVICES CORPORATION.

legal cause. See *proximate cause* under CAUSE (1).

legal custody. See CUSTODY (2).

legal death. 1. See *brain death* under DEATH. **2.** See CIVIL DEATH.

legal defense. See DEFENSE.

legal discretion. See *judicial discretion* under DISCRETION.

legal-elements test. A method of determining whether one crime is a lesser-included offense in relation to another crime, by examining the components of the greater crime to analyze whether a person who commits the greater crime necessarily commits the lesser one too.—Also termed *same-elements test*.

legal evidence. See EVIDENCE.

legal excuse. See EXCUSE.

legal fact. See FACT.

legal force. See *reasonable force* under FORCE.

legal impossibility. See IMPOSSIBILITY.

legal innocence. See INNOCENCE.

legal insanity. See INSANITY.

legality. 1. Strict adherence to law, prescription, or doctrine; the quality of being legal. **2.** The principle that a person may not be prosecuted under a criminal law that has not been previously published.—Also termed (in sense 2) *principle of legality.*

legalize, *vb.* **1.** To make lawful; to authorize or justify by legal sanction <the bill to legalize marijuana never made it to the Senate floor>. **2.** To imbue with the spirit of the law; to make legalistic <legalized conceptions of religion>.—**legalization,** *n.*

legal jeopardy. See JEOPARDY.

legal liability. See LIABILITY.

legally, *adv.* In a lawful way; in a manner that accords with the law.

legally inconsistent verdict. See VERDICT.

legally liable. See LIABLE.

legal malice. See *implied malice* under MALICE.

legal presumption. See *presumption of law* under PRESUMPTION.

legal process. See PROCESS.

legal question. See QUESTION OF LAW.

legal ruling. See RULING.

Legal Services Corporation. A corporation established by the Legal Services Corporation Act of 1974 (42 USCA § 2996) to provide legal help to clients who cannot afford legal services. See LEGAL AID.

legal willfulness. See WILLFULNESS.

legal wrong. See WRONG.

legislate, *vb.* **1.** To make or enact laws <the role of our lawmakers is to legislate, not to adjudicate>. **2.** To bring (something) into or out of existence by making laws; to attempt to control (something) by legislation <virtually every attempt to legislate morality has failed>.

legislation. 1. The process of making or enacting a law in written form, according to some type of formal procedure, by a branch of government constituted to perform this process.—Also termed *lawmaking*; *statute-making*. **2.** The law so enacted. **3.** The whole body of enacted laws.

    general legislation. Legislation that applies to the community at large.

    judicial legislation. The making of new legal rules by judges; JUDGE-MADE LAW (2).

4. A proposed law being considered by a legislature <gun-control legislation was debated in the House>. **5.** The field of study concentrating on statutes.

legislative history. The background and events leading to the enactment of a statute, including hearings, committee reports, and floor debates. • Legislative history is sometimes recorded so that it can later be used to aid in interpreting the statute.

legislative law. See STATUTORY LAW.

legislative privilege. See PRIVILEGE (3).

LEIN. *abbr.* LAW ENFORCEMENT INFORMATION NETWORK.

lenity rule. See RULE OF LENITY.

lese majesty (leez **maj**-əs-tee). [Law French "injured majesty"] **1.** A crime against the state, esp. against the ruler. See *high treason* under TREASON. **2.** An attack on a custom or traditional belief.—Also spelled *lèse-majesté*; *lèse majesty*; *leze majesty*.—Also termed *laesa majestas*.

lesser-evils defense. See DEFENSE.

lesser included offense. See OFFENSE.

lethal, *adj.* Deadly; fatal <a lethal drug>.

lethal injection. The intravenous insertion of a deadly substance into a person, usu. for the purpose of carrying out a death sentence.

lethal weapon. See *deadly weapon* under WEAPON.

lewd, *adj.* Obscene or indecent; tending to moral impurity or wantonness <lewd behavior>.

lewd and lascivious cohabitation. See *illicit cohabitation* under COHABITATION.

lewd house. See DISORDERLY HOUSE.

lewdness. Gross, wanton, and public indecency that is outlawed by many state statutes; a sexual act that the actor knows will likely be observed by someone who will be affronted or alarmed by it. See Model Penal Code § 251.1.—Also termed *open lewdness.* Cf. INDECENT EXPOSURE; OBSCENITY.

lex loci delicti (**leks loh**-sɪ də-**lik**-tɪ). [Latin] The law of the place where the offense was committed.—Often shortened to *lex delicti.*— Also termed *lex loci delictus*; *lex loci delicti commissi*; *place-of-wrong rule*; *place-of-wrong law.* Cf. LOCUS DELICTI.

lex talionis (**leks** tal-ee-**oh**-nis), *n.* [Law Latin] The law of retaliation, under which punishment should be in kind—an eye for an eye, a tooth for a tooth, and so on.—Also termed *eye for an eye*; *jus talionis*; *principle of retribution.*

leze majesty. See LESE MAJESTY.

liability, *n.* The quality or state of being legally obligated or accountable; legal responsibility to another or to society, enforceable by civil remedy or criminal punishment <liability for injuries caused by negligence>.—Also termed *legal liability.*

    accomplice liability. Criminal responsibility of one who acts with another before, during, or after a crime. See 18 USCA § 2.

enterprise liability. Criminal liability imposed on a business (such as a corporation or partnership) for certain offenses, such as public-welfare offenses or offenses for which the legislature specifically intended to impose criminal sanctions. See Model Penal Code § 2.07. See *public-welfare offense* under OFFENSE.

liable (lı-ə-bəl *also* lı-bəl), *adj.* **1.** Responsible or answerable in law; legally obligated. **2.** (Of a person) subject to or likely to incur (a fine, penalty, etc.).—Also termed *legally liable*.

libel (lı-bəl), *n.* **1.** A defamatory statement expressed in a fixed medium, esp. writing but also a picture, sign, or electronic broadcast. ● Libel is classified as both a crime and a tort but is no longer prosecuted as a crime.—Also termed *defamatory libel*. See DEFAMATION. Cf. SLANDER.

criminal libel. At common law, a malicious libel that is designed to expose a person to hatred, contempt, or ridicule and that may subject the author to criminal sanctions. ● Because of constitutional protections of free speech, libel is no longer criminally prosecuted.

obscene libel. *Archaic.* **1.** The common-law crime of publishing, with the intent to corrupt, material (esp. sexual words or pic-

415

tures) that tends to deprave or corrupt those whose minds are open to immoral influences. **2.** A writing, book, picture, or print that is so obscene that it shocks the public sense of decency.

seditious libel. Libel made with the intent of inciting sedition. ● Like other forms of criminal libel, seditious libel is no longer prosecuted. See SEDITION.

2. The act of making such a statement.

libel, *vb.* To defame (someone) in a permanent medium, esp. in writing.

liberation. The act or an instance of freeing someone or something.

liberative, *adj.* Serving or tending to free or release.

license, *n.* **1.** A revocable permission to commit some act that would otherwise be unlawful; esp., an agreement (not amounting to a lease) that it will be lawful for the licensee to enter the licensor's land to do some act that would otherwise be illegal, such as hunting game. **2.** The certificate or document evidencing such permission.—**license,** *vb.*

Lidford law (**lid**-fərd). A form of lynch law permitting a person to be punished first and tried later. ● The term took its name from the town of Lidford (now Lydford) where this type of action supposedly took place. Cf. *Jedburgh justice* under JUSTICE (1).

lie, *vb.* To tell an untruth; to speak or write falsely <she lied on the witness stand>. See PERJURY. Cf. FABRICATE.

lie detector. See POLYGRAPH.

life-qualified jury. See JURY.

lifer. See NONREMOVABLE INMATE.

life sentence. See SENTENCE.

limited admissibility. See ADMISSIBILITY.

limited appeal. See APPEAL.

Lindbergh Act. See FEDERAL KIDNAPPING ACT.

lineup. A police identification procedure in which a criminal suspect and other physically similar persons are shown to the victim or a witness to determine whether the suspect can be identified as the perpetrator of the crime.— Also termed (in BrE) *identification parade*. Cf. SHOWUP.

link-in-chain principle. The principle that a criminal defendant's Fifth Amendment right against self-incrimination protects the defendant from not only answering directly incriminating questions but also giving answers that might connect the defendant to criminal activity in the chain of evidence.

liquor offense. See OFFENSE.

litigation privilege. See PRIVILEGE (1).

loansharking, *n.* The practice of lending money at excessive and esp. usurious rates, and often threatening or using extortion to enforce repayment.—Also termed *extortionate credit transaction.*—**loan-shark,** *vb.*—**loan shark,** *n.*

lockdown. The temporary confinement of prisoners in their cells during a state of heightened alert caused by an escape, riot, or other emergency.

lockup, *n.* See JAIL.

locus criminis (**loh**-kəs **krim**-ə-nis), *n.* [Latin] The place where a crime is committed.

locus delicti (**loh**-kəs də-**lik**-tɪ). [Latin "place of the wrong"] The place where an offense is committed; the place where the last event necessary to make the actor liable occurs. Cf. LEX LOCI DELICTI.

locus poenitentiae (**loh**-kəs pen-ə-**ten**-shee-ee). [Latin "place of repentance"] A point at which it is not too late for one to change one's legal position; the possibility of withdrawing from a contemplated course of action, esp. a wrong, before being committed to it.

log, *n*. See ARREST RECORD.

loitering, *n*. The criminal offense of remaining in a certain place (such as a public street) for no apparent reason. • Loitering statutes are generally held to be unconstitutionally vague.—**loiter,** *vb*. Cf. VAGRANCY.

lumping. The imposition of a general sentence on a criminal defendant. See *general sentence* under SENTENCE.

lunacy. See INSANITY.

lying in wait. The series of acts involved in watching, waiting, and hiding from someone, with the intent of killing or inflicting serious bodily injury on that person. • Because lying in wait shows premeditation and deliberation, it can result in an increased sentence.

lynch, *vb*. To hang (a person) by mob action without legal authority.

lynch law. The administration of summary punishment, esp. death, for an alleged crime, without legal authority.

M

mace. A chemical liquid that can be sprayed in a person's face to cause dizziness and temporary immobilization.

mace-proof, *vb.* To exempt from an arrest; to secure against an arrest.

magistrate (**maj**-ə-strayt), *n.* A judicial officer with strictly limited jurisdiction and authority, often on the local level and often restricted to criminal cases.—Also termed *commissioner*.—**magisterial** (maj-ə-**stir**-ee-əl), *adj.* Cf. JUSTICE OF THE PEACE.

> *committing magistrate.* A judicial officer who conducts preliminary criminal hearings and may order that a defendant be released for lack of evidence, sent to jail to await trial, or released on bail. See EXAMINING COURT.

> *district-court magistrate.* In some states, a quasi-judicial officer given the power to set bail, accept bond, accept guilty pleas, impose sentences for traffic violations and similar offenses, and conduct informal hearings on civil infractions.

> *federal magistrate.* See UNITED STATES MAGISTRATE JUDGE.

investigating magistrate. A quasi-judicial officer responsible for examining and sometimes ruling on certain aspects of a criminal proceeding before it comes before a judge.

police magistrate. A judicial officer who has jurisdiction to try minor criminal offenses, breaches of police regulations, and similar violations.—Also termed *police justice.*

U.S. Magistrate. See UNITED STATES MAGISTRATE JUDGE.

Magistrate Judge, U.S. See UNITED STATES MAGISTRATE JUDGE.

magistrate's court (**maj**-i-strayts *or* -strits). **1.** A court with jurisdiction over minor criminal offenses. • Such a court also has the power to bind over for trial persons accused of more serious offenses.—Also termed *police court.* **2.** A court with limited jurisdiction over minor criminal and civil matters.

Magna Carta (**mag**-nə **kahr**-tə). [Latin "great charter"] The English charter that King John granted to the barons in 1215 and that Henry III and Edward I later confirmed. • It is generally regarded as one of the great common-law documents and as the foundation of constitutional liberties. The other three great charters of English liberty are the Peti-

tion of Right (3 Car. (1628)), the Habeas Cor-
pus Act (31 Car. 2 (1679)), and the Bill of
Rights (1 Will. & M. (1689)).—Also spelled
Magna Charta.

maihem. See MAIM.

mail cover. A process by which the U.S.
Postal Service provides a government agency
with information on the face of an envelope or
package (such as a postmark) for the agency's
use in locating a fugitive, identifying a coconspirator, or obtaining other evidence necessary
to solve a crime.

mail fraud. See FRAUD.

maim, *n. Archaic.* The type of injury required
for the commission of mayhem; esp., serious
injury to part of a person's body that is necessary for fighting.—Also termed *maihem.*—
maim, *vb.* See MAYHEM.

main opinion. See *majority opinion* under
OPINION.

maintainor. A person who meddles in someone else's litigation by providing money or
other assistance; a person who is guilty of
maintenance.—Also spelled *maintainer*. See
MAINTENANCE.

maintenance, *n*. Assistance in prosecuting or defending a case given to a litigant by someone who has no bona fide interest in the case; meddling in someone else's litigation. ● Though a misdemeanor at common law, maintenance is rarely punished as a crime today.

major. See ADULT.

major crime. See FELONY.

majority. The status of one who has attained the age of majority (usu. 18). See AGE OF MAJORITY. Cf. MINORITY.

majority opinion. See OPINION.

malconduct in office. See *official misconduct* under MISCONDUCT.

malfeasance (mal-**fee**-zənts), *n*. A wrongful or unlawful act; esp., wrongdoing or misconduct by a public official.—**malfeasant,** *adj*.— **malfeasor,** *n*. See MISFEASANCE.

malice, *n*. **1.** The intent, without justification or excuse, to commit a wrongful act. **2.** Reckless disregard of the law or of a person's legal rights. **3.** Ill will; wickedness of heart. ● This sense is most typical in nonlegal contexts.— **malicious,** *adj*.

actual malice. The deliberate intent to commit an injury, as evidenced by external circumstances.—Also termed *express malice*; *malice in fact*. Cf. *implied malice*.

constructive malice. See *implied malice*.

express malice. **1.** The intent to kill or seriously injure arising from a deliberate, rational mind. **2.** See *actual malice*.

general malice. Malice that is necessary for any criminal conduct; malice that is not directed at a specific person. Cf. *particular malice*.

implied malice. Malice inferred from a person's conduct.—Also termed *constructive malice*; *legal malice*; *malice in law*. Cf. *actual malice*.

malice in fact. See *actual malice*.

particular malice. Malice that is directed at a particular person.—Also termed *special malice*. Cf. *general malice*.

transferred malice. Malice directed to one person or object but instead harming another in the way intended for the first.

universal malice. The state of mind of a person who determines to take a life on slight provocation, without knowing or caring who may be the victim.

malice aforethought. The requisite mental state for common-law murder, encompassing any one of the following: (1) the intent to kill, (2) the intent to inflict serious bodily harm, (3) extremely reckless indifference to the value of human life (the so-called "abandoned and malignant heart"), or (4) the intent to commit a felony (which leads to culpability under the felony-murder rule).—Also termed *premeditated malice; preconceived malice; malice prepense; malitia praecogitata.*

malice in fact. See *actual malice* under MALICE.

malice in law. See *implied malice* under MALICE.

malice prepense. See MALICE AFORETHOUGHT.

malicious, *adj.* **1.** Substantially certain to cause injury. **2.** Without just cause or excuse.

malicious accusation. See ACCUSATION.

malicious act. An intentional, wrongful act performed against another without legal justification or excuse.

malicious arrest. See ARREST.

malicious assault with a deadly weapon.
See ASSAULT.

malicious damage. See MALICIOUS MISCHIEF.

malicious injury. See INJURY.

malicious killing. An intentional killing
without legal justification or excuse.

malicious mischief. The common-law misdemeanor of intentionally destroying or damaging another's property. ● Although modern
statutes predominantly make this offense a
misdemeanor, a few make it a felony (depending on the nature of the property or its value).
See Model Penal Code § 220.3.—Also termed
*malicious mischief and trespass; malicious in-
jury; malicious trespass; malicious damage;
maliciously damaging the property of another;*
(in the Model Penal Code) *criminal mischief.*

malicious motive. See MOTIVE.

malicious prosecution. 1. The institution of
a criminal or civil proceeding for an improper
purpose and without probable cause. **2.** The
cause of action resulting from the institution
of such a proceeding. ● Once a wrongful prosecution has ended in the defendant's favor, he
or she may sue for tort damages.

malicious trespass. See MALICIOUS MISCHIEF.

malitia (mə-**lish**-ee-ə). [Latin "malice"] An actual evil design; express malice. ● *Malitia* originally signified general wrongdoing, and did not describe a wrongdoer's state of mind; *malitia praecogitata*, for example, indicated only the seriousness of the offense, though it was eventually rendered *malice aforethought.*

Mallory **rule.** See MCNABB–MALLORY RULE.

malum in se (**mal**-əm in **say** *or* **see**), *n.* [Latin "evil in itself"] A crime or an act that is inherently immoral, such as murder, arson, or rape.—Also termed *malum per se.* Pl. *mala in se.*—*malum in se, adj.* Cf. MALUM PROHIBITUM.

malum prohibitum (**mal**-əm proh-**hib**-i-təm), *n.* [Latin "prohibited evil"] An act that is a crime merely because it is prohibited by statute, although the act itself is not necessarily immoral. ● Misdemeanors such as jaywalking and running a stoplight are *mala prohibita*, as are many regulatory violations. Pl. *mala prohibita.*—*malum prohibitum, adj.* Cf. MALUM IN SE.

malversation (mal-vər-**say**-shən), *n.* [French "ill behavior"] Official corruption; a misbehavior, esp. by someone exercising an office.

manacle (**man**-ə-kəl). A shackle; a handcuff.

mandamus (man-**day**-məs), *n.* [Latin "we command"] A writ issued by a superior court to compel a lower court or a government officer to perform mandatory or purely ministerial duties correctly.—Also termed *writ of mandamus.* Pl. **mandamuses.**—**mandamus,** *vb.*

mandatory commitment. See COMMITMENT.

mandatory instruction. See JURY INSTRUCTION.

mandatory penalty. See *mandatory sentence* under SENTENCE.

mandatory presumption. See *conclusive presumption* under PRESUMPTION.

mandatory punishment. See *mandatory sentence* under SENTENCE.

mandatory sentence. See SENTENCE.

man-endangering state of mind. See PERSON-ENDANGERING STATE OF MIND.

manifest constitutional error. See ERROR.

manifest error. See ERROR.

manifest intent. See INTENT.

manifest necessity. See NECESSITY.

manipulation. The illegal practice of raising or lowering a security's price by creating the appearance of active trading. ● Manipulation is prohibited by section 10(b) of the Securities Exchange Act of 1934. 15 USCA § 78j(b).— Also termed *market manipulation*; *stock manipulation*.

Mann Act. A federal law, enacted originally in 1948, that criminalizes the transportation of any person in interstate or foreign commerce for prostitution or similar sexual activities. 18 USCA § 2421.—Also termed *White Slave Traffic Act.*

mansion house. See DWELLING-HOUSE.

manslaughter, *n.* The unlawful killing of a human being without malice aforethought.— **manslaughter,** *vb.* Cf. MURDER.

> **involuntary manslaughter.** Homicide in which there is no intention to kill or do grievous bodily harm, but that is committed with criminal negligence or during the commission of a crime not included within the felony-murder rule.—Also termed *negligent manslaughter.* Cf. ACCIDENTAL KILLING.

429

misdemeanor manslaughter. Unintentional homicide that occurs during the commission of a misdemeanor (such as a traffic violation).

voluntary manslaughter. An act of murder reduced to manslaughter because of extenuating circumstances such as adequate provocation (arousing the "heat of passion") or diminished capacity.—Also termed *intentional manslaughter.*

manstealing. See KIDNAPPING.

Mapp **hearing.** A hearing held to determine whether evidence implicating the accused was obtained as the result of an illegal search and seizure, and should therefore be suppressed. *Mapp v. Ohio,* 367 U.S. 643, 81 S.Ct. 1684 (1961).

maraud (mə-**rawd**), *vb.* To rove about to pillage or plunder; to loot.

marital-communications privilege. See *marital privilege* (1) under PRIVILEGE (3).

marital privilege. See PRIVILEGE (3).

marital rape. See RAPE.

mariticide. 1. The murder of one's husband. **2.** A woman who murders her husband. Cf. UXORICIDE.

marked money. Money that bears a telltale mark so that the money can be traced, usu. to a perpetrator of a crime, as when marked money is given to a kidnapper as ransom.

market manipulation. See MANIPULATION.

marriage broker. One who arranges a marriage in exchange for consideration. • A marriage broker may be subject to criminal liability for public-policy reasons.

marshal, *n.* **1.** A law-enforcement officer with duties similar to those of a sheriff. **2.** A judicial officer who provides court security, executes process, and performs other tasks for the court.—**marshalship,** *n.*

> *United States Marshal.* A federal official who carries out the orders of a federal court. • U.S. Marshals are employees of the executive branch of government.

Mary Major. See JANE DOE.

Massiah **rule.** The principle that an attempt to elicit incriminating statements (usu. not during a formal interrogation) from a suspect whose right to counsel has attached but who has not waived that right violates the Sixth Amendment. *Massiah v. United States*, 377 U.S. 201, 84 S.Ct. 1199 (1964). See DELIBERATE ELICITATION.

mass murder. See MURDER.

material, *adj.* **1.** Of or relating to matter; physical <material goods>. **2.** Having some logical connection with the consequential facts <material evidence>. **3.** Of such a nature that knowledge of the item would affect a person's decision-making process; significant; essential <material alteration of the document>.—**materiality,** *n.* Cf. RELEVANT.

material allegation. See ALLEGATION.

material evidence. See EVIDENCE.

material fact. See FACT.

material witness. See WITNESS.

mathematical evidence. See EVIDENCE.

matricide (**ma**-trə-sɪd), *n.* **1.** The act of killing one's own mother. **2.** One who kills his or her mother.—**matricidal,** *adj.*

maximalist retributivism. See RETRIBUTIVISM.

maximum sentence. See SENTENCE.

mayhem (**may**-hem), *n.* **1.** The crime of maliciously injuring a person's body, esp. to impair or destroy the victim's capacity for self-defense. • Modern statutes usu. treat this as a form of aggravated battery. See BATTERY. **2.** Violent destruction. **3.** Rowdy confusion or disruption.—**maim** (for sense 1), *vb.*

mayor's court. A municipal court in which the mayor presides as the judge, with jurisdiction over minor criminal (and sometimes civil) matters, traffic offenses, and the like.

***McNabb–Mallory* rule.** The doctrine that a confession is inadmissible if obtained during an unreasonably long detention period between arrest and a preliminary hearing. • Because of the broader protections afforded under the *Miranda* rule, the *McNabb–Mallory* rule is rarely applied in modern cases. *McNabb v. United States*, 318 U.S. 332, 63 S.Ct. 608 (1943); *Mallory v. United States*, 354 U.S. 449, 77 S.Ct. 1356 (1957).—Often shortened to *Mallory rule.*

***McNaghten* rules** (mik-**nawt**-ən). The doctrine that a person is not criminally responsible for an act when a mental disability prevented the person from knowing either (1) the nature and quality of the act or (2) whether the act was right or wrong. • The federal courts and most states have adopted this test in some form. *McNaghten's Case*, 8 Eng. Rep. 718 (H.L. 1843).—Also spelled *McNaughten*

rules; *M'Naghten rules*; *M'Naughten rules.*—
Also termed *right-and-wrong test*; *right-wrong test*. See INSANITY DEFENSE.

MDV. *abbr.* MOTION FOR DIRECTED VERDICT.

mediate evidence. See *secondary evidence* under EVIDENCE.

mediate testimony. See *secondary evidence* under EVIDENCE.

medical evidence. See EVIDENCE.

medical examiner. A public official who investigates deaths, conducts autopsies, and helps the state prosecute homicide cases. ● Medical examiners have replaced coroners in many states.—Sometimes shortened to *examiner*. See CORONER.

medical jurisprudence. See FORENSIC MEDICINE.

medley (**med**-lee). An affray; sudden or casual fighting. Cf. CHANCE-MEDLEY.

Megan's law (**meg**-ən *or* **may**-gən). A statute requiring local authorities to notify a community of any resident who is a convicted sex offender released from prison. ● Although many of these statutes were enacted in the late 1980s, they took their popular name from Megan Kanka of New Jersey, a seven-year-old who in 1994 was raped and murdered by a twice-convicted sex offender who lived across the street from her house. All states have these laws, but only some require community notification (as by publishing offenders' pictures in local newspapers); in others, people must call a state hotline or submit names of persons they suspect.

memorandum decision. See *memorandum opinion* under OPINION.

memorandum opinion. See OPINION.

menacing, *n.* An attempt to commit common-law assault. • The term is used esp. in jurisdictions that have defined assault to include battery. See ASSAULT.

mens rea (**menz ree**-ə). [Law Latin "guilty mind"] The state of mind that the prosecution, to secure a conviction, must prove that a defendant had when committing a crime; criminal intent or recklessness <the *mens rea* for theft is the intent to deprive the rightful owner of the property>. • *Mens rea* is the second of two essential elements of every crime at common law, the other being the *actus reus*.— Also termed *mental element*; *criminal intent*;

435

guilty mind. Pl. *mentes reae* (**men**-teez **ree**-ee). Cf. ACTUS REUS.

general mens rea. See *general intent* under INTENT.

mental capacity. See CAPACITY.

mental element. See MENS REA.

mental incompetence. See INCOMPETENCY.

mercy. Compassionate treatment, as of criminal offenders or of those in distress; esp., imprisonment, rather than death, imposed as punishment for capital murder. See CLEMENCY.

mercy killing. See EUTHANASIA.

mercy rule. The principle that a defendant is entitled to offer character evidence as a defense to a criminal charge. ● This type of evidence is often offered by the defendant's friends and relatives. Fed. R. Evid. 404(a)(1).

mere-evidence rule. The former doctrine that a search warrant allows seizure of the instrumentalities of the crime (such as a murder weapon) or the fruits of the crime (such as stolen goods), but does not permit the seizure of items that have evidentiary value only (such as incriminating documents). ● The Supreme Court has abolished this rule, and today warrants may be issued to search for and seize all evidence of a crime. *Warden v. Hayden,* 387 U.S. 294, 87 S.Ct. 1642 (1967); Fed. R. Crim. P. 41(b).

meretricious (mer-ə-**trish**-əs), *adj.* **1.** Involving prostitution; of an unlawful sexual nature <a meretricious encounter>. **2.** (Of a romantic relationship) involving either unlawful sexual connection or lack of capacity on the part of one party <a meretricious marriage>. **3.** Superficially attractive but fake nonetheless; alluring by false show <meretricious advertising claims>.

merger. 1. The act or an instance of combining or uniting. **2.** The absorption of a lesser included offense into a more serious offense when a person is charged with both crimes, so that the person is not subject to double jeopardy. ● For example, a defendant cannot be convicted of both attempt (or solicitation) and the completed crime—though merger does not apply to conspiracy and the completed crime.—Also termed *merger of offenses.*

meritorious defense. See DEFENSE.

messuage (**mes**-wij). A dwelling house together with the curtilage, including any outbuildings. See CURTILAGE.

middle-level scrutiny. See INTERMEDIATE SCRU-
TINY.

mid-level scrutiny. See INTERMEDIATE SCRUTI-
NY.

militate (**mil**-ə-tayt), *vb.* To exert a strong
influence <the evidence of police impropriety
militates against a conviction>. Cf. MITIGATE.

***Mimms* order.** A police officer's command for
a motorist to get out of the vehicle. • A
Mimms order need not be independently justified if the initial stop was lawful. *Pennsylvania
v. Mimms*, 434 U.S. 106, 98 S.Ct. 330 (1977).

minimalist retributivism. See RETRIBUTIVISM.

minimal participant. Under the federal sentencing guidelines, a defendant who is among
the least culpable of a group of criminal actors,
as when the defendant does not understand
the scope or structure of the criminal enterprise or the actions of the other members of
the group. • The offense level for a crime of a
minimal participant can be decreased by four
levels. U.S. Sentencing Guidelines Manual
§ 3B1.2(a). Cf. MINOR PARTICIPANT.

minimal scrutiny. See RATIONAL-BASIS TEST.

minimization requirement. The mandate that police officers acting under an eaves-dropping warrant must use the wiretap in a way that will intercept the fewest possible conversations that are not subject to the warrant.

minimum scrutiny. See RATIONAL-BASIS TEST.

minimum sentence. See SENTENCE.

minor, *n.* A person who has not reached full legal age; a child or juvenile.—Also termed *infant.*

> **emancipated minor.** A minor who is self-supporting and independent of parental control, usu. as a result of a court order. See EMANCIPATION.

minor crime. See MISDEMEANOR.

minority. The state or condition of being under legal age.—Also termed *infancy*; *nonage*; *immaturity*. Cf. MAJORITY.

minority opinion. See *dissenting opinion* under OPINION.

minor participant. Under the federal sentencing guidelines, a defendant who is less culpable for a crime than the other members of the group committing the crime, but who

has more culpability than a minimal participant. • A defendant who is a minor participant
can have the offense level for the crime decreased by two levels. U.S. Sentencing Guidelines Manual § 3B1.2(b). Cf. MINIMAL PARTICI-
PANT.

***Miranda* hearing** (mə-**ran**-də). A pretrial
proceeding held to determine whether the *Miranda* rule has been followed and thus whether the prosecutor may introduce into evidence
the defendant's statements to the police made
after arrest. See MIRANDA RULE.

***Miranda* rule.** The doctrine that a criminal
suspect in police custody must be informed of
certain constitutional rights before being interrogated. • The suspect must be advised of
the right to remain silent, the right to have an
attorney present during questioning, and the
right to have an attorney appointed if the
suspect cannot afford one. If the suspect is not
advised of these rights or does not validly
waive them, any evidence obtained during the
interrogation cannot be used against the suspect at trial (except for impeachment purposes). *Miranda v. Arizona*, 384 U.S. 436, 86
S.Ct. 1602 (1966).

Mirandize (mə-**ran**-dɪz), *vb. Slang.* To read
(an arrestee) rights under the *Miranda* rule

<the suspect was arrested, Mirandized, and interrogated>. See MIRANDA RULE.

misadventure. 1. A mishap or misfortune. **2.** Homicide committed accidentally by a person doing a lawful act and having no intent to injure; ACCIDENTAL KILLING.

misbehavior in office. See *official misconduct* under MISCONDUCT.

miscarriage of justice. A grossly unfair outcome in a judicial proceeding, as when a defendant is convicted despite a lack of evidence on an essential element of the crime.—Also termed *failure of justice*.

misconduct (mis-**kon**-dəkt). **1.** A dereliction of duty; unlawful or improper behavior.

affirmative misconduct. **1.** An affirmative act of misrepresentation or concealment of a material fact; intentional wrongful behavior. • Some courts hold that there must be an ongoing pattern of misrepresentation or false promises, as opposed to an isolated act of providing misinformation. **2.** With respect to a claim of estoppel against the federal government, a misrepresentation or concealment of a material fact by a government employee—beyond a merely innocent or negligent misrepresentation.

juror misconduct. A juror's violation of the court's charge or the law, committed either during trial or in deliberations after trial, such as (1) communicating about the case with outsiders, witnesses, attorneys, bailiffs, or judges, (2) bringing into the jury room information about the case but not in evidence, and (3) conducting experiments regarding theories of the case outside the court's presence.

official misconduct. A public officer's corrupt violation of assigned duties by malfeasance, misfeasance, or nonfeasance.—Also termed *misconduct in office*; *misbehavior in office*; *malconduct in office*; *misdemeanor in office*; *corruption in office*; *official corruption*.

wanton misconduct. An act, or a failure to act when there is a duty to do so, in reckless disregard of another's rights, coupled with the knowledge that injury will probably result.—Also termed *wanton and reckless misconduct*.

willful and wanton misconduct. Conduct committed with an intentional or reckless disregard for the safety of others, as by failing to exercise ordinary care to prevent a known danger or to discover a danger.—Also termed *willful indifference to the safety of others*.

willful misconduct. Misconduct committed voluntarily and intentionally.

2. An attorney's dishonesty or attempt to persuade a court or jury by using deceptive or reprehensible methods.

misconduct in office. See *official misconduct* under MISCONDUCT.

misdemeanant (mis-də-**mee**-nənt), *n.* A person who has been convicted of a misdemeanor.

misdemeanor (mis-di-**mee**-nər). **1.** A crime that is less serious than a felony and is usu. punishable by fine, penalty, forfeiture, or confinement (usu. for a brief term) in a place other than prison (such as a county jail).—Also termed *minor crime; summary offense.* Cf. FELONY.

gross misdemeanor. A serious misdemeanor, though not a felony.

serious misdemeanor. One of a class of misdemeanors having more severe penalties than most other misdemeanors. • Conduct rising to the level of a serious misdemeanor can, in some jurisdictions, be charged as either a felony or a misdemeanor.—Also termed *high misdemeanor; indictable misdemeanor; penitentiary misdemeanor; aggravated misdemeanor.*

2. *Archaic.* Any crime, including a felony.

misdemeanor in office. See *official miscon-duct* under MISCONDUCT.

misdemeanor manslaughter. See MAN-SLAUGHTER.

misdemeanor-manslaughter rule. The doctrine that a death occurring during the commission of a misdemeanor (or sometimes a nondangerous felony) is involuntary manslaughter. ● Many states and the Model Penal Code have abolished this rule. Cf. FELONY-MUR-DER RULE.

misfeasance (mis-**fee**-zənts), *n.* **1.** A lawful act performed in a wrongful manner. **2.** More broadly, a transgression or trespass; MALFEA-SANCE.—**misfeasant,** *adj.*—**misfeasor,** *n.*

misjoinder (mis-**joyn**-dər). The improper union of offenses in a criminal case.

misprision (mis-**prizh**-ən). **1.** Concealment or nondisclosure of a serious crime by one who did not participate in the crime.

> *clerical misprision.* A court clerk's mistake or fraud that is apparent from the record.

misprision of felony. Concealment or non-disclosure of someone else's felony.

misprision of treason. Concealment or nondisclosure of someone else's treason.

negative misprision. The wrongful concealment of something that should be revealed <misprision of treason>.

positive misprision. The active commission of a wrongful act <seditious conduct against the government is positive misprision>.

2. Seditious conduct against the government. **3.** An official's failure to perform the duties of public office. **4.** Misunderstanding; mistake.

misprisor (mis-**prı**-zər). One who commits misprision of felony.

mistake. An error, misconception, or misunderstanding; an erroneous belief.

mistake of fact. The defense asserting that a criminal defendant acted from an innocent misunderstanding of fact rather than from a criminal purpose.

mistake of law. The defense asserting that a defendant did not understand the criminal consequences of certain conduct. ● This defense is generally not as effective as a mistake of fact.

mistrial. 1. A trial that the judge brings to an end, without a determination on the merits, because of a procedural error or serious misconduct occurring during the proceedings. **2.** A trial that ends inconclusively because the jury cannot agree on a verdict.

mitigate (**mit**-ə-gayt), *vb.* To make less severe or intense <the fired employee mitigated her damages for wrongful termination by accepting a new job>.—**mitigation**, *n.*—**mitigatory** (**mit**-ə-gə-tor-ee), *adj.* Cf. MILITATE.

mitigating circumstance. See CIRCUMSTANCE.

mitigation of punishment. A reduction in punishment due to mitigating circumstances that reduce the criminal's level of culpability, such as the existence of no prior convictions.

mixed larceny. See LARCENY.

mixed presumption. See PRESUMPTION.

mixed question. See MIXED QUESTION OF LAW AND FACT.

mixed question of law and fact. An issue that is neither a pure question of fact nor a

pure question of law. ● Mixed questions of law
and fact are typically resolved by juries.—Often shortened to *mixed question*.—Also termed
mixed question of fact and law.

MJOA. *abbr*. MOTION FOR JUDGMENT OF ACQUITTAL.

M'Naghten **rules.** See MCNAGHTEN RULES.

M'Naughten **rules.** See MCNAGHTEN RULES.

M.O. *abbr*. MODUS OPERANDI.

model jury charge. See *model jury instruction* under JURY INSTRUCTION.

model jury instruction. See JURY INSTRUCTION.

Model Penal Code. A proposed criminal code
drafted by the American Law Institute and
used as the basis for criminal-law revision by
many states.—Abbr. MPC.

Model Penal Code test. See SUBSTANTIAL-CAPACITY TEST.

moderate force. See *nondeadly force* under
FORCE.

modus (**moh**-dəs). [Latin "mode"] The part of a charging instrument describing the manner in which an offense was committed.

modus operandi (**moh**-dəs op-ə-**ran**-dɪ *or* -dee). [Latin "a manner of operating"] A method of operating or a manner of procedure; esp., a pattern of criminal behavior so distinctive that investigators attribute it to the work of the same person <staging a fight at the train station was part of the pickpocket's modus operandi>.—Abbr. M.O. Pl. **modi operandi.**

moiety (**moy**-ə-tee). In federal customs law, a payment made to an informant who assists in the seizure of contraband, the payment being no more than 25% of the contraband's net value (up to a maximum of $250,000). 19 USCA § 1619.

moiety act. A law providing that a portion (such as half) of an imposed fine will inure to the benefit of the informant.

mole. A person who uses a long affiliation with an organization to gain access to and betray confidential information.

molestation. 1. The persecution or harassment of someone, as in the molestation of a witness. **2.** The act of making unwanted and indecent advances to or on someone, esp. for sexual gratification.—**molest,** *vb.*—**molester,** *n.*

> *child molestation.* Any indecent or sexual activity on, involving, or surrounding a child, usu. under the age of 14. See Fed. R. Evid. 414(d).

money-laundering. See LAUNDERING.

moonshine. *Slang.* A distilled alcoholic beverage, esp. whiskey, that is illegally manufactured.

moral certainty. Absolute certainty. ● Moral certainty is not required to sustain a criminal conviction. See REASONABLE DOUBT.

moral depravity. See MORAL TURPITUDE.

moral evidence. See EVIDENCE.

moral necessity. See NECESSITY.

moral turpitude. Conduct that is contrary to justice, honesty, or morality. ● In the area of legal ethics, offenses involving moral turpitude—such as fraud or breach of trust—traditionally make a person unfit to practice law.—Also termed *moral depravity*.

moral wrong. See WRONG.

moral-wrong doctrine. The doctrine that if a wrongdoer acts on a mistaken understanding of the facts, the law will not exempt the wrongdoer from culpability when, if the facts had been as the actor believed them to be, his or her conduct would nevertheless be immoral.

Morgan presumption. A presumption that shifts the burden of proof by requiring the person against whom it operates to produce sufficient evidence to outweigh the evidence that supports the presumed fact, as in requiring a criminal defendant who was arrested while in possession of an illegal substance— and is thereby presumed to have knowingly possessed it—to produce sufficient evidence to entitle the jury to find that the defendant's evidence outweighs the evidence of knowing possession. See Edmund M. Morgan, *Instructing the Jury Upon Presumptions and Burdens of Proof,* 47 Harv. L. Rev. 59, 82–83 (1933). Cf. THAYER PRESUMPTION.

motion. 1. A written or oral application requesting a court to make a specified ruling or order. 2. A proposal made under formal parliamentary procedure.

motion for a directed verdict. See MOTION FOR DIRECTED VERDICT.

motion for a more definite statement. See MOTION FOR MORE DEFINITE STATEMENT.

motion for a new trial. See MOTION FOR NEW TRIAL.

motion for directed verdict. A party's request that the court enter judgment in its favor before submitting the case to the jury because there is no legally sufficient evidentiary foundation on which a reasonable jury could find for the other party.—Abbr. MDV.—Also termed *motion for a directed verdict*. See *directed verdict* under VERDICT.

motion for judgment of acquittal. A criminal defendant's request, at the close of the government's case or the close of all evidence, to be acquitted because there is no legally sufficient evidentiary basis on which a reasonable jury could return a guilty verdict. ● If the motion is granted, the government has no right of appeal. Fed. R. Crim. P. 29(a).—Abbr. MJOA.

motion for more definite statement. A party's request that the court require an opponent to amend a vague or ambiguous pleading to which the party cannot reasonably be required to respond.—Also termed *motion for a more definite statement*. See BILL OF PARTICULARS.

motion for new trial. A party's post-judgment request that the court vacate the judgment and order a new trial for such reasons as factually insufficient evidence, newly discovered evidence, or jury misconduct. • In many jurisdictions, this motion is required before a party can raise such matters on appeal.—Also termed *motion for a new trial.*

motion in arrest of judgment. 1. A defendant's motion claiming that a substantial error appearing on the face of the record vitiates the whole proceeding and the judgment. **2.** A post-judgment motion in a criminal case claiming that the indictment is insufficient to sustain a judgment or the verdict is somehow insufficient.

motion in limine (in **lim**-ə-nee). A pretrial request that certain inadmissible evidence not be referred to or offered at trial. • Typically, a party makes this motion when it believes that mere mention of the evidence during trial would be highly prejudicial and could not be remedied by an instruction to disregard. If, after the motion is granted, the opposing party mentions or attempts to offer the evidence in the jury's presence, a mistrial may be ordered. A ruling on a motion in limine does not always preserve evidentiary error for appellate purposes. To raise such an error on appeal, a party may be required to formally object when the evidence is actually admitted or excluded during trial.

motion to quash (kwahsh). A party's request that the court nullify process or an act instituted by the other party, as in seeking to nullify a subpoena.

motion to suppress. A request that the court prohibit the introduction of illegally obtained evidence at a criminal trial.

motion to transfer venue. A request that the court transfer the case to another district or county, usu. because the original venue is improper under the applicable venue rules or because of local prejudice. See VENUE; CHANGE OF VENUE.

motive. Something, esp. willful desire, that leads one to act.—Also termed *ulterior intent*. Cf. INTENT.

    bad motive. A person's knowledge that an act is wrongful while the person commits the act.

    malicious motive. A motive for bringing a prosecution, other than to do justice.

MPC. *abbr.* MODEL PENAL CODE.

MPC test. See SUBSTANTIAL-CAPACITY TEST.

mug book. A collection of mug shots of criminal suspects maintained by law-enforcement agencies (such as the FBI and police departments) to be used in identifying criminal offenders.

mug shot. A photograph of a person's face taken after the person has been arrested and booked.

multilevel-distribution program. See PYRAMID SCHEME.

multiple admissibility. See ADMISSIBILITY.

multiple counts. See COUNT.

multiple evidence. See EVIDENCE.

multiple hearsay. See *double hearsay* under HEARSAY.

multiple offense. See OFFENSE.

multiple sentences. See SENTENCE.

multiplicity (məl-tə-**plis**-i-tee), *n.* The improper charging of the same offense in several counts of the indictment or information. • Multiplicity violates the Fifth Amendment protection against double jeopardy.—**multiplicitous** (məl-tə-**plis**-i-təs), *adj.*

municipal court. A court having jurisdiction (usu. civil and criminal) over cases arising within the municipality in which it sits.

municipal judge. See JUDGE.

municipal ordinance. See ORDINANCE.

murder, *n.* The killing of a human being with malice aforethought. ● At common law, the crime of murder was not subdivided, but many state statutes have adopted the degree structure outlined below (though the Model Penal Code has not). See Model Penal Code § 210.2.—**murder,** *vb.*—**murderous,** *adj.* See MALICE AFORETHOUGHT. Cf. MANSLAUGHTER.

> *depraved-heart murder.* A murder resulting from an act so reckless and careless of the safety of others that it demonstrates the perpetrator's complete lack of regard for human life.

> *felony murder.* Murder that occurs during the commission of a felony (esp. a serious one).—Also termed (in English law) *constructive murder.* See FELONY-MURDER RULE.

> *first-degree murder.* Murder that is willful, deliberate, or premeditated, or that is committed during the course of another serious felony (often limited to rape, kidnapping, robbery, burglary, or arson). ● All mur-

der perpetrated by poisoning or by lying in wait is considered first-degree murder. All types of murder not involving willful, deliberate, and premeditated killing are usu. considered second-degree murder.—Also termed *murder of the first degree*; *murder one*.

mass murder. A murderous act or series of acts by which a criminal kills many victims at or near the same time, usu. as part of one act or plan. Cf. *serial murder*.

murder by torture. A murder preceded by the intentional infliction of pain and suffering on the victim.

murder of the first degree. See *first-degree murder*.

murder of the second degree. See *second-degree murder*.

murder of the third degree. See *third-degree murder*.

murder one. See *first-degree murder*.

murder two. See *second-degree murder*.

murder three. See *third-degree murder*.

second-degree murder. Murder that is not aggravated by any of the circumstances of first-degree murder.—Also termed *murder of the second degree*; *murder two*.

serial murder. A murder in which a criminal kills one of many victims over time, often as part of a pattern in which the criminal targets victims who have some similar characteristics. Cf. *mass murder*.

third-degree murder. Statutorily defined murder that is considered less heinous than first- and second-degree murder, resulting from an act that did not constitute murder at common law. • Only a few states have added to their murder statutes a third degree of murder. The other states classify all murders in two degrees. Manslaughter is not a degree of the crime of murder, but instead is a distinct offense.—Also termed *murder of the third degree*; *murder three*.

willful murder. The unlawful and intentional killing of another without excuse or mitigating circumstances.

mute, *n*. **1.** A person who cannot speak. **2.** A person (esp. a prisoner) who stands silent when required to answer or plead. • Formerly, if a prisoner stood mute, a jury was empaneled to determine whether the prisoner was intentionally mute or mute by an act of God. By the English Criminal Law Act of 1827, if a prisoner was mute by malice, the officer automatically entered a plea of not guilty and the trial proceeded. If adjudicated to be insane, the prisoner was kept in custody until the Crown determined what should be done.

mutilation, *n.* The act of cutting off or permanently damaging a body part, esp. an essential one.—**mutilate,** *vb.*—**mutilator,** *n.* See MAYHEM.

mutual affray. See MUTUAL COMBAT.

mutual-agreement program. A prisoner-rehabilitation plan in which the prisoner agrees to take part in certain self-improvement activities to receive a definite parole date.

mutual combat. A consensual fight on equal terms—arising from a moment of passion but not in self-defense—between two persons armed with deadly weapons. • A murder charge may be reduced to voluntary manslaughter if death occurred by mutual combat.—Also termed *mutual affray.* Cf. DUEL.

N

NAA. *abbr.* NEUTRON-ACTIVATION ANALYSIS.

naked confession. See CONFESSION.

narcoanalysis (nahr-koh-ə-**nal**-ə-sis). The process of injecting a "truth-serum" drug into a patient to induce semiconsciousness, and then interrogating the patient. ● This process has been utilized to enhance the memory of a witness.

narcotic, *n.* **1.** An addictive drug, esp. an opiate, that dulls the senses and induces sleep. **2.** (*usu. pl.*) A drug that is controlled or prohibited by law.—**narcotic,** *adj.*

National Institute of Corrections. A federal organization (established within the Bureau of Prisons) whose responsibilities include helping federal, state, and local authorities improve correctional programs, conducting research on correctional issues such as crime prevention, and conducting workshops for law-enforcement personnel, social workers, judges, and others involved in treating and rehabilitating offenders. 18 USCA §§ 4351–4353. See BUREAU OF PRISONS.

National Motor Vehicle Theft Act. See DYER ACT.

national-security privilege. See *state-secrets privilege* under PRIVILEGE (3).

natural death. See DEATH.

natural infancy. See INFANCY.

natural law. 1. A physical law of nature <gravitation is a natural law>. **2.** A philosophical system of legal and moral principles purportedly deriving from a universalized conception of human nature or divine justice rather than from legislative or judicial action; moral law embodied in principles of right and wrong <many ethical teachings are based on natural law>.

natural presumption. See PRESUMPTION.

natural wrong. See *moral wrong* under WRONG.

necessarily included offense. See *lesser included offense* under OFFENSE.

necessary implication. See IMPLICATION.

necessity. 1. A justification defense for a person who acts in an emergency that he or she did not create and who commits a harm that is less severe than the harm that would have occurred but for the person's actions. • For example, a mountain climber lost in a blizzard can assert necessity as a defense to theft of food and blankets from another's cabin.—Also termed *choice of evils*; *duress of circumstances*; *lesser-evils defense*. **2.** A privilege that may relieve a person from liability for trespass or conversion if that person, having no alternative, harms another's property in an effort to protect life or health.

> **manifest necessity.** A sudden and overwhelming emergency, beyond the court's and parties' control, that makes conducting a trial or reaching a fair result impossible and that therefore authorizes the granting of a mistrial. ● The standard of manifest necessity must be met to preclude a defendant from successfully raising a plea of former jeopardy after a mistrial.

> **moral necessity.** A necessity arising from a duty incumbent on a person to act in a particular way.

> **physical necessity.** A necessity involving an actual, tangible force that compels a person to act in a particular way.

necessity defense. See JUSTIFICATION (2).

necropsy (**nek**-rop-see). See AUTOPSY.

negative evidence. See EVIDENCE.

negative misprision. See MISPRISION.

negative pregnant. A denial implying its affirmative opposite by seeming to deny only a qualification of the allegation and not the allegation itself. ● An example is the statement, "I didn't steal the money last Tuesday," the implication being that the theft might have happened on another day.—Also termed *negative pregnant with an affirmative.* Cf. AFFIRMATIVE PREGNANT.

negative proof. See PROOF.

negative testimony. See *negative evidence* under EVIDENCE.

neglect, *n.* The omission of proper attention to a person or thing, whether inadvertent, negligent, or willful; the act or condition of disregarding.—**neglect,** *vb.*—**neglectful,** *adj.*

neglected child. See CHILD.

negligence, *n.* The failure to exercise the standard of care that a reasonably prudent person would have exercised in a similar situation; any conduct that falls below the legal standard established to protect others against unreasonable risk of harm, except for conduct that is intentionally, wantonly, or willfully disregardful of others' rights. • The term denotes culpable carelessness.—**negligent,** *adj.*

    criminal negligence. Gross negligence so extreme that it is punishable as a crime. • For example, involuntary manslaughter or other negligent homicide can be based on criminal negligence, as when an extremely careless automobile driver kills someone.—Also termed *culpable negligence*; *gross negligence.*

    gross negligence. **1.** A lack of slight diligence or care. **2.** A conscious, voluntary act or omission in reckless disregard of a legal duty and of the consequences to another party, who may typically recover exemplary damages.—Also termed *reckless negligence*; *wanton negligence*; *willful negligence*; *willful and wanton negligence*; *hazardous negligence*. **3.** See *criminal negligence*.

negligent escape. See ESCAPE (3).

negligent homicide. See HOMICIDE.

negligent manslaughter. See *involuntary manslaughter* under MANSLAUGHTER.

negligent offense. See OFFENSE.

negotiated plea. See PLEA.

neonaticide. See INFANTICIDE.

neutron-activation analysis. A method of identifying and analyzing physical evidence by measuring gamma rays emitted by a sample of material after that material has been bombarded with neutrons in a nuclear reactor. • This technique can be used, for example, to detect gunshot residue on the hand of someone who recently fired a gun. The analysis is usu. expensive to perform, but most courts allow the results into evidence.—Abbr. NAA.

new court commitment. See COMMITMENT.

newly discovered evidence. See EVIDENCE.

new-rule principle. A doctrine barring federal courts from granting habeas corpus relief to a state prisoner because of a rule, not dictated by existing precedent, announced after the prisoner's conviction and sentence became final.—Also termed *nonretroactivity principle*. See HABEAS CORPUS.

new ruling. A Supreme Court ruling not dictated by precedent existing when the defendant's conviction became final and thus not applicable retroactively to habeas cases. • For example, when the Court in *Ford v. Wainwright*, 477 U.S. 399, 106 S.Ct. 2595 (1986), ruled that the Eighth Amendment prohibits execution of insane prisoners, this new ruling was nonretroactive because it departed so widely from prior doctrine. *Teague v. Lane*, 489 U.S. 288, 109 S.Ct. 1060 (1989). See HABEAS CORPUS.

newsman's privilege. See *journalist's privilege* (1) under PRIVILEGE (3).

new trial. A postjudgment retrial or reexamination of some or all of the issues determined in an earlier judgment. • The trial court may order a new trial by motion of a party or on the court's own initiative. Also, when an appellate court reverses the trial court's judgment, it may remand the case to the trial court for a new trial on some or all of the issues on which the reversal is based. See MOTION FOR NEW TRIAL; REMAND.

NGRI. See *not guilty by reason of insanity* under NOT GUILTY.

night. 1. The time from sunset to sunrise. **2.** Darkness; the time when a person's face is not discernible. • This definition was used in the common-law definition of certain offenses, such as burglary. **3.** Thirty minutes after sunset and thirty minutes before sunrise, or a similar definition as set forth by statute, as in a statute requiring specific authorization for night searches. **4.** Evening.—Also termed *nighttime*.

nightwalker. 1. *Archaic*. A person who suspiciously wanders about at night and who might disturb the peace. ● Nightwalking was an example of a "common" offense requiring no specific facts to be asserted in the indictment. **2.** A sleepwalker. **3.** A prostitute who walks the streets at night; streetwalker.

nimmer. A petty thief; pilferer; pickpocket.

nitroglycerine charge. See ALLEN CHARGE.

no actus reus (noh **ak**-təs **ree**-əs). A plea in which a criminal defendant either denies involvement with a crime or asserts that the harm suffered is too remote from the criminal act to be imputable to the defendant.

no bill, *n*. A grand jury's notation that insufficient evidence exists for an indictment on a criminal charge <the grand jury returned a no bill instead of the indictment the prosecutors expected>.—**no-bill,** *vb*. <the grand jury no-billed three of the charges>. Cf. TRUE BILL.

nocent (**noh**-sənt), *adj*. [fr. Latin *nocere* "harm"] *Archaic*. **1.** Injurious; harmful. **2.** Guilty; criminal. ● This word is the little-used antonym of *innocent*.

nocent, *n. Archaic.* A person who is guilty.

no contest. A criminal defendant's plea that, while not admitting guilt, the defendant will not dispute the charge. ● This plea is often preferable to a guilty plea, which can be used against the defendant in a later civil lawsuit.— Also termed *nolo contendere; non vult contendere.*

no evidence. 1. The lack of a legally sufficient evidentiary basis for a reasonable fact-finder to rule in favor of the party who bears the burden of proof <there is no evidence in the record about his whereabouts at midnight>. **2.** Evidence that has no value in an attempt to prove a matter in issue <that testimony is no evidence of an alibi>.

no-knock search. See SEARCH.

no-knock search warrant. See SEARCH WARRANT.

nolle prosequi (**nahl**-ee **prahs**-ə-kwı), *n.* [Latin "not to wish to prosecute"] **1.** A legal notice that a case has been abandoned. **2.** A docket entry showing that the prosecution has abandoned the action.—Often shortened to *nolle.*

nolle prosequi, *vb.* To abandon (a prosecution); to have (a case) dismissed by a *nolle prosequi* <the state *nolle prosequied* the charges against Johnson>.—Often shortened to *nolle pros*; *nol-pros*; *nol-pro.*

nolo contendere (**noh**-loh kən-**ten**-də-ree). [Latin "I do not wish to contend"] See NO CONTEST.—Often shortened to *nolo.*

no-merit brief. See ANDERS BRIEF.

nominal sentence. See SENTENCE.

nonage. See MINORITY.

nonassertive conduct. See CONDUCT.

nonbailable, *adj.* **1.** (Of a person) not entitled to bail <the defendant was nonbailable because of a charge of first-degree murder>. **2.** (Of an offense) not admitting of bail <murder is a nonbailable offense>.

non compos mentis (non **kom**-pəs **men**-tis), *adj.* [Latin "not master of one's mind"] **1.** Insane. **2.** Incompetent. Cf. COMPOS MENTIS.

nonconsensual, *adj.* Not occurring by mutual consent <nonconsensual sexual relations>.

468

nonconsent. 1. Lack of voluntary agreement. **2.** In the law of rape, the refusal to engage willingly in sexual intercourse. See CONSENT.

non culpabilis (non kəl-**pay**-bə-ləs). [Latin] Not guilty.—Abbr. *non cul*.

noncustodial, *adj.* **1.** (Of an interrogation, etc.) not taking place while a person is in custody. **2.** Of or relating to someone, esp. a parent, who does not have sole or primary custody.

noncustodial sentence. See SENTENCE.

nondeadly force. See FORCE.

noninfamous crime. See CRIME.

nonjudicial punishment. See PUNISHMENT.

nonjury trial. See *bench trial* under TRIAL.

nonjusticiable question. See POLITICAL QUESTION.

nonoccupant visitor. A person who owns, co-owns, is employed by, or is a patron of a business enterprise where a search is being conducted in accordance with a search warrant.

non quieta movere (non kwɪ-**ee**-tə moh-**veer**-ee), *n.* [Latin "not to disturb what is settled"] Stare decisis. ● *Non quieta movere* expresses the same principle as *stare decisis*. It is part of the longer phrase *stare decisis et non quieta movere* ("to adhere to precedents, and not to unsettle things that are established"). See STARE DECISIS.

nonremovable inmate. An alien who, having been detained, would ordinarily be deportable but cannot be deported because the United States does not maintain diplomatic ties with the alien's country of origin.—Also termed *indefinite detainee*; *lifer*.

nonretroactivity principle. See NEW-RULE PRINCIPLE.

nonrun time. See *dead time* under TIME.

nonsupport. The failure to support a person that one is legally obliged to provide for, such as a child, spouse, or other dependent. ● Nonsupport is a crime in most states, where it is often termed *criminal nonsupport*.

nonverbal testimony. See TESTIMONY.

nonvoluntary euthanasia. See EUTHANASIA.

non vult contendere (non vəlt kən-**ten**-də-ree). [Latin "he will not contest it"] See NO CONTEST.

no-retreat rule. The doctrine that the victim of a murderous assault may use deadly force in self-defense if there is no reasonable alternative to avoid the assailant's threatened harm. • A majority of American jurisdictions have adopted this rule. Cf. RETREAT RULE.

not guilty. 1. A defendant's plea denying the crime charged. **2.** A jury verdict acquitting the defendant because the prosecution failed to prove the defendant's guilt beyond a reasonable doubt. Cf. INNOCENT.

> ***not guilty by reason of insanity. 1.*** A not-guilty verdict, based on mental illness, that usu. does not release the defendant but instead results in commitment to a mental institution. **2.** A criminal defendant's plea of not guilty that is based on the insanity defense.—Abbr. NGRI.—Also termed *not guilty on the ground of insanity.* See INSANITY DEFENSE.

not-guilty plea. See PLEA.

notice-of-alibi rule. The principle that, upon written demand from the government, a criminal defendant who intends to call an alibi witness at trial must give notice of who that witness is and where the defendant claims to have been at the time of the alleged offense. ● The government is, in turn, obligated to give notice to the defendant of what witness it intends to call to rebut the alibi testimony. See Fed. R. Crim. P. 12.1.

notice of appeal. A document filed with a court and served on the other parties, stating an intention to appeal a trial court's judgment or order. ● In most jurisdictions, filing a notice of appeal is the act by which the appeal is perfected. For instance, the Federal Rules of Appellate Procedure provide that an appeal is taken by filing a notice of appeal with the clerk of the district court from which the appeal is taken, and that the clerk is to send copies of the notice to all the other parties' attorneys, as well as the court of appeals. Fed. R. App. P. 3(a), (d).—Also termed *claim of appeal*. See APPEAL.

notice of orders or judgments. Written notice of the entry of an order or judgment, provided by the court clerk or one of the parties. ● Notice of a judgment is usu. provided by the clerk of the court in which the judgment was entered. If the court does not provide notice, a party is usu. required to provide it. Under the Federal Rules of Criminal Procedure, the clerk is required to provide immediate notice of any order or judgment to any party to the case who is not in default. Fed. R. Crim. P. 49(c).

notice of trial. A document issued by a court informing the parties of the date on which the case is set for trial. ● While the court typically provides the notice to all parties, it may instead instruct one party to send the notice to all the others.

notice to produce. See REQUEST FOR PRODUCTION.

notorious cohabitation. See COHABITATION.

not proven. An archaic jury verdict—now used only in Scots criminal law—equivalent in result to not guilty, but carrying with it a strong suspicion of wrongdoing.—Also termed *Scotch verdict*.

nullification (nəl-i-fi-**kay**-shən), *n*. **1.** The act of making something void; specif., the action of a state in abrogating a federal law, on the basis of state sovereignty. **2.** The state or condition of being void. See JURY NULLIFICATION.

nunc pro tunc (**nəngk** proh **təngk** *or* **nuungk** proh **tuungk**). [Latin "now for then"] Having retroactive legal effect through a court's inherent power <the court entered a

nunc pro tunc order to correct a clerical error in the record>.

Nuremberg defense (n[y]ər-əm-bərg). The defense asserted by a member of the military who has been charged with the crime of failing to obey an order and who claims that the order was illegal, esp. that the order would result in a violation of international law. ● The term is sometimes used more broadly to describe situations in which citizens accused of committing domestic crimes, such as degradation of government property, claim that their crimes were justified or mandated by international law.

nystagmus (ni-**stag**-məs). A rapid, involuntary jerking or twitching of the eyes, sometimes caused by ingesting drugs or alcohol. See HORIZONTAL-GAZE NYSTAGMUS TEST.

O

oath. 1. A solemn declaration, accompanied by a swearing to God or a revered person or thing, that one's statement is true or that one will be bound to a promise. ● The person making the oath implicitly invites punishment if the statement is untrue or the promise is broken. The legal effect of an oath is to subject the person to penalties for perjury if the testimony is false. **2.** A statement or promise made by such a declaration. **3.** A form of words used for such a declaration. **4.** A formal declaration made solemn without a swearing to God or a revered person or thing; AFFIRMATION.

assertory oath (ə-**sər**-tə-ree). An oath by which one attests to some factual matter, rather than making a promise about one's future conduct. ● A courtroom witness typically takes such an oath.

corporal oath (**kor**-pər-əl). An oath made solemn by touching a sacred object, esp. the Bible.

extrajudicial oath. An oath that, although formally sworn, is taken outside a legal proceeding or outside the authority of law.

judicial oath. An oath taken in the course of a judicial proceeding, esp. in open court.

pauper's oath. An affidavit or verification of poverty by a person requesting public funds or services. See *poverty affidavit* under AFFIDAVIT; IN FORMA PAUPERIS.

object (əb-**jekt**), *vb.* **1.** To state in opposition; to put forward as an objection <the prosecution objected that the defendant's discovery requests were untimely>. **2.** To state or put forward an objection, esp. to something in a judicial proceeding <the defense objected to the testimony on the ground that it was privileged>.—**objector,** *n.*

objection, *n.* A formal statement opposing something that has occurred, or is about to occur, in court and seeking the judge's immediate ruling on the point. ● The party objecting must usu. state the basis for the objection to preserve the right to appeal an adverse ruling.

   continuing objection. A single objection to all the questions in a given line of questioning. ● A judge may allow a lawyer to make a continuing objection when the judge has overruled an objection applicable to many questions, and the lawyer wants to preserve the objection for the appellate record.—Also termed *running objection.*

   general objection. An objection made without specifying any grounds in support of the objection. ● A general objection preserves only the issue of relevancy.—Also termed *broadside objection.*

speaking objection. An objection that contains more information (often in the form of argument) than needed by the judge to sustain or overrule it. ● Many judges prohibit lawyers from using speaking objections, and sometimes even from stating the grounds for objections, because of the potential for influencing the jury.

specific objection. An objection that is accompanied by a statement of one or more grounds in support of the objection.

objective method. See HYPOTHETICAL-PERSON DEFENSE.

object offense. See OFFENSE.

oblique evidence. See *circumstantial evidence* (1) under EVIDENCE.

obscene, *adj.* Extremely offensive under contemporary community standards of morality and decency; grossly repugnant to the generally accepted notions of what is appropriate. ● Under the Supreme Court's three-part test, material is legally obscene—and therefore not protected under the First Amendment—if, taken as a whole, the material (1) appeals to the prurient interest in sex, as determined by the average person applying contemporary community standards; (2) portrays sexual conduct, as specifically defined by the applicable state law, in a patently offensive way; and (3) lacks serious literary, artistic, political, or scientific value. *Miller v. California*, 413 U.S. 15, 93 S.Ct. 2607 (1973).

obscene libel. See LIBEL.

obscenity, *n.* **1.** The quality or state of being morally abhorrent or socially taboo, esp. as a result of referring to or depicting sexual or excretory functions. **2.** Something (such as an expression or act) that has this quality. See CONTEMPORARY COMMUNITY STANDARD. Cf. INDECENCY.

   commercialized obscenity. Obscenity produced and marketed for sale to the public.

obstruction of justice. Interference with the orderly administration of law and justice, as by giving false information to or withholding evidence from a police officer or prosecutor, or by harming or intimidating a witness or juror. ● Obstruction of justice is a crime in most jurisdictions. See 18 USCA §§ 1501 et seq.—Also termed *obstructing justice*; *obstructing public justice*.

obtaining property by false pretenses. See FALSE PRETENSES.

occupational crime. See CRIME.

OD. *abbr*. Overdose.

offender. A person who has committed a crime.

> ***adult offender.*** **1.** A person who has committed a crime after reaching the age of majority. **2.** A person who, having committed a crime while a minor, has been convicted after reaching the age of majority. **3.** A juvenile who has committed a crime and is tried as an adult rather than as a juvenile.

> ***career offender.*** Under the federal-sentencing guidelines, an adult who, after being convicted of two violent felonies or controlled-substance felonies, commits another such felony. U.S. Sentencing Guidelines Manual § 4B1.1.

> ***first offender.*** A person who authorities believe has committed a crime but who has never before been convicted of a crime. ● First offenders are often treated leniently at sentencing or in plea negotiations.

> ***habitual offender.*** See RECIDIVIST.

> ***repeat offender.*** A person who has been convicted of a crime more than once; RECIDIVIST.

> ***situational offender.*** A first-time offender who is unlikely to commit future crimes.

status offender. A youth who engages in conduct that—though not criminal by adult standards—is considered inappropriate enough to bring a charge against the youth in juvenile court; a juvenile who commits a status offense. Cf. *youthful offender*; JUVENILE DELINQUENT.

youthful offender. **1.** A person in late adolescence or early adulthood who has been convicted of a crime. ● A youthful offender is often eligible for special programs not available to older offenders, including community supervision, the successful completion of which may lead to erasing the conviction from the offender's record. **2.** See JUVENILE DELINQUENT.—Also termed *young offender*; *youth offender.* Cf. *status offender.*

offense (ə-**fents**). A violation of the law; a crime, often a minor one. See CRIME.

acquisitive offense. An offense characterized by the unlawful appropriation of another's property. ● This is a generic term that refers to a variety of crimes (such as larceny) rather than a particular one.

allied offense. A crime with elements so similar to those of another that the commission of the one is automatically the commission of the other.

anticipatory offense. See *inchoate offense.*

bailable offense. A criminal charge for which a defendant may be released from custody after providing proper security <misdemeanor theft is a bailable offense>.

capital offense. A crime for which the death penalty may be imposed.—Also termed *capital crime.*

cognate offense. A lesser offense that is related to the greater offense because it shares several of the elements of the greater offense and is of the same class or category. • For example, shoplifting is a cognate offense of larceny because both crimes require the element of taking property with the intent to deprive the rightful owner of that property. Cf. *lesser included offense.*

continuing offense. A crime (such as a conspiracy) that is committed over a period of time, so that the last act of the crime controls when the statute of limitations begins to run.

cumulative offense. An offense committed by repeating the same act at different times.

divisible offense. A crime that includes one or more crimes of lesser grade. • For example, murder is a divisible offense comprising assault, battery, and assault with intent to kill.

extraneous offense. An offense beyond or unrelated to the offense for which a defendant is on trial.

graded offense. A crime that is divided into various degrees of severity with corresponding levels of punishment, such as murder (first-degree and second-degree) or assault (simple and aggravated).

impeachable offense. See IMPEACHABLE OFFENSE.

inchoate offense. A step toward the commission of another crime, the step in itself being serious enough to merit punishment. • The three inchoate offenses are attempt, conspiracy, and solicitation.—Also termed *anticipatory offense*; *inchoate crime*; *preliminary crime*.

included offense. See *lesser included offense*.

index offense. One of eight classes of crimes reported annually by the FBI in the Uniform Crime Report. • The eight classes are murder (and nonnegligent homicide), rape, robbery, aggravated assault, burglary, larceny-theft, arson, and auto theft.—Also termed *index crime*.

indictable offense. A crime that can be prosecuted only by indictment. • In federal court, such an offense is one punishable by death or by imprisonment for more than one year or at hard labor. Fed. R. Crim. P. 7(a). See INDICTMENT.

joint offense. An offense (such as conspiracy) committed by the participation of two or more persons.

lesser included offense. A crime that is composed of some, but not all, of the elements of a more serious crime and that is necessarily committed in carrying out the greater crime <battery is a lesser included offense of murder>. ● For double-jeopardy purposes, a lesser included offense is considered the "same offense" as the greater offense, so that acquittal or conviction of either offense precludes a separate trial for the other.—Also termed *included offense*; *necessarily included offense.* Cf. *cognate offense.*

liquor offense. Any crime involving the inappropriate use or sale of intoxicating liquor. See DRIVING WHILE INTOXICATED.

multiple offense. An offense that violates more than one law but that may require different proof so that an acquittal or conviction under one statute does not exempt the defendant from prosecution under another.

necessarily included offense. See *lesser included offense.*

negligent offense. A violation of law arising from a defective discharge of duty or from criminal negligence. See *criminal negligence* under NEGLIGENCE.

object offense. The crime that is the object of the defendant's attempt, solicitation, conspiracy, or complicity. • For example, murder is the object offense in a charge of attempted murder.—Also termed *target offense.*

offense against property. A crime against another's personal property. • The common-law offenses against property were larceny, embezzlement, cheating, cheating by false pretenses, robbery, receiving stolen goods, malicious mischief, forgery, and uttering forged instruments. Although the term *crimes against property*—a common term in modern usage—includes crimes against real property, the term *offense against property* is traditionally restricted to personal property. Cf. CRIMES AGAINST PROPERTY.

offense against public justice and authority. A crime that impairs the administration of justice. • The common-law offenses of this type were obstruction of justice, barratry, maintenance, champerty, embracery, escape, prison breach, rescue, misprision of felony, compounding a crime, subornation of perjury, bribery, and misconduct in office.

offense against the habitation. A crime against another's house—traditionally either arson or burglary.

offense against the person. A crime against the body of another human being. • The common-law offenses against the person were murder, manslaughter, mayhem, rape, assault, battery, robbery, false imprisonment, abortion, seduction, kidnapping, and abduction. Cf. CRIMES AGAINST PERSONS.

offense against the public health, safety, comfort, and morals. A crime traditionally viewed as endangering the whole of society. • The common-law offenses of this type were nuisance, bigamy, adultery, fornication, lewdness, illicit cohabitation, incest, miscegenation, sodomy, bestiality, buggery, abortion, and seduction.

offense against the public peace. A crime that tends to disturb the peace. • The common-law offenses of this type were riot, unlawful assembly, dueling, rout, affray, forcible entry and detainer, and libel on a private person.

petty offense. A minor or insignificant crime. Cf. *serious offense.*

political offense. See POLITICAL OFFENSE.

public offense. An act or omission forbidden by law.

public-welfare offense. A minor offense that involves no moral delinquency, being intended only to secure the effective regulation of conduct in the interest of the community. ● An example is driving a car with one brake-light missing.—Also termed *regulatory offense.*

regulatory offense. **1.** A statutory crime, as opposed to a common-law crime. **2.** See *public-welfare offense.*

same offense. **1.** For double-jeopardy purposes, the same criminal act, omission, or transaction for which the person has already stood trial. See DOUBLE JEOPARDY. **2.** For sentencing and enhancement-of-punishment purposes, an offense that is quite similar to a previous one.

second offense. An offense committed after conviction for a first offense. ● The previous conviction, not the indictment, forms the basis of the charge of a second offense.

separate offense. **1.** An offense arising out of the same event as another offense but containing some differences in elements of proof. ● A person may be tried, convicted, and sentenced for each separate offense. **2.** An offense arising out of a different event entirely from another offense under consideration.

serious offense. An offense not classified as a petty offense and usu. carrying at least a six-month sentence.—Also termed *serious crime.* Cf. *petty offense.*

sexual offense. An offense involving unlawful sexual conduct, such as prostitution, indecent exposure, incest, pederasty, and bestiality.

status offense. **1.** See *status crime* under CRIME. **2.** A minor's violation of the juvenile code by doing some act that would not be considered illegal if an adult did it, but that indicates that the minor is beyond parental control. ● Examples include running away from home, truancy, and incorrigibility. See JUVENILE DELINQUENCY.

strict-liability offense. An offense that does not require a culpable mental state.

substantive offense (səb-stən-tiv). A crime that is complete in itself and is not dependent on another crime for one of its elements.—Also termed *substantive crime*.

summary offense. An offense (such as a petty misdemeanor) that can be prosecuted without an indictment. Cf. *indictable offense*.

target offense. See *object offense*.

unrelated offense. A crime that is independent from the charged offense.

violent offense. A crime characterized by extreme physical force, such as murder, forcible rape, and assault and battery with a dangerous weapon.—Also termed *violent felony*.

offense against property. See OFFENSE.

offense against public justice and authority. See OFFENSE.

offense against the habitation. See OFFENSE.

offense against the person. See OFFENSE.

offense against the public health, safety, comfort, and morals. See OFFENSE.

offense against the public peace. See OFFENSE.

offer, *n.* See ATTEMPT.

offer of proof. A presentation of evidence for the record (but outside the jury's presence) usu. made after the judge has sustained an objection to the admissibility of that evidence, so that the evidence can be preserved on the record for an appeal of the judge's ruling. • An offer of proof, which may also be used to persuade the court to admit the evidence, consists of three parts: (1) the evidence itself, (2) an explanation of the purpose for which it is offered (its relevance), and (3) an argument supporting admissibility. Such an offer may include tangible evidence or testimony (through questions and answers, a lawyer's narrative description, or an affidavit). Fed. R. Evid. 103(a)(2).—Also termed *avowal*.

officer of the court. A person who is charged with upholding the law and administering the judicial system. • Typically, *officer of the court* refers to a judge, clerk, bailiff, sheriff, or the like, but the term also applies to a lawyer, who is obliged to obey court rules and who owes a duty of candor to the court.—Also termed *court officer*.

officer of the peace. See PEACE OFFICER.

official corruption. See *official misconduct* under MISCONDUCT.

489

official misconduct. See MISCONDUCT.

official privilege. See PRIVILEGE (3).

omnibus hearing. See HEARING.

OMVI. *abbr*. Operating a motor vehicle while intoxicated. See DRIVING UNDER THE INFLUENCE.

OMVUI. *abbr*. Operating a motor vehicle under the influence. See DRIVING UNDER THE INFLUENCE.

180-day rule. 1. A rule that, in some jurisdictions, allows a person charged with a felony to be released on personal recognizance if the person has been in jail for 180 days without being brought to trial, and if the delay has not resulted from the defendant's own actions. **2.** A rule requiring all pending charges against a prison inmate to be brought to trial in 180 days or to be dismissed with prejudice.

on pain of. Followed by punishment inflicted if one does not comply with a command or condition <ordered to cease operations on pain of a $2,000 fine>.

onus probandi (**oh**-nəs prə-**ban**-dɪ). [Latin] See BURDEN OF PROOF.—Often shortened to *onus*.

op. *abbr.* OPINION.

open and notorious adultery. See ADULTERY.

open court. 1. A court that is in session, presided over by a judge, attended by the parties and their attorneys, and engaged in judicial business. • *Open court* usu. refers to a proceeding in which formal entries are made on the record. The term is distinguished from a court that is hearing evidence in camera or from a judge that is exercising merely magisterial powers. **2.** A court session that the public is free to attend. • Most state constitutions have open-court provisions guaranteeing the public's right to attend trials.

open-fields doctrine. The rule permitting a warrantless search, without probable cause, of the area outside a property owner's curtilage, which includes the home and any adjoining land (such as a yard) that is within an enclosure or otherwise protected from public scrutiny.—Also termed *open-field doctrine*; *open-fields rule*. Cf. PLAIN-VIEW DOCTRINE.

opening statement. At the outset of a trial, an advocate's statement giving the fact-finder a preview of the case and of the evidence to be presented. • Although the opening statement is not supposed to be argumentative, lawyers—purposefully or not—often include some form of argument. The term is thus sometimes referred to as *opening argument*.

open lewdness. See LEWDNESS.

open verdict. See VERDICT.

operating a motor vehicle under the influence. See DRIVING UNDER THE INFLUENCE.

operating a motor vehicle while intoxicated. See DRIVING UNDER THE INFLUENCE.

operating under the influence. See DRIVING UNDER THE INFLUENCE.

operating while intoxicated. See DRIVING UNDER THE INFLUENCE.

opinion. 1. A court's written statement explaining its decision in a given case, usu. including the statement of facts, points of law, rationale, and dicta.—Abbr. op.—Also termed *judicial opinion*. Cf. JUDGMENT; RULING.

> *advisory opinion.* A nonbinding statement by a court of its interpretation of the law on a matter submitted for that purpose. ● Federal courts are constitutionally prohibited from issuing advisory opinions by the case-or-controversy requirement, but other

courts, such as the International Court of Justice, render them routinely.

dissenting opinion. An opinion by one or more judges who disagree with the decision reached by the majority.—Often shortened to *dissent.*—Also termed *minority opinion.*

majority opinion. An opinion joined in by more than half of the judges considering a given case.—Also termed *main opinion.*

memorandum opinion. A unanimous opinion stating the decision of the court; an opinion that briefly reports the court's conclusion, usu. without elaboration because the decision follows a well-established legal principle or does not relate to any point of law.—Also termed *memorandum decision.*

minority opinion. See *dissenting opinion.*

per curiam opinion (pər **kyoor**-ee-əm). An opinion handed down by an appellate court without identifying the individual judge who wrote the opinion.—Sometimes shortened to *per curiam.*

plurality opinion. An opinion lacking enough judges' votes to constitute a majority, but receiving more votes than any other opinion.

seriatim opinions (seer-ee-**ay**-tim). A series of opinions written individually by each judge on the bench, as opposed to a single opinion speaking for the court as a whole.

2. A witness's thoughts, beliefs, or inferences about facts in dispute, as opposed to personal knowledge of the facts themselves.—Also termed (in sense 2) *conclusion*. See *opinion evidence* under EVIDENCE.

opinion evidence. See EVIDENCE.

opinion rule. The principle that a witness should testify to facts, not opinions, and that a witness's opinions are often excludable from evidence. ● Traditionally, this principle is regarded as one of the important exclusionary rules in evidence law. It is based on the idea that a witness who has observed data should provide the most factual evidence possible, leaving the jury to draw inferences and conclusions from the evidence. Under this system, the witness's opinion is unnecessary. Today, opinions are admissible if rationally based on a witness's perceptions and helpful to the factfinder.

opinion testimony. See TESTIMONY.

oppression. 1. The act or an instance of unjustly exercising authority or power. **2.** An offense consisting in the abuse of discretionary authority by a public officer who has an improper motive, as a result of which a person is injured. ● This offense does not include extortion, which is typically a more serious crime.— **oppress,** *vb.*—**oppressive,** *adj.*

oppressor. A public official who unlawfully or wrongfully exercises power under color of authority in a way that causes a person harm; one who commits oppression.

O.R. *abbr.* Own recognizance; on one's own recognizance <the prosecutor agreed not to object to releasing the suspect O.R.>. See RECOGNIZANCE; RELEASE ON RECOGNIZANCE.

oral argument. An advocate's spoken presentation before a court (esp. an appellate court) supporting or opposing the legal relief at issue.

oral confession. See CONFESSION.

order, *n.* **1.** A command, direction, or instruction. **2.** A written direction or command delivered by a court or judge.—Also termed *court order; judicial order.*

　ex parte order (eks **pahr**-tee). An order made by the court upon the application of one party to an action without notice to the other.

495

ORDER

final order. An order that is dispositive of the entire case.

interim order. **1.** A temporary court decree that takes effect until something else occurs. **2.** See *interlocutory order.*

interlocutory order (in-tər-**lok**-yə-tor-ee). An order that relates to some intermediate matter in the case; any order other than a final order. ● Most interlocutory orders are not appealable until the case is fully resolved. But by rule or statute, most jurisdictions allow some types of interlocutory orders (such as preliminary injunctions and class-certification orders) to be immediately appealed.—Also termed *interlocutory decision; interim order; intermediate order.*

show-cause order. An order directing a party to appear in court and explain why the party took (or failed to take) some action or why the court should or should not grant some relief.—Also termed *order to show cause.*

temporary restraining order. See TEMPORARY RESTRAINING ORDER.

ordinance (**or**-də-nənts). An authoritative law or decree; esp., a municipal regulation. ● Municipal governments can pass ordinances on matters that the state government allows to be regulated at the local level.—Also termed *by-law*; *municipal ordinance*.

ordinarily prudent person. See REASONABLE PERSON.

ordinary law. See STATUTORY LAW.

organic law. See CASELAW.

organizational crime. See *corporate crime* under CRIME.

organized crime. 1. Widespread criminal activities that are coordinated and controlled through a central syndicate. See RACKETEERING. **2.** Persons involved in these criminal activities; a syndicate of criminals who rely on their unlawful activities for income.

original-document rule. See BEST-EVIDENCE RULE.

original evidence. See EVIDENCE.

original jurisdiction. See JURISDICTION.

original precedent. See PRECEDENT.

original-writing rule. See BEST-EVIDENCE RULE.

ostrich defense. A criminal defendant's claim not to have known of the criminal activities of an associate.

ostrich instruction. See JURY INSTRUCTION.

OUI. *abbr.* Operating under the influence. See DRIVING UNDER THE INFLUENCE.

outlaw, *n.* **1.** A person who has been deprived of the benefit and protection of the law; a person under a sentence of outlawry. **2.** A lawless person or habitual criminal; esp., a fugitive from the law.

outlaw, *vb.* **1.** To deprive (someone) of the benefit and protection of the law; to declare an outlaw <outlaw the fugitive>. **2.** To make illegal <outlaw fireworks within city limits>. **3.** To remove from legal jurisdiction or enforcement; to deprive of legal force <outlaw a claim under the statute>.

outlawry. **1.** The state or condition of being outlawed; the status of an outlaw. **2.** Disregard or disobedience of the law.

outrageous conduct. See CONDUCT.

outstanding warrant. See WARRANT.

overt, *adj*. Open and observable; not concealed or secret <the conspirators' overt acts>.

overt act. 1. An act that indicates an intent to kill or seriously harm another person and thus gives that person a justification to use self-defense. **2.** An outward act, however innocent in itself, done in furtherance of a conspiracy, treason, or criminal attempt. ● An overt act is usu. a required element of these crimes. **3.** See ACTUS REUS.—Also termed *positive act*.

OWI. *abbr*. Operating while intoxicated. See DRIVING UNDER THE INFLUENCE.

P

packing a jury. See JURY-PACKING.

pain of, on. See ON PAIN OF.

pains and penalties, bill of. See BILL OF PAINS AND PENALTIES.

pander, *n.* One who engages in pandering.— Also termed *panderer*. See PIMP.

pandering (**pan**-dər-ing), *n.* **1.** The act or offense of recruiting a prostitute, finding a place of business for a prostitute, or soliciting customers for a prostitute.—Also termed *promoting prostitution*. **2.** The act or offense of selling or distributing textual or visual material (such as magazines or videotapes) openly advertised to appeal to the recipient's sexual interest. ● Although the concept of pandering was invoked by the U.S. Supreme Court in *Ginzburg v. United States*, 383 U.S. 463, 86 S.Ct. 942 (1966), it has seldom been discussed by the Court since then.—**pander,** *vb.*

panel attorney. A private attorney who represents indigent defendants at government expense.

pardon, *n.* The act or an instance of officially nullifying punishment or other legal consequences of a crime. ● A pardon is usu. granted by the chief executive of a government. The President has the sole power to issue pardons for federal offenses, and state governors have the power to issue pardons for state crimes.— Also termed *executive pardon.*—**pardon,** *vb.* See CLEMENCY. Cf. COMMUTATION; REPRIEVE.

> ***absolute pardon.*** A pardon that releases the wrongdoer from punishment and restores the offender's civil rights without qualification.—Also termed *full pardon*; *unconditional pardon.*

> ***conditional pardon.*** A pardon that does not become effective until the wrongdoer satisfies a prerequisite or that will be revoked upon the occurrence of some specified act.

> ***general pardon.*** See AMNESTY.

> ***partial pardon.*** A pardon that exonerates the offender from some but not all of the punishment or legal consequences of a crime.

pardon attorney. A Justice Department lawyer who considers applications for federal pardons and forwards those of promising candidates for review by the President.

parens patriae (**par**-enz **pay**-tree-ee *or* **pa**-tree-ı). [Latin "parent of his or her country"] The state regarded as a sovereign; the state in

501

its capacity as provider of protection to those unable to care for themselves <the attorney general acted as *parens patriae* in the hearing>.

parental kidnapping. See KIDNAPPING.

Parental Kidnapping Prevention Act. A federal law, enacted in 1980, providing a penalty for child-kidnapping by a noncustodial parent and requiring a state to recognize and enforce a child-custody order rendered by a court of another state. 28 USCA § 1738A; 42 USCA §§ 654, 655, 663.—Abbr. PKPA.

parental-responsibility statute. A law imposing criminal sanctions (such as fines) on parents whose minor children commit crimes as a result of the parents' failure to exercise sufficient control over them.—Also termed *control-your-kid law*.

parenticide (pə-**ren**-tə-sɪd). **1.** The act of murdering one's parent. **2.** A person who murders his or her parent.

parliamentary privilege. 1. See PRIVILEGE (1). **2.** See *legislative privilege* under PRIVILEGE (3).

parol arrest. See ARREST.

parole (pə-**rohl**), *n.* The release of a prisoner from imprisonment before the full sentence has been served. • Although not available under some sentences, parole is usu. granted for good behavior on the condition that the parolee regularly report to a supervising officer for a specified period.—**parole,** *vb.* Cf. PARDON; PROBATION.

> *bench parole.* See *bench probation* under PROBATION.

> *juvenile parole.* The conditional release of a juvenile offender from confinement.—Also termed *aftercare.*

parole board. A governmental body that decides whether prisoners may be released from prison before completing their sentences.—Also termed *board of parole; parole commission.*

parolee (pə-roh-**lee**). A prisoner who is released on parole.

parole revocation. The administrative act of returning a parolee to prison because of the parolee's failure to abide by the conditions of parole (as by committing a new offense).

parol evidence. See EVIDENCE.

parricide (**par**-ə-sɪd), *n*. **1.** The act of killing a close relative, esp. a parent. **2.** One who kills such a relative.—**parricidal,** *adj*. Cf. PATRI-CIDE.

partial evidence. See EVIDENCE.

partial insanity. See *diminished capacity* under CAPACITY.

partial pardon. See PARDON.

partial responsibility. See *diminished capacity* under CAPACITY.

partial verdict. See VERDICT.

particeps criminis (**pahr**-tə-seps **krim**-ə-nis), *n*. [Latin "partner in crime"] **1.** An accomplice or accessory. Pl. *participes criminis* (pahr-**tis**-ə-peez). See ACCESSORY. **2.** The doctrine that one participant in an unlawful activity cannot recover in a civil action against another participant in the activity. ● This is a civil doctrine only, having nothing to do with criminal responsibility.

participant. See MINIMAL PARTICIPANT; MINOR PARTICIPANT.

particular malice. See MALICE.

passive concealment. See CONCEALMENT.

passive euthanasia. See EUTHANASIA.

past recollection recorded. A document concerning events that a witness once knew about but can no longer remember. ● The document itself is evidence and, despite being hearsay, may be admitted (or read into the record) if it was prepared or adopted by the witness when the events were fresh in the witness's memory. Fed. R. Evid. 803(5).—Also termed *recorded recollection*; *past recorded recollection*. Cf. PRESENT RECOLLECTION REFRESHED.

pat-down, *n.* See FRISK.

***Pate* hearing.** A proceeding in which the trial court seeks to determine whether a criminal defendant is competent to stand trial. *Pate v. Robinson*, 383 U.S. 375, 86 S.Ct. 836 (1966); 18 USCA § 4241.—Also termed *competency hearing*; *incompetency hearing*.

pathological intoxication. See INTOXICATION.

patient-physician privilege. See *doctor-patient privilege* under PRIVILEGE (3).

patricide (pa-trə-sɪd), *n.* **1.** The act of killing one's own father. **2.** One who kills his or her father.—**patricidal,** *adj.* Cf. PARRICIDE.

patronizing a prostitute. The offense of requesting or securing the performance of a sex act for a fee; PROSTITUTION.

pattern jury charge. See *model jury instruction* under JURY INSTRUCTION.

pattern jury instruction. See *model jury instruction* under JURY INSTRUCTION.

pattern of racketeering activity. Two or more related criminal acts that amount to, or pose a threat of, continued criminal activity. • This phrase derives from the federal Racketeer Influenced and Corrupt Organizations Act. See RACKETEERING.

pauper's affidavit. See *poverty affidavit* under AFFIDAVIT.

pauper's oath. See OATH.

payoff. See KICKBACK.

payola (pay-**oh**-lə). An indirect and secret payment for a favor, esp. one relating to business; a bribe.

PCA. *abbr.* POSSE COMITATUS ACT

PCR action. See POSTCONVICTION-RELIEF PROCEEDING.

P.D. *abbr.* PUBLIC DEFENDER.

peace, *n.* A state of public tranquility; freedom from civil disturbance or hostility
<breach of the peace>.—**peaceable, peace-
ful,** *adj.*

peace, justice of. See JUSTICE OF THE PEACE.

peace bond. See BOND.

peace officer. A civil officer (such as a sheriff
or police officer) appointed to maintain public
tranquility and order. ● This term may also
include a judge who hears criminal cases or
another public official (such as a mayor) who
may be statutorily designated as a peace officer for limited purposes.—Also termed *officer
of the peace*; *conservator of the peace*.

peace warrant. See WARRANT.

peculation (pek-yə-**lay**-shən), *n.* Embezzlement, esp. by a public official.—**peculate**
(**pek**-yə-layt), *vb.*—**peculative** (**pek**-yə-lə-tiv),
adj.—**peculator** (**pek**-yə-lay-tər), *n.* Cf. DEPEC-
ULATION.

pederasty (**ped**-ər-as-tee), *n.* Anal intercourse
between a man and a boy. ● Pederasty is
illegal in all states.—**pederast** (**ped**-ə-rast), *n.*
Cf. SODOMY.

pedophile. An adult who engages in pedophilia.

pedophilia. 1. An adult's sexual disorder consisting in the desire for sexual gratification by
molesting children, esp. prepubescent children.
2. An adult's act of child molestation. • Pedophilia can but does not necessarily involve
intercourse. Cf. PEDERASTY.

Peeping Tom. A person who spies on another
(as through a window), usu. to gain sexual
pleasure; VOYEUR.—Also termed *peeper*.

penal (**pee**-nəl), *adj.* Of, relating to, or being
a penalty or punishment, esp. for a crime.

penal action. See ACTION.

penal code. A compilation of criminal laws,
usu. defining and categorizing the offenses and
setting forth their respective punishments.—
Also termed *criminal code*. See MODEL PENAL
CODE.

penal custody. See CUSTODY.

penal institution. See PRISON.

penal law. 1. See *penal statute* under STATUTE.
2. See CRIMINAL LAW.

penal redress. See REDRESS.

penal sanction. See *criminal sanction* under SANCTION.

penal statute. See STATUTE.

penalty. Punishment imposed on a wrong-doer, esp. in the form of imprisonment or fine. • Though usu. for crimes, penalties are also sometimes imposed for civil wrongs.

> *statutory penalty.* A penalty imposed for a statutory violation; esp., a penalty imposing automatic liability on a wrongdoer for violation of a statute's terms without reference to any actual damages suffered.

penalty phase. The part of a criminal trial in which the fact-finder determines the punishment for a defendant who has been found guilty.—Also termed *sentencing phase*. Cf. GUILT PHASE.

penitentiary (pen-ə-**ten**-shə-ree), *n.* A correctional facility or other place of long-term confinement for convicted criminals; PRISON.— **penitentiary,** *adj.*

penitentiary misdemeanor. See *serious misdemeanor* under MISDEMEANOR.

penology (pee-**nol**-ə-jee), *n*. The study of penal institutions, crime prevention, and the punishment and rehabilitation of criminals, including the art of fitting the right treatment to an offender.—**penological** (pee-nə-**loj**-i-kəl), *adj*.—**penologist** (pee-**nol**-ə-jist), *n*. Cf. CRIMINOLOGY.

pen register. A mechanical device that logs dialed telephone numbers by monitoring electrical impulses. ● Because a pen register does not record the telephone conversation, it does not constitute a Fourth Amendment search requiring a warrant (though it does need a court order). Some states, however, do consider the use of a pen register invasive enough to require a search warrant. Cf. WIRETAPPING.

peonage (**pee**-ə-nij), *n*. Illegal and involuntary servitude in satisfaction of a debt. See 18 USCA § 1581.—**peon,** *n*.

people. (*usu. cap.*) The citizens of a state as represented by the prosecution in a criminal case <*People v. Snyder*>.

people's court. 1. A court in which ordinary people can resolve small disputes. See *small-claims court* under COURT. **2.** In totalitarian countries, a group of nonlawyer citizens, often illiterate commoners, convened at the scene of a crime to pass judgment or impose punishment on the accused criminal. **3.** (*cap.*) In Nazi Germany, a tribunal that dealt with political offenses.

percipient witness. See WITNESS.

per curiam (pər **kyoor**-ee-əm), *adv.* & *adj.* [Latin] By the court as a whole.

per curiam, *n.* See *per curiam opinion* under OPINION.

per curiam opinion. See OPINION.

peremptory challenge. See CHALLENGE (2).

peremptory instruction. See JURY INSTRUCTION.

peremptory strike. See *peremptory challenge* under CHALLENGE (2).

perfect defense. See DEFENSE.

perfect self-defense. See SELF-DEFENSE.

perjury (**pər**-jər-ee), *n.* The act or an instance of a person's deliberately making material false or misleading statements while under oath.—Also termed *false swearing*; *false oath*; (archaically) *forswearing*.—**perjure** (**pər**-jər), *vb.*—**perjured** (pər-jərd), **perjurious** (pər-juur-ee-əs), *adj.*—**perjuror** (pər-jər-ər), *n.*

perjury-trap doctrine. The principle that a perjury indictment against a person must be dismissed if the prosecution secures it by calling that person as a grand-jury witness in an effort to obtain evidence for a perjury charge, esp. when the person's testimony does not relate to issues material to the ongoing grand-jury investigation.

permanent ward. See WARD.

permissive inference. See *permissive presumption* under PRESUMPTION.

permissive presumption. See PRESUMPTION.

perp (pərp), *n. Slang.* Perpetrator <the police brought in the perp for questioning>.

perpetrate, *vb.* To commit or carry out (an act, esp. a crime) <find whoever perpetrated this heinous deed>.—**perpetration,** *n.*

perpetrator. A person who commits a crime or offense.

per se deadly weapon. See *deadly weapon per se* under WEAPON.

personal-condition crime. See *status crime* under CRIME.

personal crime. See CRIME.

personal evidence. See TESTIMONY.

personal recognizance. See RECOGNIZANCE.

personation. See IMPERSONATION.

person-endangering state of mind. An intent to kill, inflict great bodily injury, act in wanton disregard of an unreasonable risk, or perpetrate a dangerous felony.—Also termed *man-endangering state of mind.*

persuasion burden. See BURDEN OF PERSUASION.

persuasive precedent. See PRECEDENT.

perverse verdict. See VERDICT.

Petite **policy.** The Department of Justice rule forbidding a federal prosecution after a previous state or federal prosecution based on the same acts unless (1) the prosecution has been approved by the Assistant Attorney General, (2) there is a substantial federal interest supporting the prosecution, (3) the previous prosecution failed to vindicate the federal interest, and (4) there is sufficient evidence to sustain a conviction. United States Attorneys' Manual § 9–2.031 (Sept. 1997); *Petite v. United States*, 361 U.S. 529, 80 S.Ct. 450 (1960).

petition, *n*. A formal written request presented to a court or other official body.

  juvenile petition. A petition filed in a juvenile court, alleging delinquent conduct by the accused. ● The accusations made in a juvenile petition are tried in an adjudicatory hearing. See *adjudicatory hearing* under HEARING.

petitioner. A party who presents a petition to a court or other official body, esp. when seeking relief on appeal. Cf. RESPONDENT (2).

petit juror. See JUROR.

petit jury. See JURY.

petit larceny. See LARCENY.

petit treason. See *petty treason* under TREASON.

petty, *adj*. Relatively insignificant or minor <a petty crime>. Cf. GRAND.

petty jury. See *petit jury* under JURY.

petty larceny. See *petit larceny* under LARCE-NY.

petty offense. See OFFENSE.

petty treason. See TREASON.

physical custody. See CUSTODY.

physical fact. See FACT.

physical force. See *actual force* under FORCE.

physical harm. See HARM.

physical impossibility. See *factual impossibility* under IMPOSSIBILITY.

physical injury. See *bodily injury* under INJURY.

physical necessity. See NECESSITY.

physical-proximity test. A common-law test for the crime of attempt, focusing on how much more the defendant would have needed to do to complete the offense. See ATTEMPT.

physician-client privilege. See *doctor-patient privilege* under PRIVILEGE (3).

pickpocket. A thief who steals money or property from the person of another, usu. by stealth but sometimes by physical diversion such as bumping into or pushing the victim.

pilferage (**pil**-fər-ij), *n.* **1.** The act or an instance of stealing. **2.** The item or items stolen.—**pilfer** (**pil**-fər), *vb.* See LARCENY; THEFT.

pimp, *n.* A person who solicits customers for a prostitute, usu. in return for a share of the prostitute's earnings.—**pimp,** *vb.* See PANDERING (1). Cf. BAWD.

***Pinkerton* rule.** The doctrine imposing liability on a conspirator for all offenses committed in furtherance of the conspiracy, even if those offenses are actually performed by coconspirators. *Pinkerton v. United States*, 328 U.S. 640, 66 S.Ct. 1180 (1946).

piracy, *n.* **1.** Robbery, kidnapping, or other criminal violence committed at sea. **2.** A similar crime committed aboard a plane or other vehicle; hijacking.

> ***air piracy.*** The crime of using force or threat to seize control of an aircraft; the hijacking of an aircraft, esp. one in flight.— Also termed *aircraft piracy.*

3. The unauthorized and illegal reproduction or distribution of materials protected by copyright, patent, or trademark law. See INFRINGE-MENT.—**pirate,** *vb.*—**piratical** (pɪ-**rat**-ə-kəl), *adj.*—**pirate,** *n.*

P.J. See *presiding judge* under JUDGE.

PKPA. *abbr.* PARENTAL KIDNAPPING PREVENTION ACT.

place-of-wrong law. See LEX LOCI DELICTI.

place-of-wrong rule. See LEX LOCI DELICTI.

plain error. See ERROR.

plain-feel doctrine. The principle that a police officer, while conducting a legal pat-down search, may seize any contraband that the officer can clearly identify, by touch, as being illegal or incriminating.—Also termed *plain-touch doctrine.*

plain-view doctrine. The rule permitting a police officer's warrantless seizure and use as evidence of an item observed in plain view from a lawful position or during a legal search when the officer has probable cause to believe that the item is evidence of a crime.—Also termed *clear-view doctrine*; *plain-sight rule.* Cf. OPEN-FIELDS DOCTRINE.

plea, *n.* An accused person's formal response of "guilty," "not guilty," or "no contest" to a criminal charge.

>   ***blind plea.*** A guilty plea made without the promise of a concession from either the judge or the prosecutor. Cf. *negotiated plea.*

>   ***guilty plea.*** An accused person's formal admission in court of having committed the charged offense. ● A guilty plea is usu. part of a plea bargain. It must be made voluntarily, and only after the accused has been informed of and understands his or her rights. A guilty plea ordinarily has the same effect as a guilty verdict and conviction after a trial on the merits.

>   ***insanity plea.*** See INSANITY DEFENSE.

>   ***negotiated plea.*** The plea agreed to by a criminal defendant and the prosecutor in a plea bargain. See PLEA BARGAIN. Cf. *blind plea.*

>   ***not-guilty plea.*** An accused person's formal denial in court of having committed the charged offense. ● The prosecution must then prove all elements of the charged offense beyond a reasonable doubt if the defendant is to be convicted.

plea bargain, *n.* A negotiated agreement between a prosecutor and a criminal defendant whereby the defendant pleads guilty to a lesser offense or to one of multiple charges in exchange for some concession by the prosecutor, usu. a more lenient sentence or a dismissal of the other charges.—Also termed *plea agreement*; *negotiated plea*; *sentence bargain*.— **plea-bargain,** *vb.*—**plea-bargaining,** *n.*

  charge bargain. A plea bargain in which a prosecutor agrees to drop some of the counts or reduce the charge to a less serious offense in exchange for a plea of either guilty or no contest from the defendant.

  sentence bargain. A plea bargain in which a prosecutor agrees to recommend a lighter sentence in exchange for a plea of either guilty or no contest from the defendant.

plead, *vb.* **1.** To make a specific plea, esp. in response to a criminal charge <he pleaded not guilty>. **2.** To assert or allege in a pleading <fraud claims must be pleaded with particularity>. **3.** To file or deliver a pleading <the party hasn't pleaded yet>.

pleading, *n.* **1.** A formal document in which a party to a legal proceeding (esp. a civil lawsuit) sets forth or responds to allegations, claims, denials, or defenses. ● In federal civil procedure, the main pleadings are the plaintiff's complaint and the defendant's answer.

accusatory pleading. An indictment, information, or complaint by which the government begins a criminal prosecution.

2. A system of defining and narrowing the issues in a case whereby the parties file formal documents alleging their respective positions. **3.** The legal rules regulating the statement of the plaintiff's claims and the defendant's defenses.

pleading the Fifth. The act or an instance of asserting one's right against self-incrimination under the Fifth Amendment.—Also termed *taking the Fifth.* See RIGHT AGAINST SELF-INCRIMINATION.

plea in bar. A plea that seeks to defeat the prosecutor's action completely and permanently.

general plea in bar. A criminal defendant's plea of not guilty by which the defendant denies every fact and circumstance necessary to be convicted of the crime charged.

special plea in bar. A plea that, rather than addressing the merits and denying the facts alleged, sets up some extrinsic fact showing why a criminal defendant cannot be tried for the offense charged.

plenary confession. See CONFESSION.

plenary jurisdiction. See JURISDICTION.

plurality opinion. See OPINION.

poaching, *n*. The illegal taking or killing of fish or game on another's land.—**poach,** *vb*.

pocket immunity. See IMMUNITY (2).

point of error. An alleged mistake by a lower court asserted as a ground for appeal. See ER-ROR (1); WRIT OF ERROR.

point system. A system that assigns incremental units to traffic violations, the accumulation of a certain number within a year resulting in the automatic suspension of a person's driving privileges.

poisonous-tree doctrine. See FRUIT-OF-THE-POISONOUS-TREE DOCTRINE.

police, *n*. **1.** The governmental department charged with the preservation of public order, the promotion of public safety, and the prevention and detection of crime. **2.** The officers or members of this department.

police blotter. See ARREST RECORD.

police court. See MAGISTRATE'S COURT (1).

police jury. In civil-law jurisdictions, the governing body of a parish.

police justice. See *police magistrate* under MAGISTRATE.

police magistrate. See MAGISTRATE.

police officer. A peace officer responsible for preserving public order, promoting public safety, and preventing and detecting crime. Cf. PEACE OFFICER.

police science. See CRIMINAL JUSTICE.

political asylum. See ASYLUM (2).

political offense. A crime directed against the security or governmental system of a nation, such as treason, sedition, or espionage. ● Under principles of international law, the perpetrator of a political offense cannot be extradited.—Also termed *political crime*.

political question. A question that a court will not consider because it involves the exercise of discretionary power by the executive or legislative branch of government.—Also termed *nonjusticiable question*. Cf. JUDICIAL QUESTION.

political trial. See TRIAL.

poll, *vb.* To ask how each member of (a group) individually voted <after the verdict was read, the judge polled the jury>.

polygamy (pə-**lig**-ə-mee), *n.* The state of being simultaneously married to more than one spouse; multiple marriages. See Model Penal Code § 230.1(2).—**polygamous,** *adj.*—**polygamist,** *n.* Cf. BIGAMY.

polygraph, *n.* A device used to evaluate veracity by measuring and recording involuntary physiological changes in the human body during interrogation. ● Polygraph results are inadmissible as evidence in most states but are commonly used by the police as an investigative tool.—Also termed *lie detector.*—**polygraphic,** *adj.*—**polygraphy,** *n.*

Ponzi scheme (**pon**-zee). A fraudulent investment scheme in which money contributed by later investors generates artificially high dividends for the original investors, whose example attracts even larger investments. ● Money from the new investors is used directly to repay or pay interest to old investors, usu. without any operation or revenue-producing activity other than the continual raising of new funds. This scheme takes its name from Charles Ponzi, who in the late 1920s was convicted for fraudulent schemes he conducted in Boston. Cf. PYRAMID SCHEME.

pornography, *n.* Material (such as writings, photographs, or movies) depicting sexual activity or erotic behavior in a way that is designed to arouse sexual excitement. ● Pornography is protected speech under the First Amendment unless it is determined to be legally obscene.— **pornographic,** *adj.* See OBSCENITY.

> *child pornography.* Material depicting a person under the age of 18 engaged in sexual activity. ● Child pornography is not protected by the First Amendment—even if it falls short of the legal standard for obscenity—and those directly involved in its distribution can be criminally punished.

positive act. 1. See OVERT ACT. **2.** See ACT.

positive evidence. See *direct evidence* (1) under EVIDENCE.

positive misprision. See MISPRISION.

positive proof. See PROOF.

positive testimony. See *affirmative testimony* under TESTIMONY.

positive wrong. See WRONG.

posse comitatus (**pos**-ee kom-ə-**tay**-təs), *n.* [Latin "power of the county"] A group of citizens who are called together to assist the sheriff in keeping the peace.—Often shortened to *posse*.

Posse Comitatus Act. A federal law that, with a few exceptions, prohibits the Army or Air Force from directly participating in civilian law-enforcement operations, as by making arrests, conducting searches, or seizing evidence. ● The Act was originally enacted in 1878. It does not usu. apply to members of the Navy, the National Guard, or the Coast Guard. 18 USCA § 1385.—Abbr. PCA.

possession. The fact of having or holding property in one's power; the exercise of dominion over property.

> *criminal possession.* The unlawful possession of certain prohibited articles, such as illegal drugs or drug paraphernalia, firearms, or stolen property.

post bail, *vb*. See GIVE BAIL.

postconviction-relief proceeding. A state or federal procedure for a prisoner to request a court to vacate or correct a conviction or sentence.—Also termed *postconviction-remedy proceeding*; *PCR action*; *postconviction proceeding*.

postmortem, *adj*. Done or occurring after death <a postmortem examination>.

postmortem, *n.* See AUTOPSY (1).

poverty affidavit. See AFFIDAVIT.

***Powell* doctrine.** See CORRUPT-MOTIVE DOC-TRINE.

preappointed evidence. See EVIDENCE.

precedent (**pres**-ə-dənt), *n.* **1.** The making of law by a court in recognizing and applying new rules while administering justice. **2.** A decided case that furnishes a basis for deter-mining later cases involving similar facts or issues.—**precedential,** *adj.* See STARE DECISIS.

 binding precedent. A precedent that a court must follow. ● For example, a lower court is bound by an applicable holding of a higher court in the same jurisdiction.—Also termed *authoritative precedent*; *binding authority.*

 declaratory precedent. A precedent that is merely the application of an already existing legal rule.

 original precedent. A precedent that cre-ates and applies a new legal rule.

 persuasive precedent. A precedent that a court may either follow or reject, but that is entitled to respect and careful consideration.

● For example, if the case was decided in a neighboring jurisdiction, the court might evaluate the earlier court's reasoning without being bound to decide the same way.

precedent sub silentio (səb sə-**len**-shee-oh). A legal question that was neither argued nor considered in a judicial decision that is or might be treated as a precedent.

3. See DOCTRINE OF PRECEDENT.

preconceived malice. See MALICE AFORE-THOUGHT.

predatory crime. See CRIME.

predicate act. Under RICO, one of two or more related acts of racketeering necessary to establish a pattern. See RACKETEER INFLUENCED AND CORRUPT ORGANIZATIONS ACT.

predicate fact. See FACT.

prediction theory. See BAD-MAN THEORY.

predisposition. A person's inclination to engage in a particular activity; esp., an inclination that vitiates a criminal defendant's claim of entrapment.

preferred docket. See DOCKET (2).

preferring of charges. The formal completion of a charge sheet, which includes signing
and swearing to the charges and specifications.
• Only a person subject to the Uniform Code
of Military Justice can prefer charges. Cf. INITI-
ATION OF CHARGES.

prejudice, *n.* **1.** Damage or detriment to one's
legal rights or claims.

> ***undue prejudice.*** The harm resulting from
> a fact-trier's being exposed to evidence that
> is persuasive but inadmissible (such as evi-
> dence of prior criminal conduct) or that so
> arouses the emotions that calm and logical
> reasoning is abandoned.

2. A preconceived judgment formed without a
factual basis; a strong bias.—**prejudice,** *vb.*—
prejudicial, *adj.*

prejudicial error. See *reversible error* under
ERROR.

preliminary complaint. See COMPLAINT.

preliminary crime. See *inchoate offense* under OFFENSE.

preliminary evidence. See EVIDENCE.

preliminary hearing. A criminal hearing
(usu. conducted by a magistrate) to determine

whether there is sufficient evidence to prosecute an accused person. ● If sufficient evidence exists, the case will be set for trial or bound over for grand-jury review, or an information will be filed in the trial court.—Also termed *preliminary examination*; *probable-cause hearing*; *bindover hearing*; *examining trial*. Cf. AR-RAIGNMENT.

preliminary inquiry. The initial investigation of a reported or suspected violation of the Uniform Code of Military Justice. Cf. PRETRIAL INVESTIGATION.

preliminary-inquiry officer. The person, usu. an officer, who conducts a preliminary inquiry.

preliminary warrant. See WARRANT.

premeditated, *adj.* Done with willful deliberation and planning; consciously considered beforehand <a premeditated killing>.

premeditated malice. See MALICE AFORE-THOUGHT.

premeditation, *n.* Conscious consideration and planning that precedes some act (such as committing a crime).—**premeditate,** *vb.*

preparation. The act or process of devising the means necessary to commit a crime. Cf. AT-TEMPT.

prerogative writ. See *extraordinary writ* under WRIT.

presence-of-defendant rule. The principle that a felony defendant is entitled to be present at every major stage of the criminal proceeding. Fed. R. Crim. P. 43.

present ability. The actual, immediate power to do something (esp. to commit a crime).

present case. See *case at bar* under CASE.

presentence hearing. A proceeding at which a judge or jury receives and examines all relevant information regarding a convicted criminal and the related offense before passing sentence.—Also termed *sentencing hearing*.

presentence investigation report. A probation officer's detailed account of a convicted defendant's educational, criminal, family, and social background, conducted at the court's request as an aid in passing sentence.—Abbr. PSI.—Often shortened to *presentence report*.

presenting jury. See GRAND JURY.

presentment (pri-**zent**-mənt). **1.** The act of presenting or laying before a court or other tribunal a formal statement about a matter to be dealt with legally. **2.** A formal written accusation returned by a grand jury on its own initiative, without a prosecutor's previous indictment request. ● Presentments are obsolete in the federal courts. Cf. INDICTMENT.

present recollection refreshed. A witness's memory that has been enhanced by showing the witness a document that describes the relevant events. ● The document itself is merely a memory stimulus and is not admitted in evidence. Fed. R. Evid. 612.—Also termed *refreshing recollection*; *present recollection revived*. Cf. PAST RECOLLECTION RECORDED.

present sense impression. One's perception of an event or condition, formed during or immediately after the fact. ● A statement containing a present sense impression is admissible even if it is hearsay. Fed. R. Evid. 803(1). Cf. EXCITED UTTERANCE.

president judge. See *presiding judge* under JUDGE.

president of a court-martial. The senior member in rank present at a court-martial trial.

presiding judge. See JUDGE.

presiding juror. See JUROR.

presumption. A legal inference or assumption that a fact exists, based on the known or proven existence of some other fact or group of facts. ● Most presumptions are rules of evidence calling for a certain result in a given case unless the adversely affected party overcomes it with other evidence. A presumption shifts the burden of production or persuasion to the opposing party, who can then attempt to overcome the presumption. See BURDEN OF PRODUCTION.

> *absolute presumption.* See *conclusive presumption*.

> *artificial presumption.* See *presumption of law*.

> *conclusive presumption.* A presumption that cannot be overcome by any additional evidence or argument <it is a conclusive presumption that a child under the age of seven is incapable of committing a felony>.—Also termed *absolute presumption*; *irrebuttable presumption*; *mandatory presumption*.

> *conditional presumption.* See *rebuttable presumption*.

conflicting presumption. One of two or more presumptions that would lead to opposite results.—Also termed *inconsistent presumption.*

disputable presumption. See *rebuttable presumption.*

factual presumption. See *presumption of fact.*

inconsistent presumption. See *conflicting presumption.*

irrebuttable presumption. See *conclusive presumption.*

legal presumption. See *presumption of law.*

mandatory presumption. See *conclusive presumption.*

mixed presumption. A presumption containing elements of both law and fact.

Morgan presumption. See MORGAN PRESUMPTION.

natural presumption. A deduction of one fact from another, based on common experience.

permissive presumption. A presumption that a trier of fact is free to accept or reject from a given set of facts.—Also termed *permissive inference*.

presumption of fact. A type of rebuttable presumption that may be, but as a matter of law need not be, drawn from another established fact or group of facts <the possessor of recently stolen goods is, by presumption of fact, considered the thief>.—Also termed *factual presumption*.

presumption of intent. A permissive presumption that a criminal defendant who intended to commit an act did so.

presumption of law. A legal assumption that a court is required to make if certain facts are established and no contradictory evidence is produced <by presumption of law, a criminal defendant is considered innocent until proven guilty beyond a reasonable doubt>.—Also termed *legal presumption*; *artificial presumption*.

prima facie presumption. See *rebuttable presumption*.

procedural presumption. A presumption that may be rebutted by credible evidence.

rebuttable presumption. An inference drawn from certain facts that establish a prima facie case, which may be overcome by the introduction of contrary evidence.—Also termed *prima facie presumption*; *disputable presumption*; *conditional presumption*. Cf. *conclusive presumption*.

statutory presumption. A rebuttable or conclusive presumption that is created by statute.

Thayer presumption. See THAYER PRESUMPTION.

presumption of innocence. The fundamental criminal-law principle that a person may not be convicted of a crime unless the government proves guilt beyond a reasonable doubt, without any burden placed on the accused to prove innocence.

presumptive evidence. See EVIDENCE.

presumptive proof. See *conditional proof* under PROOF.

presumptive sentence. See SENTENCE.

pretextual arrest. See ARREST.

pretrial detention. See DETENTION.

pretrial discovery. See DISCOVERY.

pretrial diversion. See DIVERSION PROGRAM.

pretrial intervention. 1. See DIVERSION PRO-GRAM. **2.** See *deferred judgment* under JUDG-MENT.

pretrial investigation. An investigation to decide whether a case should be recommended for forwarding to a general court-martial. Cf. PRELIMINARY INQUIRY.

prevarication (pri-var-ə-**kay**-shən), *n.* The act or an instance of lying or avoiding the truth; equivocation.—**prevaricate** (pri-**var**-ə-kayt), *vb.*

prevaricator (pri-**var**-ə-kay-tər). [Latin] A liar; an equivocator.

preventive custody. See CUSTODY.

preventive detention. See DETENTION.

preventive punishment. See PUNISHMENT.

priest-penitent privilege. See PRIVILEGE (3).

prima facie (**prī**-mə **fay**-shə *or* **fay**-shee), *adv.* [Latin] At first sight; on first appearance but subject to further evidence or information <the agreement is prima facie valid>.

prima facie, *adj.* Sufficient to establish a fact or raise a presumption unless disproved or rebutted <a prima facie showing>.

prima facie case. 1. The establishment of a legally required rebuttable presumption. **2.** A party's production of enough evidence to allow the fact-trier to infer the fact at issue and rule in the party's favor.

prima facie evidence. See EVIDENCE.

prima facie presumption. See *rebuttable presumption* under PRESUMPTION.

primary allegation. See ALLEGATION.

primary cause. See *proximate cause* under CAUSE (1).

primary evidence. See *best evidence* under EVIDENCE.

primary fact. See FACT.

principal, *n.* One who commits or participates in a crime. Cf. ACCESSORY; ACCOMPLICE (2).

principal in the first degree. The perpetrator of a crime.—Also termed *first-degree principal.*

principal in the second degree. One who helped the perpetrator at the time of the crime.—Also termed *accessory at the fact*; *second-degree principal.* See ABETTOR.

principal fact. See FACT.

principle of legality. See LEGALITY (2).

principle of retribution. See LEX TALIONIS.

prior, *n. Slang.* A previous conviction, esp. for a felony <because the defendant had two priors, the judge automatically enhanced his sentence>.

prior consistent statement. See STATEMENT.

prior inconsistent statement. See STATEMENT.

prior sentence. See SENTENCE.

prison. A state or federal facility of confinement for convicted criminals, esp. felons.— Also termed *penitentiary*; *penal institution*; *adult correctional institution.* Cf. JAIL.

>   *private prison.* A prison that is managed by a private company, not by a governmental agency.

prison breach. A prisoner's forcible breaking and departure from a place of lawful confinement; the offense of escaping from confinement in a prison or jail. • *Prison breach* has traditionally been distinguished from *escape* by the presence of force, but some jurisdictions have abandoned this distinction.—Also termed *prison breaking*; *breach of prison*. Cf. ESCAPE.

prison camp. A usu. minimum-security camp for the detention of trustworthy prisoners who are often employed on government projects.

prisoner. 1. A person who is serving time in prison. **2.** A person who has been apprehended by a law-enforcement officer and is in custody, regardless of whether the person has yet been put in prison.

prisoner at the bar. An accused person who is on trial.

prisoner of conscience. A person who, not having used or advocated the use of violence, has been imprisoned by reason of a political, religious, or other conscientiously held belief or by reason of ethnic origin, sex, color, or language.

prisoner's dilemma. A logic problem—often used by law-and-economics scholars to illustrate the effect of cooperative behavior—involving two prisoners who are being separately questioned about their participation in a crime: (1) if both confess, they will each receive a 5-year sentence; (2) if neither confesses, they will each receive a 3-year sentence; and (3) if one confesses but the other does not, the confessing prisoner will receive a 1-year sentence while the silent prisoner will receive a 10-year sentence.

private attorney. See ATTORNEY (1).

private prison. See PRISON.

private prosecutor. See PROSECUTOR (2).

private search. See SEARCH.

private wrong. See WRONG.

privilege. 1. A special legal right, exemption, or immunity granted to a person or class of persons; an exception to a duty.

   absolute privilege. A privilege that immunizes an actor from suit, no matter how wrongful the action might be, and even though it is done with an improper motive. Cf. *qualified privilege.*

   conditional privilege. See *qualified privilege.*

   deliberative-process privilege. A privilege permitting the government to withhold documents relating to policy formulation to encourage open and independent discussion among those who develop government policy.

litigation privilege. A privilege protecting the attorneys and parties in a case from defamation claims arising from statements made in the course of the case.

parliamentary privilege. The right of a particular question, motion, or statement to take precedence over all other business before the legislative body.

privilege from arrest. An exemption from arrest, as that enjoyed by members of Congress during legislative sessions. U.S. Const. art. I, § 6.

qualified privilege. A privilege that immunizes an actor from suit only when the privilege is properly exercised in the performance of a legal or moral duty.—Also termed *conditional privilege.* Cf. *absolute privilege.*

special privilege. A privilege granted to a person or class of persons to the exclusion of others and in derogation of the common right.

testimonial privilege. A right not to testify based on a claim of privilege; a privilege that overrides a witness's duty to disclose matters within the witness's knowledge, whether at trial or by deposition.

viatorial privilege (vī-ə-**tor**-ee-əl). A privilege that overrides a person's duty to attend court in person and to testify.

work-product privilege. See WORK-PRODUCT RULE.

2. An affirmative defense by which a defendant acknowledges at least part of the conduct complained of but asserts that the defendant's conduct was authorized or sanctioned by law. See JUSTIFICATION (2). Cf. IMMUNITY (2). **3.** An evidentiary rule that gives a witness the option to not disclose the fact asked for, even though it might be relevant; the right to prevent disclosure of certain information in court, esp. when the information was originally communicated in a professional or confidential relationship.

accountant-client privilege. The protection afforded to a client from an accountant's unauthorized disclosure of materials submitted to or prepared by the accountant.

antimarital-facts privilege. See *marital privilege* (2).

attorney-client privilege. The client's right to refuse to disclose and to prevent any other person from disclosing confidential communications between the client and the attorney.—Also termed *lawyer-client privilege*; *client's privilege*.

542

clergyman-penitent privilege. See *priest-penitent privilege.*

doctor-patient privilege. The right to exclude from evidence in a legal proceeding any confidential communication that a patient makes to a physician for the purpose of diagnosis or treatment, unless the patient consents to the disclosure.—Also termed *physician-client privilege*; *patient-physician privilege.*

editorial privilege. See *journalist's privilege* (2).

executive privilege. A privilege, based on the constitutional doctrine of separation of powers, that exempts the executive branch of the federal government from usual disclosure requirements when the matter to be disclosed involves national security or foreign policy.

husband-wife privilege. See *marital privilege.*

informant's privilege. The qualified privilege that a government can invoke to prevent disclosure of the identity and communications of its informants. ● In exercising its power to formulate evidentiary rules for federal criminal cases, the U.S. Supreme Court has consistently declined to hold that the government must disclose the identity of informants in a preliminary hearing or in a criminal trial. *McCray v. Illinois*, 386 U.S. 300, 312, 87 S.Ct. 1056, 1063 (1967). A party can, however, usu. overcome the privilege if it can demonstrate that the need for the information outweighs the public interest in maintaining the privilege.—Also termed *informer's privilege*.

joint-defense privilege. The rule that a defendant can assert the attorney-client privilege to protect a confidential communication made to a codefendant's lawyer if the communication was related to the defense of both defendants.—Also termed *common-interest doctrine*.

journalist's privilege. 1. A reporter's protection, under constitutional or statutory law, from being compelled to testify about confidential information or sources.—Also termed *reporter's privilege*; *newsman's privilege*. See SHIELD LAW (1). **2.** A publisher's protection against defamation lawsuits when the publication makes fair comment on the actions of public officials in matters of public concern.—Also termed *editorial privilege*.

judicial privilege. The privilege protecting any statement made in the course of and with reference to a judicial proceeding by any judge, juror, party, witness, or advocate.

legislative privilege. The privilege protecting (1) any statement made in a legislature by one of its members, and (2) any paper published as part of legislative business.— Also termed (in a parliamentary system) *parliamentary privilege.*

marital privilege. **1.** The privilege allowing a spouse not to testify, and to prevent another from testifying, about confidential communications with the other spouse during the marriage.—Also termed *marital-communications privilege.* **2.** The privilege allowing a spouse not to testify in a criminal case as an adverse witness against the other spouse, regardless of the subject matter of the testimony.—Also termed (in sense 2) *privilege against adverse spousal testimony*; *antimarital-facts privilege.* **3.** The privilege immunizing from a defamation lawsuit any statement made between husband and wife.—Also termed (in all senses) *spousal privilege*; *husband-wife privilege.*

national-security privilege. See *state-secrets privilege.*

newsman's privilege. See *journalist's privilege* (1).

official privilege. The privilege immunizing from a defamation lawsuit any state-

ment made by one state officer to another in
the course of official duty.

parliamentary privilege. See *legislative
privilege.*

patient-physician privilege. See *doctor-
patient privilege.*

physician-client privilege. See *doctor-patient privilege.*

priest-penitent privilege. The privilege
barring a clergy member from testifying
about a confessor's communications.—Also
termed *clergyman-penitent privilege.*

***privilege against adverse spousal testi-
mony.*** See *marital privilege* (2).

psychotherapist-patient privilege. A
privilege that a person can invoke to prevent
the disclosure of a confidential communication made in the course of diagnosis or treatment of a mental or emotional condition by
or at the direction of a psychotherapist. •
The privilege can be overcome under certain
conditions, as when the examination is ordered by a court.—Also termed *psychotherapist-client privilege.*

reporter's privilege. See *journalist's privilege* (1).

self-critical-analysis privilege. A privilege protecting individuals and entities from divulging the results of candid assessments of their compliance with laws and regulations, to the extent that the assessments are internal, the results were intended from the outset to be confidential, and the information is of a type that would be curtailed if it were forced to be disclosed. ● This privilege is founded on the public policy that it is beneficial to permit individuals and entities to confidentially evaluate their compliance with the law, so that they will monitor and improve their compliance with it.—Also termed *self-policing privilege.*

spousal privilege. See *marital privilege.*

state-secrets privilege. A privilege that the government may invoke against the discovery of a material that, if divulged, could compromise national security.—Also termed *national-security privilege.*

privilege against adverse spousal testimony. See *marital privilege* (2) under PRIVILEGE (3).

privilege against self-incrimination. See RIGHT AGAINST SELF-INCRIMINATION.

privileged, *adj.* Not subject to the usual rules or liabilities; esp., not subject to disclosure during the course of a case <a privileged document>.

privileged communication. See COMMUNICATION.

privileged evidence. See EVIDENCE.

probable cause. A reasonable ground to suspect that a person has committed or is committing a crime or that a place contains specific items connected with a crime. • Under the Fourth Amendment, probable cause—which amounts to more than a bare suspicion but less than evidence that would justify a conviction—must be shown before an arrest warrant or search warrant may be issued.—Also termed *reasonable cause*; *sufficient cause*; *reasonable grounds*. Cf. REASONABLE SUSPICION.

probable-cause hearing. See PRELIMINARY HEARING.

probable-desistance test. A common-law test for the crime of attempt, focusing on whether the defendant has exhibited dangerous behavior indicating a likelihood of committing the crime. See ATTEMPT.

probable evidence. See *presumptive evidence* under EVIDENCE.

probation. A court-imposed criminal sentence that, subject to stated conditions, releases a convicted person into the community instead of sending the criminal to jail or prison. Cf. PAROLE.

> **bench probation.** Probation in which the offender agrees to certain conditions or restrictions and reports only to the sentencing judge rather than a probation officer.—Also termed *bench parole*; *court probation*.

> **shock probation.** Probation that is granted after a brief stay in jail or prison. • Shock probation is intended to awaken the defendant to the reality of confinement for failure to abide by the conditions of probation. This type of probation is discretionary with the sentencing judge and is usu. granted within 180 days of the original sentence.—Also termed *split sentence*. Cf. *shock incarceration* under INCARCERATION.

probation before judgment. See *deferred judgment* under JUDGMENT.

probationer. A convicted criminal who is on probation.

probation officer. A government officer who supervises the conduct of a probationer.

probation termination. The ending of a person's status as a probationer by (1) the routine expiration of the probationary period, (2) early termination by court order, or (3) probation revocation.

probation without judgment. See *deferred judgment* under JUDGMENT.

probative (**proh**-bə-tiv), *adj.* Tending to prove or disprove. ● Courts can exclude relevant evidence if its probative value is substantially outweighed by the danger of unfair prejudice. Fed. R. Evid. 403.—**probativeness,** *n.*

probative evidence. See EVIDENCE.

probative fact. See FACT.

problem-oriented policing. A method that law-enforcement officers use to reduce crime by identifying and remedying the underlying causes of criminal incidents rather than merely seeking basic information (such as the identity of the perpetrator) about the crime being investigated.

procedural presumption. See PRESUMPTION.

procedure. **1.** A specific method or course of action. **2.** The judicial rule or manner for carrying on a criminal prosecution. See CRIMINAL PROCEDURE.

proceeding. **1.** The regular and orderly progression of a case, including all acts and events between the time of commencement and the entry of judgment. **2.** Any procedural means for seeking redress from a tribunal or agency.

   collateral proceeding. A proceeding brought to address an issue incidental to the principal proceeding.

   competency proceeding. A proceeding to assess a person's mental capacity. • A competency hearing may be held either in a criminal context to determine a defendant's competency to stand trial or as a civil proceeding to assess whether a person should be committed to a mental-health facility.

   contempt proceeding. A judicial or quasi-judicial hearing conducted to determine whether a person has committed contempt.

   criminal proceeding. A proceeding instituted to determine a person's guilt or innocence or to set a convicted person's punishment; a criminal hearing or trial.

   ex parte proceeding (eks **pahr**-tee). A proceeding in which not all parties are present or given the opportunity to be heard.—Also termed *ex parte hearing*.

551

in camera proceeding (in **kam**-ə-rə). A proceeding held in a judge's chambers or other private place.

informal proceeding. A trial conducted in a more relaxed manner than a typical court trial, such as an administrative hearing or a trial in small-claims court.

judicial proceeding. Any court proceeding.

process, *n.* **1.** The proceedings in any action or prosecution <due process of law>. **2.** A summons or writ, esp. to appear or respond in court <service of process>.—Also termed *judicial process*; *legal process*.

bailable process. A process instructing an officer to take bail after arresting a defendant. ● The defendant's discharge is required by law after the tender of suitable security.

compulsory process. A process, with a warrant to arrest or attach included, that compels a person to appear in court as a witness.

criminal process. A process (such as an arrest warrant) that issues to compel a person to answer for a crime.

procuring an abortion. See ABORTION.

procuring cause. See *proximate cause* under CAUSE (1).

producing cause. See *proximate cause* under CAUSE (1).

production burden. See BURDEN OF PRODUCTION.

product test. See DURHAM RULE.

proffered evidence. See EVIDENCE.

prohibition. 1. A law or order that forbids a certain action. **2.** (*cap.*) The period from 1920 to 1933, when the manufacture, transport, and sale of alcoholic beverages in the United States was forbidden by the 18th Amendment to the Constitution. ● The 18th Amendment was repealed by the 21st Amendment.

prolicide (**proh**-lə-sɪd). The killing of offspring; esp., the crime of killing a child shortly before or after birth.

promoting prostitution. See PANDERING (1).

proof, *n.* **1.** The establishment or refutation of an alleged fact by evidence; the persuasive effect of evidence in the mind of a fact-finder. **2.** Evidence that determines the judgment of a court. **3.** An attested document that constitutes legal evidence.

   affirmative proof. Evidence establishing the fact in dispute by a preponderance of the evidence.

conditional proof. A fact that amounts to proof as long as there is no other fact amounting to disproof.—Also termed *presumptive proof.*

negative proof. Proof that establishes a fact by showing that its opposite is not or cannot be true.

positive proof. Direct or affirmative proof.

presumptive proof. See *conditional proof.*

proof beyond a reasonable doubt. Proof that precludes every reasonable hypothesis except that which it tends to support.

proof, burden of. See BURDEN OF PROOF.

proper evidence. See *admissible evidence* under EVIDENCE.

property crimes. See CRIMES AGAINST PROPERTY.

proportionality review. An appellate court's analysis of whether a death sentence is arbitrary or capricious by comparing the case in which it was imposed with similar cases in which the death penalty was approved or disapproved.

pro se, *n.* One who represents oneself in a court proceeding without the assistance of a lawyer <the third case on the court's docket involving a pro se>.

prosecutable, *adj.* (Of a crime or person) subject to prosecution; capable of being prosecuted.

prosecute, *vb.* **1.** To institute and pursue a criminal action against (a person) <the notorious felon has been prosecuted in seven states>. **2.** To commence and carry out any legal action <because the plaintiff failed to prosecute its contractual claims, the court dismissed the suit>.—**prosecutory,** *adj.*

prosecuting attorney. See DISTRICT ATTORNEY.

prosecuting witness. See WITNESS.

prosecution. 1. A criminal proceeding in which an accused person is tried <the conspiracy trial involved the prosecution of seven defendants>.—Also termed *criminal prosecution.*

   deferred prosecution. See *deferred judgment* under JUDGMENT.

   selective prosecution. See SELECTIVE PROSECUTION.

   sham prosecution. A prosecution that seeks to circumvent a defendant's double-jeopardy protection by appearing to be prosecuted by another sovereignty, when it is in fact controlled by the sovereignty that already prosecuted the defendant for the same crime. • A sham prosecution is, in essence, a misuse of the dual-sovereignty rule. Under that rule, a defendant's protection against double jeopardy does not provide protection against a prosecution by a different sovereignty. For example, if the defendant was first tried in federal court and acquitted, that fact would not forbid the state authorities from prosecuting the defendant in state court. But a sham prosecution—for example, a later state-court prosecution that is completely dominated or manipulated by the federal authorities that already prosecuted the defendant, so that the state-court proceeding is merely a tool of the federal authorities—will not withstand a double-jeopardy challenge. See DUAL-SOVEREIGNTY DOCTRINE.

vindictive prosecution. A prosecution in which a person is singled out under a law or regulation because the person has exercised a constitutionally protected right. Cf. SELECTIVE ENFORCEMENT.

2. The government attorneys who initiate and maintain a criminal action against an accused defendant <the prosecution rests>.

prosecutor, *n.* **1.** A legal officer who represents the government in criminal proceedings. See DISTRICT ATTORNEY; UNITED STATES ATTORNEY; ATTORNEY GENERAL.

   public prosecutor. See DISTRICT ATTORNEY.

   special prosecutor. A lawyer appointed to investigate and, if justified, seek indictments in a particular case. See *independent counsel* under COUNSEL.

2. A private person who institutes and carries on a legal action, esp. a criminal action.—Also termed (in sense 2) *private prosecutor.*—**prosecutorial,** *adj.*

prosecutorial discretion. See DISCRETION.

prosecutorial misconduct. A prosecutor's improper or illegal act (or failure to act), esp. involving an attempt to persuade the jury to wrongly convict a defendant or assess an unjustified punishment. • If prosecutorial misconduct results in a mistrial, a later prosecution may be barred under the Double Jeopardy Clause.

prospectant evidence. See EVIDENCE.

prostitution, *n.* **1.** The act or practice of engaging in sexual activity for money or its equivalent; commercialized sex. **2.** The act of debasing.—**prostitute,** *vb.*—**prostitute,** *n.*

protection money. 1. A bribe paid to an officer as an inducement not to interfere with the criminal activities of the briber. ● Examples include payments to an officer in exchange for the officer's releasing an arrestee, removing records of traffic violations from a court's files, and refraining from making a proper arrest. **2.** Money extorted from a business owner by one who promises to "protect" the business premises, with the implied threat that if the owner does not pay, the person requesting the payment will harm the owner or damage the premises.

protection order. See RESTRAINING ORDER (1).

protective custody. See CUSTODY.

protective order. 1. A court order prohibiting or restricting a party from engaging in a legal procedure (esp. discovery) that unduly annoys or burdens the opposing party or a third-party witness. **2.** See RESTRAINING ORDER (1).

protective search. See SEARCH.

protective sweep. A police officer's quick and limited search—conducted after the officer has lawfully entered the premises—based on a reasonable belief that such a search is necessary to protect the officer or others from harm.

provisional exit. A prisoner's temporary release from prison for a court appearance, hospital treatment, work detail, or other purpose requiring a release with the expectation of return.

provocation, *n.* **1.** The act of inciting another to do something, esp. to commit a crime. **2.** Something (such as words or actions) that affects a person's reason and self-control, esp. causing the person to commit a crime impulsively.—**provoke,** *vb.*—**provocative,** *adj.*

> ***adequate provocation.*** Something that would cause a reasonable person to act without self-control and lose any premeditated state of mind. ● The usual form of adequate provocation is the heat of passion. Adequate provocation can reduce a criminal charge, as from murder to voluntary manslaughter.— Also termed *adequate cause.* See HEAT OF PASSION. Cf. SELF-DEFENSE.

proximate cause. See CAUSE (1).

prudent person. See REASONABLE PERSON.

PSI. *abbr.* PRESENTENCE INVESTIGATION REPORT.

psychopath (sı-kə-path), *n.* **1.** A person with a mental disorder characterized by an extremely antisocial personality that often leads to aggressive, perverted, or criminal behavior. **2.** Loosely, a person who is mentally ill or unstable.—Also termed *sociopath*.—**psychopathy** (sı-**kop**-ə-thee), *n.*—**psychopathic** (sı-kə-**path**-ik), *adj.*

psychotherapist-client privilege. See *psychotherapist-patient privilege* under PRIVILEGE (3).

psychotherapist-patient privilege. See PRIVILEGE (3).

public attorney. See ATTORNEY (2).

public defender. A lawyer or staff of lawyers, usu. publicly appointed, whose duty is to represent indigent criminal defendants.—Abbr. P.D.

public enemy. A notorious criminal who is a menace to society; esp., one who seems more or less immune from successful prosecution.

public intoxication. See INTOXICATION.

public offense. See OFFENSE.

public prosecutor. See DISTRICT ATTORNEY.

public-safety exception. An exception to the *Miranda* rule, allowing into evidence an otherwise suppressible statement by a defendant concerning information that the police need in order to protect the public. ● If, for example, a crime victim tells the police that an assault suspect has a gun, and upon that person's arrest the police find that the suspect is wearing a holster but no gun, the police would be entitled (before giving a *Miranda* warning) to ask the suspect where the gun is. The suspect's statement of the gun's location is admissible into evidence.

public verdict. See VERDICT.

public-welfare offense. See OFFENSE.

public wrong. See WRONG.

punishable, *adj*. **1.** (Of a person) subject to a punishment <there is no dispute that Jackson remains punishable for these offenses>. **2.** (Of a crime or tort) giving rise to a specified punishment <a felony punishable by imprisonment for up to 20 years>.—**punishability,** *n*.

punishment, *n*. A sanction—such as a fine, penalty, confinement, or loss of property, right, or privilege—assessed against a person who has violated the law.—**punish,** *vb*. See SENTENCE.

capital punishment. See DEATH PENALTY.

corporal punishment. Physical punishment; punishment that is inflicted upon the body (including imprisonment).

cruel and unusual punishment. Punishment that is torturous, degrading, inhuman, grossly disproportionate to the crime in question, or otherwise shocking to the moral sense of the community. ● Cruel and unusual punishment is prohibited by the Eighth Amendment.

cumulative punishment. Punishment that increases in severity when a person is convicted of the same offense more than once.

deterrent punishment. Punishment intended to deter others from committing crimes by making an example of the offender so that like-minded people are warned of the consequences of crime.

excessive punishment. Punishment that is not justified by the gravity of the offense or the defendant's criminal record. See *excessive fine* under FINE.

infamous punishment. Punishment by imprisonment, usu. in a penitentiary. See *infamous crime* under CRIME.

nonjudicial punishment. A procedure in which a person subject to the Uniform Code of Military Justice receives official punishment for a minor offense. ● In the Navy and Coast Guard, nonjudicial punishment is termed *captain's mast*; in the Marine Corps, it is termed *office hours*; and in the Army and Air Force, it is referred to as *Article 15*. Nonjudicial punishment is not a court-martial.

preventive punishment. Punishment intended to prevent a repetition of wrongdoing by disabling the offender.

reformative punishment. Punishment intended to change the character of the offender.

retributive punishment. Punishment intended to satisfy the community's retaliatory sense of indignation that is provoked by injustice.

punitive, *adj.* Involving or inflicting punishment.—Also termed *punitory*.

punitive articles. Articles 77–134 of the Uniform Code of Military Justice. ● These articles list the crimes in the military-justice system.

punitive segregation. See SEGREGATION.

punitive statute. See *penal statute* under STATUTE.

punitory. See PUNITIVE.

pyramid distribution plan. See PYRAMID SCHEME.

pyramiding inferences, rule against. A rule prohibiting a fact-finder from piling one inference on another to arrive at a conclusion. • Today this rule is followed in only a few jurisdictions. Cf. REASONABLE-INFERENCE RULE.

pyramid scheme. A property-distribution scheme in which a participant pays for the chance to receive compensation for introducing new persons to the scheme, as well as for when those new persons themselves introduce participants. • Pyramid schemes are illegal in most states.—Also termed *endless-chain scheme*; *chain-referral scheme*; *multilevel-distribution program*; *pyramid distribution plan*. Cf. PONZI SCHEME.

Q

Q. *abbr.* QUESTION. • This abbreviation is almost always used in deposition and trial transcripts to denote each question asked by the examining lawyer.

qualified privilege. See PRIVILEGE (1).

qualified witness. See WITNESS.

quash (kwahsh), *vb.* To annul or make void; to terminate <quash an indictment> <quash proceedings>.

quashal (**kwahsh**-əl), *n.* The act of quashing something <quashal of the subpoena>.

quasi-admission. See ADMISSION.

quasi-crime. See CRIME.

question. 1. A query directed to a witness.—Abbr. Q.

> *categorical question.* **1.** See LEADING QUESTION. **2.** (*pl.*) A series of questions, on a particular subject, arranged in systematic or consecutive order.

> *cross-question.* A question asked of a witness during cross-examination.—Abbr. XQ.

direct question. A question asked of a witness during direct examination.

hypothetical question. See HYPOTHETICAL QUESTION.

leading question. See LEADING QUESTION.

2. An issue in controversy; a matter to be determined.

certified question. See CERTIFIED QUESTION.

federal question. See FEDERAL QUESTION.

judicial question. See JUDICIAL QUESTION.

mixed question. See MIXED QUESTION OF LAW AND FACT.

question of fact. 1. An issue that has not been predetermined and authoritatively answered by the law. • An example is whether a particular criminal defendant is guilty of an offense. **2.** An issue that does not involve what the law is on a given point. **3.** A disputed issue to be resolved by the jury in a jury trial or by the judge in a bench trial.—Also termed *fact question.* See FACT-FINDER. **4.** An issue capable of being answered by way of demonstration, as opposed to a question of unverifiable opinion.

question of law. 1. An issue to be decided by the judge, concerning the application or interpretation of the law <a jury cannot decide

questions of law, which are reserved for the court>. **2.** A question that the law itself has authoritatively answered, so that the court may not answer it as a matter of discretion <under the sentencing guidelines, the punishment for a three-time offender is a question of law>. **3.** An issue about what the law is on a particular point; an issue in which parties argue about, and the court must decide, what the true rule of law is <both parties appealed on the question of law>. **4.** An issue that, although it may turn on a factual point, is reserved for the court and excluded from the jury; an issue that is exclusively within the province of the judge and not the jury <whether a contractual ambiguity exists is a question of law>.—Also termed *legal question*; *law question*.

quotient verdict. See VERDICT.

R

racket, *n.* **1.** An organized criminal activity; esp., the extortion of money by threat or violence. **2.** A dishonest or fraudulent scheme or business.

racketeer, *n.* A person who engages in racketeering.—**racketeer,** *vb.*

Racketeer Influenced and Corrupt Organizations Act. A law designed to attack organized criminal activity and preserve marketplace integrity by investigating, controlling, and prosecuting persons who participate or conspire to participate in racketeering. ● Enacted in 1970, the federal Racketeer Influenced and Corrupt Organizations Act (RICO) applies only to activity involving interstate or foreign commerce. 18 USCA §§ 1961–1968. Since then, many states have adopted laws (sometimes called "little RICO" acts) based on the federal statute. The federal and most state RICO acts provide for enforcement not only by criminal prosecution but also by civil lawsuit, in which the plaintiff can sue for treble damages.

racketeering, *n.* **1.** A system of organized crime traditionally involving the extortion of money from businesses by intimidation, violence, or other illegal methods. **2.** A pattern of illegal activity (such as bribery, extortion, fraud, and murder) carried out as part of an enterprise (such as a crime syndicate) that is owned or controlled by those engaged in the illegal activity. ● The modern sense (sense 2) derives from the federal RICO statute, which greatly broadened the term's original sense to include such activities as mail fraud, securities fraud, and the collection of illegal gambling debts. See 18 USCA §§ 1951–1960.

raid, *n.* A sudden attack or invasion by law-enforcement officers, usu. to make an arrest or to search for evidence of a crime.

railroad, *vb.* To convict (a person) hastily, esp. by the use of false charges or insufficient evidence.

raise, *vb.* To increase the stated amount of (a negotiable instrument) by fraudulent alteration <the indorser raised the check>.

raised check. See CHECK.

raising an instrument. The act of fraudulently altering a negotiable instrument, esp. a check, to increase the sum stated as being payable. See *raised check* under CHECK.

rake-off, *n.* A percentage or share taken, esp. from an illegal transaction; an illegal bribe, payoff, or skimming of profits.—**rake off,** *vb.*

ranger. 1. An officer or warden who patrols and supervises the care and preservation of a public park or forest. **2.** A member of a special state police force.

ransom, *n*. **1.** The release of a captured person or property in exchange for payment of a demanded price. **2.** Money or other consideration demanded or paid for the release of a captured person or property. See KIDNAPPING.

ransom, *vb*. **1.** To obtain the release of (a captive) by paying a demanded price. **2.** To release (a captive) upon receiving such a payment. **3.** To hold and demand payment for the release of (a captive).

rap, *n*. *Slang*. **1.** Legal responsibility for a criminal act <he took the rap for his accomplices>. **2.** A criminal charge <a murder rap>. **3.** A criminal conviction; esp., a prison sentence <a 20-year rap for counterfeiting>.

rape, *n*. **1.** At common law, unlawful sexual intercourse committed by a man with a woman not his wife through force and against her will. ● The common-law crime of rape required at least a slight penetration of the penis into the vagina. Also at common law, a husband could not be convicted of raping his wife. **2.** Unlawful sexual activity (esp. intercourse) with a person (usu. a female) without consent and usu. by force or threat of injury. • Most modern state statutes have broadened the definition along these lines. Marital status is now usu. irrelevant, and sometimes so is the victim's gender.—Also termed (in some statutes) *unlawful sexual intercourse*; *sexual assault*; *sexual battery*; *sexual abuse*.

> **acquaintance rape.** Rape committed by someone known to the victim, esp. by the victim's social companion.

> **date rape.** Rape committed by a person who is escorting the victim on a social occasion. • Loosely, *date rape* is also sometimes used in reference to what is more accurately called *acquaintance rape* or *relationship rape*.

> **marital rape.** A husband's sexual intercourse with his wife by force or without her consent. • Marital rape was not a crime at common law, but under modern statutes the marital exemption no longer applies, and in most jurisdictions a husband can be convicted of raping his wife.

> **relationship rape.** Rape committed by a person with whom the victim has had a previous sexual relationship.

> **statutory rape.** Unlawful sexual intercourse with a person under the age of consent (as defined by statute), regardless of

whether it is against that person's will. •
Generally, only an adult may be convicted of
this crime. A person under the age of consent cannot be convicted.—Also termed *rape
under age*. See AGE OF CONSENT.

3. *Archaic.* The act of seizing and carrying off
a person (esp. a woman) by force; abduction.

rape, *vb.* **1.** To commit rape against. **2.** *Archaic.* To seize and carry off by force; abduct. **3.**
To plunder or despoil.—**rapist, raper,** *n.*

rape shield law. See SHIELD LAW (2).

rape shield statute. See SHIELD LAW (2).

rape under age. See *statutory rape* under
RAPE.

rapine (**rap**-in). **1.** Forcible seizure and carrying off of another's property; pillage or plunder. **2.** *Archaic.* Rape.

rap sheet. *Slang.* A person's criminal record.

rapture. *Archaic.* Forcible seizure and carrying off of another person (esp. a woman);
abduction.

rational-basis test. A principle whereby a
court will uphold a law as valid under the

Equal Protection Clause or Due Process Clause if it bears a reasonable relationship to the attainment of some legitimate governmental objective.—Also termed *rational-purpose test*; *rational-relationship test*; *minimal scrutiny*; *minimum scrutiny*. Cf. STRICT SCRUTINY; INTERMEDIATE SCRUTINY.

rational-choice theory. The theory that criminals engage in criminal activity when they believe that the potential benefits outweigh the risks of committing the crime. Cf. CONTROL THEORY; ROUTINE-ACTIVITIES THEORY; STRAIN THEORY.

ravishment, *n. Archaic.* **1.** Forcible seizure and carrying off of another person (esp. a woman); abduction. **2.** See RAPE (1). • In this sense the term is widely considered inappropriate for modern usage, given its romantic connotations (in other contexts) of ecstasy and delight.—**ravish,** *vb.*

real evidence. See EVIDENCE.

reargument, *n.* The presentation of additional arguments, which often suggest that a controlling legal principle has been overlooked, to a court (usu. an appellate court) that has already heard initial arguments.—**reargue,** *vb.* Cf. REHEARING.

rearrest. See ARREST.

reasonable cause. See PROBABLE CAUSE.

reasonable doubt. The doubt that prevents one from being firmly convinced of a defendant's guilt, or the belief that there is a real possibility that a defendant is not guilty. • "Beyond a reasonable doubt" is the standard used by a jury to determine whether a criminal defendant is guilty. See Model Penal Code § 1.12. In deciding whether guilt has been proved beyond a reasonable doubt, the jury must begin with the presumption that the defendant is innocent. See BURDEN OF PERSUASION.

reasonable force. See FORCE.

reasonable grounds. See PROBABLE CAUSE.

reasonable-inference rule. An evidentiary principle providing that a jury, in deciding a case, may properly consider any reasonable inference drawn from the evidence presented at trial. Cf. PYRAMIDING INFERENCES, RULE AGAINST.

reasonable man. See REASONABLE PERSON.

reasonable person. 1. A hypothetical person used as a legal standard, esp. to determine whether someone acted with negligence. • The reasonable person acts sensibly, does things without serious delay, and takes proper but not excessive precautions.—Also termed *reasonable man*; *prudent person*; *ordinarily prudent person*; *reasonably prudent person*. **2.** *Archaic*. A human being.

reasonable suspicion. A particularized and objective basis, supported by specific and articulable facts, for suspecting a person of criminal activity. ● A police officer must have a reasonable suspicion to stop a person in a public place. See STOP AND FRISK. Cf. PROBABLE CAUSE.

reasonably prudent person. See REASONABLE PERSON.

rebuttable presumption. See PRESUMPTION.

rebuttal, *n*. **1.** In-court contradiction of an adverse party's evidence. **2.** The time given to a party to present contradictory evidence or arguments. Cf. CASE-IN-CHIEF.

rebuttal evidence. See EVIDENCE.

rebuttal witness. See WITNESS.

receiving stolen property. The criminal offense of acquiring or controlling property known to have been stolen by another person.

• Some jurisdictions require the additional element of wrongful intent. In some jurisdictions it is a felony, but in others it is either a felony or a misdemeanor depending on the value of the property. See Model Penal Code §§ 223.1, 223.6.—Sometimes shortened to *receiving*.—Also termed *receiving stolen goods*. See FENCE.

recidivate (ri-**sid**-ə-vayt), *vb*. To return to a habit of criminal behavior; to relapse into crime.

recidivism (ri-**sid**-ə-viz-əm), *n*. A tendency to relapse into a habit of criminal activity or behavior.—Also termed (archaically) *recidivation*.—**recidivous, recidivist,** *adj*.

recidivist (ri-**sid**-ə-vist), *n*. One who has been convicted of multiple criminal offenses, usu. similar in nature; a repeat offender <proponents of prison reform argue that prisons don't cure the recidivist>.—Also termed *habitual offender*; *habitual criminal*; *repeat offender*; *repeater*; *career criminal*.

reckless, *adj*. Characterized by the creation of a substantial and unjustifiable risk of harm to others and by a conscious (and sometimes deliberate) disregard for or indifference to that risk; heedless; rash. • Reckless conduct is much more than mere negligence: it is a gross deviation from what a reasonable person would do.—**recklessly,** *adv.* See RECKLESSNESS. Cf. WANTON.

reckless disregard. Conscious indifference to the consequences (of an act).

reckless driving. The criminal offense of operating a motor vehicle in a manner that shows conscious indifference to the safety of others.

reckless endangerment. The criminal offense of putting another person at substantial risk of death or serious injury. ● This is a statutory, not a common-law, offense.

reckless homicide. See HOMICIDE.

reckless negligence. See *gross negligence* (2) under NEGLIGENCE.

recklessness, *n.* **1.** Conduct whereby the actor does not desire harmful consequence but nonetheless foresees the possibility and consciously takes the risk. ● Recklessness involves a greater degree of fault than negligence but a lesser degree of fault than intentional wrongdoing. **2.** The state of mind in which a person does not care about the consequences of his or her actions.—Also termed *heedlessness.* Cf. WANTONNESS.

recognizance (ri-**kog**-nə-zənts). **1.** A bond or obligation, made in court, by which a person promises to perform some act or observe some condition, such as to appear when called, to pay a debt, or to keep the peace. ● Most commonly, a recognizance takes the form of a bail bond that guarantees an unjailed criminal defendant's return for a court date <the defendant was released on his own recognizance>. See RELEASE ON RECOGNIZANCE; O.R.

> *personal recognizance.* The release of a defendant in a criminal case in which the court takes the defendant's word that he or she will appear for a scheduled matter or when told to appear. ● This type of release dispenses with the necessity of the person's posting money or having a surety sign a bond with the court.

2. See *bail bond* under BOND.

reconduction, *n.* The forcible return of aliens (esp. illegal aliens, destitute or diseased aliens, or alien criminals who have served their punishment) to their country of origin.—**reconduct,** *vb.*

record, *n.* The official report of the proceedings in a case, including the filed papers, a verbatim transcript of the trial or hearing (if any), and tangible exhibits. See DOCKET (1).

recorded recollection. See PAST RECOLLECTION RECORDED.

recorder. A municipal judge with the criminal jurisdiction of a magistrate or a police judge and sometimes also with limited civil jurisdiction.

recorder's court. A court having jurisdiction over felony cases. • This court exists in only a few jurisdictions, such as Michigan, where the recorder's court hears felony cases arising within the Detroit city limits.

record on appeal. The record of a trial-court proceeding as presented to the appellate court for review.—Also termed *appellate record*. See RECORD.

recross-examination. A second cross-examination, after redirect examination.—Often shortened to *recross*. See CROSS-EXAMINATION.

recusal (ri-**kyoo**-zəl), *n.* Removal of oneself as judge or policy-maker in a particular matter, esp. because of a conflict of interest.—Also termed *recusation*; *recusement*. Cf. DISQUALIFICATION.

redirect examination. A second direct examination, after cross-examination, the scope ordinarily being limited to matters covered during cross-examination.—Often shortened to *redirect*.—Also termed (in England) *reexamination*. See DIRECT EXAMINATION.

redress (ri-**dres** *or* **ree**-dres), *n*. **1.** Relief; remedy <money damages, as opposed to equitable relief, is the only redress available>. **2.** A means of seeking relief or remedy <if the statute of limitations has run, the plaintiff is without redress>.—**redress** (ri-**dres**), *vb*.— **redressable,** *adj*.

   penal redress. A form of penal liability requiring full compensation of the injured person as an instrument for punishing the offender; compensation paid to the injured person for the full value of the loss (an amount that may far exceed the wrongdoer's benefit). See RESTITUTION (3).

   restitutionary redress. Compensation paid to one who has been injured, the amount being the pecuniary value of the benefit to the wrongdoer. See RESTITUTION (2).

reexamination, *n*. See REDIRECT EXAMINATION <the attorney focused on the defendant's alibi during reexamination>.—**reexamine,** *vb*.

referee. A type of master appointed by a court to assist with certain proceedings. ● In some jurisdictions, referees take testimony before reporting to the court.

reformative punishment. See PUNISHMENT.

reformatory, *n.* A penal institution for young offenders, esp. minors.—Also termed *reform school.*

refreshing recollection. See PRESENT RECOL-LECTION REFRESHED.

registration, *n.* The act of recording or en-rolling <the county clerk handles registration of voters>.

   criminal registration. The requirement in some communities that any felon who spends any time in the community must register his or her name with the police.

regulatory offense. See OFFENSE.

regulatory search. See *administrative search* under SEARCH.

rehabilitation, *n.* **1.** The process of seeking to improve a criminal's character and outlook so that he or she can function in society with-out committing other crimes <rehabilitation is a traditional theory of criminal punishment, along with deterrence and retribution>. Cf. DE-TERRENCE; RETRIBUTION (1). **2.** The restoration of a witness's credibility after the witness has been impeached <the inconsistencies were ex-plained away during the prosecution's rehabili-

tation of the witness>.—**rehabilitate,** *vb.*—
rehabilitative, *adj*.

rehearing. A second or subsequent hearing of
a case or an appeal, usu. held to consider an
error or omission in the first hearing <the
appellant, dissatisfied with the appellate
court's ruling, filed a petition for rehear-
ing>.—Abbr. reh'g. Cf. REARGUMENT.

reh'g. *abbr*. REHEARING.

relationship rape. See RAPE.

release, *n*. **1.** The action of freeing or the fact
of being freed from restraint or confinement
<he became a model citizen after his release
from prison>. **2.** A document giving formal
discharge from custody <after the sheriff
signed the release, the prisoner was free to
go>.—**release,** *vb*.

   conditional release. An early discharge of
   a prison inmate, who is then subject to the
   rules and regulations of parole.

   study release. A program that allows a
   prisoner to be released for a few hours at a
   time to attend classes at a nearby college or
   technical institution.—Also termed *study
   furlough*.

unconditional release. The final discharge of a prison inmate from custody.

release on recognizance. The pretrial release of an arrested person who promises, usu. in writing but without supplying a surety or posting bond, to appear for trial at a later date.—Abbr. ROR.—Also termed *release on own recognizance*; *release on O.R.* See RECOGNIZANCE.

relevant, *adj.* Logically connected and tending to prove or disprove a matter in issue; having appreciable probative value—that is, rationally tending to persuade people of the probability or possibility of some alleged fact. Cf. MATERIAL.

relevant evidence. See EVIDENCE.

remand (ri-**mand** *also* **ree**-mand), *n.* **1.** The act or an instance of sending something (such as a case, claim, or person) back for further action. **2.** An order remanding a case, claim, or person.

remand (ri-**mand**), *vb.* **1.** To send (a case or claim) back to the court or tribunal from which it came for some further action <the appellate court reversed the trial court's opinion and remanded the case for new trial>. **2.** To recommit (an accused person) to custody after a preliminary examination <the magistrate, after denying bail, remanded the defendant to custody>.

remedy, *n*. The means of enforcing a right or preventing or redressing a wrong; legal or equitable relief.

remission. A pardon granted for an offense.

remote cause. See CAUSE (1).

rendition, *n*. **1.** The action of making, delivering, or giving out, such as a legal decision. **2.** The return of a fugitive from one state to the state where the fugitive is accused or convicted of a crime.—Also termed *interstate rendition*. Cf. EXTRADITION.

rendition warrant. See WARRANT.

renunciation (ri-nən-see-**ay**-shən), *n*. Complete and voluntary abandonment of criminal purpose—sometimes coupled with an attempt to thwart the activity's success—before a crime is committed. ● Renunciation can be an affirmative defense to attempt, conspiracy, and the like. Model Penal Code § 5.01(4).—Also termed *withdrawal*; *abandonment*.—**renounce,** *vb*.—**renunciative, renunciatory,** *adj*.

reparole. A second release from prison on parole, served under the same sentence for which the parolee served the first term of parole.

repeater. See RECIDIVIST.

repeat offender. See OFFENDER.

reporter's privilege. See *journalist's privilege* (1) under PRIVILEGE (3).

reporter's record. See TRANSCRIPT.

report of proceedings. See TRANSCRIPT.

reprieve (ri-**preev**), *n*. Temporary postponement of the execution of a criminal sentence, esp. a death sentence.—**reprieve,** *vb*. Cf. COMMUTATION; PARDON.

repugnant verdict. See VERDICT.

reputational evidence. See *reputation evidence* under EVIDENCE.

reputation evidence. See EVIDENCE.

request for instructions. During trial, a party's written request that the court instruct the jury on the law as set forth in the request.—Abbr. RFI.—Also termed *request to charge*.

request for production. In pretrial discovery, a party's written request that another party provide specified documents or other tangible things for inspection and copying.— Abbr. RFP.—Also termed *notice to produce*; *demand for document inspection*.

request to charge. See REQUEST FOR INSTRUCTIONS.

required-records doctrine. The principle that the right against self-incrimination does not apply when one is being compelled to produce business records that are kept in accordance with government regulations and that involve public aspects. ● Some courts have held that certain medical records and tax forms fall within this doctrine and are thus not protected by the right against self-incrimination.

rescous (**res**-kəs). See RESCUE (2).

rescript (**ree**-skript), *n.* **1.** A judge's written order to a court clerk explaining how to dispose of a case. **2.** An appellate court's written decision, usu. unsigned, that is sent down to the trial court.

rescue, *n.* **1.** The act or an instance of saving or freeing someone from danger or captivity. **2.** The forcible and unlawful freeing of a person from arrest or imprisonment.—Also termed (in sense 2) *rescous*.

resentencing, *n.* The act or an instance of imposing a new or revised criminal sentence.— **resentence,** *vb.*

res gestae (rays **jes**-tee *also* **jes**-tɪ), *n. pl.* [Latin "things done"] The events at issue, or other events contemporaneous with them. ● In evidence law, words and statements about the res gestae are usu. admissible under a hearsay exception (such as present sense impression or excited utterance). Where the Federal Rules of Evidence or state rules fashioned after them are in effect, the use of *res gestae* is now out of place. See Fed. R. Evid. 803(1), (2).—Also termed *res gesta*.

res gestae witness. See WITNESS.

residential community treatment center. See HALFWAY HOUSE.

res ipsa loquitur test (rays **ip**-sə **loh**-kwə-tər). A method for determining whether a defendant has gone beyond preparation and has actually committed an attempt, based on whether the defendant's act itself would have indicated to an observer what the defendant intended to do.—Also termed *equivocality test*. See ATTEMPT.

resisting arrest. The crime of obstructing or opposing a police officer who is making an arrest.—Also termed *resisting lawful arrest*.

resisting unlawful arrest. The act of opposing a police officer who is making an unlawful arrest. ● Most jurisdictions have accepted the Model Penal Code position prohibiting the use of force to resist an unlawful arrest when the person arrested knows that a police officer is making the arrest. But some jurisdictions allow an arrestee to use nondeadly force to prevent the arrest. See Model Penal Code § 3.04(2)(a)(i).

respite (**res**-pit), *n*. **1.** A period of temporary delay; an extension of time. **2.** A temporary suspension of a death sentence; a reprieve. **3.** A delay granted to a jury or court for further consideration of a verdict or appeal.—**respite,** *vb*.

respondeat superior (ri-**spon**-dee-at soo-**peer**-ee-ər *or* sə-peer-ee-**or**). The doctrine holding an employer or principal liable for the employee's or agent's wrongful acts committed within the scope of the employment or agency.

respondent. 1. The party against whom an appeal is taken; APPELLEE. **2.** The party against whom a motion or petition is filed. Cf. PETITIONER.

responsibility, *n.* **1.** A person's mental fitness to answer in court for his or her actions. See COMPETENCY. **2.** Guilt.—Also termed *criminal responsibility*.—**responsible,** *adj.*

restitution, *n.* **1.** Return or restoration of some specific thing to its rightful owner or status. **2.** Compensation for benefits derived from a wrong done to another. **3.** Compensation or reparation for the loss caused to another. • In senses 2 and 3, restitution is sometimes ordered as a condition of probation.—**restitutionary,** *adj.*

restitutionary redress. See REDRESS.

restraining order. 1. A court order prohibiting or restricting a person from harassing, threatening, and sometimes even contacting or approaching another specified person. • This type of order is issued most commonly in cases of domestic violence.—Also termed *protection order*; *protective order*. **2.** See TEMPORARY RESTRAINING ORDER.

restraint, *n.* **1.** Confinement, abridgment, or limitation <a restraint on the freedom of

speech>. **2.** Prohibition of action; holding back <the victim's family exercised no restraint—they told the suspect exactly what they thought of him>.

restraint of trade. An agreement between or combination of businesses intended to eliminate competition, create a monopoly, artificially raise prices, or otherwise adversely affect the free market. ● Restraints of trade are usu. illegal, but may be declared reasonable if they are in the best interests of both the parties and the public.—Often shortened to *restraint*.—Also termed *conspiracy in restraint of trade*.

restriction. 1. A limitation or qualification. **2.** A deprivation of liberty involving moral and legal, rather than physical, restraint. ● A military restriction is imposed as punishment either by a commanding officer's nonjudicial punishment or by a summary, special, or general court-martial. Restriction is a lesser restraint because it permits the restricted person to perform full military duties. See *nonjudicial punishment* under PUNISHMENT.

  restriction in lieu of arrest. A restriction in which a person is ordered to stay within specific geographical limits, such as a base or a ship, and is permitted to perform full military duties.

retreat rule. The doctrine holding that the victim of a murderous assault must choose a safe retreat instead of resorting to deadly force in self-defense, unless (1) the victim is at home or in his or her place of business (the so-called *castle doctrine*), or (2) the assailant is a person whom the victim is trying to arrest. • A minority of American jurisdictions have adopted this rule. Cf. NO-RETREAT RULE.

retrial, *n.* A new trial of an action that has already been tried.—**retry,** *vb.* See *trial de novo* under TRIAL.

retribution, *n.* **1.** Punishment imposed as repayment or revenge for the offense committed; requital. Cf. DETERRENCE; REHABILITATION (1). **2.** Something justly deserved; repayment; reward.—**retribute,** *vb.*—**retributive,** *adj.*

retributive punishment. See PUNISHMENT.

retributivism (ri-**trib**-yə-tə-viz-əm), *n.* The legal theory by which criminal punishment is justified, as long as the offender is morally accountable, regardless of whether deterrence or other good consequences would result. • According to retributivism, a criminal is thought to have a debt to pay to society, which is paid by punishment. The punishment is also sometimes said to be society's act of paying back the criminal for the wrong done. Oppo-

nents of retributivism sometimes refer to it as
"vindictive theory."—**retributivist,** *adj. & n.*
Cf. *hedonistic utilitarianism* under UTILITARIAN-
ISM; UTILITARIAN-DETERRENCE THEORY.

> *maximalist retributivism.* The classical
> form of retributivism, espoused by scholars
> such as Immanuel Kant, under which it is
> argued that society has a duty, not just a
> right, to punish a criminal who is guilty and
> culpable, that is, someone who has no justifi-
> cation or excuse for the illegal act.

> *minimalist retributivism.* The more con-
> temporary form of retributivism, which
> maintains that no one should be punished in
> the absence of guilt and culpability (that is,
> unless punishment is deserved), and that a
> judge may absolve the offender from punish-
> ment, wholly or partially, when doing so
> would further societal goals such as rehabili-
> tation or deterrence.

retrospectant evidence. See EVIDENCE.

reversible error. See ERROR.

review, *n.* Consideration, inspection, or reexamination of a subject or thing.—**review,** *vb.*

> *appellate review.* Examination of a lower
> court's decision by a higher court, which can
> affirm, reverse, or modify the decision.

discretionary review. The form of appellate review that is not a matter of right but that occurs only with the appellate court's permission. See CERTIORARI.

judicial review. See JUDICIAL REVIEW.

revision, *n.* **1.** A reexamination or careful review for correction or improvement. **2.** The reconvening of a general or special court-martial to revise its action or to correct the record because of an improper or inconsistent action concerning the findings or the sentence. ● A revision can occur only if it will not materially prejudice the accused.

revocation hearing. See HEARING.

reward, *n.* Something of value, usu. money, given in return for some service or achievement, such as recovering property or providing information that leads to the capture of a criminal.—**reward,** *vb.*

RFI. *abbr.* REQUEST FOR INSTRUCTIONS.

RFP. *abbr.* REQUEST FOR PRODUCTION.

Richard Roe. A fictitious name for a male party to a legal proceeding, used because the party's true identity is unknown or because his real name is being withheld; esp., the second of two such parties. Cf. JOHN DOE.

RICO (**ree**-koh). *abbr.* RACKETEER INFLUENCED AND CORRUPT ORGANIZATIONS ACT.

right, *n.* **1.** That which is proper under law, morality, or ethics <know right from wrong>. **2.** Something that is due to a person by just claim, legal guarantee, or moral principle <the right of liberty>. **3.** A power, privilege, or immunity secured to a person by law <the right to dispose of one's estate>. **4.** A legally enforceable claim that another will do or will not do a given act; a recognized and protected interest the violation of which is a wrong <a breach of duty that infringes one's right>. **5.** (*often pl.*) The interest, claim, or ownership that one has in tangible or intangible property <a debtor's rights in collateral> <publishing rights>.

right against self-incrimination. A criminal defendant's or a witness's constitutional right—under the Fifth Amendment, but waivable under certain conditions—guaranteeing that a person cannot be compelled by the government to testify if the testimony might result in the person's being criminally prosecuted. ● Although this right is most often asserted during a criminal prosecution, a person can also "plead the Fifth" in a civil, legislative, administrative, or grand-jury proceeding.—Also termed *privilege against self-*

incrimination; *right to remain silent*. See
SELF-INCRIMINATION.

right-and-wrong test. See MCNAGHTEN RULES.

right to counsel. A criminal defendant's constitutional right, guaranteed by the Sixth
Amendment, to representation by a court-appointed lawyer if the defendant cannot afford
to hire one.—Also termed *access to counsel*.
See ASSISTANCE OF COUNSEL.

right to remain silent. See RIGHT AGAINST
SELF-INCRIMINATION.

right-wrong test. See MCNAGHTEN RULES.

ringing the changes. Fraud consisting in the
offender's using a large bill to pay for a small
purchase, waiting for the shopkeeper to put
change on the counter, and then, by a series of
maneuvers involving changes of mind—such
as asking for some other article of little value
or for smaller change for some of the money
on the counter—creating a confused situation
in which the offender picks up much more of
the money than is really due.

riot, *n*. An unlawful disturbance of the peace
by an assembly of usu. three or more persons
acting with a common purpose in a violent or
tumultuous manner that threatens or terroriz-

RIOT

es the public.—**riot,** *vb.*—**riotous,** *adj.* Cf. *un-lawful assembly* under ASSEMBLY; CIVIL COMMO-TION; ROUT.

risk of jury doubt. See BURDEN OF PERSUASION.

risk of nonpersuasion. See BURDEN OF PERSUA-SION.

robbery, *n.* The illegal taking of property from the person of another, or in the person's presence, by violence or intimidation; aggravated larceny.—**rob,** *vb.* See LARCENY; THEFT. Cf. BURGLARY.

aggravated robbery. Robbery committed by a person who either carries a dangerous weapon—often called *armed robbery*—or inflicts bodily harm on someone during the robbery.

armed robbery. Robbery committed by a person carrying a dangerous weapon, regardless of whether the weapon is revealed or used. ● Most states punish armed robbery as an aggravated form of robbery rather than as a separate crime.

conjoint robbery (kən-**joynt**). A robbery committed by two or more persons.

highway robbery. **1.** Robbery committed against a traveler on or near a public high-

596

way. **2.** Figuratively, a price or fee that is unreasonably high; excessive profit or advantage.

simple robbery. Robbery that does not involve an aggravating factor or circumstance.

***Rochin* rule.** The now-rejected principle that unconstitutionally obtained evidence is admissible against the accused unless the evidence was obtained in a manner that shocks the conscience (such as pumping the stomach of a suspect to obtain illegal drugs that the suspect has swallowed, as occurred in the *Rochin v. California* case). ● The Supreme Court handed down *Rochin* before the Fourth Amendment exclusionary rule applied to the states. *Rochin v. California*, 342 U.S. 165, 72 S.Ct. 205 (1952).

ROR. *abbr.* RELEASE ON RECOGNIZANCE.

rout (rowt), *n.* The offense that occurs when an unlawful assembly makes some move toward the accomplishment of its participants' common purpose. Cf. RIOT.

routine-activities theory. The theory that criminal acts occur when (1) a person is motivated to commit the offense, (2) a vulnerable victim is available, and (3) there is insufficient protection to prevent the crime. Cf. CONTROL THEORY; RATIONAL-CHOICE THEORY; STRAIN THEORY.

rubber check. See *bad check* under CHECK.

rule of lenity (len-ə-tee). The judicial doctrine holding that a court, in construing an ambiguous criminal statute that sets out multiple or inconsistent punishments, should resolve the ambiguity in favor of the more lenient punishment.—Also termed *lenity rule*.

ruling, *n.* The outcome of a court's decision either on some point of law or on the case as a whole.—Also termed *legal ruling.*—**rule,** *vb.* Cf. JUDGMENT; OPINION.

runaway. A person (usu. a juvenile) who has fled from the custody of legal guardians without permission and who has failed to return within a reasonable time.

runaway grand jury. See GRAND JURY.

running objection. See *continuing objection* under OBJECTION.

S

sabotage (sab-ə-tahzh), *n.* **1.** The destruction, damage, or knowingly defective production of materials, premises, or utilities used for national defense or for war. 18 USCA §§ 2151 et seq. **2.** The willful and malicious destruction of an employer's property or interference with an employer's normal operations, esp. during a labor dispute.—**sabotage,** *vb.*

saboteur (sab-ə-tər), *n.* A person who commits sabotage.

SAET. *abbr.* SUBSTANCE-ABUSE EVALUATION AND TREATMENT.

same-elements test. See LEGAL-ELEMENTS TEST.

same-evidence test. A test of whether the facts alleged in a given case are essentially identical to those alleged in a previous case. ● If they are the same, the Fifth Amendment's prohibition against double jeopardy will bar the later action, which is essentially a second prosecution for the same offense. This principle was first announced in *Blockburger v. United States*, 284 U.S. 299, 52 S.Ct. 180 (1932).—Also termed *Blockburger test; actual-evidence test.* See *same offense* under OFFENSE; DOUBLE JEOPARDY.

same offense. See OFFENSE.

sanction (**sangk**-shən), *n.* **1.** Official approval or authorization <the committee gave sanction to the proposal>. **2.** A penalty or coercive measure that results from failure to comply with a law, rule, or order <a sanction for discovery abuse>.

> *criminal sanction.* A sanction attached to a criminal conviction, such as a fine or restitution.—Also termed *penal sanction.*

> *shame sanction.* A criminal sanction designed to stigmatize or disgrace a convicted offender, and often to alert the public about the offender's conviction. • A shame sanction usu. publicly associates the offender with the crime that he or she committed. An example is being required to post a sign in one's yard stating, "Convicted Child Molester Lives Here."—Also termed *shaming sentence*; *scarlet-letter punishment.*

sanction, *vb.* **1.** To approve, authorize, or support <the court will sanction the trust disposition if it is not against public policy>. **2.** To penalize by imposing a sanction <the court sanctioned the attorney for violating the gag order>.

sanctionable, *adj.* (Of conduct or action) meriting sanctions; likely to be sanctioned.

sane, *adj.* Having a relatively sound and healthy mind; capable of reason and of distinguishing right from wrong.

sanity. The state or condition of having a relatively sound and healthy mind. Cf. INSANITY.

sanity hearing. 1. An inquiry into the mental competency of a person to stand trial. **2.** A proceeding to determine whether a person should be institutionalized.

sap, *n.* A club, a blackjack, a hose containing rocks in the middle, or any other object generally used as a bludgeon.

SAR. *abbr.* SUSPICIOUS-ACTIVITY REPORT.

satisfactory evidence. See EVIDENCE.

satisfactory proof. See *satisfactory evidence* under EVIDENCE.

Saturday-night special. A handgun that is easily obtained and concealed.

S.C. *abbr.* SUPREME COURT.

scalping, *n.* **1.** The practice of selling something (esp. a ticket) at a price above face value once it becomes scarce (usu. just before a high-demand event begins). **2.** The purchase of a security by an investment adviser before the adviser recommends that a customer buy the same security. ● This practice is usu. considered unethical because the customer's purchase will increase the security's price, thus enabling the investment adviser to sell at a profit. **3.** The excessive markup or markdown on a transaction by a market-maker. ● This action violates National Association of Securities Dealers guidelines.—**scalp,** *vb.*

scarlet-letter punishment. See *shame sanction* under SANCTION.

scheme. 1. A systemic plan; a connected or orderly arrangement, esp. of related concepts <legislative scheme>. **2.** An artful plot or plan, usu. to deceive others <a scheme to defraud creditors>.

scienter (sI-**en**-tər *or* see-), *n.* [Latin "knowingly"] **1.** A degree of knowledge that makes a person legally responsible for the consequences of his or her act or omission; the fact of an act's having been done knowingly, esp. as a ground for civil damages or criminal punishment. See KNOWLEDGE; MENS REA. **2.** A mental state consisting in an intent to deceive, manipulate, or defraud. ● In this sense, the term is used most often in the context of securities fraud.

scientific evidence. See EVIDENCE.

scintilla-of-evidence rule. A common-law doctrine holding that if even the slightest amount of relevant evidence exists on an issue, then a motion for summary judgment or for directed verdict cannot be granted and the issue must go to the jury. ● Federal courts do not follow this rule, but some states apply it.— Also termed *scintilla rule.*

scofflaw (**skof**-law). A person who treats the law with contempt; esp., one who avoids various laws that are not easily enforced <some scofflaws carry mannequins in their cars in order to drive in the carpool lane>.

Scotch verdict. See NOT PROVEN.

screening grand jury. See GRAND JURY.

scrivener's error. See *clerical error* under ERROR.

S.Ct. *abbr.* SUPREME COURT.

sealed verdict. See VERDICT.

search, *n.* **1.** An examination of a person's body, property, or other area that the person would reasonably be expected to consider as private, conducted by a law-enforcement officer for the purpose of finding evidence of a crime. • Because the Fourth Amendment prohibits unreasonable searches (as well as seizures), a search cannot ordinarily be conducted without probable cause.—**search,** *vb*.

administrative search. A search of public or commercial premises carried out by a regulatory authority for the purpose of enforcing compliance with health, safety, or security regulations. • The probable cause required for an administrative search is less stringent than that required for a search incident to a criminal investigation.—Also termed *regulatory search; inspection search.*

border search. **1.** A search conducted at the border of a country, esp. at a checkpoint, to exclude illegal aliens and contraband. **2.** Loosely, a search conducted near the border of a country. • Generally, searches near the border are treated no differently from those conducted elsewhere in the country.

checkpoint search. **1.** A search anywhere on a military installation. **2.** A search in which police officers set up roadblocks and stop motorists to ascertain whether the drivers are intoxicated.

Chimel search. See *protective search.*

consent search. A search conducted after a person with the authority to do so voluntarily waives Fourth Amendment rights. • The government has the burden to show that the consent was given freely—not under duress. *Bumper v. North Carolina*, 391 U.S. 543, 548–49, 88 S.Ct. 1788, 1792 (1968).

constructive search. A subpoena of a corporation's records.

emergency search. A warrantless search conducted by a police officer who has probable cause and reasonably believes that, because of a need to protect life or property, there is not enough time to obtain a warrant. See EMERGENCY DOCTRINE.

exigent search (**eks**-ə-jənt). A warrantless search carried out under exigent circumstances, such as an imminent danger to human life or a risk of the destruction of evidence. See *exigent circumstances* under CIRCUMSTANCE.

illegal search. See *unreasonable search*.

inventory search. A complete search of an arrestee's person before that person is booked into jail. • All possessions found are typically held in police custody.

no-knock search. A search of property by the police without knocking and announcing their presence and purpose before entry. • A no-knock search warrant may be issued under limited circumstances, as when a prior announcement would lead to the destruction of the objects searched for, or would endanger the safety of the police officer or another person.

private search. A search conducted by a private person rather than by a law-enforcement officer. ● Items found during a private search are generally admissible in evidence if the person conducting the search was not acting at the direction of a law-enforcement officer.

protective search. A search of a detained suspect and the area within the suspect's immediate control, conducted to protect the arresting officer's safety (as from a concealed weapon) and often to preserve evidence. ● A protective search can be conducted without a warrant. *Chimel v. California,* 395 U.S. 752, 89 S.Ct. 2034 (1969).—Also termed *search incident to arrest*; *Chimel search* (shə-**mel**).

regulatory search. See *administrative search*.

sector search. See *zone search*.

shakedown search. A usu. random and warrantless search for illicit or contraband material (such as weapons or drugs) in a prisoner's cell.—Often shortened to *shake-down*.

strip search. A search of a person conducted after that person's clothes have been removed, the purpose usu. being to find any contraband the person might be hiding.

unreasonable search. A search conducted without probable cause or other considerations that would make it legally permissible.—Also termed *illegal search*.

voluntary search. A search in which no duress or coercion was applied to obtain the defendant's consent. See *consent search*.

warranted search. A search conducted under authority of a search warrant.

warrantless search. A search conducted without obtaining a proper warrant. ● Warrantless searches are permissible under exigent circumstances or when conducted incident to an arrest. See *exigent circumstances* under CIRCUMSTANCE; *protective search*.

zone search. A search of a crime scene (such as the scene of a fire or explosion) by dividing it up into specific sectors.—Also termed *sector search*.

2. An examination of public documents or records for information. **3.** The wartime process of boarding and examining the contents of a merchant vessel for contraband. • A number of treaties regulate the manner in which the search must be conducted.

search-and-seizure warrant. See SEARCH WARRANT.

search incident to arrest. See *protective search* under SEARCH.

search warrant. A judge's written order authorizing a law-enforcement officer to conduct a search of a specified place and to seize evidence.—Also termed *search-and-seizure warrant*. See WARRANT.

anticipatory search warrant. A search warrant based on an affidavit showing probable cause that evidence of a certain crime (such as illegal drugs) will be located at a specific place in the future.

blanket search warrant. **1.** A single search warrant that authorizes the search of more than one area. **2.** An unconstitutional warrant that authorizes the seizure of everything found at a given location, without specifying which items may be seized.

no-knock search warrant. A search warrant that authorizes the police to enter premises without knocking and announcing

608

their presence and purpose before entry because a prior announcement would lead to the destruction of the objects searched for or would endanger the safety of the police or another person. See *no-knock search* under SEARCH.

Second Amendment. The constitutional amendment, ratified with the Bill of Rights in 1791, guaranteeing the right to keep and bear arms as necessary for securing freedom through a well-regulated militia.

secondary evidence. See EVIDENCE.

second-degree murder. See MURDER.

second-degree principal. See *principal in the second degree* under PRINCIPAL.

secondhand evidence. See HEARSAY.

second offense. See OFFENSE.

Secret Service. A federal law-enforcement agency—organized as a division of the Treasury Department—primarily responsible for preventing counterfeiting and protecting the President and other public officials.

sector search. See *zone search* under SEARCH.

609

sedition, *n.* An agreement, communication, or other preliminary activity aimed at inciting treason or some lesser commotion against public authority; advocacy aimed at inciting or producing—and likely to incite or produce—imminent lawless action. • At common law, sedition included defaming a member of the royal family or the government. The difference between *sedition* and *treason* is that the former is committed by preliminary steps, while the latter entails some overt act for carrying out the plan. But of course, if the plan is merely for some small commotion, even accomplishing the plan does not amount to treason.—**seditious,** *adj.* Cf. TREASON.

seditious conspiracy. See CONSPIRACY.

seditious libel. See LIBEL.

seditious speech. See SPEECH.

seduction. The offense that occurs when a man entices a woman of previously chaste character to have unlawful intercourse with him by means of persuasion, solicitation, promises, or bribes, or other means not involving force. • Many states have abolished this offense for persons over the age of legal consent. Traditionally, the parent has an action to recover damages for the loss of the child's services. But in measuring damages, the jury may consider not just the loss of services but also the distress and anxiety that the parent has suffered in being deprived of the child's comfort and companionship. Though seduction was not a crime at common law, many American states made it a statutory crime until the late 20th century.

segregation, *n*. The act or process of separating.—**segregate,** *vb*.—**segregative,** *adj*.

> ***punitive segregation.*** The act of removing a prisoner from the prison population for placement in separate or solitary confinement, usu. for disciplinary reasons.

seize, *vb*. **1.** To forcibly take possession (of a person or property). **2.** To place (someone) in possession. **3.** To be in possession (of property).

seizure, *n*. The act or an instance of taking possession of a person or property by legal right or process; esp., in constitutional law, a confiscation or arrest that may interfere with a person's reasonable expectation of privacy.

selective enforcement. The practice of law-enforcement officers who use wide or even unfettered discretion about when and where to carry out certain laws; esp., the practice of singling a person out for prosecution or punishment under a statute or regulation because the person is a member of a protected group or because the person has exercised or is planning to exercise a constitutionally protected right.—*selective prosecution.* Cf. *vindictive prosecution* under PROSECUTION.

selective prosecution. **1.** See SELECTIVE ENFORCEMENT. **2.** The practice or an instance of a criminal prosecution brought at the discretion of a prosecutor rather than one brought as a matter of course in the normal functioning of the prosecuting authority's office. ● Selective prosecution violates the Equal Protection Clause of the Fourteenth Amendment if a defendant is singled out for prosecution when others similarly situated have not been prosecuted and the prosecutor's reasons for doing so are impermissible.

self-crimination. See SELF-INCRIMINATION.

self-critical-analysis privilege. See PRIVILEGE (3).

self-defense, *n.* The use of force to protect oneself, one's family, or one's property from a real or threatened attack. ● Generally, a person is justified in using a reasonable amount of force in self-defense if he or she believes that the danger of bodily harm is imminent and that force is necessary to avoid this danger.—

Also termed *defense of self.*—**self-defender,** *n.*
Cf. *adequate provocation* under PROVOCATION.

> *imperfect self-defense.* The use of force by
> one who makes an honest but unreasonable
> mistake that force is necessary to repel an
> attack. • In some jurisdictions, such a self-
> defender will be charged with a lesser of-
> fense than the one committed.

> *perfect self-defense.* The use of force by
> one who accurately appraises the necessity
> and the amount of force to repel an attack.

self-destruction. See SUICIDE.

self-incrimination. The act of indicating
one's own involvement in a crime or exposing
oneself to prosecution, esp. by making a statement.—Also termed *self-crimination*; *self-in-
culpation.* See RIGHT AGAINST SELF-INCRIMINATION.

Self-Incrimination Clause. The clause of
the Fifth Amendment to the U.S. Constitution
barring the government from compelling criminal defendants to testify against themselves.

self-induced intoxication. See *voluntary intoxication* under INTOXICATION.

self-killing. See SUICIDE.

self-murder. See SUICIDE.

self-policing privilege. See *self-critical-analysis privilege* under PRIVILEGE (3).

self-serving declaration. See DECLARATION.

self-slaughter. See SUICIDE.

senior judge. See JUDGE.

sentence, *n.* The judgment that a court formally pronounces after finding a criminal defendant guilty; the punishment imposed on a criminal wrongdoer <a sentence of 20 years in prison>.—**sentence,** *vb.*

> *accumulative sentences.* See *consecutive sentences.*

> *aggregate sentence.* A sentence that arises from a conviction on multiple counts in an indictment.

> *alternative sentence.* A sentence other than incarceration. ● Examples include community service and victim restitution.—Also termed *creative sentence.*

> *concurrent sentences.* Two or more sentences of jail time to be served simultaneously. ● For example, if a defendant receives concurrent sentences of 5 years and 15 years, the total amount of jail time is 15 years.

conditional sentence. A sentence of confinement if the defendant fails to perform
the conditions of probation.

consecutive sentences. Two or more sentences of jail time to be served in sequence.
● For example, if a defendant receives consecutive sentences of 20 years and 5 years,
the total amount of jail time is 25 years.—
Also termed *cumulative sentences*; *accumulative sentences*.

consolidated sentence. See *general sentence.*

creative sentence. See *alternative sentence.*

death sentence. A sentence that imposes
the death penalty. See Model Penal Code
§ 210.6.—Also termed *judgment of blood*.
See DEATH PENALTY.

deferred sentence. A sentence that will not
be carried out if the defendant meets certain
requirements, such as complying with conditions of probation.

delayed sentence. A sentence that is not
imposed, allowing the defendant to satisfy
the court (usu. by complying with certain
restrictions or conditions during the delay
period) that probation is preferable to a prison sentence.

determinate sentence. A sentence for a fixed length of time rather than for an unspecified duration.—Also termed *definite sentence*; *definitive sentence*; *fixed sentence*; *flat sentence*; *straight sentence*.

excessive sentence. A sentence that gives more punishment than is allowed by law.

fixed sentence. 1. See *determinate sentence*. 2. See *mandatory sentence*.

flat sentence. See *determinate sentence*.

general sentence. An undivided, aggregate sentence in a multicount case; a sentence that does not specify the punishment imposed for each count. ● General sentences are prohibited.—Also termed *consolidated sentence*.

indeterminate sentence. 1. A sentence of an unspecified duration, such as one for a term of 10 to 20 years. 2. A maximum prison term that the parole board can reduce, through statutory authorization, after the inmate has served the minimum time required by law.—Also termed *indefinite sentence*. See INDETERMINATE SENTENCING.

intermittent sentence. A sentence consisting of periods of confinement interrupted by periods of freedom.—Also termed (when served on weekends) *weekend sentence*.

life sentence. A sentence that imprisons the convicted criminal for life—though in some jurisdictions the prisoner may become eligible for release on good behavior, rehabilitation, or the like.

mandatory sentence. A sentence set by law with no discretion for the judge to individualize punishment.—Also termed *mandatory penalty*; *mandatory punishment*; *fixed sentence.*

maximum sentence. The highest level of punishment provided by law for a particular crime.

minimum sentence. The least amount of time that a defendant must serve in prison before becoming eligible for parole.

multiple sentences. Concurrent or consecutive sentences, if a defendant is found guilty of more than one offense.

nominal sentence. A criminal sentence in name only; an exceedingly light sentence.

noncustodial sentence. A criminal sentence (such as probation) not requiring prison time.

presumptive sentence. An average sentence for a particular crime (esp. provided under sentencing guidelines) that can be raised or lowered based on the presence of mitigating or aggravating circumstances.

prior sentence. A sentence previously imposed on a criminal defendant for a different offense, whether by a guilty verdict, a guilty plea, or a nolo contendere.

split sentence. A sentence in which part of the time is served in confinement—to expose the offender to the unpleasantness of prison—and the rest on probation. See *shock probation* under PROBATION.

straight sentence. See *determinate sentence*.

suspended sentence. A sentence postponed so that the defendant is not required to serve time unless he or she commits another crime or violates some other court-imposed condition. • A suspended sentence, in effect, is a form of probation.—Also termed *withheld sentence*.

weekend sentence. See *intermittent sentence*.

sentence bargain. See PLEA BARGAIN.

sentence cap. A pretrial plea agreement in a court-martial proceeding by which a ceiling is placed on the maximum penalty that can be imposed.

sentenced to time served. A sentencing disposition in which a criminal defendant is sentenced to jail but is credited with time served in an amount equal to the sentence handed down, resulting in the defendant's release from custody. Cf. BALANCE OF SENTENCE SUSPENDED.

sentence-factor manipulation. See *sentencing entrapment* under ENTRAPMENT.

sentence-package rule. The principle that a defendant can be resentenced on an aggregate sentence—that is, one arising from a conviction on multiple counts in an indictment—when the defendant successfully challenges part of the conviction, as by successfully challenging some but not all of the counts.

sentencing council. A panel of three or more judges who confer to determine a criminal sentence. ● Sentencing by a council occurs less frequently than sentencing by a single trial judge.

sentencing entrapment. See ENTRAPMENT.

sentencing guidelines. A set of standards for determining the punishment that a convicted criminal should receive, based on the nature of the crime and the offender's criminal history. ● The federal government and several states have adopted sentencing guidelines in an effort to make judicial sentencing more consistent.

sentencing hearing. See HEARING; PRESEN-TENCE HEARING.

sentencing phase. See PENALTY PHASE.

Sentencing Reform Act of 1984. A federal statute enacted to bring greater uniformity to punishments assessed for federal crimes by creating a committee of federal judges and other officials (the United States Sentencing Commission) responsible for producing sentencing guidelines to be used by the federal courts. 28 USCA § 994(a)(1).

Sentencing Table. A reference guide used by federal courts to calculate the appropriate punishment under the sentencing guidelines by taking into account the gravity of the offense and the convicted person's criminal history.

separate count. See COUNT.

separate offense. See OFFENSE.

separate-sovereigns rule. The principle that a person may be tried twice for the same offense—despite the Double Jeopardy Clause—

if the prosecutions are conducted by separate sovereigns, as by the federal government and a state government or by two different states. See DOUBLE JEOPARDY.

separate trial. See TRIAL.

sequester, *vb.* **1.** To seize (property) by a writ of sequestration. **2.** To segregate or isolate (a jury or witness) during trial.—Also termed *sequestrate.*

sequestration (see-kwes-**tray**-shən), *n.* Custodial isolation of a trial jury to prevent tampering and exposure to publicity, or of witnesses to prevent them from hearing the testimony of others.—Also termed *jury sequestration.*

serendipity doctrine. The principle that all evidence discovered during a lawful search is eligible to be admitted into evidence at trial.

Sergeant Schultz defense. An assertion by a defendant who claims that he or she was not an active participant in an alleged scheme or conspiracy, and that he or she knew nothing, saw nothing, and heard nothing. • This defense is named after a character from the television series *Hogan's Heroes*, in which Sergeant Schultz, a German guard in charge of prisoners of war during World War II, would avoid controversy over the prisoners' schemes by proclaiming that he saw nothing and knew nothing.

serial murder. See MURDER.

seriatim opinions. See OPINION.

serious bodily harm. See *serious bodily injury* under INJURY.

serious bodily injury. See INJURY.

serious crime. 1. See *serious offense* under OFFENSE. **2.** See FELONY.

serious felony. See FELONY.

serious misdemeanor. See MISDEMEANOR.

serious offense. See OFFENSE.

servitude. The condition of a prisoner who has been sentenced to forced labor <penal servitude>.

>   ***involuntary servitude.*** The condition of one forced to labor—for pay or not—for another by coercion or imprisonment.

setting, *n.* The date and time established by a court for a trial or hearing <the defendant

sought a continuance of the imminent set-
ting>.

> *special setting.* A preferential setting on a
> court's calendar, usu. reserved for older
> cases or cases given priority by law, made
> either on a party's motion or on the court's
> own motion. ● For example, some jurisdic-
> tions authorize a special setting for cases
> involving a party over the age of 70.—Also
> termed *special trial setting*; *trial-setting pref-*
> *erence.*

settlement, *n.* An agreement ending a dispute
or lawsuit <the parties reached a settlement
the day before trial>.—**settle,** *vb.*

sexual abuse. See ABUSE.

sexual assault. See ASSAULT.

sexual battery. See BATTERY.

sexual offense. See OFFENSE.

SG. *abbr.* SOLICITOR GENERAL.

shakedown. 1. An extortion of money using
threats of violence or, in the case of a police
officer, threats of arrest. **2.** See *shakedown*
search under SEARCH.

shakedown search. See SEARCH.

sham defense. See DEFENSE.

shame sanction. See SANCTION.

shaming sentence. See *shame sanction* under SANCTION.

sham prosecution. See PROSECUTION.

shanghaiing (shang-hɪ-ing). The act or an instance of coercing or inducing someone to do something by fraudulent or other wrongful means; specif., the practice of drugging, tricking, intoxicating, or otherwise illegally inducing a person to work aboard a vessel, usu. to secure advance money or a premium.—Also termed *shanghaiing sailors*. 18 USCA § 2194.

sheriff. A county's chief peace officer, usu. elected, who in most jurisdictions acts as custodian of the county jail, executes civil and criminal process, and carries out judicial mandates within the county.

> ***deputy sheriff.*** An officer who, acting under the direction of a sheriff, may perform most of the duties of the sheriff's office. • Although *undersheriff* is broadly synonymous with *deputy sheriff*, writers have sometimes distinguished between the two, suggesting that a deputy is appointed for a special occasion or purpose, while an under-

sheriff is permanent.—Also termed *under-sheriff*; *general deputy*; *vice-sheriff*.

Sherman–Sorrells doctrine. The principle that a defendant may claim as an affirmative defense that he or she was not disposed to commit the offense until a public official (often an undercover police officer) encouraged the defendant to do so. ● This entrapment defense, which is recognized in the federal system and a majority of states, was developed in *Sherman v. United States*, 356 U.S. 369, 78 S.Ct. 819 (1958), and *Sorrells v. United States*, 287 U.S. 435, 53 S.Ct. 210 (1932).—Also termed *subjective method*. See ENTRAPMENT. Cf. HYPOTHETICAL-PERSON DEFENSE.

shield law. 1. A statute that affords journalists the privilege not to reveal confidential sources. See *journalist's privilege* under PRIVILEGE (3). **2.** A statute that restricts or prohibits the use, in rape or sexual-assault cases, of evidence about the past sexual conduct of the victim.—Also termed (in sense 2) *rape shield law*; *rape shield statute*.

shock incarceration. See INCARCERATION.

shock probation. See PROBATION.

shoplifting, *n.* Theft of merchandise from a store or business; specif., larceny of goods from a store or other commercial establishment by willfully taking and concealing the merchandise with the intention of converting the goods to one's personal use without paying the purchase price. See LARCENY.—**shoplift,** *vb.*

short summons. See SUMMONS.

shotgun instruction. See ALLEN CHARGE.

show-cause order. See ORDER.

show trial. A trial, usu. in a nondemocratic country, that is staged primarily for propagandistic purposes, with the outcome predetermined.

showup, *n.* A pretrial identification procedure in which a suspect is confronted with a witness to or the victim of a crime. ● Unlike a lineup, a showup is a one-on-one confrontation. Cf. LINEUP.

sidebar. 1. A position at the side of a judge's bench where counsel can confer with the judge beyond the jury's earshot <the judge called the attorneys to sidebar>. **2.** See SIDEBAR CONFERENCE <during the sidebar, the prosecutor accused the defense attorney of misconduct>.

sidebar comment. An unnecessary, often argumentative remark made by an attorney or witness, esp. during a trial or deposition.—Often shortened to *sidebar*.—Also termed *sidebar remark*.

sidebar conference. 1. A discussion among the judge and counsel, usu. over an evidentiary objection, outside the jury's hearing.—Also termed *bench conference*. **2.** A discussion, esp. during voir dire, between the judge and a juror or prospective juror.—Often shortened to *sidebar*.

sidebar remark. See SIDEBAR COMMENT.

signature crime. See CRIME.

signature evidence. See EVIDENCE.

silence, *n.* A restraint from speaking. ● Silence includes an arrestee's statements expressing the desire not to speak and requesting an attorney.—**silent,** *adj.*

silver-platter doctrine. The principle that a federal court could allow the admission of evidence obtained illegally by a state police officer as long as a federal officer did not participate in or request the search. ● The Supreme Court rejected this doctrine in *Elkins v. United States*, 364 U.S. 206, 80 S.Ct. 1437 (1960).

simple, *adj.* (Of a crime) not accompanied by aggravating circumstances. Cf. AGGRAVATED.

simple assault. See ASSAULT.

simple battery. See BATTERY.

simple kidnapping. See KIDNAPPING.

simple larceny. See LARCENY.

simple robbery. See ROBBERY.

single adultery. See ADULTERY.

single combat. See DUEL.

single-criminal-intent doctrine. See SINGLE-LARCENY DOCTRINE.

single-impulse plan. See SINGLE-LARCENY DOCTRINE.

single-larceny doctrine. The principle that the taking of different items of property either belonging to the same or different owners at the same time and place constitutes one act of larceny if the theft is part of one larcenous plan, as when it involves essentially one continuous act or if control over the property is exercised simultaneously. • The intent of the thief determines the number of occurrences.—

Also termed *single-impulse plan*; *single-larceny rule*; *single-criminal-intent doctrine*.

situational offender. See OFFENDER.

Sixth Amendment. The constitutional amendment, ratified with the Bill of Rights in 1791, guaranteeing in criminal cases the right to a speedy and public trial by jury, the right to be informed of the nature of the accusation, the right to confront witnesses, the right to counsel, and the right to compulsory process for obtaining favorable witnesses.

skilled witness. See *expert witness* under WITNESS.

skip bail. See JUMP BAIL.

slander, *n.* **1.** A defamatory statement expressed in a transitory form, esp. speech. ● Damages for slander—unlike those for libel— are not presumed and thus must be proved by the plaintiff (unless the defamation is slander per se). **2.** The act of making such a statement.—**slander,** *vb.*—**slanderous,** *adj.* See DEFAMATION. Cf. LIBEL.

slavery. 1. A situation in which one person has absolute power over the life, fortune, and liberty of another. **2.** The practice of keeping individuals in such a state of bondage or servi-

tude. ● Slavery was outlawed by the 13th
Amendment to the U.S. Constitution. See 18
USCA §§ 1582–1588.

slight evidence. See EVIDENCE.

slight-evidence rule. 1. The doctrine providing that, when there is evidence establishing
the existence of a conspiracy between at least
two other people, the prosecution need only
offer slight evidence of a defendant's knowing
participation or intentional involvement in the
conspiracy to secure a conviction. ● This rule
was first announced in *Tomplain v. United
States*, 42 F.2d 202, 203 (5th Cir. 1930). In the
decades after *Tomplain*, other circuits adopted
the rule, but not until the 1970s did the rule
become widespread. Since then, the rule has
been widely criticized and, in most circuits,
abolished. See, e.g., *United States v. Durrive*,
902 F.2d 1379, 1380 n.* (7th Cir. 1990). But
its vitality remains undiminished in some jurisdictions. **2.** The doctrine that only slight
evidence of a defendant's participation in a
conspiracy need be offered in order to admit a
coconspirator's out-of-court statement under
the coconspirator exception to the hearsay
rule. See Fed. R. Evid. 801(d)(2)(E).

Smith Act. A 1948 federal antisedition law
that criminalizes advocating the forcible or

violent overthrow of the government. 18 USCA § 2385.

smoking gun. A piece of physical or documentary evidence that conclusively impeaches an adversary on an outcome-determinative issue or destroys the adversary's credibility.

smuggling, *n.* The crime of importing or exporting illegal articles or articles on which duties have not been paid.—**smuggle,** *vb.* See CONTRABAND.

sobriety checkpoint. A part of a roadway at which police officers maintain a roadblock to stop motorists and ascertain whether the drivers are intoxicated.

sobriety test. A method of determining whether a person is intoxicated. • Among the common sobriety tests are coordination tests and the use of mechanical devices to measure the blood alcohol content of a person's breath sample. See BREATHALYZER; HORIZONTAL-GAZE NYSTAGMUS TEST.

    field sobriety test. A motor-skills test administered by a peace officer during a stop to determine whether a suspect has been driving while intoxicated. • The test usu. involves checking the suspect's speaking ability or coordination (as by reciting the

alphabet or walking in a straight line).—
Abbr. FST.

social harm. See HARM.

sociopath, *n*. See PSYCHOPATH.—**sociopathy,**
n.—**sociopathic,** *adj*.

SODDI defense (**sahd**-ee). *Slang*. The some-
other-dude-did-it defense; a claim that some-
body else committed a crime, usu. made by a
criminal defendant who cannot identify the
third party.

sodomy (**sod**-ə-mee), *n*. **1.** Oral or anal copulation between humans, esp. those of the same
sex. **2.** Oral or anal copulation between a human and an animal; bestiality.—**sodomize,**
vb.—**sodomitic,** *adj*.—**sodomist, sodomite,**
n. Cf. PEDERASTY.

> *aggravated sodomy.* Criminal sodomy that
> involves force or results in serious bodily
> injury to the victim in addition to mental
> injury and emotional distress. • Some laws
> provide that sodomy involving a minor is
> automatically aggravated sodomy.

sole cause. See CAUSE (1).

solicitation, *n*. **1.** The act or an instance of
requesting or seeking to obtain something; a
request or petition <a solicitation for volun-

teers to handle at least one pro bono case per year>. **2.** The offense of urging, advising, commanding, or otherwise inciting another to commit a crime <convicted of solicitation of murder>. ● Solicitation is an inchoate offense distinct from the solicited crime. Under the Model Penal Code, a defendant is guilty of solicitation even if the command or urging was not actually communicated to the solicited person, as long as it was designed to be communicated. Model Penal Code § 5.02(2).—Also termed *criminal solicitation*; *incitement*. Cf. AT-TEMPT. **3.** An offer to pay or accept money in exchange for sex <the prostitute was charged with solicitation>.—**solicit,** *vb.*

solicitation of bribe. The crime of asking or enticing another to commit bribery. See 18 USCA § 201. See BRIBERY.

solicitee. One who is solicited. See SOLICITA-TION.

solicitor. **1.** The chief law officer of a governmental body or a municipality. **2.** A prosecutor (in some jurisdictions, such as South Carolina).

solicitor general. The second-highest-ranking legal officer in a government (after the attorney general); esp., the chief courtroom

633

lawyer for the executive branch.—Abbr. SG.
Pl. **solicitors general.**

solitary confinement. Separate confinement
that gives a prisoner extremely limited access
to other people; esp., the complete isolation of
a prisoner.

somnambulism   (sahm-**nam**-byə-liz-əm).
Sleepwalking. • Generally, a person will not be
held criminally responsible for an act performed while in this state.

somnolentia (sahm-nə-**len**-shee-ə). **1.** The
state of drowsiness. **2.** A condition of incom-
plete sleep resembling drunkenness, during
which part of the faculties are abnormally
excited while the others are dormant; the combined condition of sleeping and wakefulness
producing a temporary state of involuntary
intoxication. • To the extent that it destroys
moral agency, somnolentia may be a defense to
a criminal charge.

Son-of-Sam law. A state statute that prohibits a convicted criminal from profiting by selling his or her story rights to a publisher or
filmmaker. • State law usu. authorizes prosecutors to seize royalties from a convicted criminal and to place the money in an escrow
account for the crime victim's benefit. This
type of law was first enacted in New York in

1977, in response to the lucrative book deals that publishers offered David Berkowitz, the serial killer who called himself "Son of Sam." In 1992, the U.S. Supreme Court declared New York's Son-of-Sam law unconstitutional as a content-based speech regulation, prompting many states to amend their laws in an attempt to avoid constitutionality problems. *Simon & Schuster, Inc. v. New York State Crime Victims Bd.*, 502 U.S. 105, 112 S.Ct. 501 (1992).

sororicide (sə-**ror**-ə-sɪd). **1.** The act of killing one's own sister. **2.** A person who kills his or her sister.

speaking objection. See OBJECTION.

special attorney. See *special counsel* under COUNSEL.

special circumstances. See *exigent circumstances* under CIRCUMSTANCE.

special counsel. See COUNSEL.

special court-martial. See COURT-MARTIAL.

special deputy. See DEPUTY.

special deterrence. See DETERRENCE.

special grand jury. See GRAND JURY.

special guardian. See *guardian ad litem* under GUARDIAN.

special instruction. See JURY INSTRUCTION.

special judge. See JUDGE.

special jury. See JURY.

special malice. See *particular malice* under MALICE.

special master. A judicial officer appointed to assist the court with a particular matter or case.

special-needs analysis. A balancing test used by the Supreme Court to determine whether certain searches (such as administrative, civil-based, or public-safety searches) impose unreasonably on individual rights.

special plea in bar. See PLEA IN BAR.

special privilege. See PRIVILEGE (1).

special prosecutor. See PROSECUTOR.

special setting. See SETTING.

special trial setting. See *special setting* under SETTING.

specialty doctrine. See DOCTRINE OF SPECIALTY.

special verdict. See VERDICT.

specific intent. See INTENT.

specific-intent defense. A defendant's claim that he or she did not have the capacity (often supposedly due to intoxication or mental illness) to form the intent necessary for committing the crime alleged.

specific objection. See OBJECTION.

speech. The expression or communication of thoughts or opinions in spoken words; something spoken or uttered.

> *seditious speech.* Speech advocating the violent overthrow of government. See SEDITION.

speedy trial. A trial that the prosecution, with reasonable diligence, begins promptly and conducts expeditiously. ● The Sixth Amendment secures the right to a speedy trial. In deciding whether an accused has been deprived of that right, courts generally consider the length of the delay, the reason for the delay, and the prejudice to the accused.

Speedy Trial Act of 1974. A federal statute establishing time limits for carrying out the major events (such as information, indictment, arraignment, and trial commencement) in the prosecution of federal criminal cases. 18 USCA §§ 3161–3174.

spillover theory. The principle that a severance must be granted only when a defendant can show that trial with a codefendant would substantially prejudice the defendant's case, as when the jury might wrongly use evidence against the defendant. See BRUTON RULE.

split sentence. See SENTENCE; *shock probation* under PROBATION.

split verdict. See VERDICT.

spontaneous declaration. A statement that is made without time to reflect or fabricate and is related to the circumstances of the perceived occurrence.—Also termed *spontaneous statement*; *spontaneous exclamation*; *spontaneous utterance*. See EXCITED UTTERANCE; PRESENT SENSE IMPRESSION.

spousal abuse. See ABUSE.

spousal privilege. See *marital privilege* under PRIVILEGE (3).

spouse-breach. See ADULTERY.

stalking. 1. The act or an instance of following another by stealth. **2.** The offense of following or loitering near another, often surreptitiously, with the purpose of annoying or harassing that person or committing a further crime such as assault or battery. • Some statutory definitions include an element that the person being stalked must reasonably feel harassed, alarmed, or distressed about personal safety or the safety of one or more persons for whom that person is responsible. And some definitions state that acts such as telephoning another and remaining silent during the call amount to stalking. Cf. CYBER-STALKING.

stand. See WITNESS STAND.

standard instruction. See JURY INSTRUCTION.

standby counsel. See COUNSEL.

stand mute. 1. (Of a defendant) to refuse to enter a plea to a criminal charge. • Standing mute is treated as a plea of not guilty. **2.** (Of any party) to raise no objections.

stand trial. To submit to a legal proceeding, esp. a criminal prosecution.

stare decisis (**stahr**-ee di-**si**-sis *or* **stair**-ee), *n.* [Latin "to stand by things decided"] The doctrine of precedent, under which it is necessary for a court to follow earlier judicial decisions when the same points arise again in litigation. See PRECEDENT; NON QUIETA MOVERE. Cf. LAW OF THE CASE.

state criminal. See CRIMINAL.

statement. 1. A verbal assertion or nonverbal conduct intended as an assertion. **2.** A formal and exact presentation of facts. **3.** An account of a person's (usu. a suspect's) knowledge of a crime, taken by the police pursuant to their investigation of the offense. Cf. CONFESSION.

consonant statement. A prior declaration of a witness, testified to by a person to whom the declaration was made and allowed into evidence only after the witness's testimony has been impeached. ● This type of evidence would, but for the impeachment of the witness, be inadmissible hearsay.

false statement. **1.** An untrue statement knowingly made with the intent to mislead. See PERJURY. **2.** Any one of three distinct federal offenses: (1) falsifying or concealing a material fact by trick, scheme, or device; (2) making a false, fictitious, or fraudulent representation; and (3) making or using a false document or writing. 18 USCA § 1001.

incriminating statement. A statement that tends to establish the guilt of an accused.

prior consistent statement. A witness's earlier statement that is consistent with the witness's trial testimony. • A prior consistent statement is not hearsay if it is offered to rebut a charge that the testimony was improperly influenced or fabricated. Fed. R. Evid. 801(d)(1)(B).

prior inconsistent statement. A witness's earlier statement that conflicts with the witness's testimony at trial. • In federal practice, extrinsic evidence of an unsworn prior inconsistent statement is admissible—if the witness is given an opportunity to explain or deny the statement—for impeachment purposes only. Fed. R. Evid. 613(b). Sworn statements may be admitted for all purposes. Fed. R. Evid. 801(d)(1)(A).

sworn statement. A statement given under oath; an affidavit.

voluntary statement. A statement free from duress, coercion, or inducement.

statement of facts. A party's written presentation of the facts leading up to or surrounding a legal dispute, usu. recited toward the beginning of a brief.

statement of particulars. See BILL OF PARTIC-
ULARS.

state of mind. 1. The condition or capacity of
a person's mind; MENS REA. **2.** Loosely, a person's reasons or motives for committing an
act, esp. a criminal act.

state-of-mind exception. The principle that
an out-of-court declaration of an existing motive is admissible, even when the declarant
cannot testify in person. ● This principle constitutes an exception to the hearsay rule.

state police. The department or agency of a
state government empowered to maintain order, as by investigating and preventing crimes,
and making arrests.

state police power. The power of a state to
enforce laws for the health, welfare, morals,
and safety of its citizens, if the laws are reasonably calculated to protect those legitimate
state interests.

state's attorney. See DISTRICT ATTORNEY.

state secret. A governmental matter that
would be a threat to the national defense or
diplomatic interests of the United States if
revealed, and is therefore protected against

disclosure by a witness in an ordinary judicial proceeding.

state-secrets privilege. See PRIVILEGE (3).

state's evidence. See EVIDENCE.

state's evidence, turn. See TURN STATE'S EVIDENCE.

state trial. See TRIAL.

stationhouse. 1. A police station or precinct. **2.** The lockup at the police precinct.

stationhouse bail. See *cash bail* under BAIL.

statistical-decision theory. A method for determining whether a panel of potential jurors was selected from a fair cross section of the community, by calculating the probabilities of selecting a certain number of jurors from a particular group to analyze whether it is statistically probable that the jury pool was selected by mere chance. ● This method has been criticized because a pool of potential jurors is not ordinarily selected by mere chance; potential jurors are disqualified for a number of legitimate reasons. See FAIR-CROSS-SECTION REQUIREMENT; ABSOLUTE DISPARITY; COMPARATIVE DISPARITY; DUREN TEST.

status crime. See CRIME.

status offender. See OFFENDER.

status offense. See OFFENSE.

statute. A law passed by a legislative body.

    criminal statute. A law that defines, classifies, and sets forth punishment for one or more specific crimes. See PENAL CODE.

    penal statute. A law that defines an offense and prescribes its corresponding fine, penalty, or punishment.—Also termed *penal law*; *punitive statute.*

statute-making. See LEGISLATION (1).

statute of limitations. A statute establishing a time limit for prosecuting a crime, based on the date when the offense occurred.

statutory arson. See ARSON (2).

statutory burglary. See BURGLARY (2).

statutory crime. See CRIME.

statutory extortion. See EXTORTION (2).

statutory law. The body of law derived from statutes rather than from constitutions or judicial decisions.—Also termed *legislative law*; *ordinary law*. Cf. COMMON LAW; CONSTITUTIONAL LAW.

statutory penalty. See PENALTY.

statutory presumption. See PRESUMPTION.

statutory rape. See RAPE.

stay, *n.* **1.** The postponement or halting of a proceeding, judgment, or the like. **2.** An order to suspend all or part of a judicial proceeding or a judgment resulting from that proceeding.—Also termed *stay of execution.*—**stay,** *vb.*—**stayable,** *adj.*

stay of execution. See STAY.

steal, *vb.* **1.** To take (personal property) illegally with the intent to keep it unlawfully. **2.** To take (something) by larceny, embezzlement, or false pretenses.

stickup. An armed robbery in which the victim is threatened by the use of weapons.—Also termed *holdup*. See *armed robbery* under ROBBERY.

stifling of a prosecution. An agreement, in exchange for money or other benefit, to abstain from prosecuting a person.

645

sting. An undercover operation in which law-enforcement agents pose as criminals to catch actual criminals engaging in illegal acts.

stock manipulation. See MANIPULATION.

stocks, *n.* A punishment device consisting of two boards that together form holes for trapping an offender's feet and hands.

stolen property. Goods acquired by larceny, robbery, or theft.

stop, *n.* Under the Fourth Amendment, a temporary restraint that prevents a person from walking away.

stop and frisk, *n.* A police officer's brief detention, questioning, and search of a person for a concealed weapon when the officer reasonably suspects that the person has committed or is about to commit a crime. • The stop and frisk, which can be conducted without a warrant or probable cause, was held constitutional by the Supreme Court in *Terry v. Ohio*, 392 U.S. 1, 88 S.Ct. 1868 (1968).—Also termed *investigatory stop*; *field stop*; *Terry stop*; *investigatory detention*. See REASONABLE SUSPICION.

straight sentence. See *determinate sentence* under SENTENCE.

straight up. See S.U.

strain theory. The theory that people commit crimes to alleviate stress created by the disjunction between their station in life and the station to which society has conditioned them to aspire. Cf. CONTROL THEORY; RATIONAL-CHOICE THEORY; ROUTINE-ACTIVITIES THEORY.

street crime. See CRIME.

street gang. See GANG.

street time. The time that a convicted person spends on parole or on other conditional release. • If the person's parole is revoked, this time may or may not be credited toward the person's sentence, depending on the jurisdiction and the particular conditions of that person's parole. See *dead time* under TIME.

strict-liability crime. See CRIME.

strict-liability offense. See OFFENSE.

strict scrutiny. The standard applied to suspect classifications (such as race) in equal-protection analysis and to fundamental rights (such as voting rights) in due-process analysis. • Under strict scrutiny, the state must establish that it has a compelling interest that justifies and necessitates the law in question.

STRICT SCRUTINY

See COMPELLING-STATE-INTEREST TEST; SUSPECT
CLASSIFICATION; FUNDAMENTAL RIGHT. Cf. INTERME-
DIATE SCRUTINY; RATIONAL-BASIS TEST.

strike, *n.* **1.** The removal of a prospective
juror from the jury panel <a peremptory
strike>. See CHALLENGE (2). **2.** A failure or
disadvantage, as by a criminal conviction <a
strike on one's record>.

strike, *vb.* **1.** To remove (a prospective juror)
from a jury panel by a peremptory challenge or
a challenge for cause <the prosecution struck
the panelist who indicated an opposition to the
death penalty>. See *peremptory challenge* under CHALLENGE (2). **2.** To expunge, as from a
record <motion to strike the prejudicial evi-
dence>.

striking a jury. The selecting of a jury out of
all the candidates available to serve on the
jury; esp., the selecting of a special jury. See
special jury under JURY.

strip search. See SEARCH.

struck jury. See JURY.

study furlough. See *study release* under RE-
LEASE.

study release. See RELEASE.

s.u. *abbr.* Straight up. • When a prosecutor writes this on a defendant's file, it usu. means that the prosecutor plans to try the case—that is, not enter into a plea bargain.

subjective method. See SHERMAN–SORRELLS DOCTRINE.

suborn (sə-**born**), *vb.* **1.** To induce (a person) to commit an unlawful or wrongful act, esp. in a secret or underhanded manner. **2.** To induce (a person) to commit perjury. **3.** To obtain (perjured testimony) from another.—**suborna-tion** (səb-or-**nay**-shən), *n.*—**suborner** (sə-**bor**-nər), *n.*

subornation of perjury. The crime of per-suading another to commit perjury.—Some-times shortened to *subornation*.

subpoena (sə-**pee**-nə), *n.* [Latin "under pen-alty"] A writ commanding a person to appear before a court or other tribunal, subject to a penalty for failing to comply.—Also spelled *subpena.* Pl. **subpoenas.**

> *alias subpoena* (**ay**-lee-əs sə-**pee**-nə). A subpoena issued after an initial subpoena has failed.

> *subpoena ad testificandum* (sə-**pee**-nə ad tes-tə-fi-**kan**-dəm). [Law Latin] A subpoena

ordering a witness to appear and give testimony.

subpoena duces tecum (sə-**pee**-nə **d[y]oo**-seez **tee**-kəm *also* **doo**-səz **tay**-kəm). [Law Latin] A subpoena ordering the witness to appear and to bring specified documents or records.

subpoena, *vb.* **1.** To call before a court or other tribunal by subpoena <subpoena the material witnesses>. **2.** To order the production of (documents or other things) by subpoena duces tecum <subpoena the corporate records>.—Also spelled *subpena.*

subpoenal (sə–**pee**-nəl), *adj.* Required or done under penalty, esp. in compliance with a subpoena.

substance-abuse evaluation and treatment. A drug offender's court-ordered participation in a drug rehabilitation program. ● This type of treatment is esp. common in DUI cases.—Abbr. SAET.

substantial-capacity test. The Model Penal Code's test for the insanity defense, stating that a person is not criminally responsible for an act if, as a result of a mental disease or defect, the person lacks substantial capacity either to appreciate the criminality of the conduct or to conform the conduct to the law. ●

SUBSTANTIVE EVIDENCE

This test combines elements of both the *McNaghten* rules and the irresistible-impulse test by allowing consideration of both volitional and cognitive weaknesses. This test was formerly used by the federal courts and many states, but since 1984 many jurisdictions (including the federal courts)—in response to the acquittal by reason of insanity of would-be presidential assassin John Hinckley—have narrowed the insanity defense and adopted a new test resembling the *McNaghten* rules, although portions of the substantial-capacity test continue to be used. Model Penal Code § 4.01.—Also termed *Model Penal Code test*; *MPC test*; *American Law Institute test*; *ALI test*. See INSANITY DEFENSE.

substantial evidence. See EVIDENCE.

substantial-step test. The Model Penal Code's test for determining whether a person is guilty of attempt, based on the extent of the defendant's preparation for the crime, the criminal intent shown, and any statements personally made that bear on the defendant's actions. Model Penal Code § 5.01(1)(c). See ATTEMPT.

substantive crime. See *substantive offense* under OFFENSE.

substantive evidence. See EVIDENCE.

SUBSTANTIVE OFFENSE

substantive offense. See OFFENSE.

substitutionary evidence. See *secondary evidence* under EVIDENCE.

subterfuge arrest. See ARREST.

subversive activity. A pattern of acts designed to overthrow a government by force or other illegal means.

successive-writ doctrine. The principle that a second or supplemental petition for a writ of habeas corpus may not raise claims that were heard and decided on the merits in a previous petition. Cf. ABUSE-OF-THE-WRIT DOCTRINE.

sudden heat. See HEAT OF PASSION.

sudden heat of passion. See HEAT OF PASSION.

sudden passion. See HEAT OF PASSION.

sufficiency-of-evidence test. 1. The guideline for a grand jury considering whether to indict a suspect: if all the evidence presented were uncontradicted and unexplained, it would warrant a conviction by the fact-trier. **2.** A standard for reviewing a criminal conviction on appeal, based on whether enough evidence exists to justify the fact-trier's finding of guilt beyond a reasonable doubt.—Also termed *sufficiency-of-the-evidence test*.

sufficient cause. See PROBABLE CAUSE.

sufficient evidence. See *satisfactory evidence* under EVIDENCE.

suggestive interrogation. See LEADING QUESTION.

suggestive question. See LEADING QUESTION.

suicide, *n.* **1.** The act of taking one's own life.—Also termed *self-killing*; *self-destruction*; *self-slaughter*; *self-murder*; *felony de se*.

  assisted suicide. A suicide committed with the aid of a person who provides the medical means or medical knowledge needed to carry it out.—Also termed *assisted self-determination*. Cf. EUTHANASIA.

  attempted suicide. An unsuccessful suicidal act.

2. A person who has taken his or her own life.—**suicidal,** *adj.*

summary conviction. See CONVICTION.

summary court-martial. See COURT-MARTIAL.

summary jurisdiction. See JURISDICTION.

summary jury trial. See TRIAL.

summary offense. See OFFENSE; MISDEMEANOR.

summation. See CLOSING ARGUMENT.

summing up. See CLOSING ARGUMENT.

summons, *n.* **1.** Formerly, a writ directing a sheriff to summon a defendant to appear in court. **2.** A writ or process commencing the plaintiff's action and requiring the defendant to appear and answer. **3.** A notice requiring a person to appear in court as a juror or witness. Pl. **summonses.**

   alias summons. A second summons issued after the original summons has failed for some reason.

   John Doe summons. A summons to a person whose name is unknown at the time of service.

   short summons. A summons having a response time less than that of an ordinary summons, usu. served on a fraudulent or nonresident debtor.

sumptuary law (**səmp**-choo-er-ee). **1.** A statute, ordinance, or regulation that limits the expenditures that people can make for personal gratification or ostentatious display. **2.** More broadly, any law whose purpose is to regulate conduct thought to be immoral, such as prostitution, gambling, or drug abuse.

Sup. Ct. *abbr.* SUPREME COURT.

superseding cause. See CAUSE (1).

supervening cause. See *intervening cause* under CAUSE (1).

suppress, *vb.* To put a stop to, put down, or prohibit; to prevent (something) from being seen, heard, known, or discussed <the defendant tried to suppress the incriminating evidence>.—**suppression,** *n.*—**suppressible, suppressive,** *adj.*

suppression hearing. See HEARING.

suppression of evidence. 1. A trial judge's ruling that evidence that a party has offered should be excluded because it was illegally acquired. **2.** The destruction of evidence or the refusal to give evidence at a criminal proceeding. ● This is usu. considered a crime. See OBSTRUCTION OF JUSTICE. **3.** The prosecution's withholding from the defense of evidence that is favorable to the defendant.

supreme court. 1. (*cap.*) SUPREME COURT OF THE UNITED STATES. **2.** An appellate court existing in most states, usu. as the court of last resort. **3.** In New York, a court of general jurisdiction with trial and appellate divisions. • The Court of Appeals is the court of last resort in New York.—Abbr. S.C.; S.Ct.; Sup. Ct.

Supreme Court of the United States. The court of last resort in the federal system, whose members are appointed by the President and approved by the Senate. • The Court was established in 1789 by Article III of the U.S. Constitution, which vests the Court with the "judicial power of the United States."—Often shortened to *Supreme Court*.—Also termed *United States Supreme Court*.

surrender, *n.* The act of yielding to another's power or control.

surrender by bail. A surety's delivery of a prisoner, who had been released on bail, into custody.

surrender of a criminal. An officer's delivery of a prisoner to the authorities in the appropriate jurisdiction. See EXTRADITION; RENDITION.

surreptitious (sər-əp-**tish**-əs), *adj.* (Of conduct) unauthorized and clandestine; stealthily and usu. fraudulently done <surreptitious interception of electronic communications is prohibited under wiretapping laws>.

surreptitious-entry warrant. See WARRANT.

surveillance (sər-**vay**-lənts), *n.* Close observation or listening of a person or place in the hope of gathering evidence.—**surveil** (sər-**vayl**), *vb.*

suspect, *n.* A person believed to have committed a crime or offense.

suspect classification. A statutory classification based on race, national origin, or alienage, and thereby subject to strict scrutiny under equal-protection analysis. ● Examples of suspect classifications are a law permitting only U.S. citizens to receive welfare benefits and a law setting quotas for the government's hiring of minority contractors. See STRICT SCRUTINY. Cf. FUNDAMENTAL RIGHT.

suspended sentence. See SENTENCE.

suspicion. The imagination or apprehension of the existence of something wrong based only on slight or no evidence, without definitive proof. See REASONABLE SUSPICION.

suspicious-activity report. A form that, as of 1996, a financial institution must complete and submit to federal regulatory authorities if it suspects that a federal crime has occurred in the course of a monetary transaction. ● This form superseded two earlier forms, the criminal-referral form and the suspicious-transaction report.—Abbr. SAR.

suspicious character. In some states, a person who is strongly suspected or known to be a habitual criminal and therefore may be arrested or required to give security for good behavior.

sweating. The illegal interrogation of a prisoner by use of threats or similar means to extort information.

swift witness. See *zealous witness* under WITNESS.

sworn statement. See STATEMENT.

syndicalism (**sin**-di-kə-liz-əm), *n.* A direct plan or practice implemented by trade-union workers seeking to control the means of production and distribution, esp. by using a general strike.—**syndicalist,** *n.*

   criminal syndicalism. Any doctrine that advocates or teaches the use of illegal methods to change industrial or political control.

syndicate (**sin**-di-kit), *n*. A group organized for a common purpose; esp., an association formed to promote a common interest, carry out a particular business transaction, or (in a negative sense) organize criminal enterprises.—**syndicate** (**sin**-di-kayt), *vb*.—**syndication** (sin-di-**kay**-shən), *n*.—**syndicator** (**sin**-di-kay-tər), *n*. See ORGANIZED CRIME.

T

tacit admission. See *implied admission* under ADMISSION.

taint, *n.* **1.** A conviction of felony. **2.** A person so convicted. See ATTAINDER.

tainted evidence. See EVIDENCE.

taking, *n.* The act of seizing an article, with or without removing it, but with an implicit transfer of possession or control.

> ***constructive taking.*** An act that does not equal an actual appropriation of an article but that does show an intention to convert it, as when a person entrusted with the possession of goods starts using them contrary to the owner's instructions.

taking a case from the jury. See *directed verdict* under VERDICT.

taking the Fifth. See PLEADING THE FIFTH.

tampering, *n.* **1.** The act of altering a thing; esp., the act of illegally altering a document or product, such as written evidence or a consumer good. See Model Penal Code § 224.4, § 241.8; 18 USCA § 1365. **2.** The act or an instance of engaging in improper or underhanded dealings, esp. in an attempt to influence. ● Tampering with a witness or jury is a criminal offense. See WITNESS TAMPERING; OBSTRUCTION OF JUSTICE; EMBRACERY.

tangible evidence. See *demonstrative evidence* under EVIDENCE.

tapping, *n.* See WIRETAPPING.

target offense. See *object offense* under OFFENSE.

target witness. See WITNESS.

tax evasion. The willful attempt to defeat or circumvent the tax law in order to illegally reduce one's tax liability. ● Tax evasion is punishable by both civil and criminal penalties.—Also termed *tax fraud*.

TBC. *abbr.* Trial before the court. See *bench trial* under TRIAL.

technical error. See *harmless error* under ERROR.

temporary detention. See *pretrial detention* under DETENTION.

temporary insanity. See INSANITY.

temporary judge. See *visiting judge* under
JUDGE.

temporary restraining order. A court order
preserving the status quo until a litigant's
application for a preliminary or permanent
injunction can be heard. ● A temporary restraining order may sometimes be granted
without notifying the opposing party in advance.—Abbr. TRO.—Often shortened to *restraining order*.

temporary ward. See WARD.

ten-percent bond. See BOND.

terrorism, *n*. The use or threat of violence to
intimidate or cause panic, esp. as a means of
affecting political conduct.—**terrorist,** *adj*. &
n.

terroristic threat. See THREAT.

Terry **stop.** See STOP AND FRISK.

testify, *vb*. **1.** To give evidence as a witness
<she testified that the Ford Bronco was at the
defendant's home at the critical time>. **2.** (Of
a person or thing) to bear witness <the incom-
plete log entries testified to his sloppiness>.

testimonial evidence. See EVIDENCE.

testimonial immunity. See IMMUNITY (2).

testimonial incapacity. See INCAPACITY.

testimonial privilege. See PRIVILEGE (1).

testimony, *n*. Evidence that a competent witness under oath or affirmation gives at trial or in an affidavit or deposition.—Also termed *personal evidence*.—**testimonial,** *adj*.

> *affirmative testimony.* Testimony about whether something occurred or did not occur, based on what the witness saw or heard at the time and place in question.—Also termed *positive testimony*. See *direct evidence* under EVIDENCE.

> *cumulative testimony.* Identical or similar testimony by more than one witness, and usu. by several, offered by a party usu. to impress the jury with the apparent weight of proof on that party's side. • The trial court typically limits cumulative testimony.

> *dropsy testimony.* A police officer's false testimony that a fleeing suspect dropped an illegal substance that was then confiscated by the police and used as probable cause for arresting the suspect. • Dropsy testimony may be given when an arrest has been made without probable cause, as when illegal sub-

stances have been found through an improper search.

expert testimony. See *expert evidence* under EVIDENCE.

false testimony. Testimony that is untrue. • This term is broader than *perjury*, which has a state-of-mind element. Unlike perjury, false testimony does not denote a crime.— Also termed *false evidence*.

interpreted testimony. Testimony translated because the witness cannot communicate in the language of the tribunal.

lay opinion testimony. Evidence given by a witness who is not qualified as an expert but who testifies to opinions or inferences. • In federal court, the admissibility of this testimony is limited to opinions or inferences that are rationally based on the witness's perception and that will be helpful to a clear understanding of the witness's testimony or the determination of a fact in issue. Fed. R. Evid. 701.

mediate testimony. See *secondary evidence* under EVIDENCE.

negative testimony. See *negative evidence* under EVIDENCE.

nonverbal testimony. A photograph, drawing, map, chart, or other depiction used to aid a witness in testifying. ● The witness need not have made it, but it must accurately represent something that the witness saw. See *demonstrative evidence* under EVIDENCE.

opinion testimony. Testimony based on one's belief or idea rather than on direct knowledge of the facts at issue. ● Opinion testimony from either a lay witness or an expert witness may be allowed in evidence under certain conditions. See *opinion evidence* under EVIDENCE.

positive testimony. See *affirmative testimony.*

testimony de bene esse (dee **bee**-nee **es**-ee *also* day **ben**-ay **es**-ay). Testimony taken because it is in danger of being lost before it can be given at a trial or hearing, usu. because of the impending death or departure of the witness. ● Such testimony is taken in aid of a pending case, while testimony taken under a bill to perpetuate testimony is taken in anticipation of future litigation.

written testimony. **1.** Testimony given out of court by deposition. ● The recorded writing, signed by the witness, is considered testimony. **2.** In some administrative agencies and courts, direct narrative testimony that is reduced to writing, to which the witness swears at a hearing or trial before cross-examination takes place in the traditional way.

Thayer presumption. A presumption that requires the party against whom the presumption operates to come forward with evidence to rebut the presumption, but that does not shift the burden of proof to that party. See James B. Thayer, *A Preliminary Treatise on Evidence* 31–44 (1898). ● Most presumptions that arise in civil trials in federal court are interpreted in this way. Fed. R. Evid. 301. Cf. MORGAN PRESUMPTION.

theft, *n.* **1.** The felonious taking and removing of another's personal property with the intent of depriving the true owner of it; larceny. **2.** Broadly, any act or instance of stealing, including larceny, burglary, embezzlement, and false pretenses. ● Many modern penal codes have consolidated such property offenses under the name "theft." See LARCENY.

cybertheft. See CYBERTHEFT.

theft by deception. The use of deception to obtain another's property, esp. by (1) creating or reinforcing a false impression (as about value), (2) preventing one from obtaining information that would affect one's judgment about a transaction, or (3) failing to disclose, in a property transfer, a known lien or other legal impediment. Model Penal Code § 223.3.

theft by extortion. Larceny in which the perpetrator obtains property by threatening to (1) inflict bodily harm on anyone or commit any other criminal offense, (2) accuse anyone of a criminal offense, (3) expose any secret tending to subject any person to hatred, contempt, or ridicule, or impair one's credit or business reputation, (4) take or withhold action as an official, or cause an official to take or withhold action, (5) bring about or continue a strike, boycott, or other collective unofficial action, if the property is not demanded or received for the benefit of the group in whose interest the actor purports to act, (6) testify or provide information or withhold testimony or information with respect to another's legal claim or defense, or (7) inflict any other harm that would not benefit the actor. Model Penal Code § 223.4.—Also termed *larceny by extortion*. See EXTORTION.

theft by false pretext. The use of a false pretext to obtain another's property.

theft of property lost, mislaid, or delivered by mistake. Larceny in which one obtains control of property the person knows to be lost, mislaid, or delivered by mistake (esp. in the amount of property or identity of recipient) and fails to take reasonable measures to restore the property to the rightful owner. Model Penal Code § 223.5.—Also termed *larceny of property lost, mislaid, or delivered by mistake.*

theft of services. The act of obtaining services from another by deception, threat, coercion, stealth, mechanical tampering, or using a false token or device. See Model Penal Code § 223.7.

theftuous (**thef**-choo-əs), *adj.* **1.** (Of an act) characterized by theft. **2.** (Of a person) given to stealing.—Also spelled *theftous.*

thief. One who steals, esp. without force or violence; one who commits theft or larceny. See THEFT.

common thief. A thief who has been convicted of theft or larceny more than once.—Also termed *common and notorious thief.*

thieve, *vb.* To steal; to commit theft or larceny. See THEFT.

third degree, *n.* The process of extracting a confession or information from a suspect or prisoner by prolonged questioning, the use of threats, or physical torture <the police gave the suspect the third degree>.

third-degree instruction. See ALLEN CHARGE.

third-degree murder. See MURDER.

third-party consent. A person's agreement to official action (such as a search of premises) that affects another person's rights or interests. ● To be effective for a search, third-party consent must be based on the consenting person's common authority over the place to be searched or the items to be inspected. See COMMON-AUTHORITY RULE.

threat, *n.* **1.** A communicated intent to inflict harm or loss on another or on another's property, esp. one that might diminish a person's freedom to act voluntarily or with lawful consent <a kidnapper's threats of violence>.

> ***terroristic threat.*** A threat to commit any crime of violence with the purpose of (1) terrorizing another, (2) causing the evacuation of a building, place of assembly, or facility of public transportation, (3) causing serious public inconvenience, or (4) recklessly disregarding the risk of causing such terror or inconvenience. Model Penal Code § 211.3.

2. An indication of an approaching menace <the threat of bankruptcy>. **3.** A person or thing that might well cause harm <Mrs. Harrington testified that she had never viewed her

husband as a threat>.—**threaten,** *vb.*—
threatening, *adj.*

three-strikes law. A statute prescribing an
enhanced sentence, esp. life imprisonment, for
a repeat offender's third felony conviction. •
About half the states have enacted a statute of
this kind.—Also termed *three-strikes-and-
you're-out law.*

threshold confession. See CONFESSION.

ticket speculator. A person who buys tickets
and then resells them for more than their face
value; a scalper.

till-tapping. *Slang.* Theft of money from a
cash register.

time. 1. A measure of duration. **2.** A point in
or period of duration at or during which something is alleged to have occurred. **3.** *Slang.* A
convicted criminal's period of incarceration.

> *dead time.* Time that does not count for a
> particular purpose; esp., time not credited
> toward a prisoner's sentence. • The time
> during which a prisoner has escaped, for
> example, is not credited toward the prison-
> er's sentence.—Also termed *nonrun time.*

> *earned time.* A credit toward a sentence
> reduction awarded to a prisoner who takes

part in activities designed to lessen the chances that the prisoner will commit a crime after release from prison. ● Earned time, which is usu. awarded for taking educational or vocational courses, working, or participating in certain other productive activities, is distinct from good time, which is awarded simply for refraining from misconduct. Cf. *good time*.

flat time. A prison term that is to be served without the benefit of time-reduction allowances for good behavior and the like.

good time. The credit awarded to a prisoner for good conduct, which can reduce the duration of the prisoner's sentence. Cf. GOOD BEHAVIOR; *earned time*.

nonrun time. See *dead time*.

totality-of-the-circumstances test. A standard for determining whether hearsay (such as an informant's tip) is sufficiently reliable to establish probable cause for an arrest or search warrant. ● Under this test—which replaced *Aguilar–Spinelli*'s two-pronged approach—the reliability of the hearsay is weighed by focusing on the entire situation as described in the probable-cause affidavit, and not on any one specific factor. *Illinois v. Gates*, 462 U.S. 213, 103 S.Ct. 2317 (1983). Cf. AGUILAR–SPINELLI TEST.

traces, *n.* See *retrospectant evidence* under EVI-
DENCE.

trading with the enemy. The federal offense
of carrying on commerce with a nation or with
a subject or ally of a nation with which the
United States is at war.

traditionary evidence. See EVIDENCE.

traffic, *vb.* To trade or deal in (goods, esp.
illicit drugs or other contraband) <trafficking
in heroin>.

traitor, *n.* **1.** A person who commits treason
against his or her country. **2.** One who betrays
a person, a cause, or an obligation.—**traito-
rous,** *adj.*

transactional immunity. See IMMUNITY (2).

transcarceration. The movement of prisoners or institutionalized mentally ill persons
from facility to facility, rather than from a
prison or an institution back to the community, as when a prisoner is transferred to a
halfway house or to a drug-treatment facility.

transcript, *n.* A handwritten, printed, or
typed copy of testimony given orally; esp., the
official record of proceedings in a trial or hearing, as taken down by a court reporter.—Also
termed *report of proceedings*; *reporter's record.*

transfer hearing. See HEARING.

transfer of venue. See CHANGE OF VENUE.

transferred intent. See INTENT.

transferred-intent doctrine. The rule that if one person intends to harm a second person but instead unintentionally harms a third, the first person's criminal or tortious intent toward the second applies to the third as well. ● Thus, the offender may be prosecuted for an intent crime or sued by the third person for an intentional tort. See INTENT.

transferred malice. See MALICE.

Travel Act. A federal law, enacted in 1961, that prohibits conduct intended to promote, direct, or manage illegal business activities in interstate commerce. ● This statute was enacted to create federal jurisdiction over many criminal activities traditionally handled by state and local governments to help those jurisdictions cope with increasingly complex interstate criminal activity. 18 USCA § 1952.

traverse jury. See *petit jury* under JURY.

treason, *n.* The offense of attempting to overthrow the government of the state to which one owes allegiance, either by making war against the state or by materially supporting its enemies. See 18 USCA § 2381.—Also termed *high treason*.—**treasonable, treasonous,** *adj.* Cf. SEDITION.

>   ***petty treason.*** *Archaic.* Murder of one's employer or husband. ● Until 1828, this act was considered treason under English law.—Also spelled *petit treason.*

trespass (**tres**-pəs *or* **tres**-pas), *n.* **1.** An unlawful act committed against the person or property of another; esp., wrongful entry on another's real property. **2.** At common law, a legal action for injuries resulting from an unlawful act of this kind.—**trespass,** *vb.*—**trespassory** (**tres**-pə-sor-ee), *adj.*

>   ***criminal trespass.*** **1.** A trespass on property that is clearly marked against trespass by signs or fences. **2.** A trespass in which the trespasser remains on the property after being ordered off by a person authorized to do so.

trespasser. One who commits a trespass; one who intentionally and without consent or privilege enters another's property.

trial. A formal judicial examination of evidence and determination of legal claims in an adversary proceeding.

bench trial. A trial before a judge without
a jury. ● The judge decides questions of fact
as well as questions of law.—Also termed
trial to the bench; *nonjury trial*; *trial before
the court* (abbr. TBC); *judge trial*.

bifurcated trial. A trial that is divided into
two stages, such as for guilt and punishment.—Also termed *two-stage trial*.

fair trial. See FAIR TRIAL.

joint trial. A trial involving two or more
parties; esp., a criminal trial of two or more
persons for the same or similar offenses.

judge trial. See *bench trial*.

jury trial. A trial in which the factual
issues are determined by a jury, not by the
judge.—Also termed *trial by jury*.

nonjury trial. See *bench trial*.

political trial. **1.** A trial (esp. a criminal
prosecution) in which either the prosecution
or the defendant (or both) uses the proceedings as a platform to espouse a particular
political belief. **2.** A trial of a person for a
political crime. See SHOW TRIAL.

separate trial. The individual trial of each
of several persons jointly accused of a crime.
Fed. R. Crim. P. 14.

show trial. See SHOW TRIAL.

speedy trial. See SPEEDY TRIAL.

state trial. A trial for a political offense.

summary jury trial. A settlement technique in which the parties argue before a mock jury, which then reaches a nonbinding verdict that will assist the parties in evaluating their positions.

trial before the court. See *bench trial.*

trial by jury. See *jury trial.*

trial by the country. See *trial per pais.*

trial by the record. A trial in which one party insists that a record exists to support its claim and the opposing party denies the existence of such a record. ● If the record can be produced, the court will consider it in reaching a verdict—otherwise, it will rule for the opponent.

trial de novo (dee *or* di **noh**-voh). A new trial on the entire case—that is, on both questions of fact and issues of law—conducted as if there had been no trial in the first instance.

trial on the merits. A trial on the substantive issues of a case, as opposed to a motion hearing or interlocutory matter.

trial per pais (pər **pay** *or* **pays**). [Law French "trial by the country"] Trial by jury.—Also termed *trial by the country*.

trial to the bench. See *bench trial*.

trifurcated trial. A trial that is divided into three stages, such as for liability, general damages, and special damages.

two-stage trial. See *bifurcated trial*.

trial before the court. See *bench trial* under TRIAL.

trial brief. Counsel's written submission, usu. just before trial, outlining the legal issues before the court and arguing one side's position.

trial by jury. See *jury trial* under TRIAL.

trial by the country. See *trial per pais* under TRIAL.

trial by the record. See TRIAL.

trial calendar. See DOCKET (2).

trial de novo. See TRIAL.

trial judge. See JUDGE.

trial jury. See *petit jury* under JURY.

trial on the merits. See TRIAL.

trial *per pais*. See TRIAL.

trial-setting preference. See *special setting* under SETTING.

trial to the bench. See *bench trial* under TRIAL.

trier of fact. See FACT-FINDER.

trifurcated trial. See TRIAL.

trigamy (**trig**-ə-mee), *n.* The act of marrying a person while being legally married to someone else and bigamously married to yet another.

TRO (tee-ahr-**oh**). *abbr.* TEMPORARY RESTRAINING ORDER.

truancy (**troo**-ən-see), *n.* The act or state of shirking responsibility; esp., willful and unjustified failure to attend school by one who is required to attend.—**truant,** *adj.* & *n.*

truancy officer. An official responsible for enforcing laws mandating school attendance for minors of specified ages (usu. 16 and under).—Also termed *truant officer*; *attendance officer*.

true bill, *n.* A grand jury's notation that a criminal charge should go before a petty jury for trial <the grand jury returned a true bill, and the state prepared to prosecute>.—Also termed *billa vera*. Cf. NO BILL.

true-bill, *vb.* To make or deliver a true bill on <the grand jury true-billed the indictment>.

true defense. See DEFENSE.

true legal impossibility. See *legal impossibility* (1) under IMPOSSIBILITY.

true verdict. See VERDICT.

trusty, *n.* A convict or prisoner who is considered trustworthy by prison authorities and therefore given special privileges.

turncoat witness. See WITNESS.

turn state's evidence, *vb.* To cooperate with prosecutors and testify against other criminal defendants <after hours of intense negotiations, the suspect accepted a plea bargain and agreed to turn state's evidence>.

turpitude (tər-pə-t[y]ood). See MORAL TURPI-
TUDE.

twelve-day rule. A rule in some jurisdictions
requiring that a person charged with a felony
be given a preliminary examination no later
than 12 days after the arraignment on the
original warrant.

twist, *n.* An informant who provides testimony in exchange for leniency in sentencing,
rather than for money. See INFORMANT.

two-stage trial. See *bifurcated trial* under
TRIAL.

two-witness rule. 1. The rule that, to support a perjury conviction, two independent
witnesses (or one witness along with corroborating evidence) must establish that the alleged perjurer gave false testimony. **2.** The
rule, as stated in the U.S. Constitution, that
no person may be convicted of treason without
two witnesses to the same overt act—or unless
the accused confesses in open court. U.S.
Const. art. IV, § 2, cl. 2.

U

UCMJ. *abbr.* UNIFORM CODE OF MILITARY JUSTICE.

UCR. *abbr.* UNIFORM CRIME REPORTS.

ulterior intent. See INTENT.

ultimate fact. See FACT.

unauthorized use of a vehicle. See JOYRIDING.

unconditional pardon. See *absolute pardon* under PARDON.

unconditional release. See RELEASE.

unconscionable (ən-**kon**-shə-nə-bəl), *adj.* **1.** (Of a person) having no conscience; unscrupulous <an unconscionable used-car salesman>. **2.** (Of an act or transaction) showing no regard for conscience; affronting the sense of justice, decency, or reasonableness <the contract is void as unconscionable>.

unconscious, *adj.* Without awareness; not conscious. ● A person who commits a criminal act while unconscious may be relieved from liability for the act.

uncontrollable impulse. See IMPULSE.

681

undercover agent. See AGENT.

undersheriff. See *deputy sheriff* under SHER-IFF.

under the influence. (Of a driver, pilot, etc.) deprived of clearness of mind and self-control because of drugs or alcohol. See DRIVING UNDER THE INFLUENCE.

undisputed fact. See FACT.

undue prejudice. See PREJUDICE.

unfair hearing. See HEARING.

Uniform Code of Military Justice. 1. See CODE OF MILITARY JUSTICE. **2.** A model code promulgated by the National Conference of Commissioners on Uniform State Laws to govern state military forces when not in federal service. 11 U.L.A. 335 et seq. (1974).—Abbr. UCMJ.

Uniform Controlled Substances Act. A uniform act, adopted by many states and the federal government, governing the sale, use, and distribution of drugs. 21 USCA §§ 801 et seq.

Uniform Crime Reports. A series of annual criminological studies (each entitled *Crime in* *the United States*) prepared by the FBI. • The reports include data on eight index offenses, statistics on arrests, and information on offenders, crime rates, and the like.—Abbr. UCR.

Uniform Mandatory Disposition of Detainers Act. A law, promulgated in 1958 and adopted by several states, requiring a state to timely dispose of any untried charges against a prisoner in that state, on the prisoner's written request. See INTERSTATE AGREEMENT ON DETAINERS ACT.

unindicted coconspirator. See *unindicted conspirator* under CONSPIRATOR.

unindicted conspirator. See CONSPIRATOR.

United States Attorney. A lawyer appointed by the President to represent, under the direction of the Attorney General, the federal government in civil and criminal cases in a federal judicial district.—Also termed *United States District Attorney*. Cf. DISTRICT ATTORNEY.

United States Code. A multivolume published codification of federal statutory law. • In a citation, it is abbreviated as USC, as in 42 USC § 1983.

UNITED STATES CODE ANNO.

United States Code Annotated. A multi-volume publication of the complete text of the United States Code with historical notes, cross-references, and casenotes of federal and state decisions construing specific Code sections.—Abbr. USCA.

United States District Attorney. See UNITED STATES ATTORNEY.

United States District Court. A federal trial court having jurisdiction within its judicial district.—Abbr. U.S.D.C.

United States Magistrate Judge. A federal judicial officer who hears civil and criminal pretrial matters and who may conduct civil trials or criminal misdemeanor trials. 28 USCA §§ 631–639.—Also termed *federal magistrate* and (before 1990) *United States Magistrate*.

United States Marshal. See MARSHAL.

United States Reports. The official printed record of U.S. Supreme Court cases. • In a citation, it is abbreviated as U.S., as in 388 U.S. 14 (1967).

United States Sentencing Commission. An independent commission of the federal judiciary responsible for promulgating sentenc-

ing guidelines to be used in the federal courts.
● The Commission is made up of seven members (three of whom must be federal judges) appointed by the President.

United States Supreme Court. See SUPREME COURT OF THE UNITED STATES.

universal malice. See MALICE.

unlawful, *adj.* **1.** Not authorized by law; illegal <in some cities, jaywalking is unlawful>. **2.** Criminally punishable <unlawful entry>. **3.** Involving moral turpitude <the preacher spoke to the congregation about the unlawful activities of gambling and drinking>.—**unlawfully,** *adv.*

unlawful act. Conduct that is not authorized by law; a violation of a civil or criminal law.

unlawful assembly. See ASSEMBLY.

unlawful entry. See ENTRY.

unlawful force. See FORCE.

unlawful sexual intercourse. See RAPE.

unreasonable search. See SEARCH.

unrelated offense. See OFFENSE.

unsecured bail bond. See BOND.

unsworn, *adj.* Not sworn <an unsworn statement>.

unsworn declaration under penalty of perjury. See DECLARATION (2).

unwritten evidence. See EVIDENCE.

upward departure. See DEPARTURE.

U.S. *abbr.* **1.** United States. **2.** UNITED STATES REPORTS.

USC. *abbr.* UNITED STATES CODE.

USCA. *abbr.* UNITED STATES CODE ANNOTATED.

U.S.D.C. *abbr.* UNITED STATES DISTRICT COURT.

use/derivative use immunity. See IMMUNITY (2).

use immunity. See IMMUNITY (2).

useless-gesture exception. An exception to the knock-and-announce rule by which police are excused from having to announce their purpose before entering the premises to execute a warrant when it is evident from the circumstances that the authority and purpose of the police are known to those inside. See KNOCK-AND-ANNOUNCE RULE.

use of force. The application of physical power or pressure to bring about a result, such as the arrest of a criminal suspect. Model Penal Code § 3.07.

U.S. Magistrate. See UNITED STATES MAGISTRATE JUDGE.

usury (**yoo**-zhə-ree) *n.* **1.** Historically, the lending of money with interest. **2.** Today, the charging of an illegal rate of interest. **3.** An illegally high rate of interest.—**usurious** (yoo-**zhuur**-ee-əs), *adj.*—**usurer** (**yoo**-zhər-ər), *n.*

usury law. A law that prohibits moneylenders from charging illegally high interest rates.

utilitarian-deterrence theory. The legal theory that a person should be punished only if it is for the good of society—that is, only if the punishment would further the prevention of future harmful conduct. See *hedonistic utilitarianism* under UTILITARIANISM. Cf. RETRIBUTIVISM.

utilitarianism. A philosophy that the goal of public action should be the greatest happiness to the greatest number of people.

hedonistic utilitarianism. The theory that the validity of a law should be measured by determining the extent to which it would promote the greatest happiness to the greatest number of citizens. • This theory is found most prominently in the work of Jeremy Bentham, whose "Benthamite utilitarianism" greatly influenced legal reform in nineteenth-century Britain. Hedonistic utilitarianism generally maintains that pleasure is intrinsically good and pain intrinsically bad. Therefore, inflicting pain, as by punishing a criminal, is justified only if it results in a net increase of pleasure by deterring future harmful behavior.—Also termed *Benthamism*. See *utilitarian-deterrence theory.* Cf. RETRIBUTIVISM.

uttering. The crime of presenting a false or worthless instrument with the intent to harm or defraud.—Also termed *uttering a forged instrument.* See FORGERY.

uxoricide (ǝk-**sor**-ǝ–sɪd *or* ǝg-**zor**-). **1.** The murder of one's wife. **2.** A man who murders his wife. Cf. MARITICIDE.

V

v. *abbr.* VERSUS.—Also abbreviated *vs.*

vagrancy (**vay**-grən-see), *n.* **1.** The state or condition of wandering from place to place without a home, job, or means of support. ● Vagrancy is generally considered a course of conduct or a manner of living rather than a single act. But under some statutes, a single act has been held sufficient to constitute vagrancy. One court held, for example, that the act of prowling about and creeping up on parked cars and their occupants at night, under circumstances suggesting an intent to commit a crime, constitutes vagrancy. See *Smith v. Drew*, 26 P.2d 1040 (Wash. 1933). Many state laws prohibiting vagrancy have been declared unconstitutionally vague.—Also termed *vagrantism*. **2.** An instance of such wandering. Cf. LOITERING.

vagrant, *adj.* **1.** Of, relating to, or characteristic of a vagrant; inclined to vagrancy. **2.** Nomadically homeless.

vagrant, *n.* **1.** At common law, anyone belonging to the several classes of idle or disorderly persons, rogues, and vagabonds. **2.** One who, not having a settled habitation, strolls from place to place; a homeless, idle wanderer. ● The term often refers to one who spends time in idleness, lacking any property and without

689

any visible means of support. Under some statutes, a vagrant is an offender against or menace to the public peace, usu. liable to become a
public burden.

vagrantism. See VAGRANCY.

vandal. A malicious destroyer or defacer of
works of art, monuments, buildings, or other
property.

vandalism, *n*. **1.** Willful or ignorant destruction of public or private property, esp. of artistic, architectural, or literary treasures. **2.** The
actions or attitudes of one who maliciously or
ignorantly destroys or disfigures public or private property; active hostility to anything that
is venerable or beautiful.—**vandalize,** *vb*.—
vandalistic, *adj*.

variance. A difference or disparity between
two statements or documents that ought to
agree; esp., in criminal procedure, a difference
between the allegations in a charging instrument and the proof actually introduced at trial.—Also termed *variation*.

> **fatal variance.** A variance that either de-
> prives the defendant of fair notice of the
> charges or exposes the defendant to the risk
> of double jeopardy. • A fatal variance is
> grounds for reversing a conviction.

immaterial variance. A variance that is too slight to mislead or prejudice the defendant, and is thus harmless error.

vehicular homicide. See HOMICIDE.

vendetta (ven-**det**-ə), *n.* A private blood feud in which family members seek revenge on a person outside the family (often members of another family); esp., a private war in which the nearest of kin seek revenge for the slaying of a relative.

venire (və-**nɪ**-ree *or* -**neer**-ee *or* -**nɪr** *or* -**neer**). **1.** A panel of persons who have been selected for jury duty and from among whom the jurors are to be chosen.—Also termed *array*; *jury panel*; *jury pool*. **2.** See VENIRE FACIAS.

venire de novo. See *venire facias de novo* under VENIRE FACIAS.

venire facias (və-**nɪ**-ree [*or* -**neer**-ee *or* -**nɪr** *or* -**neer**] **fay**-shee-əs). A writ directing a sheriff to assemble a jury.—Often shortened to *venire.*—Also termed *venire facias juratores* (juur-ə-**tor** -eez).

venire facias ad respondendum (ad ree-spon-**den**-dəm). A writ requiring a sheriff to summon a person against whom an indict-

ment for a misdemeanor has been issued. •
A warrant is now more commonly used.

venire facias de novo (dee *or* di **noh**-voh).
A writ for summoning a jury panel anew
because of some impropriety or irregularity
in the original jury's return or verdict so
that no judgment can be given on it. • The
result of a new venire is a new trial. In
substance, this is a motion for new trial, but
when the party objects to the verdict because of an error in the course of the proceeding (and not on the merits), the form of
motion was traditionally for a venire facias
de novo.—Often shortened to *venire de novo*.

veniremember (və-**nɪ**-ree-mem-bər *or* və-
neer-ee- *or* və-**neer**-). A prospective juror; a
member of a jury panel.—Also termed *venire-
man*; *venireperson*.

venue (**ven**-yoo). [Law French "coming"] **1.**
The proper or a possible place for the trial of a
case, usu. because the place has some connection with the events that have given rise to the
case. **2.** The county or other territory over
which a trial court has jurisdiction. Cf. JURIS-
DICTION. **3.** Loosely, the place where a conference or meeting is being held. **4.** In a pleading,
the statement establishing the place for trial.
5. In an affidavit, the designation of the place
where it was made.

venue, change of. See CHANGE OF VENUE.

verdict. 1. A jury's finding or decision on the factual issues of a case. **2.** Loosely, in a non-jury trial, a judge's resolution of the issues of a case.

> *chance verdict.* A now-illegal verdict, arrived at by hazard or lot.—Also termed *gambling verdict; verdict by lot.*

> *compromise verdict.* A verdict that is reached when jurors concede some issues so they can settle other issues in their favor.

> *defective verdict.* A verdict on which a judgment cannot be based because of irregularities or legal inadequacies.

> *directed verdict.* A judgment entered on the order of a trial judge who takes over the fact-finding role of the jury because the evidence is so compelling that only one decision can reasonably follow or because it fails to establish a prima facie case.—Also termed *instructed verdict.*

> *false verdict.* A verdict so contrary to the evidence and so unjust that the judge may set it aside.

> *gambling verdict.* See *chance verdict.*

693

general verdict. A verdict by which the jury finds in favor of one party or the other, as opposed to resolving specific fact questions. Cf. *special verdict.*

general verdict with interrogatories. A general verdict accompanied by answers to written interrogatories on one or more issues of fact that bear on the verdict.

guilty verdict. A jury's formal pronouncement that a defendant is guilty of the charged offense.

instructed verdict. See *directed verdict.*

legally inconsistent verdict. A verdict in which the same element is found to exist and not to exist, as when a defendant is acquitted of one offense and convicted of another, when the offenses arise from the same set of facts and an element of the second offense requires proof that the first offense has been committed.

open verdict. A verdict of a coroner's jury finding that the subject "came to his death by means to the jury unknown" or "came to his death at the hands of a person or persons to the jury unknown." • This verdict leaves open either the question whether any crime was committed or the identity of the criminal.

partial verdict. A verdict by which a jury finds a criminal defendant innocent of some charges and guilty of other charges.

perverse verdict. A jury verdict so contrary to the evidence that it justifies the granting of a new trial.

public verdict. A verdict delivered by the jury in open court.

quotient verdict. An improper verdict that a jury arrives at by totaling their individual damage awards and dividing by the number of jurors.

repugnant verdict. A verdict that contradicts itself in that the defendant is convicted and acquitted of different crimes having identical elements. • Sometimes the inconsistency occurs in a single verdict (*repugnant verdict*), and sometimes it occurs in two separate verdicts (*repugnant verdicts*). Both terms are used mainly in New York.

sealed verdict. A written verdict put into a sealed envelope when the jurors have agreed on their decision but when court is not in session at the time. • Upon delivering a sealed verdict, the jurors may separate. When court convenes again, this verdict is officially returned with the same effect as if the jury had returned it in open court before separating. This type of verdict is useful to

695

avoid detaining the jurors until the next session of court.

special verdict. A verdict that gives a written finding for each issue, leaving the application of the law to the judge. Cf. *general verdict*.

split verdict. **1.** A verdict finding a defendant guilty on one charge but innocent on another. **2.** A verdict of guilty for one defendant and of not guilty for a codefendant.

true verdict. A verdict that is reached voluntarily—even if one or more jurors freely compromise their views—and not as a result of an arbitrary rule or order, whether imposed by the jurors themselves, the court, or a court officer.

verdict by lot. See *chance verdict*.

verdict contrary to law. A verdict that the law does not authorize a jury to render because the conclusion drawn is not justified by the evidence.

verdict subject to opinion of court. A verdict that is subject to the court's determination of a legal issue reserved to the court upon the trial, so that judgment is ultimately entered depending on the court's ruling on a point of law.

versus, *prep.* Against.—Abbr. v.; vs.

viatorial privilege. See PRIVILEGE (1).

vicarious disqualification. See DISQUALIFICA-
TION.

vicecomital. See VICONTIEL.

vice crime. See CRIME.

vice-sheriff. See *deputy sheriff* under SHERIFF.

vicinage (**vis**-ə-nij). [Law French "neighborhood"] **1.** Vicinity; proximity. **2.** The place
where a crime is committed or a trial is held;
the place from which jurors are to be drawn
for trial; esp., the locale from which the accused is entitled to have jurors selected.

vicious propensity. An animal's tendency to
endanger the safety of persons or property.

vicontiel (vi-**kon**-tee-əl). Of or relating to a
sheriff.—Also spelled *vicountiel.*—Also termed
vicecomital.

victim, *n.* A person harmed by a crime, tort,
or other wrong.—**victimize,** *vb.*—**victimiza-
tion,** *n.*

victim allocution. See ALLOCUTION.

victim-impact statement. A statement read into the record during sentencing to inform the judge or jury of the financial, physical, and psychological impact of the crime on the victim and the victim's family.

victimless crime. See CRIME.

victim-related adjustment. An increase in punishment available under federal sentencing guidelines when the defendant knew or should have known that the victim was unusually vulnerable (because of age or condition) or otherwise particularly susceptible to the criminal conduct.

view, *n.* A jury's inspection of a place relevant to a case it is considering; the act or proceeding by which a tribunal goes to observe an object that cannot be produced in court because it is immovable or inconvenient to remove. ● The appropriate procedures are typically regulated by state statute. At common law, and today in many civil cases, the trial judge's presence is not required. The common practice has been for the jury to be conducted to the scene by "showers" who are commissioned for this purpose. Parties and counsel are generally permitted to attend, although this is a matter typically within the trial judge's discretion.

view of an inquest. A jury's inspection of a place or property to which an inquiry or inquest refers.

vigilante (vij-ə-**lan**-tee). A person who seeks to avenge a crime by taking the law into his or her own hands.

vigilantism (vij-ə-**lan**-tiz-əm). The act of a citizen who takes the law into his or her own hands by apprehending and punishing suspected criminals.

vindicate, *vb.* **1.** To clear (a person or thing) from suspicion, criticism, blame, or doubt <the serial killer will never be vindicated in the minds of the victims' families>. **2.** To assert, maintain, or affirm (one's interest) by action <the claimants sought to vindicate their rights through a class-action proceeding>. **3.** To defend (one's interest) against interference or encroachment <the borrower vindicated its interest in court when the lender attempted to foreclose>. **4.** To clear from censure or suspicion by means of demonstration.—**vindication,** *n.*—**vindicator,** *n.*

vindictive prosecution (vin-**dik**-tiv). See PROSECUTION.

violation, *n.* **1.** An infraction or breach of the law; a transgression. See INFRACTION. **2.** The act of breaking or dishonoring the law; the contravention of a right or duty. **3.** Rape; ravishment. **4.** Under the Model Penal Code, a public-welfare offense. ● In this sense, a violation is not a crime. See Model Penal Code § 1.04(5).—**violate,** *vb.*—**violative** (vɪ-ə-lay-tiv), *adj.*—**violator,** *n.*

violence. Unjust or unwarranted use of force, usu. accompanied by fury, vehemence, or outrage; physical force unlawfully exercised with the intent to harm. ● Some courts have held that violence in labor disputes is not limited to physical contact or injury, but may include picketing conducted with misleading signs, false statements, erroneous publicity, and veiled threats by words and acts.

> ***domestic violence.*** Violence between members of a household, usu. spouses; an assault or other violent act committed by one member of a household against another. See BAT-TERED-CHILD SYNDROME; BATTERED-WOMAN SYNDROME.

violent, *adj.* **1.** Of, relating to, or characterized by strong physical force <violent blows to the legs>. **2.** Resulting from extreme or intense force <violent death>. **3.** Vehemently or passionately threatening <violent words>.

violent crime. See CRIME.

violent death. See DEATH.

violent felony. See *violent offense* under OF-FENSE.

violent offense. See OFFENSE.

visible crime. See *street crime* under CRIME.

visiting judge. See JUDGE.

voice exemplar. A sample of a person's voice used for the purpose of comparing it with a recorded voice to determine whether the speaker is the same person. ● Although voice-print identification was formerly inadmissible, the trend in recent years has been toward admissibility. See Fed. R. Evid. 901.

voiceprint. A distinctive pattern of curved lines and whorls that are made by a machine that measures human vocal sounds for the purpose of identifying an individual speaker. ● Like fingerprints, voiceprints are thought to be unique to each person.

volitional test. See IRRESISTIBLE-IMPULSE TEST.

voluntary, *adj.* **1.** Done by design or inten-tion <voluntary act>. **2.** Unconstrained by interference; not impelled by outside influence <voluntary statement>.—**voluntariness,** *n.*

voluntary escape. See ESCAPE (3).

voluntary euthanasia. See EUTHANASIA.

voluntary intoxication. See INTOXICATION.

voluntary manslaughter. See MANSLAUGHTER.

voluntary search. See SEARCH.

voluntary statement. See STATEMENT.

voyeur (voy-yər *also* vwah-yər), *n.* A person who observes something without participating; esp., one who gains pleasure by secretly observing another's sexual acts. See PEEPING TOM.

voyeurism, *n.* Gratification derived from observing the sexual organs or acts of others, usu. secretly.—**voyeuristic,** *adj.*

vs. *abbr.* VERSUS.

W

***Wade* hearing.** A pretrial hearing in which the defendant contests the validity of his or her out-of-court identification. ● If the court finds that the identification was tainted by unconstitutional methods, the prosecution cannot use the identification and must link the defendant to the crime by other means. *United States v. Wade*, 388 U.S. 218, 87 S.Ct. 1926 (1967).

waif (wayf), *n.* A stolen article thrown away by a thief in flight, usu. through fear of apprehension. ● At common law, if a waif was seized by a public officer or private person before the owner reclaimed it, the title vested in the Crown, but today the general rule is that a waif passes to the state in trust for the true owner, who may regain it by proving ownership.

waiting period. A period that must expire before some legal right or remedy can be enjoyed or enforced. ● For example, many states have waiting periods for the issuance of marriage licenses or the purchase of handguns.

waiver hearing. See *transfer hearing* under HEARING.

waiver of counsel. A criminal defendant's intentional relinquishment of the right to legal representation. ● To be valid, a waiver of counsel must be made knowingly and intelligently.

Walsh Act. A statute, originally enacted in 1926, giving federal courts the power to subpoena and compel the return, testimony, and (if requested) production of documents or other items of U.S. citizens or residents who are abroad. ● The subpoena is available for criminal proceedings, including grand-jury proceedings. 28 USCA § 1783.

wanted person. A person sought by the police because the person has escaped from custody or an arrest warrant has been issued for the person's arrest.

wanton (**wahn**-tən), *adj.* Unreasonably or maliciously risking harm while being utterly indifferent to the consequences. ● In criminal law, *wanton* usu. connotes malice, while *reckless* does not. Cf. RECKLESS; WILLFUL.

wanton and reckless misconduct. See *wanton misconduct* under MISCONDUCT.

wanton misconduct. See MISCONDUCT.

wanton negligence. See *gross negligence* (2) under NEGLIGENCE.

wantonness. Conduct indicating that the actor is aware of the risks but indifferent to the results. ● Wantonness usu. suggests a greater degree of culpability than recklessness, and it often connotes malice. Cf. RECKLESSNESS.

war crime. Conduct that violates international laws governing war. ● Examples of war crimes are the killing of hostages, abuse of civilians in occupied territories, abuse of prisoners of war, and devastation that is not justified by military necessity.

ward. 1. A person, usu. a minor, who is under a guardian's charge or protection.

> *permanent ward.* A ward who has been assigned a permanent guardian, the rights of the natural parents having been terminated by a juvenile court.

> *temporary ward.* A minor who is under the supervision of a juvenile court but whose parents' parental rights have not been terminated.

2. A territorial division in a city, usu. defined for purposes of city government.

warden. A person in charge of something <game warden> <port warden>; esp., the official in charge of a prison or jail <prison warden>.

warrant, *n.* A writ directing or authorizing someone to do an act, esp. one directing a law enforcer to make an arrest, a search, or a seizure.

 administrative warrant. A warrant issued by a judge at the request of an administrative agency. ● This type of warrant is sought to conduct an administrative search. See *administrative search* under SEARCH.

 anticipatory search warrant. See SEARCH WARRANT.

 arrest warrant. A warrant, issued only on probable cause, directing a law-enforcement officer to arrest and bring a person to court.—Also termed *warrant of arrest.*

 bench warrant. A warrant issued directly by a judge to a law-enforcement officer, esp. for the arrest of a person who has been held in contempt, has been indicted, has disobeyed a subpoena, or has failed to appear for a hearing or trial.

 blanket search warrant. See SEARCH WARRANT.

 commitment warrant. See *warrant of commitment.*

 death warrant. A warrant authorizing a warden or other prison official to carry out a death sentence. ● A death warrant typically sets the time and place for a prisoner's execution.

escape warrant. A warrant directing a peace officer to rearrest an escaped prisoner.

extradition warrant. A warrant for the return of a fugitive from one jurisdiction to another. Cf. *rendition warrant.*

fugitive warrant. A warrant that authorizes law-enforcement officers to take into custody a person who has fled from one state to another to avoid prosecution or punishment.

general warrant. A warrant that gives a law-enforcement officer broad authority to search and seize unspecified places or persons; a search or arrest warrant that lacks a sufficiently particularized description of the person or thing to be seized or the place to be searched. ● General warrants are unconstitutional because they fail to meet the Fourth Amendment's specificity requirements.

John Doe warrant. A warrant for the arrest of a person whose name is unknown. ● A John Doe warrant may be issued, for example, for a person known by sight but not by name. This type of warrant is permitted in a few states, but not in federal practice.

justice's warrant. See *peace warrant.*

no-knock search warrant. See SEARCH WARRANT.

outstanding warrant. An unexecuted arrest warrant.

peace warrant. A warrant issued by a justice of the peace for the arrest of a specified person.—Also termed *justice's warrant.*

preliminary warrant. A warrant to bring a person to court for a preliminary hearing on probable cause.

rendition warrant. A warrant requesting the extradition of a fugitive from one jurisdiction to another. Cf. *extradition warrant.*

search warrant. See SEARCH WARRANT.

surreptitious-entry warrant. A warrant that authorizes a law officer to enter and observe an ongoing criminal operation (such as an illegal drug lab).

warrant of arrest. See *arrest warrant.*

warrant of commitment. A warrant committing a person to custody.—Also termed *commitment warrant.*

warrant upon indictment or informa- tion. An arrest warrant issued at the re- quest of the prosecutor for a defendant named in an indictment or information. Fed. R. Crim. P. 9.

Warrant Clause. The clause of the Fourth Amendment to the U.S. Constitution requiring that warrants be issued on probable cause.

warranted arrest. See ARREST.

warranted search. See SEARCH.

warrantless arrest. See ARREST.

warrantless search. See SEARCH.

warrant of arrest. See *arrest warrant* under WARRANT.

warrant of commitment. See WARRANT.

warrant upon indictment or information. See WARRANT.

weapon. An instrument used or designed to be used to injure or kill someone.

concealed weapon. A weapon that is car- ried by a person but that is not visible by ordinary observation.

dangerous weapon. An object or device that, because of the way it is used, is capable of causing serious bodily injury.

deadly weapon. Any firearm or other device, instrument, material, or substance that, from the manner it is used or is intended to be used, is calculated or likely to produce death.—Also termed *lethal weapon.* Cf. DANGEROUS INSTRUMENTALITY.

deadly weapon per se. A weapon that is deadly in and of itself or would ordinarily result in death by its use <a gun is a deadly weapon per se>.—Also termed *per se deadly weapon.*

lethal weapon. See *deadly weapon.*

weekend sentence. See *intermittent sentence* under SENTENCE.

weight of the evidence. The persuasiveness of some evidence in comparison with other evidence <because the verdict is against the great weight of the evidence, a new trial should be granted>. See BURDEN OF PERSUASION.

Wharton's rule ([h]**wor**-tən). The doctrine that an agreement by two or more persons to commit a particular crime cannot be prosecuted as a conspiracy if the crime could not be committed except by the actual number of participants involved. ● But if an additional person participates so as to enlarge the scope of the agreement, all the actors may be charged with conspiracy. The doctrine takes its name from the influential criminal-law author Francis Wharton (1820–1889).—Also termed *Wharton rule*; *concert-of-action rule*.

wheel conspiracy. See CONSPIRACY.

whipping, *n.* A method of corporal punishment formerly used in England and a few American states, consisting of inflicting long welts on the skin, esp. with a whip.

whistleblower, *n.* An employee who reports employer illegality to a governmental or law-enforcement agency. ● Federal and state laws protect whistleblowers from employer retaliation.—**whistleblowing,** *n.*

whistleblower act. A federal or state law protecting employees from retaliation for disclosing employer illegality, such as during an investigation by a regulatory agency. ● Federal laws containing whistleblower provisions include the Occupational Safety and Health Act (29 USCA § 660), CERCLA (42 USCA § 9610), and the Air Pollution and Control Act (42 USCA § 7622).

711

whitecapping. The criminal act of threatening a person—usu. a member of a minority group—with violence in an effort to compel the person either to move away or to stop engaging in a certain business or occupation. ● Whitecapping statutes were originally enacted to curtail the activities of the Ku Klux Klan.

white-collar crime. A nonviolent crime usu. involving cheating or dishonesty in commercial matters. ● Examples include fraud, embezzlement, bribery, and insider trading.

Whiteley rule. See FELLOW-OFFICER RULE.

white slavery. The practice of forcing a female (or, rarely, a male) to engage in commercial prostitution. ● Trafficking in white slavery is prohibited by the Mann Act (18 USCA §§ 2421–2424).

White Slave Traffic Act. See MANN ACT.

willful, *adj.* Voluntary and intentional, but not necessarily malicious.—Sometimes spelled *wilful.*—**willfulness,** *n.* Cf. WANTON.

willful and wanton misconduct. See MISCONDUCT.

willful and wanton negligence. See *gross negligence* (2) under NEGLIGENCE.

willful blindness. Deliberate avoidance of knowledge of a crime, esp. by failing to make a reasonable inquiry about suspected wrongdoing despite being aware that it is highly probable. • A person acts with willful blindness, for example, by deliberately refusing to look inside an unmarked package after being paid by a known drug dealer to deliver it. Willful blindness creates an inference of knowledge of the crime in question. See Model Penal Code § 2.02(7).

willful homicide. See HOMICIDE.

willful indifference to the safety of others. See *willful and wanton misconduct* under MISCONDUCT.

willful misconduct. See MISCONDUCT.

willful murder. See MURDER.

willful negligence. See *gross negligence* (2) under NEGLIGENCE.

willfulness. 1. The fact or quality of acting purposely or by design; deliberateness; intention. • Willfulness does not necessarily imply malice, but it involves more than just knowledge. **2.** The voluntary, intentional violation or disregard of a known legal duty.—Also termed *legal willfulness.*

713

willful wrong. See *intentional wrong* under
WRONG.

wire fraud. See FRAUD.

wiretapping, *n.* Electronic or mechanical
eavesdropping, usu. done by law-enforcement
officers under court order, to listen to private
conversations. • Wiretapping is regulated by
federal and state law.—**wiretap,** *vb.*—**wiretap,** *n.*—Often shortened to *tapping*. See BUG-
GING; EAVESDROPPING. Cf. PEN REGISTER.

withdrawal, *n.* **1.** The act of taking back or
away; removal <withdrawal of consent>. **2.**
The act of retreating from a place, position, or
situation <withdrawal from the standoff with
police>. **3.** See RENUNCIATION <withdrawal
from the conspiracy to commit arson>.—**withdraw,** *vb.*

withdrawal of charges. The removal of
charges by the one bringing them, such as a
prosecutor. See NOLLE PROSEQUI.

withdrawal of counsel. An attorney's termination of his or her role in representing a
party in a case. • An attorney usu. must
obtain the court's permission to withdraw
from a case. Such permission is usu. sought by
a written motion (1) explaining the reason for
the requested withdrawal (often, a conflict be-

tween attorney and client over a matter such as strategy or fees), and (2) stating whether the client agrees.

withdrawing a juror. The act or an instance of removing a juror, usu. to obtain a continuance in a case or, sometimes in English practice, to end the case, as when the case has settled, the parties are too anxious to proceed to verdict, or the judge recommends it because the action is not properly before the court.

withheld sentence. See *suspended sentence* under SENTENCE.

withholding of evidence. The act or an instance of obstructing justice by stifling or suppressing evidence knowing that it is being sought in an official investigation or a judicial proceeding. See OBSTRUCTION OF JUSTICE.

witness, *n.* **1.** One who sees, knows, or vouches for something <a witness to the accident>. **2.** One who gives testimony under oath or affirmation (1) in person, (2) by oral or written deposition, or (3) by affidavit <the prosecution called its next witness>.—**witness,** *vb.*

> *accomplice witness.* An accomplice in a criminal act. ● A codefendant cannot be convicted solely on the testimony of an accomplice witness.

adverse witness. See *hostile witness.*

alibi witness. A witness who testifies that the defendant was in a location other than the scene of the crime at the relevant time; a witness that supports the defendant's alibi.

attesting witness. One who vouches for the authenticity of another's signature by signing an instrument that the other has signed <proof of the will requires two attesting witnesses>.

character witness. A witness who testifies about another person's character traits or community reputation. See *character evidence* under EVIDENCE.

competent witness. A witness who is legally qualified to testify. ● A lay witness who has personal knowledge of the subject matter of the testimony is competent to testify. Fed. R. Evid. 601–602.

corroborating witness. A witness who confirms or supports someone else's testimony.

credible witness. A witness whose testimony is believable.

disinterested witness. A witness who is legally competent to testify and has no private interest in the matter at issue.

expert witness. A witness qualified by knowledge, skill, experience, training, or education to provide a scientific, technical, or other specialized opinion about the evidence or a fact issue. Fed. R. Evid. 702–706.—Also termed *skilled witness*. See EXPERT; DAUBERT TEST.

going witness. *Archaic.* A witness who is about to leave a court's jurisdiction, but not the country. ● An example is the witness who leaves one state to go to another.

grand-jury witness. A witness who is called to testify in a matter under inquiry by a grand jury.

hostile witness. A witness who is biased against the examining party or who is unwilling to testify. ● A hostile witness may be asked leading questions on direct examination. Fed. R. Evid. 611(c).—Also termed *adverse witness*.

interested witness. A witness who has a direct and private interest in the matter at issue.

lay witness. A witness who does not testify as an expert and who therefore may only give an opinion or make an inference that is based on firsthand knowledge and helpful in understanding the testimony or in determining facts. Fed. R. Evid. 701.

material witness. A witness who can testify about matters having some logical connection with the consequential facts, esp. if few others, if any, know about those matters.

percipient witness. A witness who perceived the things he or she testifies about.

prosecuting witness. A person who files the complaint that triggers a criminal prosecution and whose testimony the prosecution usu. relies on to secure a conviction.

qualified witness. A witness who, by explaining the manner in which a company's business records are made and kept, is able to lay the foundation for the admission of business records under an exception to the hearsay rule. Fed. R. Evid. 803(6).

rebuttal witness. A witness who contradicts or attempts to contradict evidence previously presented.

res gestae witness. A witness who, having been at the scene of an incident, can give a firsthand account of what happened. See RES GESTAE.

skilled witness. See *expert witness.*

swift witness. See *zealous witness.*

target witness. **1.** The person who has the knowledge that an investigating body seeks.

2. A witness who is called before a grand jury and against whom the government is also seeking an indictment.

turncoat witness. A witness whose testimony was expected to be favorable but who becomes (usu. during the trial) a hostile witness.

zealous witness (**zel**-əs). A witness who is unduly zealous or partial to one side of a case and shows bias through extreme readiness to answer questions or volunteer information advantageous to that side.—Also termed *swift witness.*

witness box. See WITNESS STAND.

witness-protection program. A federal or state program in which a person who testifies against a criminal is assigned a new identity and relocated to another part of the country to avoid retaliation by anyone convicted as a result of that testimony. ● The Federal Witness Protection Program was established by the Organized Crime Control Act of 1970 and is administered by the marshals of the U.S. Justice Department.

witness stand. The space in a courtroom, usu. a boxed area, occupied by a witness while testifying.—Often shortened to *stand.*—Also termed *witness box.*

witness tampering. The act or an instance of obstructing justice by intimidating, influencing, or harassing a witness before or after the witness testifies. ● Several state and federal laws, including the Victim and Witness Protection Act of 1982 (18 USCA § 1512), provide criminal penalties for tampering with witnesses or other persons in the context of a pending investigation or official proceeding. See OBSTRUCTION OF JUSTICE.

wobbler. *Slang.* A crime that can be charged as either a felony or a misdemeanor.

work-furlough program. See WORK-RELEASE PROGRAM.

workhouse. A jail for criminals who have committed minor offenses and are serving short sentences.

work-product rule. The rule providing for qualified immunity of an attorney's work product from discovery or other compelled disclosure. Fed. R. Civ. P. 26(b)(3). ● The exemption was primarily established to protect an attorney's litigation strategy. *Hickman v. Taylor*, 329 U.S. 495, 67 S.Ct. 385 (1947).—Also termed *work-product immunity*; *work-product privilege*; *work-product exemption*.

work-release program. A correctional program allowing a prison inmate—primarily one being readied for discharge—to hold a job outside prison.—Also termed *work-furlough program*. See HALFWAY HOUSE.

worthless check. See *bad check* under CHECK.

writ (rit). A court's written order, in the name of a state or other competent legal authority, commanding the addressee to do or refrain from doing some specified act.

> *alias writ.* An additional writ issued after another writ of the same kind in the same case. ● It derives its name from a Latin phrase that formerly appeared in alias writs: *sicut alias praecipimus*, meaning "as we at another time commanded."

> *concurrent writ.* A duplicate of an original writ (esp. a summons), issued either at the same time as the original writ or at any time while the original writ is valid.

> *counterpart writ.* A copy of an original writ, to be sent to a court in another county when a defendant resides in, or is found in, that county.

> *extraordinary writ.* A writ issued by a court exercising unusual or discretionary power. ● Examples are certiorari, habeas

corpus, mandamus, and prohibition.—Also termed *prerogative writ.*

judicial writ. Any writ issued by a court.

writ of capias. See CAPIAS.

writ of certiorari. See CERTIORARI.

writ of error. A writ issued by an appellate court directing a lower court to deliver the record in the case for review.

writ of habeas corpus. See HABEAS CORPUS.

writ of injunction. See INJUNCTION.

writ of mandamus. See MANDAMUS.

writ of protection. A writ to protect a witness in a judicial proceeding who is threatened with arrest.

written testimony. See TESTIMONY.

wrong, *n.* Breach of one's legal duty; violation of another's legal right.—**wrong,** *vb.*

intentional wrong. A wrong in which the *mens rea* amounts to intention, purpose, or design.—Also termed *willful wrong.*

legal wrong. An act that is a violation of the law; an act authoritatively prohibited by a rule of law.

moral wrong. An act that is contrary to the rule of natural justice.—Also termed *natural wrong.* See MORAL-WRONG DOCTRINE.

positive wrong. A wrongful act, willfully committed.

private wrong. An offense committed against a private person and dealt with at the instance of the person injured.

public wrong. An offense committed against the state or the community at large, and dealt with in a proceeding to which the state is itself a party. ● Not all public wrongs are crimes. For example, a person that breaches a contract with the government commits a public wrong, but the offense is a civil one, not a criminal one.

willful wrong. See *intentional wrong.*

wrongdoer, *n.* One who violates the law <both criminals and tortfeasors are wrongdoers>.—**wrongdoing,** *n.*

wrongful, *adj.* **1.** Characterized by unfairness or injustice <wrongful military invasion>. **2.** Contrary to law; unlawful <wrongful termination>. **3.** (Of a person) not entitled to the

position occupied <wrongful possessor>.—
wrongfully, *adv.*

wrongful act. See WRONGFUL CONDUCT.

wrongful conduct. An act taken in violation
of a legal duty; an act that unjustly infringes
on another's rights.—Also termed *wrongful
act.*

XYZ

XQ. See *cross-question* under QUESTION (1).

XYY-chromosome defense. A defense, usu. asserted as the basis for an insanity plea, whereby a male defendant argues that his criminal behavior is due to the genetic abnormality of having an extra Y chromosome, which causes him to have uncontrollable aggressive impulses. ● Most courts have rejected this defense because its scientific foundations are uncertain.—Also termed *XYY defense*. See INSANITY DEFENSE.

XYY syndrome. The abnormal presence of an extra Y chromosome in a male, theoretically resulting in increased aggressiveness and antisocial behavior often resulting in criminal conduct.

year-and-a-day rule. The common-law principle that an act causing death is not homicide if the death occurs more than a year and a day after the act was committed.

young offender. See *youthful offender* under OFFENDER.

Youth Correction Authority Act. A model act, promulgated by the American Law Institute in 1940, that proposed the creation of central state commissions responsible for set-

725

ting up appropriate agencies that would determine the proper treatment for each youthful offender committed to the agency by the courts. ● The Act is noteworthy for its emphasis on rehabilitating juvenile offenders, as opposed to punishing them.

youthful offender. See OFFENDER.

youth offender. See *youthful offender* under OFFENDER.

zealous witness. See WITNESS.

zero-tolerance law. A statute—esp. one dealing with specified criminal conduct—that the enacting authority claims will be enforced zealously and without exception.

zone search. See SEARCH.

Appendix A

Bill of Rights to the U.S. Constitution

Amendment I [1791]

Congress shall make no law respecting an establishment of religion, or prohibiting the free exercise thereof; or abridging the freedom of speech, or of the press; or the right of the people peaceably to assemble, and to petition the Government for a redress of grievances.

Amendment II [1791]

A well regulated Militia, being necessary to the security of a free State, the right of the people to keep and bear Arms, shall not be infringed.

Amendment III [1791]

No Soldier shall, in time of peace be quartered in any house, without the consent of the Owner, nor in time of war, but in a manner to be prescribed by law.

Amendment IV [1791]

The right of the people to be secure in their persons, houses, papers, and effects, against unreasonable searches and seizures, shall not be violated, and no Warrants shall issue, but upon probable cause, supported by Oath or affirmation, and particularly describing the place to be searched, and the persons or things to be seized.

Amendment V [1791]

No person shall be held to answer for a capital, or otherwise infamous crime, unless on a presentment or indictment of a Grand Jury, except in cases arising in the land or naval forces, or in the Militia, when in actual service in time of War or public danger; nor shall any person be subject for the same offence to be twice put in jeopardy of life or limb; nor shall be compelled in any criminal case to be a witness against himself, nor be deprived of life, liberty, or property, without due process of law; nor shall private property be taken for public use, without just compensation.

Amendment VI [1791]

In all criminal prosecutions, the accused shall enjoy the right to a speedy and public trial, by an impartial jury of the State and district wherein the crime shall have been committed, which district shall have been previously ascertained by law, and to be informed of the nature and cause of the accusation; to be confronted with the witnesses against him; to have compulsory process for obtaining witnesses in his favor, and to have the Assistance of Counsel for his defence.

Amendment VII [1791]

In Suits at common law, where the value in controversy shall exceed twenty dollars, the right of trial by jury shall be preserved, and no fact tried by jury, shall be otherwise re-examined in any Court of the United States, than according to the rules of the common law.

Amendment VIII [1791]

Excessive bail shall not be required, nor excessive fines imposed, nor cruel and unusual punishments inflicted.

Amendment IX [1791]

The enumeration in the Constitution, of certain rights, shall not be construed to deny or disparage others retained by the people.

Amendment X [1791]

The powers not delegated to the United States by the Constitution, nor prohibited by it to the States, are reserved to the States respectively, or to the people.

Appendix B

Legal Maxims

Legal scholars have long warned that maxims are not the decisive points in actual cases. They are about as helpful as proverbs are in everyday life: some are little better than fortune-cookie messages, while others capsulize fundamental legal principles. The context in which they're invoked is crucial. So take them only for what they're worth. What follows is a list of those most commonly cited in criminal-law contexts.

Accusator post rationabile tempus non est audiendus, nisi se bene de omissione excusaverit. A person who makes an accusation after a reasonable time has passed is not to be heard unless the person makes a satisfactory excuse for the omission.

Acta exteriora indicant interiora secreta. Outward acts indicate the thoughts hidden within.

Actus me invito factus non est meus actus. An act done (by me) against my will is not my act.

Actus non reum facit nisi mens sit rea. An act does not make a person guilty unless his mind (or intention) is guilty.

Affectus punitur licet non sequatur effectus. The intention is punished even if the object is not achieved.

Agentes et consentientes pari poena plectentur. Acting and consenting parties will be liable to the same punishment.

Audi alteram partem. Hear the other side. • No one should be condemned unheard.

Baratriam committit qui propter pecuniam justitiam baractat. A person is guilty of barratry who sells justice for money.

Carcer ad homines custodiendos, non ad puniendos, dari debet. Imprisonment should be imposed for keeping people in confinement, not for punishing them (further).

Cogitationis poenam nemo patitur. No one is punished for his thoughts.

Commodum ex injuria sua non habere debet. (The wrongdoer) should not derive any benefit from his own wrong.

Confessio facta in judicio omni probatione major est. A confession made in court is of greater effect than any proof.

Confessus in judicio pro judicato habetur et quodammodo sua sententia damnatur. A person who has confessed his guilt when arraigned is considered to have been tried and is, as it were, condemned by his own sentence.

Consentientes et agentes pari poena plectentur. Those consenting and those perpetrating will receive the same punishment.

Contrectatio rei alienae animo furandi est furtum. Touching or taking another's property with an intention of stealing is theft.

Crescente malitia crescere debet et poena. With increase of malice, punishment ought also to increase.

Crimen laesae majestatis omnia alia crimina excedit quoad poenam. The crime of treason exceeds all other crimes in its punishment.

Crimen omnia ex se nata vitiat. Crime taints everything that springs from it.

Crimen trahit personam. The crime brings with it the person. ● That is, the commission of a crime gives the courts of the place where it is committed jurisdiction over the person of the offender.

Crimina morte extinguuntur. Crimes are extinguished by death.

Culpae poena par esto. Let the punishment be equal to the crime.

Cum confitente sponte mitius est agendum. One making a voluntary confession is to be dealt with more leniently.

Debet quis juri subjacere ubi delinquit. Any offender should be subject to the law of the place where he offends.

Deceptis, non decipientibus, jura subveniunt. The laws help persons who have been deceived, not those deceiving.

Delinquens per iram provocatus puniri debet mitius. A wrongdoer provoked by anger ought to be punished less severely.

Dolus est machinatio, cum aliud dissimulat aliud agit. Deceit is an artifice, since it pretends one thing and does another.

Domus sua cuique est tutissimum refugium. Everyone's house is his safest refuge.

Domus tutissimum cuique refugium atque receptaculum sit. Everyone's house should be his safest refuge and shelter.

Dona clandestina sunt semper suspiciosa. Clandestine gifts are always suspicious.

Ejus nulla culpa est cui parere necesse sit. No guilt attaches to a person who is compelled to obey.

Ex frequenti delicto augetur poena. Punishment increases with repeated offense.

Facinus quos inquinat aequat. Guilt makes equal those whom it stains.

Facta sunt potentiora verbis. Deeds (or facts) are more powerful than words.

Factum infectum fieri nequit. What is done cannot be undone.

Fatetur facinus qui judicium fugit. A person who flees judgment confesses guilt.

Felonia, ex vi termini, significat quodlibet capitale crimen felleo animo perpetratum. Felony, by force of the term, signifies any capital crime perpetrated with a malicious intent.

Felonia implicatur in quolibet proditione. Felony is implied in every treason.

Fraus est celare fraudem. It is a fraud to conceal a fraud.

Fraus et dolus nemini patrocinari debent. Fraud and deceit should excuse no one.

Fraus et jus nunquam cohabitant. Fraud and justice never dwell together.

Furiosus solo furore punitur. An insane person is punished by insanity alone.

Furtum est contrectatio rei alienae fraudulenta, cum animo furandi, invito illo domino cujus res illa fuerat. Theft is the fraudulent handling of another's property, with an intention of stealing, against the will of the proprietor, whose property it had been.

Furtum non est ubi initium habet detentionis per dominium rei. There is not theft where the holder has a beginning of detention (began holding the object) through ownership of the thing.

Habemus optimum testem, confitentem reum. We have the best witness, a confessing defendant.

Idem est facere et nolle prohibere cum possis. It is the same thing to commit an act and to refuse to prohibit it when you can.

Ignorantia facti excusat, ignorantia juris non excusat. Ignorance of fact excuses; ignorance of law does not excuse. ● Every person must be considered cognizant of the law; otherwise, there is no limit to the excuse of ignorance.

Ignorantia legis neminem excusat. Ignorance of law excuses no one.

Ignoscitur ei qui sanguinem suum qualiter redemptum voluit. A person is forgiven who chose to purchase his own blood (or life) upon any terms whatsoever. ● Whatever a person may do under the fear of losing life or limb will not be held binding upon him in law.

Illud quod alias licitum non est, necessitas facit licitum, et necessitas inducit privilegium quod jure privatur. That which is not otherwise lawful, necessity makes lawful; and necessity brings in as a privilege what is denied by right.

Impunitas continuum affectum tribuit delinquendi. Impunity provides a constant inclination to wrongdoing.

Impunitas semper ad deteriora invitat. Impunity invites (an offender) to ever worse offenses.

In alta proditione nullus potest esse accessorius sed principalis solummodo. In high treason no one can be an accessory but only a principal.

In atrocioribus delictis punitur affectus licet non sequatur effectus. In the more atrocious crimes, the intent (or attempt) is punished even if the effect does not follow.

In civilibus ministerium excusat, in criminalibus non item. In civil matters, agency (or service) excuses, but not so in criminal matters.

In criminalibus sufficit generalis malitia intentionis cum facto paris gradus. In criminal matters, a general malice of intention is sufficient if combined with an act of equal or corresponding degree.

In criminalibus voluntas reputabitur pro facto. In criminal matters, the intent will be reckoned as the deed. • In criminal attempts or conspiracy, the intention is considered in place of the act.

In favorem vitae, libertatis, et innocentiae omnia praesumuntur. All presumptions are in favor of life, liberty, and innocence.

In haeredes non solent transire actiones quae poenales ex maleficio sunt. Penal actions arising from anything of a criminal nature do not pass to heirs.

Injuria non excusat injuriam. A wrong does not excuse a wrong.

Injuria non praesumitur. A wrong is not presumed.

Injuria propria non cadet beneficium facientis. No benefit shall accrue to a person from his own wrongdoing.

In maleficiis voluntas spectatur, non exitus. In criminal offenses, the intention is regarded, not the event.

In quo quis delinquit, in eo de jure est puniendus. In whatever matter one offends, in that the person is rightfully to be punished.

Insanus est qui, abjecta ratione, omnia cum impetu et furore facit. The person is insane who, having cast aside reason, does everything with violence and rage.

Intentio caeca mala. A concealed intention is an evil one.

Intentio inservire debet legibus, non leges intentioni. The intention ought to be subject to the laws, not the laws to the intention.

Intentio mea imponit nomen operi meo. My intent gives a name to my act.

Interest reipublicae ne maleficia remaneant impunita. It is in the interest of the state that crimes not remain unpunished.

Interest reipublicae quod homines conserventur. It is in the interest of the state that people should be protected.

Interest reipublicae ut carceres sint in tuto. It is in the interest of the state that prisons should be secure.

Ira furor brevis est. Anger is a short insanity.

Jus est norma recti; et quicquid est contra normam recti est injuria. The law is the rule of right; and whatever is contrary to the rule of right is an injury.

LEGAL MAXIMS

Jus et fraus nunquam cohabitant. Right and fraud never abide together.

Jus ex injuria non oritur. A right does not arise from a wrong.

Justitia nemini neganda est. Justice is to be denied to no one.

La ley favour la vie d'un home. The law favors a man's life.

Le salut du peuple est la suprême loi. The safety of the people is the highest law.

Lex citius tolerare vult privatum damnum quam publicum malum. The law would sooner endure a private loss than a public evil.

Lex deficere non potest in justitia exhibenda. The law cannot fail in dispensing justice.

Lex est dictamen rationis. Law is the dictate of reason.

Lex est norma recti. Law is a rule of right.

Lex punit mendaciam. The law punishes false-hood.

Maihemium est homicidium inchoatum. Mayhem is incipient homicide.

Maihemium est inter crimina majora minimum, et inter minora maximum. Mayhem is the least of great crimes, and the greatest among small.

*Maihemium est membri mutilatio, et dici po-
terit, ubi aliquis in aliqua parte sui corporis
effectus sit inutilis ad pugnandum.* Mayhem is
the mutilation of a limb, and can be said (to occur)
when a person is injured in any part of his body so
as to be useless in a fight.

*Majore poena affectus quam legibus statuta
est non est infamis.* A criminal afflicted with a
greater punishment than is provided by law is not
infamous.

*Maleficia non debent remanere impunita, et
impunitas continuum affectum tribuit delinquendi.* Evil deeds ought not to remain unpunished, and impunity affords continual incitement to
wrongdoing.

Maleficia propositis distinguuntur. Evil deeds
are distinguished by their evil purposes.

Malitia est acida, est mali animi affectus. Malice is sour; it is the quality of a bad mind.

Malitiis hominum est obviandum. The malicious designs of men must be thwarted.

*Malum non habet efficientem sed deficientem
causam.* Evil has not an efficient but a deficient
cause.

Malum non praesumitur. Evil is not presumed.

Malum quo communius eo pejus. The more common the evil, the worse.

Maxime paci sunt contraria vis et injuria. The greatest enemies to peace are force and wrong.

Melior est justitia vere praeveniens quam severe puniens. Justice that truly prevents a crime is better than that which severely punishes it.

Melius est omnia mala pati quam malo consentire. It is better to suffer every wrong than to consent to wrong.

Mentiri est contra mentem ire. To lie is to go against the mind.

Minatur innocentibus qui parcit nocentibus. A person threatens the innocent who spares the guilty.

Minima poena corporalis est major qualibet pecuniaria. The smallest bodily punishment is greater than any pecuniary one.

Mors dicitur ultimum supplicium. Death is called the extreme penalty.

Mortis momentum est ultimum vitae momentum. The moment of death is the last moment of life.

Necessitas facit licitum quod alias non est licitum. Necessity makes lawful what otherwise is unlawful.

Necessitas quod cogit defendit. Necessity defends what it compels.

Nec veniam effuso sanguine casus habet. Where blood has been spilled, the case is unpardonable.

Nemo bis punitur pro eodem delicto. No one is punished twice for the same offense.

Nemo cogitationis poenam patitur. No one suffers punishment for his thoughts.

Nemo contra factum suum (proprium) venire potest. No one can contradict his own deed.

Nemo debet bis puniri pro uno delicto. No one ought to be punished twice for the same offense.

Nemo est supra leges. No one is above the laws.

Nemo ex dolo suo proprio relevetur aut auxilium capiat. Let no one be relieved or gain advantage by his own fraud.

Nemo potest nisi quod de jure potest. No one is able to do a thing unless he can do it lawfully.

Nemo praesumitur ludere in extremis. No one is presumed to trifle at the point of death.

Nemo praesumitur malus. No one is presumed to be bad.

Nemo prohibetur pluribus defensionibus uti. No one is forbidden to employ several defenses.

Nemo punitur pro alieno delicto. No one is punished for the crime or wrong of another.

Nemo punitur sine injuria, facto, seu defalta. No one is punished unless for some wrong, act, or default.

Nemo qui condemnare potest absolvere non potest. No one who can condemn is unable to acquit.

Nemo tenetur jurare in suam turpitudinem. No one is bound to swear to his own criminality.

Nemo tenetur prodere seipsum. No one is bound to betray himself. ● In other words, no one can be compelled to incriminate himself.

Nemo tenetur seipsum accusare. No one is bound to accuse himself.

Nemo videtur fraudare eos qui sciunt et consentiunt. No one is considered as deceiving those who know and consent.

Nihil consensui tam contrarium est quam vis atque metus. Nothing is so opposite to consent as force and fear.

Nihil nequam est praesumendum. Nothing wicked is to be presumed.

Non alio modo puniatur aliquis, quam secundum quod se habet condemnatio. A person may not be punished otherwise than according to what the sentence enjoins.

Non bis in idem (or imperative, ne bis in idem). Not twice for the same thing. ● That is, a person shall not be twice tried for the same crime. This maxim of the civil law expresses the same principle as the familiar rule against "double jeopardy."

Non officit conatus nisi sequatur effectus. An attempt does not harm unless a consequence follows.

Nullum tempus occurrit regi. Lapse of time does not bar the right of the Crown. ● Literally, no time runs against the king.

Nullum tempus occurrit reipublicae. No time runs against the commonwealth (or state).

Nullus dicitur accessorius post feloniam sed ille qui novit principalem feloniam fecisse, et illum receptavit et comfortavit. No one is called an accessory after the fact but that person who knew the principal to have committed a felony, and received and comforted him.

Nullus dicitur felo principalis nisi actor aut qui praesens est, abettans aut auxilians actorem ad feloniam faciendam. No one is called a principal felon except the party actually committing the felony, or the party who was present aiding and abetting the perpetrator in its commission.

Obedientia est legis essentia. Obedience is the essence of the law.

Officit conatus si effectus sequatur. The attempt becomes of consequence if the effect follows.

Omne actum ab intentione agentis est judicandum. Every act is to be judged by the intention of the doer.

Omne crimen ebrietas et incendit et detegit.
Drunkenness both inflames and reveals every
crime.

Omne sacramentum debet esse de certa scientia. Every oath ought to be founded on certain
knowledge.

Omnis indemnatus pro innoxio legibus habetur. Every uncondemned person is held by the law
as innocent.

Peccatum peccato addit qui culpae quam facit patrocinium defensionis adjungit. A person
adds one offense to another, who, when he commits
a crime, joins to it the protection of a defense.

Perjuri sunt qui servatis verbis juramenti decipiunt aures eorum qui accipiunt. Those who
preserve the words of an oath but deceive the ears
of those who accept it are perjurors.

Plus peccat auctor quam actor. The instigator of
a crime is a worse offender than the perpetrator.

Plus valet unus oculatus testis quam auriti decem. One eyewitness is better than ten earwitnesses.

Poena ad paucos, metus ad omnes perveniat.
Let punishment be inflicted on a few, dread upon
all.

Poenae potius molliendae quam exasperandae sunt. Punishments should rather be softened than
aggravated.

Poenae sunt restringendae. Punishments should be restrained.

Poena ex delicto defuncti haeres teneri non debet. The heir ought not to be bound by a penalty for the crime of the deceased.

Poena suos tenere debet actores et non alios. Punishment should take hold of the guilty (who commit the wrong), and not others.

Poena tolli potest, culpa perennis erit. The punishment can be removed, but the guilt will be perpetual.

Praesumatur pro justitia sententiae. Let there be a presumption of sentence's justice.

Quae sunt minoris culpae sunt majoris infamiae. Offenses that are of lesser guilt are of greater infamy.

Quando aliquid prohibetur ex directo, prohibetur et per obliquum. When anything is prohibited directly, it is also prohibited indirectly.

Quando aliquid prohibetur, prohibetur omne per quod devenitur ad illud. When anything is prohibited, everything by which it is arrived at is prohibited.

Qui accusat integrae famae sit et non criminosus. Let the one who accuses be of honest reputation and not implicated in a crime.

Quicquid est contra normam recti est injuria. Whatever is against the rule of right is a wrong.

Qui facit per alium facit per se. A person who acts through another acts himself. • The acts of an agent are considered the acts of the principal.

Qui male agit odit lucem. A person who does wrong hates the light (of discovery).

Qui mandat ipse fecisse videtur. A person who commands (a thing to be done) is considered to have done it himself.

Qui non improbat approbat. A person who does not disapprove approves.

Qui non negat fatetur. A person who does not deny admits.

Qui non obstat quod obstare potest, facere videtur. A person who does not prevent what he can prevent is considered to act.

Qui non propulsat injuriam quando potest infert. A person who does not repel an injury when he can brings it on.

Qui parcit nocentibus innocentes punit. A person who spares the guilty punishes the innocent.

Qui peccat ebrius, luat sobrius. Let him who offends while drunk be punished when sober.

Qui per alium facit per seipsum facere videtur. A person who does anything through another is considered as doing it himself.

Qui potest et debet vetare, tacens jubet. A person who can and ought to forbid a thing (as much as) orders it, if he keeps silent.

Quod alias bonum et justum est, si per vim vel fraudem petatur, malum et injustum efficitur. What is otherwise good and just, if it is sought by force or fraud, becomes bad and unjust.

Quod alias non fuit licitum necessitas licitum facit. Necessity makes lawful what otherwise was unlawful.

Quod a quoque poenae nomine exactum est id eidem restituere nemo cogitur. What has been exacted from someone as a penalty no one is obliged to restore to him.

Quodcunque aliquis ob tutelam corporis sui fecerit jure id fecisse videtur. Whatever one does in defense of his person, he is considered to have done legally.

Quod est necessarium est licitum. What is necessary is lawful.

Quod necessitas cogit, defendit. What necessity compels, it justifies.

Regula est, juris quidem ignorantiam cuique nocere, facti vero ignorantiam non nocere. The rule is that ignorance of the law is harmful (or prejudicial) to anyone, but ignorance of a fact is not. ● Ignorance of a fact may excuse a party from the legal consequences of his conduct, but not ignorance of law.

Rei turpis nullum mandatum est. There is no mandate for a thing immoral (or illegal). ● Hence, there is no action for failing to act upon such a mandate.

Res accessoria sequitur rem principalem. An accessory follows its principal.

Respondeat superior. Let the principal answer.

Reus laesae majestatis punitur, ut pereat unus ne pereant omnes. A traitor is punished that one may die lest all perish.

Sacramentum si fatuum fuerit, licet falsum, tamen non committit perjurium. A foolish oath, though false, does not make perjury.

Salus populi (est) suprema lex. The safety of the people is the supreme law. ● The phrase is sometimes put in the imperative: *Salus populi suprema lex esto* (let the safety of the people be the supreme law).

Salus reipublicae suprema lex. The safety of the state is the supreme law.

Scienti et volenti non fit injuria. A wrong is not done to one who knows and assents to it.

Si quis unum percusserit cum alium percutere vellet, in felonia tenetur. If a person kills one when he meant to kill another, he is held guilty of felony.

Stare decisis et non quieta movere. To stand by previous decisions and not to disturb settled matters. ● To adhere to precedents, and not to depart from established principles.

Summa caritas est facere justitiam singulis et omni tempore quando necesse fuerit. The greatest charity is to do justice to each individual and at every time when it is necessary.

Suppressio veri, expressio falsi. Suppression of the truth (is equivalent to) the expression of what is false.

Suppressio veri, suggestio falsi. Suppression of the truth (is equivalent to) the suggestion of what is false.

Testimonia ponderanda sunt, non numeranda. Testimonies are to be weighed, not counted.

Transgressione multiplicata, crescat poenae inflictio. When transgression is repeated, let the infliction of punishment be increased.

Tutius semper est errare in acquietando quam in puniendo, ex parte misericordiae quam ex parte justitiae. It is always safer to err in acquitting than in punishing, (and) on the side of mercy than of justice.

Ubi culpa est, ibi poena subesse debet. Where the fault is, there the punishment should be imposed.

Ubi non est principalis, non potest esse accessorius. Where there is no principal, there can be no accessory.

Ubi quis delinquit ibi punietur. Where anyone commits an offense, there will he be punished.

Ultimum supplicium esse mortem solam interpretamur. We consider death alone to be the extreme punishment.

LEGAL MAXIMS

Ut poena ad paucos, metus ad omnes perveniat. So that punishment afflict few, (and) fear affect all.

Vani timoris justa excusatio non est. There is no legal excuse based on a groundless fear.

Veniae facilitas incentivum est delinquendi. Ease of winning pardon is an incentive to committing crime.

Verba sunt indices animi. Words are indications of the intention.

Vim vi repellere licet, modo fiat moderamine inculpatae tutelae, non ad sumendam vindictam, sed ad propulsandam injuriam. It is lawful to repel force by force; but let it be done with the self-control of blameless defense—not to take revenge, but to repel injury.

Vis legibus est inimica. Force is inimical to the laws.

Volenti non fit injuria. There is no injury to one who consents.

Voluntas et propositum distinguunt maleficia. The will and the purpose distinguish crimes.